THE BOOK OF JESUS

~

A TREASURY
OF THE GREATEST
STORIES AND
WRITINGS
ABOUT CHRIST

EDITED BY CALVIN MILLER

A Touchstone Book
Published by Simon & Schuster

TOUCHSTONE
Rockefeller Center
1230 Avenue of the Americas
New York, NY 10020

First Touchstone Edition 1998

This edition of the book is substantially similar to the hardcover edition, but
some passages from the hardcover edition have been deleted from this paperback.

TOUCHSTONE and colophon are registered trademarks
of Simon & Schuster Inc.

DESIGNED BY BARBARA MARKS
Manufactured in the United States of America

1 3 5 7 9 10 8 6 4 2

The Library of Congress has cataloged the Simon & Schuster
edition as follows:
The book of Jesus : a treasury of the greatest stories and writings
about Christ / edited by Calvin Miller.
p.   cm.
Includes bibliographical references and index.
1. Jesus Christ—Literary collections.   I. Miller, Calvin,
PN6071.J4B66   1996
808.8'0351—dc20   96-14822   CIP

ISBN 0-684-81559-1
ISBN 0-684-83150-3 (Pbk)

Pages 563–569 constitute an extension of the copyright page.

Acknowledgments

〜

THIS PROJECT OWES any significance it owns to a great many people beyond myself. I would like to call attention to five wonderful friends who have helped to make this endeavor a reality. First, Deron Spoo, my teaching and research assistant, who not only helped me gather this anthology but devoted himself to a thousand hours of working with permissions. Second, to Cassie Jones of Simon & Schuster, whose cheerful creativity and coordination kept me highly motivated throughout the project. Third, to Dominick Anfuso of Simon & Schuster for believing in the project. Fourth, to Greg Johnson of Alive Communications for encouraging me in undertaking the project, and above all, to Barbara for her tireless effort in creating from thousands of books and articles this splendid offering of devotion.

To Barbara

My lifelong companion

The champion of all my dreams

The essence of all things real

The soul of every worthy venture

And graciously my own.

CONTENTS

~

II   JESUS: HIS BIRTH   93

III JESUS: HIS FRIENDSHIP WITH US ALL 157

IV   JESUS: HIS BECOMING ONE OF US   201

V JESUS: HIS MIRACLES 229

VI JESUS: HIS TEACHINGS 263

VII Jesus: His Cross   343

VIII JESUS: HIS RESURRECTION 407

IX JESUS: HIS CONTINUING REIGN 437

X   JESUS: HIS SECOND COMING   525

INTRODUCTION

JESUS. WHO WAS HE? Who is he? When was he born? Can anybody born that long ago be anything more than history? Can we say with certainty that there ever was a Jesus?

This book does not set out to answer every question of Christ that might be asked. It will seek to paint his reality with such bold strokes that few would dare to say that this man of widespread influence is not of everlasting importance. Not all who read this book will say with that centurion at the foot of his cross, "Surely this was the Son of God" (Matthew 27:54). Much of the world has yet to say that. However, most of the world's population does believe there was once a man named Jesus. Ask on the street of any major city if anyone believes in Jesus. Someone will say an enthusiastic yes. The question will take none by surprise, nor would the name of Christ be unfamiliar. Still, when most tell you they believe in Jesus, they are not giving you their statement of faith. They are not answering as though they were a Christian. They are not claiming to believe the Apostles' Creed. They are simply saying that they believe there once was a Jesus. They believe in Jesus the same way they believe in Genghis Khan or Marco Polo. They are merely agreeing with the record. Historically, the world has voted: there was a Jesus.

Christians themselves take the issue of believing a good deal further. They are not interested in talking about the Jesus who *was*. They are interested only in the Christ who *is*. The academic, historical Jesus is not to be compared with the Christ of the *right now*. This is not the Christ of theology or of history, but the Christ of faith. For Christians, it is not the Christ who once reckoned with Pilate that they find vital but the Christ who remains a contemporary of American presidents or British prime ministers. This Jesus gets involved in their daily affairs and helps them make sense of their tangled lives. It is this Jesus that 40 percent of Americans worship each Sunday.

The name *Jesus,* or *Joshua,* literally means *Jehovah saves.* And the word *Christ* means *the anointed one.* Both names taken together mean Christ is the celebrated Messiah of the gospels. He is presented as a miracle worker and a teacher of great authority (John 7:46). Through his resurrection from the dead, Jesus became the center of God's redeeming plan for all the ages (1 Corinthians 15). He was a storyteller whose stories, known worldwide, exist timelessly in his eighteen major parables (some scholars, reckoning in different manners, say there are as many as thirty). The Bible also records that he did other, less story-centered sermons and talks—twenty-eight or so in number—including his world-famous Sermon on the Mount. This sermon, as recorded by Matthew, can be preached in eighteen minutes or so and contains the most wonderfully radical and remarkable ethics for all relationships.

Not only was Jesus a storyteller and teacher; he was also a miracle worker. While the Bible clearly admits to thirty-three recorded miracles, John says that this was by no means all that Jesus did. "There are also many other things that Jesus did, which if they were written one by one, I suppose that even the world itself could not contain the books that would be written," said John (John 21:25).

The gospel writers who wrote of Jesus compiled an almost endless list of names by which he is called. In the first chapter of John alone he is called the creating Word (1:1–3), the Life (1:4), the Light (1:5), the Glory of God (1:14), one full of grace (1:17), and one who makes the Father known (1:18). In John 3:16 he is called the Only-begotten of the Father, in John 4:14 the Water of Life, and in John 6:41 the Bread of Life. In John 10:7, Jesus is called the Door, and in John 10:1, 7, 9, Jesus is called the Door of the Sheepfold. In John 11:25, he is called the Resurrection and the Life, and in John 14:6 the Way, the Truth, and the Life.

Long genealogies in both Matthew and Luke trace his ancestry through the Jewish patriarchs. These genealogies are careful to show his ancestry through David the king. He was baptized by a kinsman named John bar Zechariah at the outset of his brief three years of ministry. By official decree the sign above his gallows was lettered in three languages, stating his name and his claim of messiahship. The Latin letters on that sign were *I.N.R.I., Iesus Nazarenus Rex Iudaeorum,* Jesus of Nazareth, King of the Jews. The Roman initials have become perhaps the most famous four letters in English.

Most fascinating of all that he taught was his Second Coming. His Second Coming would be preceded by natural calamities and great cosmic disturbances (Matthew, chapters 13, 24, 25). This idea of the great and terrible Day of the Lord has haunted Christians of every era of time, who have always anticipated this worldwide, cosmic event. That theme is exalted in Julia Ward Howe's "Battle Hymn":

Mine eyes have seen the glory of the coming of the Lord:
He is trampling out the vintage where the grapes of wrath are stored;
He has loosed the fateful lightning of his terrible swift sword:
  His truth is marching on.

I have seen Him in the watch-fires of a hundred circling camps;
They have builded Him an altar in the evening dews and damps;
I can read His righteous sentence by the dim and flaring lamps.
  His day is marching on.

His apocalypse is a fascinating concept of the end of the world, and that drama lies at the heart of all he taught concerning his Second Coming.

Perhaps even before we define how others felt about him, we ought to let Jesus define himself. In his first sermon, which according to the gospel writer Luke took place back in his hometown, Nazareth, Jesus stood up in the synagogue to read the ancient scroll of Isaiah. He read these words:

The Spirit of the Lord is upon me,
Because He has anointed me to preach the gospel to the poor.
He has sent me to heal the brokenhearted,
To preach deliverance to the captives
And recovery of sight to the blind,
To set at liberty those who are oppressed,
To preach the acceptable year of the Lord.

Luke 4:18–19

Then, after Jesus had read this passage, he said, "Today this scripture is fulfilled in your hearing" (Luke 4:21). Those of Nazareth who knew him quite well were not hasty to believe that he was the Messiah. In fact a storm of protest broke out over who Jesus really was.

And they said, "Is not this Joseph's son?" And he said to them, "You will surely say this proverb to me, Physician heal yourself. What we have heard done in Capernaum, do also here in your country." Then he said, "Assuredly, I say to you, no prophet is accepted in his own country."

• • •

Then all those in the synagogue, when they heard these things, were filled with wrath, and rose up and thrust him out of the city; and they led him to the brow of the hill on which their city was built, that they might throw him down over the cliff. Then passing through the midst of them, he went his way.

Luke 4:22–24, 28–30

The disastrous crush of public opinion begins with Jesus' very first sermon in his hometown. Although he was able to escape this first scrape with premature execution, the tide of the swelling public outcry at last resulted in his cross three years later.

What did Jesus mean when he talked about the gospel? The word is an old English contraction of two words, the *god spell,* or *good news.* What *is* the good news? The good news is that the sins of all people have been forgiven. Further, the gospel means that the long alienation between the remote God and the human race has been bridged. The good news really means that God became one of us in Jesus Christ. He is no longer separate in the heavens. He is Emmanuel, God with us. Jesus Christ ended the remoteness of God by coming to earth as a man himself. He is one of us. We don't have to be afraid of God; we can have peace with God. We have been reconciled to God (2 Corinthians 5:19). The austere God who spoke to the Old Testament heroes in thunder and lightning is now as real and touchable, as human, as flesh and blood can make him. Charles Wesley wrote of the glory of God coming to us in human form in his powerful Christmas message:

Hark the herald angels sing, Glory to the newborn King.
Peace on Earth and mercy mild, God and sinners reconciled.

• • •

Veiled in flesh the Godhead see. Hail the incarnate Trinity.
Pleased as man with men to dwell, Jesus Our Immanuel.

The good news then means that the estrangement is over. In Jesus we know who God is and what he is like. Indeed, if we want to know the nature of God, we have only to look at Jesus, for he is the very picture of God (Colossians 1:15). Jesus is not the God of thunderbolts but the Son of God the loving Father, Abba. Humanity is simply God's children, and therefore the brothers and sisters of Jesus. Jesus is God's Son, like us, but so obedient and pleasing to God that God proclaimed in a loud voice that thundered above the Jordan River at Jesus' baptism, "You are My beloved Son, in whom I am well pleased" (Mark 1:11).

This towering Jesus, while rooted firmly in the scripture, is finished only in the individual hearts of those who believe. No two people know quite the same things about him or see him in quite the same way. The children's Christmas carol speaks volumes about our highly individualistic vision of Jesus: "Some children see him bronzed and brown,/The Lord of heav'n to earth come down/. . . Some children see him lily white,/The baby Jesus born this night." Some see him as a judge, coming to scourge the nations. Others see him primarily as a lover of little children. Scholars tend to see him in scholarly ways. Poets see him more poetically. Preachers see him as a preacher, teachers as a teacher. Carpenters like remembering he was one of them.

Somewhere along the line we are all shocked by some actual truths about Jesus that don't fit our cozy, privatized, inner conceptions of Jesus. I remember as a child having to learn for the first time that Jesus was a Jew. How odd this seemed to me and how remote it made me feel toward Jesus for a while. Later I had to learn that he died a bachelor at around thirty-three years of age. Again, that seemed very non-Oklahoman, when almost all men had married by twenty-five or so. Then, when I learned that Nazareth was halfway around the globe from my Oklahoma home, I had to understand what all maturing Christians have to learn, that we are ever having to blend the Christ of unstudied adoration with the one whom only critical scholarship can inform us about.

Harmonizing the Christ of worship and the Christ of study is difficult. As we have pointed out, the Christ of our adoration is always remarkably like ourselves. The Christ of scholarship is less so. We are always trying to get the Christ of critical thought to be a little more like us. Certain Nazi theologians, in an attempt to harmonize the real New Testament Jesus with one who would more logically fit into the anti-Semitism of the Third Reich, taught that Jesus was in truth Aryan, the child of a German legionnaire—wouldn't you know it?—and Mary of Nazareth. Fortunately, this theologically hybridized monstrosity of a Messiah did not survive World War II. Still, this Nazi Nazarene is evidence of how far some have been willing to modify Jesus to keep him acceptable to their privatized worldview. Most examples are not so extreme, but I suspect the Christ of suburbia looks remarkably suburbanite and the Christ of Appalachia looks quite rural. Still, if everyone is always constructing his or her own private view of Jesus, how are we ever to arrive at who he actually was?

This question of who he was has been with us from the very beginning. Jesus once asked his disciples, "Who do people say I am?" (Matthew 16:13). The disciples told Christ that there were various ideas about him.

Some felt that he was a resurrected prophet or some ancient Jewish luminary returning for another go at history. The answers to Jesus' question came within the framework of Jewish understanding but, other than that, were nearly as varied then as they are now. Still, some great commonalities remain in all views. To most Christians around the world, Jesus is the anointed Son of God, born of the Virgin, resurrected from the dead. He is quite alive at the present and reigning at the right hand of God's throne. Others, more skeptical, see him only as an inspired teacher, helpful but never to be venerated for worship. Some believe he is merely one more human being. To many he is a complete myth.

Many Christian scholars believe that there is a kernel of truth to the gospel narratives but that not all the New Testament says of Jesus should be considered true. Rudolph Bultmann earlier in this century tried to arrive at what he called the "Christ of faith." He challenged the church to ask the question "Did Jesus create the New Testament church or did the New Testament church create Jesus?" It was Bultmann's contention that the early disciples loved Jesus so much they "wrote him up" as more spectacular than he really was. The New Testament, taught Bultmann, is not the cold, calculating biography of researchers; it is the testimony of believers, giving their highly privatized account of Jesus. Every new generation produces its own set of researchers, who seem to have less of a need to endorse the Christ of faith than they do to arrive at what they believe is the more genuine Christ of scholarship.

Here at the end of the twentieth century, Robert Funk and the Jesus Seminar, like Bultmann before, are trying to strip away the mythical elements of the New Testament Christ in an attempt to arrive at just how much of the gospel story is true. These seemingly sincere scholars meet in closed sessions, where they consider the sayings of Jesus one at a time. They pass the hat of collective opinion around each of the sayings of Jesus. Various scholars, having considered the saying of Jesus in question, vote their conscience. They cast in a black bead if they consider the supposed saying of Jesus completely false. They vote with other shades, of red and white, to voice their opinions on other levels of authenticity.

Across from those who play marbles with Jesus' authenticity are people like Richard Miller of the Brethren in Christ, who says, "There was a virgin birth. Jesus was born all-powerful. He was brought to save man. He was God made flesh, God walking the earth. He was man and God." On the other hand, Jon Murray, president of American Atheists, says, "There was no such person in the history of the world as Jesus Christ. There was no historical, living, breathing, sentient human being by that name. The Bible is a fictional, nonhistorical narrative. The myth is good for business." Robert Funk called Jesus a "subversive sage." Muslims see Jesus as the greatest prophet to come upon the human scene before Mohammed himself. Harvey Cox of Harvard Divinity School reminds us that Gandhi found Jesus gloriously commendable because he lived out his teachings among his neighbors and enemies. John Cardinal O'Connor, archbishop of New York, reminds us that in any question of who Jesus is, faith makes the difference. "I don't see how, without the gift of faith, you would believe He was the Son of God. Faith makes the difference. You can study Scriptures till your eyes fall out, and without the gift of faith you're not going to believe Christ was the Son of God."

The creeds have always formed the strongest statement of who Jesus is. At the Council of Nicea in 325 A.D., one of the earliest of the creeds was suggested by Eusebius of Caesarea, an early church historian. In the creed Eusebius formulated for use in his own church, he said of Jesus:

> We believe in one God, the Father, all sovereign, the Maker of things visible and invisible; and in one Lord Jesus Christ, the Word of God, God of God, Light of Light, Son only-begotten, Firstborn of all Creation, begotten of the Father before all ages, through whom also all things were made; who was made flesh for our salvation and lived among men, and suffered, and rose again on the third day, and ascended to the Father, who shall come again in glory to judge the living and the dead.

Beyond the opinion of the scholars and the creeds, however, there is the more practical and usable question "Who is Jesus to me?" My suspicion is that your interest in this book is your own never-ending attempt to answer this more immediate question. The Reformers were overwhelmingly consumed by this question. On January 1, 1519, Huldrych Zwingli ran through Grossmünster Church in Zürich and smashed the images of the various saints. He did this in an attempt to end what he believed was idolatry in Christianity. He drew up sixty-seven conclusions, which he confessed to have preached in the city of Zürich. Some of those conclusions were:

> Christ is the only way to salvation.
> Christ is the only eternal high priest.
> Christ, having sacrificed himself once, is to eternity a certain and valid sacrifice for the sins of all faithful.
> Christ is the only mediator between God and man.

When we pray for each other on earth we do so believing that
all things are given to us through Christ alone.
Christ is our righteousness.

The Reformers were wholly intent on arriving at who Jesus was outside
of the liturgical and traditional structures of the church. They wanted to
arrive again at Jesus of Nazareth by intentionally bypassing the Jesus that
had become so encrusted with medieval lore.

It is the purpose of such a small volume as this not to acquaint you
with the Jesus of the creeds, or of the Reformers, or of the scholars.
Rather, I want to present the Christ of universal reflection in an attempt
to help you arrive at the Christ of your own understanding. I will not
spend your time or mine on those who doubt Jesus or attack him. Rather,
my own reverent bias that Jesus was God's Son has determined the prevailing view of this volume.

This entire book is a celebration of his greatness. If you are looking
for material to buttress some different opinion of Jesus, you must look
elsewhere. This book is set as a reflection of hundreds of human beings.
They did not all see him alike, but they all saw him as utterly unique. It is
their views of Jesus that are united here in the hope that you will be
joined in the scope of their vast agreement.

I

JESUS:

~

WHO HE WAS

CHRIST founded his church on the confession of Peter while on retreat with his disciples near the little town of Caesarea. Christ seemed to be asking about the public consensus when he asked, "Who am I?" It was Peter who answered, "You are the Christ" (Matthew 16:16). Peter's confession was later flawed in a crisis when he denied Christ by saying, "I do not know the man!" (Matthew 26:72).

The truth is that the immensity of Christ towers over Western civilization. Most Christians find their best definition rising from their need. To the hurting, he is the great Physician. To the confused, he is the Light. To the lost, he is the Way. To the hungry, he is the Bread of Life. To the thirsty, he is the Water of Life. To the broken, he is the Balm in Gilead. These diverse definitions of Christ are sometimes reminiscent of the story of the six blind men who touched an elephant and then were asked to describe him. One, falling against his side, said the elephant was rather like a wall. Another, who wrapped his arms around the elephant's gigantic leg, replied that the elephant was rather like a tree. A third, grasping its tail, said the elephant was more like a rope. The one who touched the elephant's ear described him as a fan, and so forth. Each of us defines Jesus from his or her own perspective. "A pig's god," said the philosopher, "would have a snout and bristles."

What then shall we say? What is an elephant? One thing is clear: an elephant cannot be defined by those with separate, exclusive streams of information. Still, the question does depend to some degree on whom you ask. Consider the Nazarene synagogue where Jesus first preached. At the conclusion of his sermon, a few seemed to believe that he was indeed the Christ. Most felt, however, that he was only a carpenter (Luke 4:16–30). To be sure, those who heard him preach and thought him only a carpenter were most likely those who had few emotional or physical needs. Those who are well fed can always afford to greet Jesus philosophically. Those, on the other hand, who felt that Jesus was the Christ may have been those whose needs were so desperate they had no time to riffle through the various philosophies of their day. Most debates over the existence of God come from well-fed philosophers sitting at a full table, warmed by the glow of the fire and their own laughter. Free from need and pain, most of these have none too great a need for a faith definition of Jesus.

Jesus' great question, "Who do men say that I am?" is never so much a question of *his* identity. It is more a question of *ours*. It is always out of our need to discover ourselves that we feel the need to answer Jesus' question. And what he is to us, we tend to see him as being to all.

> Going through a long line of prophets, God has been addressing our ancestors in different ways for centuries. Recently he spoke to us directly through his Son. By his Son, God created the world in the beginning, and it will all belong to the Son at the end. This Son perfectly mirrors God, and is stamped with God's nature. He holds everything together by what he says—powerful words!
>
> After he finished the sacrifice for sins, the Son took his honored place high in the heavens right alongside God, far higher than any angel in rank and rule. Did God ever say to an angel, "You're my Son; today I celebrate you"? Or, "I'm his Father, he's my Son"? When he presented his honored Son to the world, He says, "All angels must worship him."
>
> Hebrews 1:1–6, *The Message*

JESUS AS THEY SAW HIM

WILLIAM BARCLAY

William Barclay, one of the most esteemed British scholars in modern times, was an authority on the life of Christ. Here, as we begin to think about who Jesus was, we need to consider Barclay's definition of the meaning of Jesus' name.

IN HEBREW THE names Joshua and Jehoshua, which, as we have seen, become Jesus in Greek, mean, "Jehovah is my help," or, "Jehovah is rescue," or, "The help of Jehovah." "You shall give him the name Jesus," the angel said, "for he will save his people from their sins" (Matt. 1.21). The very name stamps Jesus as Saviour. He is God's divinely appointed and divinely sent Rescuer, whose function it is to deliver men from their sins. He came to rescue men from the estrangement and the alienation from God which is the consequence of their past sins, and for the future to liberate them from the bondage to sin, from the moral frustration and the continuous and inevitable defeat which are the result of sin. He came to bring friendship for fear, and victory for defeat.

This is in fact a meaning of the name Jesus which all true Jews would recognize. In Ecclesiasticus Jesus the Son of Sirach speaks of Joshua the son of Nun (Jesus the son of Nave is what he calls him): "Jesus the son of Nave was valiant in the wars, and was the successor of Moses in prophecies, who according to his name was made great for the saving of the elect of God" (Ecclus. 46.1). Joshua the son of Nun, Jesus the son of Nave, as his name denotes, rescued his people from their enemies; Jesus of Nazareth is the great Rescuer from sin.

❧

HE COULD HAVE BEEN HIGHBROW AND UPPITY

MAX LUCADO

Max Lucado, a Texas pastor, has distinguished himself as a beloved writer on the life of Christ. His sensitive descriptions of the life and times of Jesus have endeared him to the faithful across America. Jesus, to Lucado, was not just the Son of God but a real man whose humanity soars with emotion and human understanding. The energy Lucado imparts to the simple, straightforward biographies of the gospels has given many Christians in our day a new sense of the reality of the New Testament Christ.

BIG DEAL? I think so. I think it's significant that common folk in a little town enjoyed being with Jesus. I think it's noteworthy that the Almighty didn't act high and mighty. The Holy One wasn't holier-than-thou. The One who knew it all wasn't a know-it-all. The One who made the stars didn't keep his head in them. The One who owns all the stuff of earth never strutted it.

Never. He could have. Oh, how he could have!

He could have been a name-dropper: *Did I ever tell you of the time Moses and I went up on the mountain?*

He could have been a showoff: *Hey, want me to beam you into the twentieth century?*

He could have been a smart-aleck: *I know what you're thinking. Want me to prove it?*

He could have been highbrow and uppity: *I've got some property on Jupiter . . .*

Jesus could have been all of these, but he wasn't. His purpose was not to show off but to show up. He went to great pains to be as human as the guy down the street. He didn't need to study, but still went to the synagogue. He had no need for income, but still worked in the workshop. He had known the fellowship of angels and heard the harps of heaven, yet still went to parties thrown by tax collectors. And upon his shoulders rested the challenge of redeeming creation, but he still took time to walk ninety miles from Jericho to Cana to go to a wedding.

As a result, people liked him. Oh, there were those who chafed at his claims. They called him a blasphemer, but they never called him a braggart. They accused him of heresy, but never arrogance. He was branded as a radical, but never called unapproachable.

There is no hint that he ever used his heavenly status for personal gain. Ever. You just don't get the impression that his neighbors grew sick of his haughtiness and asked, "Well, who do you think made you God?"

His faith made him likable, not detestable. Would that ours would do the same!

Where did we get the notion that a good Christian is a solemn Christian? Who started the rumor that the sign of a disciple is a long face? How did we create this idea that the truly gifted are the heavy-hearted?

May I state an opinion that may raise an eyebrow? May I tell you why I think Jesus went to the wedding? I think he went to the wedding to

—now hold on, hear me out, let me say it before you heat the tar and pluck the feathers—I think Jesus went to the wedding to have fun.

Think about it. It's been a tough season. Forty days in the desert. No food or water. A standoff with the devil. A week breaking in some greenhorn Galileans. A job change. He's left home. It hasn't been easy. A break would be welcome. Good meal with some good wine and some good friends . . . well, it sounds pretty nice.

So off they go.

His purpose wasn't to turn the water to wine. That was a favor for his friends.

His purpose wasn't to show his power. The wedding host didn't even know what Jesus did.

His purpose wasn't to preach. There is no record of a sermon.

Really leaves only one reason. Fun. Jesus went to the wedding because he liked the people, he liked the food, and heaven forbid, he may have even wanted to swirl the bride around the dance floor a time or two. (After all, he's planning a big wedding himself. Maybe he wanted the practice?)

So, forgive me, Deacon Drydust and Sister Somberheart. I'm sorry to rain on your dirge, but Jesus was a likable fellow. And his disciples should be the same. I'm not talking debauchery, drunkenness, and adultery. I'm not endorsing compromise, coarseness, or obscenity. I am simply crusading for the freedom to enjoy a good joke, enliven a dull party, and appreciate a fun evening.

Maybe these thoughts catch you by surprise. They do me. It's been awhile since I pegged Jesus as a party-lover. But he was. His foes accused him of eating too much, drinking too much, and hanging out with the wrong people! (See Matt. 11:19.) I must confess: It's been awhile since I've been accused of having too much fun. How about you?

We used to be good at it. What has happened to us? What happened to clean joy and loud laughter? Is it our neckties that choke us? Is it our diplomas that dignify us? Is it the pew that stiffens us?

Couldn't we learn to be children again?

No God but These

JOHN BANNISTER TABB

I had no God but these,
The sacerdotal Trees,
And they uplifted me.
"I hung upon a tree."

The sun and moon I saw,
And reverential awe
Subdued me day and night.
"I am the perfect Light."

Within a lifeless Stone—
All other gods unknown—
I sought Divinity.
"The Corner-Stone am I."

For sacrificial feast,
I slaughtered man and beast,
Red recompense to gain.
"So I, a lamb, was slain."

"Yea; such My hungering Grace
That whereso'er My face
Is hidden, none may grope
Beyond eternal Hope."

∾

He Was Everybody, Only a Little Taller

HERBERT C. GABHART

The Christian church has always contained at its heart a glorious
paradox: how do you make Jesus fully human but not make him merely
human? Only if he is fully a human being can he fully understand
how human beings feel the common hurt and hope of living in a world
where death and disease and pain are so much with us. On the other

hand, only if he is more than a human being, with divine power, can he really do anything to help the woes of our earthly existence. It is to this issue that many scholars and thinkers have written, and this issue is the compelling reason behind this Gabhart selection.

"He shall grow up before him as a tender plant, and as a root out of a dry ground: he hath no form nor comeliness; and when we shall see him, there is no beauty that we should desire him."

Isaiah 53:2

"For in him dwelleth all the fulness *of the Godhead bodily."*

Colossians 2:9

IN JANUARY 1952 I was on the campus of Union University in Jackson, Tennessee, as guest speaker for Christian Emphasis Week. One afternoon I was meeting with an English class and saw on the classroom wall a John Hancock Insurance advertisement with a picture of Abraham Lincoln in the center. These words were at the top of the ad: "He was everybody, only a little taller."

I thought then, and I still think, that Lincoln was a great person, but no one meets that description like Jesus. He was everyone, only much taller.

Let us call the roll of some of the professions:

To artists, He is the One altogether lovely.

To architects, He is the Chief Cornerstone.

To physicians, He is the Great Physician.

To preachers, He is the Word of God.

To philosophers, He is the Wisdom of God.

To the dying, He is the Resurrection and the Life.

To geologists, He is the Rock of ages.

To farmers, He is the Lord of the harvest.

To professors, He is the Master Teacher.

To prodigals, He is the forgiving Father.

To the lost sheep, He is the Good Shepherd.

To thirsty souls, He is the Water of life.

To the hungry, He is the Bread of life.

To philanthropists, He is God's Unspeakable Gift.

Nineteen centuries after His sojourn on earth, His shadow is larger and growing larger than ever before. No one can measure His height or His influence.

JOHN THE BAPTIST'S TESTIMONY ABOUT JESUS

CLARENCE JORDAN

Clarence Jordan offered his Cotton Patch Version *of the New Testament as a contemporary paraphrase of scripture. He sets the gospel into the modern social scene as though Jesus and the disciples lived and taught in Georgia.*

FOLLOWING THIS, JESUS and his students went to south Georgia, and he spent a while there with them and was doing some baptizing. John was baptizing at Eufaula near Georgetown, because there was plenty of water there, and people were coming to him and getting immersed. (This was before John had been thrown in jail.) Well, John's students and a Methodist got into a fuss over dipping and sprinkling. So they came to John and told him, "Reverend, you remember that fellow who was with you on the other side of the Chattahoochee, who you yourself praised? Guess what! Now he's dipping and everybody is joining up with *him!*" John answered, "A man can't take an office that hasn't been given him from above. You yourselves can bear me out that I told you, 'I am not the Leader, but I was sent ahead of him.' The man with the bride is the bridegroom. The best man stands with the groom and shares his joy. That's why I'm so happy. That man must grow, while I must fade out."

• • •

The one who springs from above is over everything. The earthling, being from the earth, speaks in terms of the earth. The spiritual person, however, is above all this. While he does talk about what he has seen and heard, nobody takes him seriously. When one does take him seriously, one becomes evidence that God is true. The God-sent man bears God's message, for God fully equips him with the Spirit. The Father loves the Son and has put him in charge of everything. When one lives by the Son, one has spiritual life. When one disobeys the Son, one won't catch a glimpse of life; rather, God's displeasure hangs over him.

ENOCH'S WITNESS FROM THE APOCRYPHA

WILLIAM BARCLAY

The Apocrypha is a kind of third testament included in some versions of the Bible between the Old and New Testaments. It is generally not considered to carry the same weight of authenticity, either in content or authorship, as the books of the Old and New Testaments.

And there I saw One who had a head of days,
And His head was white like wool,
And with Him there was another whose countenance had the appearance
  of a man,
And his face was full of graciousness, like one of the holy angels.
And I asked the angel who went with me and showed me all the hidden
  things, concerning that Son of Man, who he was, and whence he
  was, and why he went with the Head of Days? And he answered
  and said unto me:
This is the Son of Man who hath righteousness,
With whom dwelleth righteousness,
And who revealeth all the treasures of that which is hidden,
Because the Lord of Spirits hath chosen him,
And whose lot hath the pre-eminence before the Lord of Spirits in
  uprightness for ever.
And this Son of Man whom thou hast seen
Shall put down the kings and mighty from their seats,
And the strong from their thrones,
And shall loosen the reins of the strong
And break the teeth of sinners.
And he shall put down the kings from their thrones and kingdoms
Because they do not extol and praise Him,
Nor humbly acknowledge whence the kingdom was bestowed upon
  them.
And he shall put down the countenance of the strong,
And shall fill them with shame.
And darkness shall be their dwelling,
And worms shall be their bed,
And they shall have no hope of rising from their beds,
Because they do not extol the name of the Lord of Spirits.

Enoch 46:1—6

And at that hour that Son of Man was named
In the presence of the Lord of Spirits,
And his name before the Head of Days.
Yea, before the sun and the signs were created,
Before the stars of the heaven were made,
His name was named before the Lord of Spirits.
He shall be a staff to the righteous whereon to stay themselves and not
   fall,
And he shall be the light of the Gentiles,
And the hope of those who are troubled in heart.
All who dwell on earth shall fall down and worship before him,
And will praise and bless and celebrate with song the Lord of Spirits
And for this reason hath he been chosen and hidden before Him,
Before the creation of the world and for evermore.
And the wisdom of the Lord of Spirits hath revealed to him the holy and
   righteous;
For he hath preserved the lot of the righteous,
Because they have hated and despised this world of unrighteousness,
And have hated all its works and ways in the name of Lord of Spirits;
For in his name they are saved,
And according to his good pleasure hath it been in regard to their life.
In these days downcast in countenance shall the kings of earth have
   become,
And the strong who possess the land because of the work of their hands,
For on the day of their anguish and affliction they shall not be able to save
   themselves,
And I will give them over into the hands of Mine elect:
As straw in the fire so shall they burn before the face of the holy:
As lead in the water shall they sink before the face of the righteous.
And no trace of them shall any more be found.
And on the day of their affliction there shall be rest on the earth,
And before them they shall fall and not rise again:
And there shall be no one to take them with his hands and raise them;
For they have denied the Lord of Spirits and His Anointed.
The name of the Lord of Spirits be blessed.

               Enoch 48.2–10

And one portion of them shall look on the other,
And they shall be terrified,
And they shall be downcast of countenance,
And pain shall seize them,

When they see that Son of Man
Sitting on the throne of his glory.
And the kings and the mighty and all who possess the earth shall bless
    and glorify and extol him who rules over all, who was hidden.
For from the beginning the Son of Man was hidden,
And the Most High preserved him in the presence of His might,
And revealed him to the elect.
And the congregation of the elect and holy shall be sown,
And all the elect shall stand before him on that day.
And all the kings and the mighty and the exalted and those who rule the
    earth
Shall fall down before him on their faces,
And worship and set their hope upon that Son of Man,
And petition him and supplicate him for mercy at his hands.
Nevertheless the Lord of Spirits will so press them
That they shall hastily go forth from His presence,
And their faces shall be filled with shame,
And darkness grow deeper on their faces.
And He will deliver them to the angels for punishment,
To execute vengeance on them because they have oppressed His children
    and His elect;
And they shall be a spectacle for the righteous and for His elect:
They shall rejoice over them,
Because the wrath of the Lord of Spirits resteth upon them,
And His sword is drunk with their blood.
And the righteous and elect shall be saved on that day,
And they shall never thenceforward see the face of the sinners and
    unrighteous.
And the Lord of Spirits will abide over them,
And with the Son of Man shall they eat
And lie down and rise up for ever and ever.
And the righteous and elect shall have risen from the earth,
And ceased to be of downcast countenance.
And they shall have been clothed with garments of glory,
And these shall be the garments of life from the Lord of Spirits;
And your garments shall not grow old,
Nor your glory pass away before the Lord of Spirits.

Enoch 62:5–16

And after that their faces shall be filled with darkness
And shame before that Son of Man,

And they shall be driven from his presence,
And the sword shall abide before his face in their midst.

Enoch 63:11

And there was great joy among them,
And they blessed and gloried and extolled
Because the name of that Son of Man had been revealed unto them.
And he sat on the throne of his glory,
And the sum of judgement was given unto the Son of Man,
And he caused the sinners to pass away and be destroyed from off the
      face of the earth,
And those who have led the world astray
With chains shall they be bound,
And in their assemblage-place of destruction shall they be imprisoned,
And all their works vanish from the face of the earth.
And from henceforth there shall be nothing corruptible;
For that Son of Man has appeared,
And has seated himself on the throne of his glory,
And all evil shall pass away before his face,
And the word of that Son of Man shall go forth
And be strong before the Lord of Spirits.

Enoch 69:26–29

Finally, of the translation of Enoch it is said:

And it came to pass after this that his name during his lifetime
was raised aloft to that Son of Man and to the Lord of Spirits
from amongst those who dwell on the earth.

Enoch 70:1

ABOUT THIS TIME LIVED JESUS

FLAVIUS JOSEPHUS

Josephus was a Jewish historian of antiquity. He often commented on early Christianity but he himself was not a Christian.

ABOUT THIS TIME lived Jesus, a wise man, if it be proper to call him a man; for he was a doer of wonderful works,—a teacher of such men as receive the truth with pleasure. He drew over to him both many of the Jews and many of the Greeks. He was the Christ. And when Pilate, at the instigation of the principal men among us, had condemned him to the cross, those who had loved him at first did not forsake him. For he appeared to them alive again on the third day; the divine prophets having foretold these and many other wonderful things concerning him. And the sect of Christians, so named after him, are not extinct to this day.

❧

THE MYSTERY OF CHRIST

ELTON TRUEBLOOD

Christianity was born in the Greco-Roman arena, a multicultural age not unlike our own. The prominent religion of the day was of course that of the Olympian gods and goddesses. This religion, which erected temples all over the Roman Empire, sought to define the reasons for the phenomena of the natural world in terms of the activities of those gods and goddesses. The point that worshippers of the Olympians made was that behind every unanswerable issue of life, there was a pat answer.

Christianity was born as one of the mystery religions; it taught that Christ did not come to supply a pat answer to all that could not be answered. Life is always going to be full of problems that cannot be quickly answered. Jesus himself cannot be explained. How can we ever give logical, genetic explanations of his Virgin Birth, or rational reasons for his Resurrection? Christians do not set themselves to give reasons for Jesus' miracles but to attest that the mystery holds more meaning than the pat Olympian explanations of what it means to have an origin and destiny.

As CHRIST CAME into Galilee, He exhibited at once all of the major elements of His ministry. These elements were three. In the first place, He proclaimed a message. What made this remarkable was its mood and tense. The mood was personal and urgent. The consequence is that we are told relatively little of what Christ said on those early occasions, but much of how He said it. Christ did not begin by telling of the glorious acts of God in the past, nor of the glittering hope of the future. Instead He spoke of the living, immediate *present*. "The time," He said, "is fulfilled." Such a message, given with burning passion, is inevitably exciting because the completed present is the most moving of all tenses. The past is irretrievably gone and the future may never be, but the present is vivid and real. The good news started with the message of *God in the present tense*.

The second element of Christ's ministry, which appeared in the opening scene, was the direct calling of individual men. He needed helpers and He found them early. The primary extension of Christ's kingdom comes when men and women are reached one by one, as occurred in the recruitment of the unlearned fishermen of Galilee. There is no reason to suppose that these four men, Simon, Andrew, James, and John, were seeing Jesus for the first time, but the call to participation was undoubtedly fresh and new. It was given with such confidence that it was answered without hesitation.

The third characteristic element of Christ's ministry, which appeared at the beginning, was that of *healing*. Exactly how He healed we do not know, but it is unhistorical to stress Christ's teaching without equal emphasis upon release from human suffering. We cannot present Christ accurately if we present Him merely as Teacher, or Leader, or Healer, for He was all three, and He was all three all the time. The pattern appeared early and was continually repeated.

❧

THERE IS A MAN

JEAN-BAPTISTE-HENRI LACORDAIRE

THERE IS A Man whose tomb is guarded by love, there is a Man whose sepulchre is not only glorious as a prophet declared, but whose sepulchre is loved. There is a Man whose ashes, after eighteen centuries, have not grown cold; who daily lives again in the thoughts of an innumerable multitude of men; who is visited in His cradle by shepherds and by kings, who vie with each other in bringing to Him gold and frankincense and myrrh. There is a Man whose steps are unweariedly retrodden by a large portion of mankind, and who, although no longer present, is followed by that throng in all the scenes of His bygone pilgrimage, upon the knees of His mother, by the borders of the lakes, to the tops of the mountains, in the byways of the valleys, under the shade of the olive trees, in the still solitude of the deserts. There is a Man, whose every word still vibrates and produces more than love, produces virtues fructifying in love. There is a Man, who eighteen centuries ago was nailed to a gibbet, and whom millions of adorers daily detach from this throne of His suffering, and, kneeling before Him, prostrating themselves as low as they can without shame, there, upon the earth, they kiss His bleeding feet with unspeakable ardour. There is a Man, who was scourged, killed, crucified, whom an ineffable passion raises from death and infamy, and exalts to the glory of love unfailing which finds in Him peace, honour, joy, and even ecstasy. There is a Man, pursued in His sufferings and in His tomb by undying hatred, and who, demanding apostles and martyrs from all posterity, finds apostles and martyrs in all generations. There is a Man, in fine, and only one, who has founded His love upon earth, and that Man is thyself, O Jesus! who hast been pleased to baptize me, to anoint me, to consecrate me in Thy love, and whose name alone now opens my very heart, and draws from it those accents which overpower me and raise me above myself.

THIS YOUR GREATEST GIFT

JOHN BAILLIE

O GOD, WHO has proven Your love for all humanity by sending us Jesus Christ our Lord, and has illuminated our human life by the radiance of His presence, I give You thanks for this Your greatest gift.

For my Lord's days upon the earth:
For the record of His deeds of love:
For the words He spoke for my guidance and help:
For His obedience unto death:
For His triumph over death:

For the presence of His Spirit within me now:
I thank you, O God.

Grant that the remembrance of the blessed Life that once was lived out on this common earth under these ordinary skies may remain with me in all the tasks and duties of this day. Let me remember—

His eagerness, not to be ministered unto, but to minister:
His sympathy with suffering of every kind:
His bravery in the face of His own suffering:
His meekness of bearing, so that, when reviled, He reviled not again:
His steadiness of purpose in keeping to His appointed task:
His simplicity:
His self-discipline:
His serenity of spirit:
His complete reliance upon You, His Father in Heaven.

And in each of these ways give me grace to follow in His footsteps. Amen.

OUR BELOVED PHYSICIAN

CHARLES H. SPURGEON

Christ is venerated for many reasons among the faithful, but one of his great exaltations comes from the title—long given him by the church —"the Great Physician." In both Catholic and Protestant traditions, Jesus is seen as the healer. Jesus is credited in scripture with thirty-five specific miracles and many unspecified miracles, most of which had to do with healing. This reverence will always be central in his church.

"Great multitudes followed Him, and He healed them all."
Matthew 12:15

WHAT A MASS of hideous sickness Jesus must have seen. Yet He was not disgusted but patiently healed them all. What a variety of evils He must have seen. What sickening ulcers and festering sores. Yet He was prepared for every type of evil and was victorious over its every form. Let the arrows fly from any angle, He quenches their fiery power.

The heat of fever, the cold of fluid buildup, the lethargy of paralysis, the rage of madness, the filth of leprosy, the darkness of blindness: All knew the power of His word and fled at His command. In every corner of the field, He triumphed over evil and received honor from the delivered captives. He came, He saw, and He conquered everywhere.

He is the same this morning. Whatever my case may be, the beloved Physician can heal me. Whatever the state of others whom I remember in prayer, I have hope in Jesus that they will be healed. My child, my friend, or my dearest one, I have hope for each and all when I remember the healing power of my Lord.

In my own situation, however severe my struggle with sin and infirmities, I too may be of good cheer. He who on earth walked the hospitals still dispenses His grace and works wonders among His children. Let me earnestly go to Him at once.

Let me praise Him this morning as I remember how He wrought His spiritual cures. He took on Himself our sicknesses. "By His stripes we are healed" (Isaiah 53:5). The church on earth is full of souls healed by our beloved Physician. The inhabitants of heaven confess that "He healed them all."

Come then and spread the virtue of His grace. Let it be "an everlasting sign that shall not be cut off" (Isaiah 55:13).

∾

I Believe

FYODOR MIKHAYLOVICH DOSTOYEVSKY

Jesus is unquestionably the primary literary symbol of the West. Nowhere does Jesus more dominate novels as the primary literary symbol than in the Russian novels of the nineteenth century. Both Tolstoy and Dostoyevsky were imbued with a faith that marked their novels with a ready evidence of all they believed about Christ. While they rarely stated their faith in direct creedal statements of their own, they did freely give this office to their fictional characters. Such is the case of this inclusion from The Brothers Karamazov.

I BELIEVE THERE is nothing lovelier, deeper, more sympathetic and more perfect than the Saviour; I say to myself with jealous love that not only is there no one else like Him, but that there could be no one. I would say even more. If any one could prove to me that Christ is outside the truth, and if the truth really did exclude Christ, I should prefer to stay with

Christ and not with truth. There is in the world only one figure of
absolute beauty: Christ. That infinitely lovely figure is as a matter of
course an infinite marvel.

◆

THE GOOD SHEPHERD

BILLY GRAHAM

THE WONDERFUL PICTURE of God as our Shepherd is found in many places
in the Old Testament. One of the Psalms begins, "Hear us, O Shepherd
of Israel, you who lead Joseph like a flock" (Psalm 80:1). It's great to
think that the Everlasting God, the Almighty Creator, condescends to be
the Shepherd of His people.

David makes the relationship a personal one in the best known of all
Psalms. "The Lord is my shepherd," he cries exultantly, "I shall lack
nothing" (Psalm 23:1). The rest of the Psalm tells us what we shall not
lack. It speaks of the shepherd's provision as He leads us to the green
pastures, His guidance along the paths of righteousness (that means the
right paths), His presence with us in the dark valley. No wonder David
testifies, "My cup overflows" (verse 5)—such are God's boundless
blessings.

Isaiah adds a further touch to the picture when he says, "He tends
his flock like a shepherd: He gathers the lambs in his arms and carries
them close to his heart" (Isaiah 40:11). The figure here indicates the
tender care with which the Lord supports His people on their journey
and the strong love with which He enfolds them.

In the New Testament, Jesus uses this same figure and applies it to
Himself. He says, "I am the good shepherd. The good shepherd lays down
his life for the sheep. The hired hand is not the shepherd who owns the
sheep. So when he sees the wolf coming, he abandons the sheep and runs
away. Then the wolf attacks the flock and scatters it. . . . I am the good
shepherd; I know my sheep and my sheep know me" (John 10:11–14).

Note four things about Jesus the Good Shepherd.

He owns the sheep: they belong to Him.

He guards the sheep: He never abandons them when danger is near.

He knows the sheep, knows them each by name and leads them out
(see verse 3).

And He lays down His life for the sheep, such is the measure of His love.

How thankful we should be, weak, wandering, and foolish as we are, that we have such a shepherd. Let's learn to keep close to Him, to listen to His voice, and follow Him.

∽

THE GREAT NAME

PÈRE DIDON

We are never real without a name. God, in the Old Testament, gave Moses his name in terms of his being. When Moses asks God for a name, God says simply, "I am who I am" (Exodus 3:4). But the birth story of Matthew declares that an angel appears to Joseph with the particular instruction that he is to name the boy Jesus, or Joshua (Matthew 1:21). Joshua means Jehovah saves in Hebrew. It is by this highly significant name that Jesus is reverenced worldwide. His proper name in Hebrew would have been Jesus bar Joseph, or Jesus the son of Joseph.

JESUS CHRIST IS the great name in history. There are others for whom men have died; He alone is adored by all people, in all nations, and in all times.

He who bears this name is known throughout the world. Even among the savage and degenerate tribes of the human race, His apostles preach without ceasing that He died upon the cross; and the offscourings of mankind may be saved by loving Him. Those who are neutral, in the modern world, recognize that none is better for the weak and miserable.

The greatest intellects of the past would be forgotten if memorials, as palaces, obelisks or tombs; if written testimonies, as papyrus or parchments, bricks, columns or medals, had not preserved their memory. Jesus survives in the conscience of the faithful: there is His witness and indestructible monument. The Church founded by Him fills time and space with His name. She knows Him, she loves Him, she adores Him.

A Symposium on Jesus' Identity

JOHN BLANCHARD

"Who is Jesus?" is a question the whole world has ever asked. The issue of his identity has long remained hidden in miracle and mystery. He means something very individual and special to as many as have ever spoken of him or written about him. John Blanchard here presents the words of but a few.

When Jesus came to earth he did not cease to be God; when he returned to heaven he did not cease to be man.

Christ was a complete man.

AUGUSTINE

Jesus Christ is God in the form of man; as completely God as if he were not man; as completely man as if he were not God.

A. J. F. Behrends

Jesus Christ, the condescension of divinity, and the exaltation of humanity.

Phillips Brooks

Christ uncrowned himself to crown us, and put off his robes to put on our rags, and came down from heaven to keep us out of hell. He fasted forty days that he might feast us to all eternity; he came from heaven to earth that he might send us from earth to heaven.

W. Dyer

Jesus became as like us as God can be.

Donald English

Jesus did not become identical to us; he did become identified with us.

Donald English

It pleases the Father that *all* fulness should be in Christ; therefore there is nothing but emptiness anywhere else.

W. Gadsby

Christ's humanity is the great hem of the garment, through which we can touch his Godhead.

Richard Glover

If ever the Divine appeared on earth, it was in the person of Christ.

Johann Wolfgang von Goethe

Christ is our temple, in whom by faith all believers meet.

Matthew Henry

In Christ Jesus heaven meets earth and earth ascends to heaven.

Henry Law

Surely royalty in rags, angels in cells, is not descent compared to Deity in flesh!

Henry Law

A man who was merely a man and said the sort of things Jesus said wouldn't be a great moral teacher. He'd be either a lunatic—on a level with a man who says he's a poached egg—or else he'd be the devil of hell. You must make your choice. Either this man was and is the Son of God, or else a madman or something worse. . . . But don't let us come up with any patronizing nonsense about his being a great human teacher. He hasn't left that open to us. He didn't intend to.

C. S. Lewis

Jesus was man in guise, not in disguise.

Handley C. G. Moule

He suffered not as God, but he suffered who was God.

John Owen

The impression of Jesus which the gospels give . . . is not so much one of deity reduced as of divine capacities restrained.

J. I. Packer

If the life and death of Socrates are those of a philosopher, the life and death of Jesus Christ are those of a God.

Jean-Jacques Rousseau

If you want to know what God has to say to you, see what Christ was and is.

Remember, Christ was not a deified man, neither was he a humanized God. He was perfectly God and at the same time perfectly man.

Charles H. Spurgeon

Christ was not half a God and half a man; he was perfectly God and perfectly man.

James Stalker

Because Christ was God, did he pass unscorched through the fires of Gethsemane and Calvary? Rather let us say, because Christ was God he underwent a suffering that was absolutely infinite.

Augustus H. Strong

∾

CHRIST IS GOOD

A. E. GARVIE

THERE HAVE BEEN great teachers and leaders of the souls of men, but none of them claimed to do or did what Jesus has done. Through Moses came a law to be obeyed; Mohammed was the prophet of a truth about God; Gautama offered man the secret of a salvation which must be secured by their own efforts. Christ brings men to God and God to men in an immediacy of relation, in an intimacy of communion, in a sufficiency and an efficacy of divine grace through human faith which is a new creation of man in his inmost, highest life. It is because of the sufficiency and efficacy both of His revelation of God, and His redemption of man, the transcendence of what He has done for man over all that other teachers and leaders of the soul have accomplished, the absolute quality of the relation of man to God through Him, that we must confess that this work is not of man, even at his very best; but this God and God alone can have wrought. This cannot, of course, be demonstrated by merely intellectual arguments to those who have not had the experience of what Christ has done; but for those who have that experience, there need be no other evidence. They have the witness in themselves that He is God.

We believe that Christ is God not because He mysteriously possessed a divine nature united to a human, but because as He is as man we find God in Him, and God finds us through Him. We behold the glory of the Only

Begotten of the Father in the Word incarnate, and find Him full of grace and truth. God making Himself known and even giving Himself in love to us. This and nothing less is what believing in the divinity of Christ means.

∾

A GATHERING OF ANGELS

CALVIN MILLER

There are any number of fictional quips and short stories that cannot be put on a par with either the veracity of holy scripture or the sincere work of dedicated scholars. Yet while these tales do not define historical truth, they do derive from the heart of truth, and their fictional mode should be allowed to define the theological truth they intend to emphasize. There are many of these scattered throughout this book. They accent the truth that Jesus always quickens artistic and literary imagination.

CHRISTMAS EVE HAD come at last. Gabriel and Michael sat talking.

"What time is it, Gabriel?" asked Michael.

Gabriel looked down at a rather immense calendar watch, studied it a moment, and looked back up.

"It's exactly the fourteenth year of Augustus . . . you know, *annus quattuordecimus,* as these Romans say."

"No, no, no! I want it in the new time. I can't remember! Is it B.C. or A.D.?"

Gabriel looked again at the big watch.

"It's about time for the changeover! Tonight at midnight, the Lord God puts the new star on that elliptical orbit that passes over Bethlehem . . . then all the angels have to set their watches ahead to A.D."

Michael scratched his head.

"A.D.? What's that mean?"

"How do I know what it means? The Lord God's the only one who knows everything. I think it stands for some more of those Roman words, *anno Domini* or something like that. Anyway, it just means Jesus Time. The whole world is going to use it; it all becomes official as soon as the Lord God takes the brakes off that new star."

Michael cautiously ventured one final question:

"Look, Gabriel, how are they coming on that new star?"

Gabriel looked excited.

"I just flew by the Star Foundry yesterday. Mike, this is going to be a big one. Bright too. You remember how all the angels were wearing sunglasses when the Lord God started dumping the hydrogen in Andromeda? Well, I swear! This one's bigger and brighter. It makes Halley's comet look like a sulfur match."

"Sulfur match?"

"Never mind, Michael. They're pumping the helium in now. This is going to be some star. It's gonna slam smack into the middle of the constellation Pisces. There's some astrologers out in the desert at a big stargazers convention. Those guys are really in for a surprise. Remember how mixed up they were during the last meteorite shower? Think what it'll do to their charts when Redeemer I comes a-slicin' through the sky."

Michael beamed. "Redeemer I . . . I like that. Is that what they're calling it: Redeemer I?"

"That's what it is, Michael."

"Man, what a name for the Jesus star! Say, speaking of Jesus, where is he, Gabe?"

"Still tucked up under the heart of Mary, but not for long. Mike, I'm so excited!"

"Me too. I've been practicing the Christmas music all day long. I hate scaring those shepherds like we're going to have to do. Still, I know I can't hold my song past midnight."

"Me either, Gabe. I understand the whole anthem is going to be in Aramaic. Of course, I really sing it best in Latin—you know, like *Gloria in excelsis Deo.* But you know the Lord God. Those shepherds don't know a word of Latin, so we're going to do the whole thing in Aramaic."

"Man, this is some anthem. I can't remember. Is it *double p* or *double f* on the refrain?" he asked, studying the sheet music.

"*Triple f.* We start out loud; and we just keep the whole piece a-swelling. I have the tenor obbligato. *Crashing crescendo,* it is going to be quite a night. Still, why is time draggin' so . . . will A.D. never get here?"

Michael paused and walked a few steps and looked over the crystal balustrades.

"Look, Gabriel. See the little couple down there? They've been traveling for three days."

Gabriel leaned out and looked over. He struggled to fight back tears before he spoke. "He's been to all six inns in the city. She's in so much pain she can hardly stand it. She's only eighteen and this is her first baby. How time flies! I was just down in Nazareth nine months ago talking to her. She's a beautiful girl. You wanna hear the song she wrote, Michael? It was pretty good for an earthling.

My soul doth magnify the Lord
And my spirit rejoiceth in God my Savior
For he hath regarded the low estate of his handmaiden,
For behold from henceforth all generations will call me blessed.
For he that is mighty hath done to me great things,
And holy is his name.
And his mercy is on them that
Fear him from generation to generation.

Gabriel stopped. Michael went on, "Wow, that's some poetry, Gabe. When did she write that?"

"Right after she found out that she was going to be the mother of the Messiah."

"Look! Gabriel, they're going toward the stable. It must be getting time."

"It's time all right! Say, what's the name of that unfriendly place?"

"It's Bethlehem. Why?"

"Bethlehem? Why in the world Bethlehem? I mean, why not Athens or Rome or Thebes? Where's this Bethlehem, anyway?"

"It's about six miles from Jerusalem; that's where King David was from."

"Couldn't it be somewhere more cosmopolitan than Bethlehem?"

"I suppose the Lord God could have picked a bigger place, but after all, this isn't a world's fair, you know. Besides, half a millennium or so back, Micah said it would have to be Bethlehem. You know Micah, don't you?"

"Well, of course, I know Micah, doesn't everyone? I just saw him and Jeremiah and a couple of the minor prophets the other day. But I didn't know he said it would have to be Bethlehem."

"I even heard him telling a couple of the younger cherubim the way."

"The way where?"

"The way to Bethlehem. He was real insistent to them. Told them to watch their altitude and steer clear of Mount Hermon. 'Set the glide pattern at thirty thousand feet,' he said, 'and fly left at Damascus.' "

"Say, what the . . . what's that light?"

"Wow, Gabe, look. It's Redeemer I. Better get into your choir robe." Quickly Gabriel slipped into his choir robe.

"Can I set my watch on A.D. now?" he asked.

"Not yet, Gabe! Not yet!"

Gabriel looked like he was about to burst. In a nervous minute, he asked again.

"Please, can I set my watch now, Mike?"

"Shhh! Not yet, Gabe. Now be quiet."

Redeemer I rolled out into the night sky and spilled its light.

Everything was all golden!

It was magnificent!

Down below, the astrologers panicked in the splendor of the light. Nervously Gabriel continued to play with the stem of his watch. Ten thousand angels stood in rapt attention waiting for the downbeat of the Aramaic anthem.

Far to the left of Damascus, the shepherds gazed out into the night silently. The universe was hushed. Nothing moved.

Then the great Lord God of all the universe raised his hands. The great Redeemer I rolled right over Bethlehem. The prophet Micah beamed from ear to ear. And the Lord God dropped his hand.

And distinctly every angel heard a faint redeeming sound above the sleeping world. At that very moment when God dropped his hand, they heard it. A baby cried!

And Gabriel set his watch to run a billion years on Jesus Time.

❧

THAT NIGHT

AUTHOR UNKNOWN

That night when in the Judean skies
    The mystic star dispensed its light,
A blind man moved in his sleep—
    And dreamed that he had sight.

That night when shepherds heard the song
    Of hosts angelic choiring near,
A deaf man stirred in slumber's spell—
    And dreamed that he could hear!

That night when in the cattle stall
    Slept Child and mother cheek by jowl,
A cripple turned his twisted limbs—
    And dreamed that he was whole.

That night when o'er the newborn Babe
  The tender Mary rose to lean,
A loathsome leper smiled in sleep—
  And dreamed that he was clean.

That night when to the mother's breast
  The little King was held secure,
A harlot slept a happy sleep—
  And dreamed that she was pure!

That night when in the manger lay
  The Sanctified who came to save,
A man moved in the sleep of death—
  And dreamed there was no grave.

❧

HIS GREATNESS

BLAISE PASCAL

JESUS CHRIST, WITHOUT worldly riches, without the exterior productions of science, was infinitely great in His sublime order of holiness. He neither published inventions nor possessed kingdoms; but He was humble, patient, pure before God, terrible to evil spirits, and without spot of sin. Oh, with what illustrious pomp, with what transcendent magnificence did He come attended, to such as beheld with the eyes of the heart, and with those faculties which are the judges and discerners of true wisdom!

It had been needless for our Lord Jesus Christ to have assumed the state of an earthly king, for the illustration of His kingdom of holiness. But how great, how excellent did He appear in the brightness of His proper order!

It is most unreasonable to be scandalised at the mean condition of our Lord, as if it were opposed in the same order and kind to the greatness which He came to display. Let us consider this greatness in His life, in His sufferings, in His solitude, in His death, in the choice of His attendants, in their act of forsaking Him, in the privacy of His resurrection, and in all the other parts of His history; we shall find it so truly raised and noble, as to leave no ground for our being offended at a meanness which was quite of another order.

CHRIST IN GALILEE

ANDREW MARTIN FAIRBAIRN

One of the aspects of Christianity that sets it in such great contradis-
tinction to other religions is the great detail that is given geographi-
cally of the life of its founder, Christ. Jesus' life is set historically in a
time that was a real time. This inclusion speaks casually of those
definite times and places in which Jesus lived and taught.

JESUS CAME INTO Galilee, preaching the gospel of the kingdom of God.
He will appear before us as a Jew, lowly born, humbly bred, without the
manners of the court or the capital, without the learning of the school,
or the culture of the college; a mere peasant, as it were, just like the
unlettered workmen of Nazareth, or the toil-stained rustics of Galilee. He
becomes a preacher, just as Amos the herdsman of Tekoah and multitudes
more of His people had done, but He is flouted by the Pharisees, contradicted by the scribes, hated and persecuted by the priests. In a word, He
is despised and rejected of the official guardians of religion, and heard
gladly by the common people alone. The men He gathers round Him are,
like Himself, without the delicate thought or the fastidious speech—not
always accurate or pure—of the man of conscious culture, or the thorough
knowledge of all that is superficial in man, which marks the person high
in place and familiar with affairs. Now, what would men accustomed to a
perspective given by those who are accounted pillars in Church and State
think of this preacher and His rustic band? Pascal puts the matter far too
mildly when he says Jesus Christ lived in such obscurity that the great
historians of the world who are concerned with the affairs of State have
hardly noticed Him. He who from the heavens watcheth the ways of men
might well laugh in infinite irony as He heard the poet praise Caesar as
divine, or the historian bid all eyes to behold the acts of Pilate, and blind
as death to the deeds of Christ. If the historian had tried to notice and to
describe Him, what would he have said? Something like this: "In those
days one Jesus of Nazareth, a carpenter, began to preach, and gathered
around Him certain ignorant fisher-folk after the manner of His kind, but
all the people of repute held aloof, and the chief priest, with adroit and
most excellent diplomacy, when this Jesus became troublesome, induced
the procurator to crucify Him." Had we depended on the historian of
great deeds there would have been the limit of his vision, and it would
mark the immensity of his ignorance and our own. Happily, eyes truer
and keener of sight watched His coming, and by their help we can see the
entrance into the world of the greatest person and the most creative truth,
and the process by which they slowly penetrated the spirit of man, and

worked his saving. It was Godlike that He should enter and begin in silent lowliness. All God's great works are silent. They are not done amid rattle of drums and flare of trumpets. Light as it travels makes no noise, utters no sound to the ear. Creation is a silent process; nature rose under the Almighty hand without clang or clamor, or noises that distract and disturb. So, when Jesus came, being of God, His coming was lowly.

∾

THE BOGUS DESCRIPTION OF CHRIST

EDGAR JOHNSON GOODSPEED

A DOCUMENT KNOWN as "The Description of Christ" has of late reappeared in religious papers and books in various parts of the United States. In recent years I have received copies of it from all parts of the country. In a well-known berry ranch near Los Angeles the document is on display, together with a portrait of Christ.

Because it is presented as an ancient and presumably authentic document, it is worth while to state the facts about it.

The "Description" probably originated in Italy in the thirteenth century. In its earliest form it appeared as a simple statement beginning: "It is read in the annals books of the Romans that our Lord Jesus Christ, who was called by the Gentiles the prophet of truth, was of stature middling tall, and comely . . ." It was probably based on the books of instructions of the Greek miniature painters who illustrated medieval manuscripts. These instructions, which still exist, contain descriptions of the personal appearance of all the leading figures in the New Testament, as well as the heroes of Troy.

In a number of medieval manuscripts, the description appears in the longer form of a letter from Publius Lentulus, Governor of Judea, to the Roman Senate.

This is the version given by Montague R. James in his *Apocryphal New Testament* (1924), but somewhat modernized:

> A certain Lentulus, a Roman, being an official for the Romans in the province of Judea in the time of Tiberius Caesar, upon seeing Christ, and noting his wonderful works, his preaching, his endless miracles, and other amazing things about him, wrote thus to the Roman Senate:

There has appeared in these times, and still is, a man of great power named Jesus Christ, who is called by the Gentiles the prophet of truth, whom his disciples call the Son of God: raising the dead and healing diseases, a man in stature middling tall, and comely, having a reverend countenance, which they that look upon may love and fear; having hair of the hue of an unripe hazel-nut and smooth almost down to his ears, but from the ears in curling locks somewhat darker and more shining, waving over his shoulders; having a parting at the middle of the head according to the fashion of the Nazareans; a brow smooth and very calm, with a face without wrinkle or any blemish, which a moderate color makes beautiful; with the nose and mouth no fault at all can be found; having a full beard of the color of his hair, not long, but a little forked at the chin; having an expression simple and mature, the eyes grey, glancing, and clear; in rebuke terrible, in admonition kind and lovable, cheerful yet keeping gravity; sometimes he has wept, but never laughed; in stature of body tall and straight, with hands and arms fair to look upon; in talk grave, reserved and modest (so that he was rightly called by the prophet) fairer than the children of men.

THE DEATH OF CHRIST

JOHN R. W. STOTT

CHRISTIANITY IS A rescue religion. It declares that God has taken the initiative in Jesus Christ to deliver us from our sins. This is the main theme of the Bible.

> "You shall call his name Jesus, for he will save his people from their sins."

> "The Son of man came to seek and to save the lost."

> "The saying is sure and worthy of full acceptance, that Christ Jesus came into the world to save sinners."

"We have seen and testify that the Father has sent his Son as the Saviour of the world."

More particularly, since sin has three principal consequences, . . . "salvation" includes man's liberation from them all. Through Jesus Christ the Saviour we can be brought out of exile and reconciled to God; we can be born again, receive a new nature and be set free from our moral bondage; and we can have the old discords replaced by a fellowship of love. The first aspect of salvation Christ made possible by his suffering of death, the second by the gift of his Spirit and the third by the building of his church.

I KNOW MEN

NAPOLEON BONAPARTE

Perhaps it needs to be pointed out here that even those figures of history who didn't much carry out the teachings of Jesus were still impressed with his worthiness. Napoleon, like despots before and after him, cannot be called a man of deep faith. Yet it is a tribute to Jesus that even politicians and despots reverence his example.

I KNOW MEN; and I tell you that Jesus Christ is not a man. Superficial minds see a resemblance between Christ and the founders of empires, and the gods of other religions. That resemblance does not exist. There is between Christianity and whatever other religions the distance of infinity. . . .

Everything in Christ astonishes me. His spirit overawes me, and his will confounds me. Between him and whoever else in the world there is no possible term of comparison. He is truly a being by himself. His ideas and his sentiments, the truth which he announces, his manner of convincing, are not explained either by human organisation or by the nature of things.

The nearer I approach, the more carefully I examine, everything is above me; everything remains grand,—of a grandeur which overpowers. His religion is a revelation from an intelligence which certainly is not that of man. There is there a profound originality which has created a series of words and of maxims before unknown. Jesus borrowed nothing from our science. One can absolutely find nowhere, but in him alone, the imitation or the example of his life.

. . . I search in vain in history to find the similar to Jesus Christ, or anything which can approach the gospel. Neither history, nor humanity, nor the ages, nor nature, offer me anything with which I am able to compare it or to explain it. Here everything is extraordinary. The more I consider the gospel, the more I am assured that there is nothing there which is not beyond the march of events, and above the human mind.

༄

ALL THINGS TO ALL MEN

GILES FLETCHER

He is a path, if any be misled;
  He is a robe, if any naked be;
If any chance to hunger, he is bread;
  If any be a bondman, he is free;
  If any be but weak, how strong is he!
To dead men life He is, to sick men health;
To blind men sight, and to the needy wealth;
A pleasure without loss, a treasure without stealth.

༄

JESUS WHO FASCINATES AND THE CHRIST WHO SAVES

C. S. LEWIS

In this selection taken from The Screwtape Letters, *Screwtape, Lewis's senior demon is writing to his inferior minion, Wormwood, to instruct him as how to ensnare his "client" in an apparently "good truth" that will keep him from believing the "best truth."*

Many, when saying they believe in Christ, are really saying that they believe that there was a man named Jesus. The confession that this Jesus is God's only Son and Savior of the world is what makes a person a Christian. C. S. Lewis, a mainstream twentieth-century Protestant writer, is speaking to the difference between the Jesus of history and the Jesus who is to be worshipped by his church.

YOU WILL FIND that a good many Christian political writers think that Christianity began going wrong, and departing from the doctrine of its Founder, at a very early stage. Now, this idea must be used by us to encourage once again the conception of a "historical Jesus" to be found by clearing away later "accretions and perversions" and then to be contrasted with the whole Christian tradition. In the last generation we promoted the construction of such a "historical Jesus" on liberal and humanitarian lines; we are now putting forward a new "historical Jesus" on Marxian, catastrophic, and revolutionary lines. The advantages of these constructions, which we intend to change every thirty years or so, are manifold. In the first place they all tend to direct men's devotion to something which does not exist, for each "historical Jesus" is unhistorical. The documents say what they say and cannot be added to; each new "historical Jesus" therefore has to be got out of them by suppression at one point and exaggeration at another, and by that sort of guessing (*brilliant* is the adjective we teach humans to apply to it) on which no one would risk ten shillings in ordinary life, but which is enough to produce a crop of new Napoleons, new Shakespeares, and new Swifts in every publisher's autumn list. In the second place, all such constructions place the importance of their "historical Jesus" in some peculiar theory He is supposed to have promulgated. He has to be a "great man" in the modern sense of the word—one standing at the terminus of some centrifugal and unbalanced line of thought—a crank vending a panacea. We thus distract men's minds from Who He is, and what He did. We first make Him solely a teacher, and then conceal the very substantial agreement between His teachings and those of all other great moral teachers. For humans must not be allowed to notice that all great moralists are sent by the Enemy, not to inform men, but to remind them, to restate the primeval moral platitudes against our continual concealment of them. We make the Sophists; He raises up a Socrates to answer them. Our third aim is, by these constructions, to destroy the devotional life. For the real presence of the Enemy, otherwise experienced by men in prayer and sacrament, we substitute a merely probable, remote, shadowy, and uncouth figure, one who spoke a strange language and died a long time ago. Such an object cannot in fact be worshipped. Instead of the Creator adored by its creature, you soon have merely a leader acclaimed by a partisan, and finally a distinguished character approved by a judicious historian. And fourthly, besides being unhistorical in the Jesus it depicts, religion of this kind is false to history in another sense. No nation, and few individuals, are really brought into the Enemy's camp by the historical study of the biography of Jesus, simply as biography. Indeed, materials for a full biography have been withheld from men. The earliest converts were converted by a single historical fact (the Resurrection) and a single theological doctrine (the Redemption) operating on a sense of sin which they already had—and sin, not against some new fancy-dress law produced as a novelty by a "great man," but against the old, platitudinous, universal moral law which they had been taught by their nurses and mothers. The "Gospels" come later, and were written, not to make Christians, but to edify Christians already made.

The "historical Jesus," then, however dangerous he may seem to be to us at some particular point, is always to be encouraged.

∽

JESUS CAME PREACHING

GEORGE A. BUTTRICK

Was Jesus a preacher or was he a teacher? He was both, and while he generally referred to himself as a teacher, or the Teacher, his teachings were often given as sermons, such as his Sermon on the Mount. What is the difference between a teaching and a sermon? It is an oversimplification, but somewhat true, to say that teaching concerns itself with what should be believed, and preaching more with what we should do because of what we believe. Jesus spoke in both ways. In this inclusion, the emphasis is more on his preaching.

"JESUS CAME PREACHING." He trusted His most precious sayings to the blemished reputation and the precarious memory of His friends. Hosts of scribes had traced on papyri their interpretations of the Law. Jesus could have followed their example; thereby He might have saved Himself much journeying and a violent death. But would we exchange His cross or our fragmentary record of the words of the Cross for any treatise He might have written? Of a truth it is a printed New Testament that remains, but its vital power is drawn from a word and a Person. Being spoken, that word was sharp to pierce where the written word would have made no mark. The gospel was and is a living impact. "Jesus came preaching"—and wisdom is justified of her children.

WHAT ARE WE TO MAKE OF CHRIST?

C. S. LEWIS

Christian faith comes from believing that Jesus was who he said he was, the Son of God. But there is also inherent in the idea of accepting or rejecting Christ the idea of Christian conversion. The great Christians and martyrs of history often became believers after long periods of internal questioning and intellectual struggle. C. S. Lewis was one of those, and in this inclusion he discusses some of the great either/or issues of becoming a Christian. Lewis believed that Christ is the dividing point of choice. This is a choice everyone must make. It is not a choice that can be ignored, for even deciding not to decide is a decision of sorts.

"WHAT ARE WE to make of Christ?" There is no question of what we can make of Him, it is entirely a question of what He intends to make of us. You must accept or reject the story.

The things He says are very different from what any other teacher has said. Others say, "This is the truth about the Universe. This is the way you ought to go," but He says, "*I* am the Truth, and the Way, and the Life." He says, "No man can reach absolute reality, except through Me. Try to retain your own life and you will be inevitably ruined. Give yourself away and you will be saved." He says, "If you are ashamed of me, if, when you hear this call, you turn the other way, I also will look the other way when I come again as God without disguise. If anything whatever is keeping you from God and from Me, whatever it is, throw it away. If it is your eye, pull it out. If it is your hand, cut it off. If you put yourself first you will be last. Come to Me everyone who is carrying a heavy load, I will set that right. Your sins, all of them, are wiped out, I can do that. I am Re-birth, I am Life. Eat Me, drink Me, I am your Food. And finally, do not be afraid, I have overcome the whole Universe." That is the issue.

GOD IS A POET

FREDERICK BUECHNER

Frederick Buechner, one of contemporary Christianity's most important writers, shows how the era of mere words was over and the era of the Word become flesh (John 1:14) had begun.

GOD IS POET, say, searching for the right word. Tries Noah, but Noah is a drinking man, and tries Abraham, but Abraham is a little too Mesopotamian with all those wives and whiskers. Tries Moses, but Moses himself is trying too hard; and David too handsome for his own good; Elisha, who sicks the bears on the children. Tries John the Baptist with his locusts and honey, who might almost have worked except for something small but crucial like a sense of the ridiculous or a balanced diet.

Word after word God tries and then finally tries once more to say it right, to get it all into one final Word what he is and what human is and why the suffering of love is precious and how the peace of God is a tiger in the blood.

❧

HE WAS HIMSELF

GEORGE A. BUTTRICK

Jesus was a Jew. But one cannot escape the feeling that while the Jews were and are the chosen people, Jesus was out to redefine the word chosen *to denote all those who would willingly receive the grace and goodness of his Father in heaven. In this selection is painted that wide, wide definition that Jesus is the Savior to all.*

THE ETHNIC FAITHS predated Christ: He was Himself the ultimate flower of Judaism. They have been here longer than He to bid for the suffrages of mankind. That men should have said, "for neither is there any other name," was not a bigotry or a theology: it was confession that they had tried the clutter of cults with which their world was filled and found them vain, and then tried Christ to find Him true. No other Name has ever won such diverse allegiance—Paul and Tolstoi, Roosevelt and St. Francis, Grenfell and Schweitzer. No other face is a "Face like all men's faces." No other voice speaks to every man "in his own tongue." If other nations refuse Him at our hands, it is not because He lacks authority but because our hands have not been clean. Despite our unclean hands His purity shines through, and His gospel now is read in over three hundred different tongues. He has become mankind's other self. Well might that soldier say: "The soul stands at salute when He passes by." Well might that little Chinese girl confess: "I have known Him all my life, and one day I learned His name."

This is not He alone
Whom I have known,
   This is all Christs since time began
The blood of all the dead
His veins have shed,
   For He is God and Ghost and Everyman.

∽

THE TRINITY

BILLY GRAHAM

The word trinity *comes from contracting two words,* tri-unity. *The idea is one of the hardest of the Christian faith to define. The word really means the* three in one, *and Christians forbid the world to talk about the Father, Son, and Holy Spirit as three separate gods. We Christians are indebted to Judaism, which precedes us and from which we borrow our origins—monotheists. God as he creates, we call Father; as he saves, we call Son; and as he lives in our current hearts we call the Holy Spirit (as any one woman may be wife, daughter, and mother). There is no completely adequate way to picture this mystery we call the Trinity. How can the three be one? As a child I liked thinking of it in this way: H_2O is always water. Yet if we cool it to less than zero Celsius, it becomes a solid, and if we warm it to over one hundred degrees Celsius, it becomes a vapor; but in any of the three states it is still water. Most theologians I know do not want to pin down the mystery of the Trinity, for the mystery is too grand for such elementary definitions as I have given (indeed they smack of an early Trinitarian heresy called Modalism). I must agree that they are right. In the following selection Billy Graham is commenting on this glorious and inscrutable truth at the heart of the Christian faith.*

WHEN I FIRST began to study the Bible years ago, the doctrine of the Trinity was one of the most complex problems I had to encounter. I have never fully resolved it, for it contains an aspect of mystery. Though I do not totally understand it to this day, I accept it as a revelation of God.

The Bible teaches us that the Holy Spirit is a living being. He is one of the three persons of the Holy Trinity. To explain and illustrate the Trinity is one of the most difficult assignments to a Christian. Dr. David

McKenna once told me that he was asked by his small son, Doug, "Is God the Father God?"

He answered, "Yes."

"Is Jesus Christ God?"

"Yes."

"Is the Holy Spirit God?"

"Yes."

"Then how can Jesus be His own Father?"

David thought quickly. They were sitting in their old 1958 Chevrolet at the time. "Listen, son," he replied, "under the hood is one battery. Yet I can use it to turn on the lights, blow the horn, and start the car." He said, "How this happens is a mystery—but it happens!"

This is a terribly difficult subject—far beyond the ability of our limited minds to grasp fully. Nevertheless, it is extremely important to declare what the Bible holds, and be silent where the Bible is silent. God the Father is fully God. God the Son is fully God. God the Holy Spirit is fully God. The Bible presents this as fact. It does not explain it.

∾

RAGMAN

WALTER WANGERIN

Walter Wangerin is one of the most profound religious thinkers and artists of our time. In this wholly fictional tale, he show how Christ meets everyone's special needs in a very special way. The uniqueness of the Christian experience is that Jesus is just what he needs to be to meet anyone's particular need.

I SAW A strange sight. I stumbled upon a story most strange, like nothing my life, my street sense, my sly tongue had ever prepared me for.

Hush, child. Hush, now, and I will tell it to you.

EVEN BEFORE THE dawn one Friday morning I noticed a young man, handsome and strong, walking the alleys of our city. He was pulling an old cart filled with clothes both bright and new, and he was calling in a clear, tenor voice: "Rags!" Ah, the air was foul and the first light filthy to be crossed by such sweet music.

"Rags! New rags for old! I take your tired rags! Rags!"

"Now, this is a wonder," I thought to myself, for the man stood six-feet-four, and his arms were like tree limbs, hard and muscular, and his eyes flashed intelligence. Could he find no better job than this, to be a ragman in the inner city?

I followed him. My curiosity drove me. And I wasn't disappointed.

Soon the Ragman saw a woman sitting on her back porch. She was sobbing into a handkerchief, sighing, and shedding a thousand tears. Her knees and elbows made a sad X. Her shoulders shook. Her heart was breaking.

The Ragman stopped his cart. Quietly, he walked to the woman, stepping round tin cans, dead toys, and Pampers.

"Give me your rag," he said so gently, "and I'll give you another."

He slipped the handkerchief from her eyes. She looked up, and he laid across her palm a linen cloth so clean and new that it shined. She blinked from the gift to the giver.

Then, as he began to pull his cart again, the Ragman did a strange thing: he put her stained handkerchief to his own face; and then *he* began to weep, to sob as grievously as she had done, his shoulders shaking. Yet she was left without a tear.

"This *is* a wonder," I breathed to myself, and I followed the sobbing Ragman like a child who cannot turn away from mystery.

"Rags! Rags! New rags for old!"

In a little while, when the sky showed grey behind the rooftops and I could see the shredded curtains hanging out black windows, the Ragman came upon a girl whose head was wrapped in a bandage, whose eyes were empty. Blood soaked her bandage. A single line of blood ran down her cheek.

Now the tall Ragman looked upon this child with pity, and he drew a lovely yellow bonnet from his cart.

"Give me your rag," he said, tracing his own line on her cheek, "and I'll give you mine."

The child could only gaze at him while he loosened the bandage, removed it, and tied it to his own head. The bonnet he set on hers. And I gasped at what I saw: for with the bandage went the wound! Against his brow it ran a darker, more substantial blood—his own!

"Rags! Rags! I take old rags!" cried the sobbing, bleeding, strong, intelligent Ragman.

The sun hurt both the sky, now, and my eyes; the Ragman seemed more and more to hurry.

"Are you going to work?" he asked a man who leaned against a telephone pole. The man shook his head.

The Ragman pressed him: "Do you have a job?"

"Are you crazy?" sneered the other. He pulled away from the pole, revealing the right sleeve of his jacket—flat, the cuff stuffed into the pocket. He had no arm.

"So," said the Ragman. "Give me your jacket, and I'll give you mine."

Such quiet authority in his voice!

The one-armed man took off his jacket. So did the Ragman—and I trembled at what I saw: for the Ragman's arm stayed in its sleeve, and when the other put it on he had two good arms, thick as tree limbs; but the Ragman had only one.

"Go to work," he said.

After that he found a drunk, lying unconscious beneath an army blanket, an old man, hunched, wizened, and sick. He took that blanket and wrapped it round himself, but for the drunk he left new clothes.

AND NOW I had to run to keep up with the Ragman. Though he was weeping uncontrollably, and bleeding freely at the forehead, pulling his cart with one arm, stumbling for drunkenness, falling again and again, exhausted, old, old, and sick, yet he went with terrible speed. On spider's legs he skittered through the alleys of the City, this mile and the next, until he came to its limits, and then he rushed beyond.

I wept to see the change in this man. I hurt to see his sorrow. And yet I needed to see where he was going in such haste, perhaps to know what drove him so.

The little old Ragman—he came to a landfill. He came to the garbage pits. And then I wanted to help him in what he did, but I hung back, hiding. He climbed a hill. With tormented labor he cleared a little space on that hill. Then he sighed. He lay down. He pillowed his head on a handkerchief and a jacket. He covered his bones with an army blanket. And he died.

Oh, how I cried to witness that death! I slumped in a junked car and wailed and mourned as one who has no hope—because I had come to love the Ragman. Every other face had faded in the wonder of this man, and I cherished him, but he died. I sobbed myself to sleep.

I did not know—how could I know?—that I slept through Friday night and Saturday and its night, too.

But then, on Sunday morning, I was wakened by a violence.

Light—pure, hard, demanding light—slammed against my sour face, and I blinked, and I looked, and I saw the last and the first wonder of all. There was the Ragman, folding the blanket most carefully, a scar on his forehead, but alive! And, besides that, healthy! There was no sign of sorrow nor of age, and all the rags that he had gathered shined for cleanliness.

Well, then I lowered my head and, trembling for all that I had seen, I myself walked up to the Ragman. I told him my name with shame, for I was a sorry figure next to him. Then I took off all my clothes in that place, and I said to him with dear yearning in my voice: "Dress me."

He dressed me. My Lord, he put new rags on me, and I am a wonder beside him. The Ragman, the Ragman, the Christ!

∾

THE SON OF MAN CAME EATING AND DRINKING

I. F.

This brief poem points out that Jesus ate and drank meanly and sparsely, like the common people among whom he lived. There was always a heresy among Christians that taught Christ was not a real person who had biological qualities like hunger and thirst. Heretics taught that Jesus only seemed *to be real but was not fully human. They were called Docetists (from the Greek word* dokeo, *to seem). Much of the gospel of John was written to prove that Jesus was real, that is, fully human.*

> He loved not sloth—unprofitable rest—
> Which eats and feeds, and only feeds and eats:
> Excess of feeding he hath not professed,
> To surfeit in variety of meats:
> His diet was not change, or choice: his dish—
> Sometimes a barley loaf, sometimes a fish.

LOVING THE DISGUISED CHRIST

MOTHER TERESA OF CALCUTTA

Mother Teresa, a recent Nobel Peace Prize winner, is admired by all for pointing out the doctrine she affirms in this selection.

FEEDING THE HUNGRY Christ.
    Clothing the naked Christ.
    Visiting the sick Christ.
    Giving shelter to the homeless Christ.
    Teaching the ignorant Christ.

WE ALL LONG for heaven where God is, but we have it in our power to be in heaven with Him right now—to be happy with Him at this very moment. But being happy with Him now means loving like He loves, helping like He helps, giving as He gives, serving as He serves, rescuing as He rescues, being with Him twenty-four hours a day—touching Him in his distressing disguise.

TRAPPED BETWEEN PERSON AND IDEA

EARL PALMER

Jesus saves as a real person. But even those who might never believe he existed could wish that such a person might have existed for them. The wonder of the idea of a man like Jesus haunts even those who might not be willing to say he was the Son of God. Atheists, in considering Jesus, become aware of a kind of longing for such a man.

"I CAN'T GET Jesus Christ out of my mind," he said. "If I dismiss him as an idea he haunts me as a person. If I dismiss him as a person he haunts me as an idea."

IS JESUS REAL?

LOIS A. CHENEY

IS JESUS REAL? I mean *really* real? Did a group of men just sort of get together and decide to pull off the biggest con trick of all time? And did they write down some stories—quite alike, but not too much alike? And are they sitting on some fat cloud somewhere laughing themselves sick?

I could believe that. But what would I do with all those people who talk to me in gentleness, those with Christ twinkling in their eyes? If he didn't exist, how'd he get inside so many people? Over and over, men drop their lives and walk in Christ. Spend a day looking for Christ living in others. He's in the most unlikely people and places. If Jesus isn't real, then you're going to have to exterminate thousands who live in him.

I love it when people argue that there is no love, and then stand stupid before an act of love. I love it when people argue that there is no mercy, and then whistle and glance the other way when an act of mercy looms in front of them. I love it when people say there is no Christ, and frown and mumble at the life that lives in Jesus, who is stalking the world.

&

THE PRINCE OF PEACE

WILLIAM JENNINGS BRYAN

William Jennings Bryan became famous for being the lawyer who took the creationist position in the famous Scopes Monkey Trial. Known in his day as one of the greatest Christian orators who had ever lived, here he explores the humility of Christ.

HUMILITY IS A rare virtue. If one is rich he is apt to be proud of his riches; if he has distinguished ancestry, he is apt to be proud of his lineage; if he is well educated, he is apt to be proud of his learning. Some one has suggested that if one becomes humble he soon becomes proud of his humility. Christ, however, possessed of all power, was the very personification of humility.

The most difficult of all the virtues to cultivate is the forgiving spirit. Revenge seems to be natural to the human heart; to want to get even with an enemy is a common sin. It has even been popular to boast of vindictiveness; it was once inscribed on a monument to a hero that he had repaid both friends and enemies more than he had received. This was not the spirit of Christ. He taught forgiveness; and in that incomparable prayer which He left as a model for our petitions He made our willingness to forgive the measure by which we may claim forgiveness. He not only taught forgiveness, but He exemplified His teachings in His life. When those who persecuted Him brought Him to the most disgraceful of all deaths, His spirit of forgiveness rose above His sufferings and He prayed, "Father, forgive them, for they know not what they do!"

But love is the foundation of Christ's creed. The world had known love before; parents had loved children, and children parents; husband had loved wife, and wife husband; and friend had loved friend; but Jesus gave a new definition of love. His love was as boundless as the sea; its limits were so far-flung that even an enemy could not travel beyond it. Other teachers sought to regulate the lives of their followers by rule and formula, but Christ's plan was first to purify the heart and then to leave love to direct the footsteps.

WHAT CONCLUSION IS to be drawn from the life, the teachings and the depth of this historic figure? Reared in a carpenter shop; with no knowledge of literature, save Bible literature; with no acquaintance with philosophers living or with the writings of sages dead, this young man gathered disciples about Him, promulgated a higher code of morals than the world had ever known before, and proclaimed Himself the Messiah. He taught and performed miracles for a few brief months and then was crucified; His disciples were scattered and many of them put to death; His claims were disputed, His resurrection denied and His followers persecuted, and yet from this beginning His religion has spread until millions take His name with reverence upon their lips and thousands have been willing to die rather than surrender the faith which he put into their hearts. How shall we account for Him? "What think ye of Christ?" It is easier to believe Him divine than to explain in any other way what He said and did and was. And I have greater faith even than before since I have visited the Orient and witnessed the successful contest which Christianity is waging against the religions and philosophies of the East.

I was thinking a few years ago of the Christmas which was then approaching and of Him in whose honor the day is celebrated. I recalled the message, Peace on earth, good will to men, and then my thoughts ran back to the prophecy uttered centuries before His birth, in which He was described as the Prince of Peace. To reinforce my memory I reread the prophecy and found immediately following a verse which I had forgotten

—a verse which declares that of the increase of His peace and government there shall be no end, for, adds Isaiah, "He shall judge His people with justice and with judgment." Thinking of the prophecy, I have selected this theme that I may present some of the reasons which lead me to believe that Christ has fully earned the title, The Prince of Peace, and that in the years to come it will be more and more applied to Him. Faith in Him brings peace to the heart and His teachings, when applied, will bring peace between man and man. And if He can bring peace to each heart, and if His creed will bring peace throughout the earth, who will deny His right to be called The Prince of Peace?

• • •

Christ gave us proof of immortality, and yet it would hardly seem necessary that one should rise from the dead to convince us that the grave is not the end. To every created thing God has given a tongue that proclaims a resurrection.

If the Father deigns to touch with divine power the cold and pulseless heart of the buried acorn and to make it burst forth from its prison walls, will He leave neglected in the earth the soul of man, made in the image of his Creator? If He stoops to give to the rosebush, whose withered blossoms float upon the autumn breeze, the sweet assurance of another springtime, will He refuse the words of hope to the sons of men when the frosts of winter come? If matter, mute and inanimate, though changed by the forces of nature into a multitude of forms, can never die, will the spirit of man suffer annihilation when it has paid a brief visit like a royal guest to this tenement of clay? No, I am as sure that there is another life as I am that I live today!

In Cairo I secured a few grains of wheat that had slumbered for more than three thousand years in an Egyptian tomb. As I looked at them this thought came into my mind: If one of those grains had been planted on the banks of the Nile the year after it grew, and all its lineal descendants planted and replanted from that time until now, its progeny would today be sufficiently numerous to feed the teeming millions of the world. There is in the grain of wheat an invisible something which has power to discard the body that we see, and from earth and air fashion a new body so much like the old one that we cannot tell the one from the other. If this invisible germ of life in the grain of wheat can thus pass unimpaired through three thousand resurrections, I shall not doubt that my soul has power to clothe itself with a body suited to its new existence when this earthly frame has crumbled into dust.

A belief in immortality not only consoles the individual, but it exerts a powerful influence in bringing peace between individuals. If one really thinks that man dies as the brute dies, he may yield to the temptation to do injustice to his neighbor when the circumstances are such as to promise security from detection. But if one really expects to meet again and live eternally with those whom he knows today, he is restrained from evil deeds by the fear of endless remorse. We do not know what rewards are in store for us or what punishments may be reserved, but if there were no other punishment it would be enough for one who deliberately and consciously wrongs another to have to live forever in the company of the person wronged and have his littleness and selfishness laid bare. I repeat, a belief in immortality must exert a powerful influence in establishing justice between men and thus laying the foundation for peace.

❧

THE GRAND INQUISITOR

FYODOR MIKHAYLOVICH DOSTOYEVSKY

This selection taken from The Brothers Karamazov *contains the story that seeks to show that the politics of the church have always been unfriendly to the real Jesus. Jesus often battled the politics of official Judaism in his own day.*

"EVEN THIS MUST have a preface—that is, a literary preface," laughed Ivan, "and I am a poor hand at such things. You see, my story takes place in the sixteenth century. At that time, as you probably learned at school, it was customary in poetry to bring down heavenly powers on earth. Dante was not the only one to do this. In France, clerks, as well as monks in monasteries, used to give regular performances in which the Madonna, the saints, the angels, Christ, and God Himself were brought on the stage. In those days it was done in all simplicity. In Victor Hugo's *Notre Dame de Paris* an edifying and gratuitous spectacle was provided for the people in the Hotel de Ville of Paris in the reign of Louis XI in honor of the birth of the dauphin. It was called 'The good judgment of the very saintly and gracious Virgin Mary,' and she appears herself on the stage and pronounces her 'good judgment.' Similar plays, based on the Old Testament, were occasionally performed in Moscow too, up to the time of Peter the Great. But besides plays there were all sorts of legends and ballads scattered about the world, in which the saints and angels and all the powers of Heaven took part when required."

• • •

"My story is laid in Spain, in Seville, in the most terrible time of the Inquisition, when fires were lighted every day to the glory of God, and 'in the splendid act of faith the wicked heretics were burnt.' Oh, of course, this was not the coming in which He will appear according to His promise at the end of time in all His heavenly glory, and which will be sudden 'as lightening flashing from east to west.' No, He visited His children only for a moment, and then where the flames were crackling round the heretics. In His infinite mercy He came among men in that human shape in which He walked among men for three years fifteen centuries ago. He came down to the 'hot pavement' of the southern town in which on the day before almost a hundred heretics had, 'for the greater glory of God,' been burned by the cardinal, the Grand Inquisitor, in a magnificent 'act of faith.' They had been burned in the presence of the king, the court, the knights, the cardinals, the most charming ladies of the court, and the whole population of Seville.

"He came softly, unobserved, and yet, strange to say, everyone recognized Him. . . . This might be one of the best passages in the poem, I mean, why they recognized Him. . . . The people are irresistibly drawn to Him, they surround Him, they flock about Him, follow Him. He moves silently in their midst with a gentle smile of infinite compassion. The sun of love burns in His heart, light and power shine from His eyes, and their radiance, shed on the people, stirs their hearts with responsive love. He holds out His hands to them, blesses them, and a healing virtue comes from contact with Him, even with His garments. An old man in the crowd, blind from childhood, cries out: 'O Lord, heal me and I shall see Thee!' And, as it were, scales fall from his eyes and the blind man sees Him. The crowd weeps and kisses the earth under His feet. Children throw flowers before Him, sing, and cry hosanna. 'It is He. It is He!' all repeat. 'It must be He, it can be no one but Him!' He stops at the steps of the Seville cathedral at the moment when the weeping mourners are bringing in a little open white coffin. In it lies a child of seven, the only daughter of a prominent citizen. The dead child lies hidden in flowers. 'He will raise your child,' the crowd shouts to the weeping mother. The priest, coming to meet the coffin, looks perplexed, and frowns, but the mother of the dead child throws herself at His feet with a wail. 'If it is Thou, raise my child!' she cries, holding out her hands to Him. The procession halts, the coffin is laid on the steps at His feet. He looks with compassion, and His lips once more softly pronounce: 'Maiden arise!' And the maiden arises. The little girl sits up in the coffin and looks around smiling, with wide-open wondering eyes, holding a bunch of white roses they had put in her hand.

"There are cries, sobs, confusion among the people, and at that

moment the cardinal himself, the Grand Inquisitor, passes by the cathedral. He is an old man, almost ninety, tall and erect, with a withered face
and sunken eyes, in which there is still a gleam of light. He is not dressed
in his brilliant cardinal's robes, as he was the day before, when he was
burning the enemies of the Roman Church—at this moment he is wearing
his coarse, old, monk's cassock. At a distance behind him come his gloomy
assistants and slaves and the 'holy guard.' He stops at the sight of the
crowd and watches it from a distance. He sees everything; he sees them
set the coffin down at His feet, sees the child rise up. His face darkens.
He knits his thick gray brows and his eyes gleam with a sinister fire. He
holds out his finger and bids his guards arrest Him. And such is his
power, so completely are the people cowed into submission and trembling
obedience to him, that the crowd immediately makes way for the guards.
And in the midst of deathlike silence the guards lay hands on Him and
lead Him away. The crowd instantly bows down to the earth, like one
man, before the old inquisitor. He blesses the people in silence and
passes on.

"The guards lead their Prisoner to the close, gloomy vaulted prison
in the ancient palace of the Holy Inquisition and lock Him in it. The day
passes and is followed by the dark, burning 'breathless' night of Seville.
The air is 'fragrant with laurel and lemon.' In the pitch darkness the iron
door of the prison is suddenly opened and the Grand Inquisitor himself
comes in with a light in his hand. He is alone. The door is closed at once
behind him. He stands in silence and for a minute or two gazes into His
face. At last he goes up slowly, sets the light on the table and speaks.

" 'Is it Thou? Thou?' But receiving no answer, he adds at once,
'Don't answer, be silent. What canst Thou say, indeed? I know too well
what Thou wouldst say. And Thou hast no right to add anything to what
Thou hadst said of old. Why, then, art Thou come to hinder us? For Thou
hast come to hinder us, and Thou knowest that. But dost Thou know what
will be tomorrow? I know not who Thou art and care not to know
whether it is Thou or only a semblance of Him. But tomorrow I shall
condemn Thee and burn Thee at the stake as the worst of heretics. And
the very people who have today kissed Thy feet, tomorrow at the faintest
sign from me will rush to heap up the embers of Thy fire. Knowest Thou
that? Yes, maybe Thou knowest it,' he added with thoughtful penetration,
never for a moment taking his eyes off the Prisoner."

• • •

" 'Hast Thou the right to reveal to us one of the mysteries of that
world from which Thou hast come?' my old man asks Him, and answers
the question for Him. 'No, Thou hast not; Thou mayest not add to what

has been said of old, and mayest not take from men the freedom which Thou didst exalt when Thou wast on earth. Whatsoever Thou revealest anew will encroach on men's freedom of faith; for it will be manifest as a miracle, and the freedom of their faith was dearer to Thee than anything else in those days fifteen hundred years ago. Didst Thou not often say then: "I will make you free"? But now Thou has seen these "free" men,' the old man adds suddenly, with a pensive smile. 'Yes, we've paid dearly for it,' he goes on, looking sternly at Him, 'but at last we have completed that work in Thy name. For fifteen centuries we have been wrestling with Thy freedom, but now it is ended and over for good. Dost Thou not believe that it's over for good? Thou lookest meekly at me and deignest not even to be angry with me. But let me tell Thee that now, today, people are more persuaded than ever that they have perfect freedom, yet they have brought their freedom to us and laid it humbly at our feet. But that has been our doing. Was this what Thou didst? Was this Thy freedom?"

• • •

" 'Thou hast had no lack of warnings, but Thou didst not listen to those warnings. Thou didst reject the only way by which men might be made happy. But fortunately, departing Thou didst hand on the work to us. Thou hast promised, Thou hast established by Thy word, Thou hast given to us the right to bind and to unbind, and now, of course, Thou canst not think of taking it away. Why, then, hast Thou come to hinder us?' "

• • •

" 'But now that fifteen hundred years have passed, we see that everything in those three questions was so justly divined and foretold, and has been so truly fulfilled, that nothing can be added to them or taken from them.

" 'Judge Thyself who was right—Thou or he who questioned Thee then? Remember the first question. Its meaning was this: "Thou wouldst go into the world, and art going with empty hands, with some promise of freedom which men in their simplicity and their natural unruliness cannot even understand, which they fear and dread—for nothing has ever been more insupportable for a man and a human society than freedom. But seest Thou these stones in this parched and barren wilderness? Turn them into bread, and mankind will run after Thee like a flock of sheep, grateful and obedient, though forever trembling, lest Thou withdraw Thy hand and deny them Thy bread." But Thou wouldst not deprive man of freedom and didst reject the offer, thinking, what is that freedom worth, if obedience is bought with bread? Thou didst reply that man lives not by bread alone. But dost Thou know that for the sake of that earthly bread the spirit of the earth will rise up against Thee and will strive with Thee and overcome Thee? And all will follow him crying: "Who can compare with this beast? He has given us fire from heaven!" Dost Thou know that the ages will pass, and humanity will proclaim by the lips of their sages that there is no crime, and therefore no sin; there is only hunger? "Feed men, and then ask of them virtue!" that's what they'll write on the banner, which they will raise against Thee, and with which they will destroy Thy temple. Where Thy temple stood will rise a new building; the terrible tower of Babel will be built again. And though, like the one of old, it will not be finished, yet Thou mightest have prevented that new tower and have cut short the sufferings of men for a thousand years; for they will come back to us after a thousand years of agony with their tower. They will seek us again, hidden underground in the catacombs, for we shall be again persecuted and tortured. They will find us and cry to us: "Feed us, for those who have promised us fire from heaven haven't given it!" And then we shall finish building their tower, for he finishes the building who feeds them. And we alone shall feed them in Thy name, declaring falsely that it is in Thy name. Oh, never, never can they feed themselves without us! No science will give them bread so long as they remain free. In the end they will lay their freedom at our feet, and say to us: "Make us your slaves, but feed us." They will understand at last, that freedom and bread enough for all are inconceivable together. Never, never will they be able to have both together! They will be convinced, too, that they can never be free, for they are weak, vicious, worthless, and rebellious.

" 'Thou didst promise them the bread of Heaven, but, I repeat again, can it compare with earthly bread in the eyes of the weak, ever sinful and ignoble race of man? And if for the sake of the bread of Heaven thousands and tens of thousands shall follow Thee, what is to become of the millions and tens of thousands of millions of creatures who will not have the strength to forego the earthly bread for the sake of the heavenly? Or dost Thou care only for the tens of thousands of the great and strong, while the millions, numerous as the sands of the sea, who are weak but love Thee, must exist only for the sake of the great and strong? No, we care for the weak too. They are sinful and rebellious, but in the end they too will become obedient. They will marvel at us and look on us as gods, because we are ready to endure the freedom which they have found so dreadful and to rule over them—so awful it will seem to them to be free. But we shall tell them that we are Thy servants and rule them in Thy name. We shall deceive them again, for we will not let Thee come to us again. That deception will be our suffering, for we shall be forced to lie.

" 'This is the significance of the first question in the wilderness, and this is what Thou hast rejected for the sake of that freedom which Thou hast exalted above everything. Yet in this question lies hidden the great secret of this world. Choosing "bread," Thou wouldst have satisfied the universal and everlasting craving of humanity——to find someone to worship. So long as man remains free he strives for nothing so incessantly and so painfully as to find someone to worship. But man seeks to worship what is established beyond dispute, so that all men would agree at once to worship it. For these pitiful creatures are concerned not only to find what one or the other can worship, but to find something that all would believe in and worship; what is essential is that all may be *together* in it. This craving for *community* of worship is the chief misery of every man individually and of all humanity from the beginning of time. For the sake of common worship they've slain each other with the sword. They have set up gods and challenged one another: "Put away your gods and come and worship ours, or we will kill you and your gods!" And so it will be to the end of the world, even when gods disappear from the earth; they will fall down before idols just the same. Thou didst know, Thou couldst not but have known, this fundamental secret of human nature. But Thou didst reject the one infallible banner which was offered Thee to make all men bow down to Thee alone——the banner of earthly bread. And Thou hast rejected it for the sake of freedom and the bread of Heaven.

" 'Behold what Thou didst further. And again in the name of freedom! I tell Thee that man is tormented by no greater fear than to find someone quickly to whom he can hand over that gift of freedom with which he is born. But only one who can appease his conscience can take over his freedom. In bread there was offered Thee an invincible banner; give bread, and man will worship Thee, for nothing is more certain than bread. But if someone else gains possession of his conscience——oh! then he will cast away Thy bread and follow after him who has ensnared his conscience: In that Thou wast right. For the secret of man's being is not only to live but to have something to live for. Without a stable conception of the object of life, man would not consent to go on living, and would rather destroy himself than remain on earth, though he had bread in abundance. That is true. But what happened? Instead of taking men's freedom from them, Thou didst make it greater than ever! Didst Thou forget that man prefers peace, and even death, to freedom of choice in the knowledge of good and evil? Nothing is more seductive for man than his freedom of conscience, but nothing is a greater cause of suffering. And behold, instead of giving a firm foundation for setting the conscience of man at rest forever, Thou didst choose all that is exceptional, vague and puzzling. Thou didst choose what was utterly beyond the strength of men, acting as though Thou didst not love them at all—Thou who didst come to give Thy life for them! Instead of taking possession of men's freedom, Thou didst increase it, and burdened the spiritual kingdom of mankind with its sufferings forever. Thou didst desire man's free love, that he should follow Thee freely, enticed and taken captive by Thee. In place of the rigid ancient law, man must hereafter with free heart decide for himself what is good and what is evil, having only Thy image before him as his guide. But didst Thou not know he would at last reject even Thy image and Thy truth, if he is weighed down with the fearful burden of free choice? They will cry aloud at last that the truth is not in Thee, for they could not have been left in greater confusion and suffering than Thou hast caused, laying upon them so many cares and unanswerable problems.

" 'So that, in truth, Thou didst Thyself lay the foundation for the destruction of Thy kingdom, and no one is more to blame for it. Yet what was offered Thee?' "

• • •

" 'Thou didst crave for free love and not the base raptures of the slave before the might that has overawed him forever. But Thou didst think too highly of men therein, for they are slaves, of course, though rebellious by nature. Look round and judge; fifteen centuries have passed, look upon them. Whom hast Thou raised up to Thyself? I swear, man is weaker and baser by nature than Thou hast believed him! Can he, can he do what Thou didst? By showing him so much respect, Thou didst, as it were, cease to feel for him, for Thou didst ask far too much from him—Thou who hast loved him more than Thyself! Respecting him less, Thou wouldst have asked less of him. That would have been more like love, for his burden would have been lighter. He is weak and vile. He is weak and vile though he is everywhere now rebelling against our power, and proud of his rebellion! It is the pride of a child and a schoolboy! They are little children rioting and barring out the teacher at school. But their childish delight will end; it will cost them dearly. They will cast down temples and drench the earth with blood. But they will see at last the foolish children, that, though they are rebels, they are impotent rebels, unable to keep up their own rebellion. Bathed in their foolish tears, they will recognize at last that He who created them rebels must have meant to mock at them. They will say this in despair, and their utterance will be a blasphemy which will make them more unhappy still, for man's nature cannot bear blasphemy, and in the end always avenges it on itself. And so unrest, confusion and unhappiness—that is the present lot of man after Thou didst bear so much for his freedom!

" 'Thy great prophet tells in vision and in image, that he saw all those who took part in the first resurrection and that there were of each tribe twelve thousand. But if there were so many of them, they must have been not men but gods. They had borne thy cross, they had endured scores of years in the barren, hungry wilderness, living upon locusts and roots—and Thou mayest indeed point with pride at those children of freedom, of free love, of free and splendid sacrifice for thy name. But remember that they were only some thousands; and what of the rest? And how are the other weak ones to blame, because they could not endure what the strong have endured? How is the weak soul to blame that it is unable to receive such terrible gifts? Canst Thou have simply come to the elect and for the elect? If so, it is a mystery and we cannot understand it. And if it is a mystery, we too have a right to preach a mystery, and to teach men that it's not the free judgment of their hearts, not love that matters, but a mystery which they must follow blindly, even against their conscience. So we have done. We have corrected Thy work and have founded it upon *miracle, mystery* and *authority.* And men rejoiced that they were again led like sheep and that the terrible gift that had brought them such suffering was, at last, lifted from their hearts. Were we right teaching them this? Speak! Did we not love mankind, so meekly acknowledging their feebleness, lovingly lightening their burden, and permitting their weak nature even sin with our sanction? Why hast Thou come now to hinder us? And why dost Thou look silently and searchingly at me with Thy mild eyes? Be angry. I don't want Thy love, for I love Thee not. And what use is it for me to hide anything from Thee? Don't I know to Whom I am speaking? All that I can say is known to Thee already. And is it for me to conceal from Thee our mystery? Perhaps it is Thy will to hear it from my lips. Listen, then. We are not working with Thee, but with *him* —that is our mystery. It's long—eight centuries—since we have been on *his* side and not on Thine.

" 'Just eight centuries ago, we took from *him,* the wise and mighty spirit in the wilderness, what Thou didst reject with scorn, that last gift *he* offered Thee, showing Thee all the kingdoms of the earth. We took from *him* Rome and the sword of Caesar, and proclaimed ourselves sole rulers of the earth, though we have not yet been able to complete our work. But whose fault is that? Oh, the work is only beginning, but it has begun. It has long to await completion and the earth has yet much to suffer, but we shall triumph and shall be Caesars, and then we shall plan the universal happiness of man. But Thou mightest have taken even then the sword of Caesar. Why didst Thou reject that last gift? Had Thou accepted that last offer of the mighty spirit, Thou wouldst have accomplished all that man seeks on earth—that is, someone to worship, someone to keep his conscience, and some means of uniting all in one unanimous and harmonious ant heap, because the craving for universal unity is the third and last anguish of men. Mankind as a whole has always striven to organize a universal state. There have been many great nations with great histories, but the more highly they were developed the more unhappy they were, for they felt more acutely than other people the craving for worldwide union. The great conquerors, Timours and Genghis-Khans, whirled like hurricanes over the face of the earth striving to subdue its people, and they too were but the unconscious expression of the same craving for universal unity. Hadst Thou taken the world and Caesar's purple, Thou wouldst have founded the universal state and have given universal peace. For who can rule men if not he who holds their conscience and their bread in his hands.

" 'We have taken the sword of Caesar, and in taking it, of course, have rejected Thee and followed *him*. Oh, ages are yet to come of the confusion of free thought, of their science and cannibalism. For having begun to build their tower of Babel without us, they will end, of course, with cannibalism. But then the beast will crawl to us and lick our feet and spatter them with tears of blood. And we shall sit upon the beast and raise the cup, and on it will be written: "Mystery." But then, and only then, the reign of peace and happiness will come for men. Thou art proud of Thine elect, but Thou hast only the elect, while we give rest to all. And besides, how many of those elect, those mighty ones who could become elect, have grown weary waiting for Thee, and have transferred and will transfer the powers of their spirit and the warmth of their heart to the other camp, and end by raising their *free* banner against Thee? Thou didst Thyself lift up that banner. But with us all will be happy and will no more rebel nor destroy one another as under Thy freedom. Oh, we shall persuade them that they will only become free when they renounce their freedom to us and submit to us. And shall we be right or shall we be lying? They will be convinced that we are right, for they will remember the horrors of slavery and confusion to which Thy freedom brought them. Freedom, free thought and science, will lead them into such straits and will bring them face to face with such marvels and insoluble mysteries, that some of them, the fierce and rebellious, will destroy themselves. Others, rebellious but weak, will destroy one another. The rest, weak and unhappy, will crawl fawning to their feet and whine to us: "Yes, you were right, you alone possess His mystery, and we come back to you. Save us from ourselves!"

" 'Receiving bread from us, they will see clearly that we take the bread made by their hands from them, to give it to them, without any miracle. They will see that we do not change the stones to bread, but in truth they will be more thankful for taking it from our hands than for the bread itself! For they will remember only too well that in old days, without our help, even the bread they made turned to stones in their hands, while since they have come back to us, the very stones have turned to bread in their hands. Too, too well they know the value of complete submission! And until men know that, they will be unhappy. Who is most to blame for their not knowing it? Speak! Who scattered the flock and sent it astray on unknown paths?' "

· · ·

" 'It is prophesied that Thou wilt come again in victory, Thou wilt come with Thy chosen, the proud and strong. But we will say that they have only saved themselves, but we have saved all. We are told that the harlot who sits upon the beast, and holds in her hands the *mystery,* shall be put to shame, that the weak will rise up again, and will rend her royal purple and will strip naked her loathsome body. But then I will stand up and point out to Thee the thousand millions of happy creatures who have known no sin. And we who have taken their sins upon us for their happiness will stand up before Thee and say: "Judge us if Thou canst and darest." Know that I fear Thee not. Know that I too have been in the wilderness, I too have lived on roots and locusts, I too prized the freedom with which Thou hast blessed men, and I too was striving to stand among Thy elect, among the strong and powerful, thirsting "to make up the number." But I awakened and would not serve madness. I turned back and joined the ranks of those *who have corrected Thy work.* I left the proud and went back to the humble, for the happiness of the humble.

" 'What I say to Thee will come to pass, and our dominion will be built up. I repeat, tomorrow Thou shalt see that obedient flock who at a sign from me will hasten to heap up the hot cinders about the pile on which I shall burn Thee for coming to hinder us. For if anyone has ever deserved our fires, it is Thou. Tomorrow I shall burn Thee. . . . I have spoken.' "

· · ·

"When the Inquisitor stopped speaking he waited some time for his Prisoner to answer him. His silence weighed down upon him. He saw that the Prisoner had listened carefully all the time, looking gently in his face. But evidently he did not want to reply. The old man longed for Him to say something, however bitter and terrible. But He suddenly approached the old man in silence and softly kissed him on the forehead. That was his answer. The old man shuddered. His lips moved. He went to the door, opened it and said to Him: 'Go, and come no more. . . . Come not at all, never, never!' And he let Him out into the dark alleys of the town. The Prisoner went away."

❧

NATURE OF MAN

KARL RAHNER

Karl Rahner, one of the most significant Catholic thinkers of our time, described in this selection the inner wrangling that most Christians go through when they try to figure out why Christ sometimes seems to ignore those who really believe in him and to bless with significance all of those who ignore him. At the heart of the church's dilemma has always lain Job's age-old question, "Why do the righteous suffer?"

LOOK AT THE vast majority of men, Lord—and excuse me if I presume to pass judgment on them—but do they often think of You? Are You the First Beginning and Last End for them, the One without whom their minds and hearts can find no rest? Don't they manage to get along perfectly well without You? Don't they feel quite at home in this world which they know so well, where they can be sure of just what they have to reckon with? Are You anything more for them than the One who sees to it that the world stays on its hinges, so that they won't have to call on You? Tell me, are You the God of *their* life?

❧

YESHUA

SHOLEM ASCH

IN SHOLEM ASCH'S gripping account of Yeshua, his brothers ask him about his intention to reveal his identity to the world. Yeshua replies that his time is not yet. Mary, his mother, alone knew the secret that would soon unfold. The following scene takes place after a religious "argument" between Jesus and his brothers over the nature of faith in the new order of truth Jesus was bringing into being.

Miriam [Mary] was well aware of the conflict in their hearts. She knew their thoughts because they were as dear and close to her as her own life. She rejoiced in their learning and uprightness and in their good name among the people of Nazareth. But she would have liked to see her sons shine, like many candles on a single stick, in one blended flame—the flame the Lord had lighted in her eldest. She wished to see the others sit at Yeshua's [Jesus] feet, as one sits about a rabbin, and drink at the fount of his wisdom. But it was clear today that her younger sons were not fitted to partake of Yeshua's sanctity. Not learning, nor even piety, could open a man's heart to Yeshua's teaching. A special ray of grace issued from the hearts of those poor artisans who listened to him and fused with him as light fuses with light. Utter strangers who had never looked on him before perceived in Yeshua some mystic quality which was veiled from his own flesh and blood.

Jacob, her second son, was coming slowly toward her on the garden path. He walked with difficulty, like a man newly crippled.

"I know not who my brother is," he said, coming close, "and I cannot judge how far his rights extend. I know only that God will justify him in his doings. But we, we have nothing in our hands but the guide rope of the Law. And he who cuts this rope, whoever he may be, cuts off our path to God."

"My son, my son," said Miriam passionately, "pray God that He plant a new spirit in you, that you may see the new path to the Lord which your brother lays out for the poor and simple. Without God's help you shall never see your brother's light, for what he does is not done according to the laws of men but in accordance with the will of God."

Jacob's sunken eyes opened wide as he stared at his mother. He dropped his head shamefully and stammered out in a choked voice:

"*Ema*, Mother, who is Yeshua?"

Miriam laid her hand on his arm.

"It is not for me to reveal the mysteries of God. When the time is ripe it shall be known to you, my son."

CHILD JESUS

JOHN OXENHAM

John Oxenham fictionalizes this account of a menial job that Jesus and his father, Joseph, who were both carpenters, performed together. The church has never been able to get beyond the beautiful idea that Jesus was not by profession a scholar.

JOSEPH AND JESUS worked at our house for three days, putting up shelves and cupboards and arranging our things, and on the third day we went into it. It was very much smaller than our house at Ptolemais, but it was big enough for two of us and my mother was well pleased with it. For me, the joy of having that boy as neighbor would have more than made up for even a smaller house still.

I had worked with Jesus and his father these three days, handing them tools and fetching and carrying, and the more I saw of this boy the more I liked him. He was a clever little workman and so even-tempered that nothing ever put him out, not even when he once hit his thumb with a hammer, a blow that made his eyes water. It was really my fault again; for I had asked him something and he had looked over his shoulder to answer me.

He made a little face at me for a moment, then rubbed the thumb violently and sucked it for a time, and then went on with his work as gaily as ever.

That first night I went up on the roof with my mother to watch the sun set between the hills along the valley. There were hills all round, but they fell back towards the east and west and our house stood so high that we could see well both ways and over the white houses of the village.

Behind the house was our plot of land enclosed by a rough stone wall. There were some vines in it and two tall cypress trees, and a wide-spreading fig-tree full of big leaves and the little knobs of coming figs.

"We can grow all we need," said my mother. "But we shall have to work, little son. We are but poor folk now."

"I will work hard, Mother——" And then we heard a joyous shout below, and saw Joseph's boy bounding along the stony track that led past his house and ours along the hillside.

"He is a beautiful boy," said my mother, as we stood watching him.

And beautiful he was, with the sunset gold in his hair, and his face all alight and his eyes shining.

WHAT WAS JESUS?

DR. R. J. CAMPBELL

IT IS REMARKABLE that in the gospels we have so little reference to a subject on which modern readers would greatly desire information. What was Jesus like in appearance? Was He tall or short, robust or frail, handsome or the reverse? Did He resemble in any degree the conventional portrait of Him which has now become all but universal in Christendom? How did He dress; and what characteristic features, if any, did He possess? What sort of voice, look, gesture, such as we are wont to associate with those dear to us, would those who knew Him always remember as specially His?

On all these points the evangelists are strangely silent. All we can gather from them is—and they are impressively at one in regard thereto—that He carried with Him a suggestion of great personal force and at the same time of wonderful winsomeness.

There is one incident which illustrates this even more than the saying "Suffer little children to come unto Me," which finds a place in all the synoptics, and that is the placing of a little child in the midst of the wondering circle of quarrelling men and bidding them imitate him if they would attain to membership in the Kingdom of God. This child must have been content to stand between Jesus' knees with Jesus' arms around him; no hint is offered to the contrary. And where did He find the child? The suggestion is that he was there already, standing looking up into the Master's face, and that Jesus had simply drawn him to His side to point His discourse. Children could have felt no fear of Jesus. Evidently, therefore, there must have been something attractive and kind in His very look when it rested on a little one, something tender and winning.

The erring and the downtrodden discerned this also. The woman taken in adultery remained near Him when her accusers fled discomfited, the woman that was a sinner washes His feet with her tears, regardless of the opinion of those about her; little Zacchaeus blurts out his promise of amendment in the presence of a company that scorned him, sure of the Master's sympathy and understanding—all that was good in him rose up and found expression under the serene gaze of those kind eyes.

And what eyes Jesus must have had. All of the evangelists repeatedly draw attention to the way in which He looked at people. Evidently they were struck by this. Those who listened to Jesus habitually must often have spoken about it—that look at Peter in the judgment hall, for instance, the look that He gave to the churlish Pharisees before the act of healing in the synagogue; most of all, perhaps, the smiling sympathy with which He regarded the rich young ruler. As to His voice, we are told that "the common people heard Him gladly," which they would not have done if there had not been a certain charm in the cadences of the voice that uttered the words of eternal life. "Never man spake like this man," was the testimony of the officers of the Sanhedrin sent to arrest Him. In their absorption in what He was saying and in His way of saying it they forgot their commission, and later felt they could not carry it out.

His dress, His walk, His demeanour would all be in keeping. There would be a dignity and simplicity about these which accord with the rest of what we are told about Jesus. He was not rich, so His garments must have been those of the ordinary person of His class in that day. Perhaps it is not very different now. He may have worn the praying shawl of white with coloured edges which was common in that day, as at present, principally in the synagogue, but also outside. The long straight undergarment worn by natives of Palestine by night and day, and extending from the neck to the ankles, no doubt formed part of Jesus' costume. This too may have been white, and was probably fastened with a girdle. On His head would be a large white or coloured napkin, folded diagonally. A sleeveless cloak or coat of goat's or camel's hair or wool, for outdoor use, and sandals for the feet would complete the wearing apparel, as in Tissot's realistic pictures.

II

JESUS:

~

HIS BIRTH

*W*HEN asked what he considered to be the most important date in history, Ignazio Silone said December 25, the year zero. Because of calendar revisions by Pope Gregory XIII, we now know, Jesus was probably born in the year we call 4 B.C. Nevertheless, the date is established. Around his birth, time in the West divides into A.D. and B.C. (or C.E. and B.C.E.). In truth, the year is about as close as we can get to the date, for we know neither the season nor the month when Jesus was born.

We do know it was an age heavy with expectancy. Scripture says that a star appeared announcing Jesus' birth. This too was not all that unusual. The birth of Moses, the lawgiver, had many motifs in common with Jesus' birth. A star, according to tradition, had also appeared when Moses was born. In the Nile delta of Egypt, Pharaoh, to keep down the burgeoning population of the Hebrews, orders the slaughter of the innocents, just as Herod did in an attempt to locate and destroy the infant Jesus. Jesus was miraculously born of a virgin, and Moses' life was miraculously spared by Pharaoh's court.

But perhaps the most spectacular event of Jesus' coming was the adoration of various people. First the shepherds, then the Magi, then old Anna and Simeon. From the very first, the infant Jesus was recognized by some as the Son of God, by others as the Messiah, and by still others as a king. There are many other sacred writings not accepted as biblical that tell of the infant Christ. Some of these say that, even as a child, Jesus was a miracle worker. One of these accounts says that Jesus, shortly after he was born, sat up in the manger and announced to Mary, his mother, that he was indeed The Son of God. There are accounts in *I* and *II Infancy,* second- and third-century false accounts, that relate stories of Jesus' swaddling clothes being taken from his body and laid on the sick and infirm to heal them.

But in the gospel accounts of Matthew and Luke we have none of these child miracle stories. In the biblical account, Jesus is born, and his birth is celebrated by angels and human beings.

His birth seems to have become connected quite early with the Roman holiday of Saturnalia, a festival of merriment set near the year's end. The holiday honored Saturn, the God of time. *Christmas* (a term growing out of the Christian year from two words, *Christ* and *masse*) became the day the church chose to celebrate the birth of Christ. In the following centuries, the season of Advent became built around Christmas itself. As the name implies, Advent is a time of high anticipation of Christ's Second Coming, based on the glorious celebration of his first. The Christmas season comes to an official end on January 6 (the twelfth day of Christmas) with the celebration of Epiphany, or the *manifestation.* On this day Jesus was manifested to the world as God's Son, the Messiah and Savior of the world.

> After Jesus was born in Bethlehem village, Judah territory—this was during Herod's kingship—a band of scholars arrived in Jerusalem from the East. They asked around, "Where can we find and pay homage to the newborn King of the Jews? We observed a star in the eastern sky that signaled his birth. We're on pilgrimage to worship him."
>
> When word of their inquiry got to Herod, he was terrified—and not Herod alone, but most of Jerusalem as well. Herod lost no time. He gathered all the high priests and religion scholars in the city together and asked, "Where is the Messiah supposed to be born?"

They told him, "Bethlehem, Judah territory. The prophet Micah wrote it plainly:

'It's you, Bethlehem, in Judah's land,
　　no longer bringing up the rear.
From you will come the leader
　　who will shepherd-rule my people, my Israel.' "

Herod then arranged a secret meeting with the scholars from the East. Pretending to be as devout as they were, he got them to tell him exactly when the birth-announcement star appeared.

Matthew 2:1–7, The Message

∾

SOME QUESTIONS FOR JOSEPH

MAX LUCADO

Max Lucado imagines some very supposable questions that any of us might like to ask. In this passage is seen the poetic and keen insight that has made Max Lucado's scholarship so important in our own day.

KNOTHOLES AND SNAPSHOTS and "I wonders." You'll find them in every chapter about every person. But nothing stirs so many questions as does the birth of Christ! Characters appear and disappear before we can ask them anything. The innkeeper too busy to welcome God—did he ever learn who he turned away? The shepherds—did they ever hum the song the angels sang? The wise men who followed the star—what was it like to worship a toddler? And Joseph, especially Joseph. I've got questions for Joseph.

Did you and Jesus arm wrestle? Did he ever let you win?
Did you ever look up from your prayers and see Jesus listening?
How do you say "Jesus" in Egyptian?
What ever happened to the wise men?
What ever happened to you?

We don't know what happened to Joseph. His role in Act I is so crucial that we expect to see him the rest of the drama—but with the exception of a short scene with twelve-year-old Jesus in Jerusalem, he never reappears. The rest of his life is left to speculation, and we are left with our questions.

But of all my questions, my first would be about Bethlehem. I'd like to know about the night in the stable. I can picture Joseph there. Moonlit pastures. Stars twinkle above. Bethlehem sparkles in the distance. There he is, pacing outside the stable.

What was he thinking while Jesus was being born? What was on his mind while Mary was giving birth? He'd done all he could do—heated the water, prepared a place for Mary to lie. He'd made Mary as comfortable as she could be in a barn and then he stepped out. She'd asked to be alone, and Joseph has never felt more so.

In that eternity between his wife's dismissal and Jesus' arrival, what was he thinking? He walked into the night and looked into the stars. Did he pray?

For some reason, I don't see him silent; I see Joseph animated, pacing. Head shaking one minute, fist shaking the next. This isn't what he had in mind. I wonder what he said . . .

THIS ISN'T THE way I planned it, God. Not at all. My child being born in a stable? This isn't the way I thought it would be. A cave with sheep and donkeys, hay and straw? My wife giving birth with only the stars to hear her pain?

This isn't at all what I imagined. No, I imagined family. I imagined grandmothers. I imagined neighbors clustered outside the door and friends standing at my side. I imagined the house erupting with the first cry of the infant. Slaps on the back. Loud laughter. Jubilation.

That's how I thought it would be.

The midwife would hand me my child and all the people would applaud. Mary would rest and we would celebrate. All of Nazareth would celebrate.

But now. Now look. Nazareth is five days' journey away. And here we are in a . . . in a sheep pasture. Who will celebrate with us? The sheep? The shepherds? The stars?

This doesn't seem right. What kind of husband am I? I provide no midwife to aid my wife. No bed to rest her back. Her pillow is a blanket from my donkey. My house for her is a shed of hay and straw.

The smell is bad, the animals are loud. Why, I even smell like a shepherd myself.

Did I miss something? Did I, God?

When you sent the angel and spoke of the son being born—this isn't what I pictured. I envisioned Jerusalem, the temple, the priests, and the people gathered to watch. A pageant perhaps. A parade. A banquet at least. I mean, this is the Messiah!

Or, if not born in Jerusalem, how about Nazareth? Wouldn't Nazareth have been better? At least there I have my house and my business. Out here, what do I have? A weary mule, a stack of firewood, and a pot of warm water. This is not the way I wanted it to be! This is not the way I wanted my son.

Oh my, I did it again. I did it again, didn't I, Father? I don't mean to do that; it's just that I forget. He's not my son . . . he's yours.

The child is yours. The plan is yours. The idea is yours. And forgive me for asking but . . . is this how God enters the world?

∾

THE WONDERFUL TEACHER

ELIJAH P. BROWN

His name shall be called wonderful.

Isaiah 9:6

IN OLDEN TIMES all names meant something, and this is still the case among Indians and all other people who are living in a primitive way. Whenever you know an Indian's name and the meaning of it, you know something about the Indian. Such names as Kill Deer, Eagle Eye, Buffalo Face and Sitting Bull tell us something about the men who possessed them.

This tendency to use names that are expressive still crops out in camp life, and whenever men are thrown together in an unconventional way. In mining, military and lumber camps nearly every man has a nickname that indicates some peculiarity or trait of character. Usually a man's nickname is nearer the real man than his right name.

All of our family names today had their origin in something that meant something. All Bible names have a meaning, and when you read the Scriptures it will always help you to a better understanding of their meaning to look up the definition of all proper names.

There are two hundred and fifty-six names given in the Bible for the Lord Jesus Christ, and I suppose this was because He was infinitely beyond all that any one name could express.

Of the many names given to Christ it is my purpose at this time to briefly consider this one: "His name shall be called Wonderful." Let us look into it somewhat and see whether He was true to the name given Him in a prophecy eight hundred years before He was born. Does the name fit Him? Is it such a name as He ought to have?

Wonderful means something that is transcendently beyond the common; something that is away beyond the ordinary. It means something that is altogether unlike anything else. We say that Yellowstone Park, Niagara Falls and the Grand Cañon of the Colorado are wonderful because there is nothing else like them.

When David killed Goliath with his sling he did a wonderful thing, because nobody else ever did anything like it. It was wonderful that the Red Sea should open to make a highway for Israel, and wonderful that the sun should stand still for Joshua. Let us see whether Jesus was true to His name.

His birth was wonderful, for no other ever occurred that was like it. It was wonderful in that He had but one human parent, and so inherited the nature of man and the nature of God. He came to be the Prince of princes, and the King of kings, and yet His birth was not looked forward to in glad expectation, as the birth of a prince usually is in the royal palace, and celebrated with marked expressions of joy all over the country, as has repeatedly happened within the recollection of many who are here.

There was no room for Him at the inn, and He had to be born in a stable, and cradled in a manger, and yet angels proclaimed His birth with joy from the sky, to a few humble shepherds in sheepskin coats, who were watching their flocks by night.

Mark how He might have come with all the pomp and glory of the upper world. It would have been a great condescension for Him to have been born in a palace, rocked in a golden cradle and fed with golden spoons, and to have had the angels come down and be His nurses. But He gave up all the glory of that world, and was born of a poor woman, and His cradle was a manger.

Think what He had come for. He had come to bless, and not to curse; to lift up, and not to cast down. He had come to seek and to save that which was lost. To give sight to the blind; to open prison doors and set captives free; to reveal the Father's love; to give rest to the weary; to be a blessing to the whole world, and yet there was no room for Him. He came to do that, and yet many of you have no room for Him in your hearts.

His birth was also wonderful in this, that the wise men of the East were guided from far across the desert to His birthplace by a star. Nothing like this ever announced the coming of any one else into this world. As soon as His birth was known the king of the country sought His life, and ordered the slaughter of the Innocents at Bethlehem. The babies were the first Christian martyrs.

His character was wonderful, for no other has ever approached it in perfection. It is wonderful that the greatest character ever known should have come out of such obscurity, to become the most famous in all history. That such a time and such a country and such a people should have produced Jesus Christ can be accounted for on no other ground than His divinity. On his return from a trip to the Holy Land a minister was asked what had made the greatest impression upon him while there. "Nazareth," he answered, and for this reason:

"The same kind of people are living there to-day as in the time of Jesus, and they are about the worst specimens of humanity I have seen anywhere. Lazy, lustful, ignorant and unspeakably wicked, and to think of His coming out from such a people is to me a sure proof of His divinity. Had I not been a believer in His divinity before going there, I should have to believe in it now."

His life was wonderful. Wonderful for its unselfishness, its sinlessness and its usefulness. Even His enemies could not bring against Him any graver charge than that He claimed God for His Father, and that He would do good on the Sabbath day. Not the slightest evidence of selfishness or self-interest can be found in the story of His life. He was always helping others, but not once did He do anything to help Himself. He had the power to turn stones into bread, but went hungry forty days without doing it. While escaping from enemies who were determined to put Him to death He saw a man who had been blind from birth, and stopped to give him sight, doing so at the risk of His life. He never sought His own in any way, but lived for others every day of His life. His first miracle was performed, not before a multitude to spread His own fame, but in a far-away hamlet, to save a peasant's wife from humiliation. He had compassion on the hungry multitude and wept over Jerusalem, but He never had any mercy on Himself.

His teaching was wonderful. It was wonderful for the way in which He taught; for its simplicity and clearness, and adaptation to the individual. Nowhere do you find Him seeking the multitude, but He never avoided the individual. And His teaching was always adapted to the comprehension of those whom He taught. It is said that the common people heard Him gladly, and this shows that they understood what He said. He put the cookies on the lower shelf. No man had to take a dictionary with him when he went to hear the Sermon on the Mount. He illustrated His thought and made plain His meaning by the most wonderful word-pictures. The preacher who would reach the people must have something to say, and know how to say it so that those who hear will know just what he means.

Jesus made His meaning clear by using plenty of illustrations. He didn't care a rap what the scribes and Pharisees thought about it, or said about it. He wanted the people to know what He meant, and that is why He was always so interesting. The preacher who can't make his preaching interesting has no business in the pulpit. If he can't talk over ten minutes without making people begin to snap their watches and go to yawning all over the house, he has misunderstood the Lord about his call to preach. Jesus was interesting because He could put the truth before people in an interesting way. We are told that without a parable He spake not to any man. He made people see things, and see them clearly. It is wonderful that this humble Galilean peasant, who may never have gone to school a day in His life, should have made Himself a Teacher of teachers for all time. The pedagogy of to-day is modeling after the manner of Christ closer and closer every day.

He was wonderful in His originality. The originality of Jesus is a proof of His divinity. The human mind cannot create anything in an absolute sense. It can build out of almost any kind of material, but it cannot create. There is no such thing as out-and-out originality belonging to man. You cannot imagine anything that does not resemble something you have previously seen or heard of.

I grant that you can take a cow and a horse and a dog and a sheep and from them make animals enough to fill Noah's ark, but you must have the cow and the horse and the dog and the sheep for a beginning. Everything you make will simply be a modification of the various forms and properties of them.

There is said to be nothing new under the sun, and there is a sense in which it is true. Everything is the outgrowth of something else. The first railway cars looked like the old stage-coaches, and the first automobiles looked like carriages. It is that way about everything. No man ever made a book, or even a story, that was altogether unlike all others.

The stories we hear to-day on the Irish and Dutch are older than the Irish and Dutch. You can find stories like them in the earliest literature, but you can't find any stories anywhere in any literature that even in the remotest way resemble the parables of Jesus. Such parables as the prodigal son and the Good Samaritan are absolutely new creations, and so proclaim Jesus as divine, because He could create.

His teaching was wonderful, not only in the way He taught, but in what He taught. He taught that He was greater than Moses. Think of the audacity of it! Making such claims as that to the Jews, who regarded Moses as being almost divine. Think of the audacity of some man of obscure and humble parentage standing before us Americans and trying to make us think he was greater than George Washington.

Jesus also declared that He fulfilled the prophecies and the law of Moses, and the only effort He ever made to prove His claim was to point to the works that He did. The first thing an impostor always does is to overprove his case. Jesus never turned His hand over to try to convince His enemies that He was the Christ. You have to explain a coal-oil lamp, but you don't need to waste any breath in giving information about the power of the sun. The springtime will do that by making all nature burst into bud, flower and leaf, and the power of Christ is shown just as convincingly in the changed lives of men and women who believe in Him.

Jesus taught that all would be lost who did not believe on Him. I have seen multitudes of saved people, but I have yet to see one who did not get his salvation by believing on Christ. Find the place in this world that comes the nearest to being like hell itself, and you will find it filled with those who are haters of Jesus Christ. You can't argue it. Go into saloons, gambling halls, and such places, and the people you find there are all haters of Jesus Christ, and the more of them you find the more the place in which you find them will be like hell itself.

Jesus taught that He was equal to God. He said, "He that hateth Me hateth My Father also" (John 15:23). Did you ever know of anybody else making such claims? He said, "Come unto Me, all ye that labor and are heavy laden, and I will give you rest." Offering to bear the burden of the whole world. Think of it! He said, "I am come that they might have life, and that they might have it more abundantly." And He said, "I am the resurrection and the life; and he that believeth in Me, though he were dead, yet shall he live. And whosoever liveth and believeth in Me shall never die." Surely He was wonderful in what He taught.

It is not surprising that He so stirred them in the Capernaum synagogue, where He taught them not as the scribes, but as one having authority. Is it any wonder that they were right after Him for heresy? Let any one to-day begin to teach in our churches something as entirely new as the teachings of Jesus were, and see what will happen.

He was wonderful in what He prophesied of Himself. He foretold how He would die, and when He would die. It was wonderful that He should have been betrayed into the hands of those who sought His life, by one of His own trusted disciples, and wonderful that He should have been sold for so low a price.

Wonderful, too, that He should have been condemned to death in the way in which He was, by both the religious and civil authorities, and on the testimony of false witnesses, in the name of God, when all the laws of God were defied in the trial. It was wonderful that He was tormented and tortured so cruelly before being sent to the cross, and that He should have been put to death in the brutal manner in which He was. The time of His death was also wonderful; on the day of the Passover, thus Himself becoming the real Passover, to which the passover lamb had so long pointed.

The great publicity of His death was also wonderful. It is doubtful if any other death was ever witnessed by so many people. Hundreds of thousands of people were in Jerusalem, who had come from everywhere to attend the Passover. The sky was darkened, and the sun hid his face from the awful scene. A great earthquake shook the city; the dead came out of their graves, and went into the city, appearing unto many, and the veil of the temple was rent from top to bottom. And remember that up to that time no eye had been allowed to look behind that veil, except that of the high priest, and then only once a year, on the great Day of Atonement.

His resurrection was wonderful. He had foretold it to His disciples, and had done so frequently, always saying, whenever He spoke of His death, that He would rise again on the third day, and yet every one of them appeared to forget all about it, and not one of them was expecting it. None of them thought of going to the sepulcher on the morning of the third day, except the women, and they only to prepare His body more fully for the grave. Womanhood has always been on the firing line.

This shows how fully they had abandoned all hope when they saw Him dead. Some left the city, for we are told of two who went to Emmaus. The manner of His resurrection was godlike. No human mind could ever have imagined such a scene. Had some man described it in the way in which he thought it should have occurred, he would have had earthquakes and thunders and a great commotion in the heavens. A sound like that of the last trump would have proclaimed to all the terrified inhabitants of Jerusalem that He was risen. But see how far different it was.

An angel rolled away the stone from the mouth of the sepulcher as quietly as the opening of the buds in May, and the women, who were early there, found no disorder in the grave, but the linen clothes with which they had tenderly robed His body were neatly folded and tidily placed.

And then how wonderful are the recorded appearances after the resurrection, again so different from what man would have had them. He appeared to every one of His friends, and to His best friends, but not a single one of His enemies got to see Him. I know that this story of the resurrection is true, because none but God would have had things happen in the order that they did, and in the way in which they occurred. Had the story been false the record would have made Jesus go to Pilate and the high priest, and to the others who had put Him to death, to prove that He was risen.

The effect of His teaching upon the world has been wonderful. Remember that He left no great colleges to promulgate His doctrines, but committed them to a few humble fishermen, whose names are now the most illustrious in all history. Looked at from the human side alone, how great was the probability that everything He had said would be forgotten within a few years. He never wrote a sermon. He published no books. Not a thing He said was engraved upon stone or scrolled upon brass, and yet His doctrines have endured for two thousand years. They have gone to the ends of the earth, and have wrought miracles wherever they have gone. They have lifted nations out of darkness and degradation and sin, and have made the wilderness to blossom as the rose.

When Jesus began His ministry Rome ruled the world, and her invincible legions were everywhere, but now through the teachings of the humble Galilean peasant, whom her minions put to death, her power and her religion are gone. The great temple of Diana of the Ephesians is in ruins, and no worshipper of her can be found.

When Jesus fed the five thousand with a few loaves and fishes, and healed the poor woman who touched the hem of His garment, there wasn't a church, or a hospital, or an insane asylum, or other eleemosynary institution in the world, and now they are nearly as countless as the sands upon the seashore. When the bright cloud hid Him from the gaze of those who loved Him with a devotion that took them to martyrdom, the only record of His sayings was graven upon their hearts, but now libraries are devoted to the consideration of them. No words were ever so weighty or so weighed as those of Him who was so poor that He had no where to lay His head. The scholarship of the world has sat at His feet with bared head, and has been compelled to say again and again, "Never man spake as He spake." His utterances have been translated into every known tongue, and have carried healing on their wings wherever they have gone. No other book has ever had a tithe of the circulation of that which contains His words, and not only that, but His thoughts and the story of His life are so interwoven in all literature that if a man should never read a line in the Bible, and yet be a reader at all he could not remain ignorant of the Christ.

He is true to His name because He is a wonderful Savior now. You have only to lift your eyes and look about you to see that His wonderful salvation is going on everywhere to-day. This vast audience throws the lie back into your teeth when you say the religion of Jesus Christ is dying out. There has never been a time when the love of Christ gripped the hearts of humanity as it does to-day.

THE SHEPHERD'S FIELD

JEAN-BAPTISTE-HENRI LACORDAIRE

THE FIELD OF the shepherds is still there; flocks feed in winter under the olives, as in the days of Jesus, in the fields where the grass still grows green, and the anemones flower. Worship has never left the place where shone the brightness of the birthday dawn of Christ. On Christmas evening the people of Bethlehem flock to the church of St. Helena, of which only the ruins remain, and in its desolate crypt they pray to the shepherds of Beir-Saour, their ancestors, who were the first apostles. Clad in their long white veils, seated in groups on the broken walls, beneath the shade of the circling olives, the women, seen from afar, recall the mysterious beings who heralded the advent of Jesus. The crowd has an air of cheerfulness and calm, which harmonizes well with the memories of which the plain is full; and with that Eastern light which colours the whole and gives to the sterile rock itself an appearance of richness and of life.

TWENTY-FIVE QUESTIONS FOR MARY

MAX LUCADO

WHAT WAS IT like watching him pray?

How did he respond when he saw other kids giggling during the service at the synagogue?

When he saw a rainbow, did he ever mention a flood?

Did you ever feel awkward teaching him how he created the world?

When he saw a lamb being led to the slaughter, did he act differently?

Did you ever see him with a distant look on his face as if he were listening to someone you couldn't hear?

How did he act at funerals?

Did the thought ever occur to you that the God to whom you were praying was asleep under your own roof?

Did you ever try to count the stars with him . . . and succeed?

Did he ever come home with a black eye?

How did he act when he got his first haircut?

Did he have any friends by the name of Judas?

Did he do well in school?

Did you ever scold him?

Did he ever have to ask a question about Scripture?

What do you think he thought when he saw a prostitute offering to the highest bidder the body he made?

Did he ever get angry when someone was dishonest with him?

Did you ever catch him pensively looking at the flesh on his own arm while holding a clod of dirt?

Did he ever wake up afraid?

Who was his best friend?

When someone referred to Satan, how did he act?

Did you ever accidentally call him Father?

What did he and his cousin John talk about as kids?

Did his other brothers and sisters understand what was happening?

Did you ever think, *That's God eating my soup?*

THE CHRIST OF BETHLEHEM IS THE MESSIAH

ALFRED EDERSHEIM

PASSING THE NARROW bounds of obscure Judea, and breaking down the walls of national prejudice and isolation, He has made the sublimer teaching of the Old Testament the common possession of the world, and founded a great Brotherhood, of which the God of Israel is the Father. He alone also has exhibited a life, in which absolutely no fault could be found; and promulgated a teaching, to which absolutely no exception can be taken. Admittedly, He was *the One perfect Man*—the ideal of humanity, His doctrine the one absolute teaching. The world has known none other, none equal. And the world has owned it, if not by the testimony of words, yet by the evidence of facts. Springing from such a people; born, living, and dying in circumstances, and using means, the most unlikely of such results—the Man of Nazareth has, by universal consent, been the mightiest Factor in our world's history: alike politically, socially, intellectually, and morally. If He be not the Messiah, He has at least thus far done the Messiah's work. If He be not the Messiah, there has at least been none other, before or after Him. If He be not the Messiah, the world has not, and never can have, a Messiah.

❧

CHRISTMAS DAY SERMON

MARTIN LUTHER

Martin Luther was incensed by various fund-raising techniques of the sixteenth-century church, and when, on Halloween 1517, he nailed his Ninety-Five Theses to the wall of the parish church in Wittenberg, the Reformation was born. Although he is hailed historically for challenging religious tradition and calling the church to reformation, he was and is known also as one of the great communicators of history.

IT IS WRITTEN in Haggai 2, 6–7, that God says: "I will shake the heavens; and the precious things of all nations shall come." This is fulfilled to-day, for the heavens were shaken, that is, the angels in the heavens sang praises to God. And the earth was shaken, that is the people on the earth were agitated; one journeying to this city, another to that throughout the whole land, as the Gospel tells us. It was not a violent, bloody uprising, but rather a peaceable one awakened by God who is the God of peace.

• • •

First, behold how very ordinary and common things are to us that transpire on earth, and yet how high they are regarded in heaven. On earth it occurs in this wise: Here is a poor young woman, Mary of Nazareth, not highly esteemed, but of the humblest citizens of the village. No one is conscious of the great wonder she bears, she is silent, keeps her own counsel, and regards herself as the lowliest in the town. She starts out with her husband Joseph; very likely they had no servant, and he had to do the work of master and servant, and she that of mistress and maid. They were therefore obliged to leave their home unoccupied, or commend it to the care of others.

• • •

The Evangelist shows how, when they arrived at Bethlehem, they were the most insignificant and despised, so that they had to make way for others until they were obliged to take refuge in a stable, to share with the cattle, lodging, table, bedchamber and bed, while many a wicked man sat at the head in the hotels and was honored as lord. No one noticed or was conscious of what God was doing in that stable. He lets the large houses and costly apartments remain empty, lets their inhabitants eat, drink and be merry; but this comfort and treasure are hidden from them. O what a dark night this was for Bethlehem, that was not conscious of that glorious light!

• • •

But the birth itself is still more pitiful. There was no one to take pity on this young wife who was for the first time to give birth to a child; no one to take to heart her condition that she, a stranger, did not have the least thing a mother needs in a birth-night. There she is without any preparation, without either light or fire, alone in the darkness, without any one offering her service as is customary for women to do at such times. Every thing is in commotion in the inn, there is a swarming of guests from all parts of the country, no one thinks of this poor woman. It is also possible that she did not expect the event so soon, else she would probably have remained at Nazareth.

Just imagine what kind of swaddling clothes they were in which she wrapped the child. Possible her veil or some article of her clothing she could spare. But that she should have wrapped him in Joseph's trousers, which are exhibited at Aix-la-Chapelle, appears entirely too false and frivolous. It is a fable, the like of which there are more in the world. Is it not strange that the birth of Christ occurs in cold winter, in a strange land, and in such a poor and despicable manner?

Some argue as to how this birth took place, as if Jesus was born while Mary was praying and rejoicing, without any pain, and before she was conscious of it. While I do not altogether discard that pious supposition, it was evidently invented for the sake of simple minded people. But we must abide by the Gospel, that he was born of the virgin Mary. There is no deception here, for the Word clearly states that it was an actual birth.

It is well known what is meant by giving birth. Mary's experience was not different from that of other women, so that the birth of Christ was a real natural birth, Mary being his natural mother and he being her natural son. Therefore her body performed its functions of giving birth, which naturally belonged to it, except that she brought forth without sin, without shame, without pain and without injury, just as she had conceived without sin.

• • •

When we look at this birth, and reflect upon how the sublime Majesty moves with great earnestness and inexpressable love and goodness upon the flesh and blood of this virgin, we see how here all evil lust and every evil thought is banished.

No woman can inspire such pure thoughts in a man as this virgin; nor can any man inspire such pure thought in a woman as this child. If in reflecting on this birth we recognize the work of God that is embodied in it, only chastity and purity spring from it.

But what happens in heaven concerning this birth? As much as it is despised on earth, so much and a thousand times more is it honored in heaven. If an angel from heaven came and praised you and your work, would you not regard it of greater value than all the praise and honor the world could give you, and for which you would be willing to bear the greatest humility and reproach? What exalted honor is that when all the angels in heaven can not restrain themselves from breaking out in rejoicing, so that even poor shepherds in the fields hear them preach, praise God, sing and pour out their joy without measure?

• • •

Behold how very richly God honors those who are despised of men, and that very gladly. Here you see that his eyes look into the depths of humility, as is written, "He sitteth above the cherubim" and looketh into the depths. Nor could the angels find princes or vallient men to whom to communicate the good news; but only unlearned laymen, the most humble people on earth. Could they not have addressed the high priests, who it was supposed knew so much concerning God and the angels? No, God chose poor shepherds, who, though they were of low esteem in the sight of men, were in heaven regarded as worthy of such great grace and honor.

• • •

The Gospel teaches that Christ was born, and that he did and suffered everything in our behalf, as is here declared by the angel: "Behold, I bring you good tidings of great joy which shall be to all the people; for there is born to you this day a Saviour, who is Christ the Lord." In these words you clearly see that he is born for us.

He does not simply say, Christ is born, but to *you* he is born, neither does he say, I bring glad tidings, but to *you* I bring glad tidings of great joy. Furthermore, this joy was not to remain in Christ, but it shall be to all the people.

• • •

We see here how Christ, as it were, takes our birth from us and absorbs it in his birth, and grants us his, that in it we might become pure and holy, as if it were our own, so that every Christian may rejoice and glory in Christ's birth as much as if he had himself been born of Mary as was Christ. Whoever does not believe this, or doubts, is no Christian.

O, this is the great joy of which the angel speaks. This is the comfort and exceeding goodness of God that, if a man believes this, he can boast of the treasure that Mary is the rightful mother, Christ his brother, and God his father. For these things actually occurred and are true, but we must believe. This is the principal thing and the principal treasure in every Gospel, before any doctrine of good works can be taken out of it. Christ must above all things become our own and we become his, before we can do good works.

But this can not occur except through the faith that teaches us rightly to understand the Gospel and properly to lay hold of it. This is the only way in which Christ can be rightly known so that the conscience is satisfied and made to rejoice. Out of this grow love and praise to God who in Christ has bestowed upon us such unspeakable gifts. This gives courage to do or leave undone, and living or dying, to suffer every thing that is well pleasing to God. This is what is meant by Isaiah 9:6, "Unto us a child is born, unto us a son is given," to us, to us, to us is born, and to us is given this child.

I HAVE A ROOM

SIR MATTHEW HALE

But art Thou come, dear Saviour? Hath Thy love
Thus made Thee stoop, and leave Thy throne above
The lofty heavens, and thus Thyself to dress
In dust to visit mortals? Could no less
A condescension serve? And after all,
The mean reception of a cratch and stall?
Dear Lord, I'll fetch Thee thence; I have a room.
'Tis poor, but 'tis my best, if Thou wilt come
Within so small a cell, where I would fain
Mine and the world's Redeemer entertain.
I mean my heart; 'tis sluttish. I confess,
And will not mend Thy lodging, Lord, unless
Thou send before Thy harbinger, I mean
Thy pure and purging grace, to make it clean
And sweep its nasty comers; then I'll try
To wash it also with a weeping eye;
And when 'tis swept and washed, I then will go
And, with thy leave, I'll fetch some flowers that grow
In Thine own garden, faith and love to Thee;
With those I'll dress it up; and these shall be
My rosemary and bays; yet when my best
Is done, the room's not fit for such a guest,
　　But here's the cure; Thy presence, Lord, alone
　　Will make a stall a court, a cratch a throne.

GOD CAME NEAR

MAX LUCADO

We must be careful lest we romanticize the birth of Christ beyond reality. Nativity scenes have a way of making Jesus' birth unreasonably fairy-tale-like. What Jesus really endured in becoming a human being was to enter this world of harsh reality. Here in the midst of an inhuman humanity, he navigated existence to show us all the way.

SHE LOOKS INTO the face of the baby. Her son. Her Lord. His Majesty. At this point in history, the human being who best understands who God is and what he is doing is a teenage girl in a smelly stable. She can't take her eyes off him. Somehow Mary knows she is holding God. *So this is he.* She remembers the words of the angel. "His kingdom will never end."

He looks like anything but a king. His face is prunish and red. His cry, though strong and healthy, is still the helpless and piercing cry of a baby. And he is absolutely dependent upon Mary for his well-being.

Majesty in the midst of the mundane. Holiness in the filth of sheep manure and sweat. Divinity entering the world on the floor of a stable, through the womb of a teenager and in the presence of a carpenter.

❧

JESUS' BIRTH

CLARENCE JORDAN

Clarence Jordan sets the nativity in Georgia instead of Palestine. Somehow, in "telling it like he did," he managed to "tell it like it is."

WHEN JESUS WAS born in Gainesville, Georgia, during the time that Herod was governor, some scholars from the Orient came to Atlanta and inquired, "Where is the one who was born to be governor of Georgia? We saw his star in the Orient, and we came to honor him." This news put Governor Herod and all his Atlanta cronies in a tizzy. So he called a meeting of the big-time preachers and politicians, and asked if they had any idea where the Leader was to be born. "In Gainesville, Georgia," they replied, "because there's a Bible prophecy which says:

> 'And you, Gainesville, in the state of Georgia,
> Are by no means the least in the Georgia delegation;
> From you will come forth a governor,
> Who will wisely guide my chosen people.' "

Then Herod called in the scholars privately and questioned them in detail about the exact time of the star's appearance. And he sent them off to Gainesville with this instruction: "Go and find out the facts about the child. Then tell me what you've learned, so that I too may come and honor him." They listened to the governor and left. And you know, the star which they saw in the Orient went ahead of them until it came and stood above the place where the child was. (Just looking at the star flooded them with great happiness.) So they went inside the house and saw the baby with his mother, Mary. They bowed down and honored him, and opened the presents they had brought to him—gifts of jewelry, incense, and perfume. And having gotten the word in a dream not to revisit Herod, they went back to their own country by another route.

After they had checked out, the Lord's messenger made connection with Joseph in a dream and said, "Get moving, and take your wife and baby and highball it to Mexico. Then stay put until I get word to you, because Herod is going to do his best to kill the baby." So he got right up, took the baby and its mother and checked out by night for Mexico. He stayed there until the death of Herod. (This gave meaning to what the Lord said through the prophet: "I summoned my son from Mexico.")

∾

THE CHRIST OF CHRISTMAS

PAM WHITLEY

THE WORD

In the beginning was the Word, and the Word was with God, and the Word was God. He was in the beginning with God. All things came into being by Him, and apart from Him, nothing came into being that has come into being. In him was life, and the life was the light of men . . . And the Word became flesh and dwelt among us (John 1:1–4,14a).

This Christ of Christmas shines down through the ages like a gem with many facets. Each facet (or Hebrew name) reveals a different aspect of His personality, love, and provision of humanity.

The name of the Lord is a strong tower: the righteous runs into it and is safe (Proverbs 18:10).

ELOHIM

In the beginning God (Elohim) created the heaven and the earth (Genesis 1:1).

El . . . Mighty or strong
Him . . . plural (Father, Son, Holy Spirit)
Total power and might

This Christ of Christmas is the Creator, mighty and strong. He saw us in our mother's womb (Psalm 139). He created us and has a special plan for every life.

JEHOVAH-ROHI

Jehovah my Shepherd

Psalm 23

This Christ of Christmas is our *Shepherd*. He desires to lead us through paths of righteousness.

Jehovah-Rohi says,
I am the Good Shepherd: The good Shepherd lays down His life for the sheep.
John 10:11

JEHOVAH-M'KADDESH

Jehovah who sanctifies

Exodus 31:13

Sanctify = Consecrate, dedicate

This Christ of Christmas desires to set us apart to walk in holiness, because He is *our* God.

For this is the will of God, even your sanctification.
I Thessalonians 4:3a

JEHOVAH-RAPHA

I am the Lord that healeth thee.
Exodus 15:26

This Christ of Christmas is our healer; body, soul, and spirit.

He Himself took our infirmities, and carried away our diseases.
Matthew 8:16–17

JEHOVAH-NISSI

"The Lord our banner"
Exodus 17:12b,13,15

The Christ of Christmas is our banner (Victory)! Lift Him up.

And I, if I be lifted up from the earth, will draw all men to myself.
John 12:32

EL SHADDAI

"The One Who is more than enough"

This Christ of Christmas is more than enough to meet our needs in *every* situation. What seemingly impossible need can we bring Him?

Now unto Him that is able to do exceeding abundantly above all that we ask or think according to the power that worketh in us.
Ephesians 3:20

JEHOVAH-TSIDKENU

Jehovah Our Righteousness
Jeremiah 23:5–6

This Christ of Christmas is our Righteousness.

For He hath made Him to be sin for us, who knew no sin: that we might be made the righteousness of God in Him.
II Corinthians 5:21

JEHOVAH-JIREH

"The Lord will Provide" a sacrifice
Genesis 22:13–14

This Christ of Christmas is our Lamb of Provision! All may partake of His free gift of eternal life.

Behold the Lamb of God who takes away the Sin of the World.
John 1:29

LET US BOW BEFORE HIM.

THE BIRTH

GENE EDWARDS

THE YOUNG COUPLE accompanied the three Magi to the barn where they had earlier stabled their camels.

"You are sure it is all right if we keep the gold and the myrrh and the frankincense?" asked Mary incredulously.

"They are small gifts for so great a king," assured Caspin.

"Well, you could stay the night," said Joseph. "There is an inn here in our village. And it is not crowded. In fact," he added with a grin, "I do not recall its being filled for over a year now."

"No," replied Gazerim as he mounted his camel. "We must return to Jerusalem with this great news. There are those waiting to hear."

"What do you mean?" asked Mary.

"We have promised to report back to the wise men of your religion, the ones who told us of the prophecy that the great king would be born here in this village."

"And more," said Akard. "Yesterday it was our privilege to meet your present king. He was very pleased to know that there might be one born to equal greatness to himself. He asked us to return to him and tell him if we found the child who was born under David's star."

Joseph looked up into the face of Akard, "You met Herod the Great? He knows of the birth of our son?"

"Yes," said Akard. "We met him in his own palace. He was quite warm and hospitable. And he was very excited about the news."

Mary's face grew ashen. Joseph spoke, his words direct and strong.

"Before you return to speak to the king and to our leaders, would you first ask our God for wisdom? It may be that our Lord would have the birth of this child be kept secret for a while longer."

The three men exchanged glances and then nodded in assent. Before mounting his camel, Caspin walked over to Mary and planted a kiss on the forehead of the young boy she held in her arms. He then added a blessing in his heathen tongue.

As they rode off, Joseph wondered out loud, "What does this mean?" Mary crossed her arms as if to ward off a sudden chill. "Can it mean . . ." The sentence remained unfinished.

Joseph completed the sentence, saying what they both were thinking. ". . . that the gentiles will come to worship Him just as much as may His own people?"

They made the short walk back to their small home in silence. As they arrived at the door, Mary revealed her anxious thoughts. "Herod . . . he knows. This is *not* good."

"Not good at all," agreed Joseph.

"Joseph, please, what shall we do? I am very uneasy. In fact, I am worried. That wicked man in Jerusalem is the most evil creature who ever lived. He wishes nothing good for our child."

Joseph put his arm around Mary and led her into the house. Long into the night the young couple shared their thoughts about what they might do; but unable to come to any conclusion, they at last fell asleep. A few moments later, the Door from the other realm opened into the small living room where the young couple and their child lay sleeping.

Gabriel knelt beside Joseph and stared into the young carpenter's face. Joseph turned restlessly. Gabriel did not move. Rather, he continued his motionless vigil. At last the archangel touched Joseph's forehead. Then, standing, he stepped back through the Door.

Joseph woke with a start.

"Mary," he cried. "A dream. I have had another dream! We must leave here immediately. It is some dreadful thing. Some monstrous evil. Herod will seek the life of our child. I know the dream is true. It was that same angel who appeared to me before. I saw him!"

Joseph sat up and turned toward Mary. "You are not going to like this, but I dare not disobey. The angel told me that we must take the baby out of Judea."

"Oh, Joseph, another move? Please, Joseph, not Nazareth."

"Mary, I told you, you are not going to like this. We are to go into *Egypt*."

"Egypt!" cried Mary. "Never! They worship bugs in Egypt!"

"Mary, we are not going to disobey the very angel who appeared to you, and who also has this odd habit of haunting *my* sleep. We are going to Egypt. We must. In the dream I heard the wail of thousands of mothers. I felt the death of little children all over our land."

Mary sat up, "The gold. This is why God sent us the gold. I knew we were not supposed to be rich. We are to use the gold to flee into Egypt."

Mary threw off the covers, speaking in an unbroken stream of words as she did. "We must leave immediately. Tonight. Joseph, wake that friend of yours, the owner of the stable. You know, Azzan. Buy a camel. We will use the camel for carrying our belongings and food and water. And buy a new donkey. A young, strong donkey. That floppy eared old donkey of yours will never make it to Egypt."

"What about all those bugs?" replied Joseph good-naturedly, still savoring the fact he had so quickly won this one.

"Joseph," responded Mary thoughtfully, ignoring his last remark, "there is something else we must do. The wrath of Satan has been kindled against our child, and the Lord has delivered us. But there are two children involved here. John is in as much danger as is Jesus. We must go to Elizabeth and Zachariah and warn them of the danger their child faces. They *must* go with us to Egypt."

"No, Mary, I forbid it. We do not have time. Every minute puts our son at greater risk. I will send Zachariah and Elizabeth some of our gold. I will send it by one of my trusted kinsmen, along with a letter. The three of them can flee, perhaps, into the wilderness. There they can hide among the Essenes or some of the nomads. Herod's forces will never be able to cover all of the southern wastelands. That is as much as we dare to do. We must believe that the Lord will take care of John, just as He is taking care of our son."

That night the young couple bought a camel they laughingly named Pharaoh, and the largest, strongest donkey they had ever seen, named Bashan. At dawn Joseph and Mary took Jesus and began their flight across the Sinai desert and into the land where men did, indeed, worship bugs.

It would be of Egypt that the young child, Jesus, would have His earliest memories. Nor would He forget that among the first things He ever learned was that He was a fugitive and a wayfarer upon this earthen ball.

❧

The Virgin Birth Is Nothing Compared to Incarnation

MADELEINE L'ENGLE

The Virgin Birth is that name we assign to the theological idea that a baby could be born beyond the ordinary process of conception. The strain of explaining what some might call a genetic monstrosity of a doctrine has led some theologians to be skeptical of the Virgin Birth teaching. But Saint Anselm long ago taught that the monstrosity lies not in asking God how he did it but why would he do it. The Christian church for the most part does not ask the how of God becoming a man but the why.

THE VIRGIN BIRTH has never been a major stumbling block in my struggle with Christianity; it's far less mind-boggling than the Power of all Creation stooping so low as to become one of us. But I find myself disturbed at the changing, by some committee or other, of the myth which brought God and the human creature together in marvelous at-one-ment, as Jacob's ladder brought heaven and earth together. That's the wonder that God can reach out and become one with that which has been created.

∾

AN ADVENT MONOLOGUE

WALTER WANGERIN

In this imaginary soliloquy God is reasoning how to make Mary his friend and consort in bringing to pass the conception of Jesus Christ. It is a tender summons to a mortal to spend her fears in that submission by which human redemption will become possible.

I LOVE A child.

But she is afraid of me.

I want to help this child, so terribly in need of help. For she is hungry; her cheeks are sunken to the bone; but she knows little of food, less of nutrition. I know both these things. She is cold, and she is dirty; she lives at the end of a tattered hallway, three flights up in a tenement whose landlord long forgot the human bodies huddled in that place. But I know how to build a fire; and I know how to wash a face.

She is retarded, if the truth be told, thick in her tongue, slow in her mind, yet aware of her infirmity and embarrassed by it. But here am I, well-traveled throughout the universe, and wise, and willing to share my wisdom.

She is lonely all the day long. She sits in a chair with her back to the door, her knees tucked tight against her breasts, her arms around these, her head down. And I can see how her hair hangs to her ankles; but I cannot see her face. She's hiding. If I could but see her face and kiss it, why I could draw the loneliness out of her.

She sings a sort of song to pass the time, a childish melody, though she is a woman in her body by its shape, a swelling at her belly. She sings, "Puss, puss." I know the truth, that she is singing of no cat at all, but of her face, sadly, calling it ugly. And I know the truth, that she is right. But

I am mightily persuasive myself, and I could make it lovely by my love alone.

I love the child.

But she is afraid of me.

THEN HOW CAN I come to her, to feed and to heal her by my love?

Knock on the door? Enter the common way?

No. She holds her breath at a gentle tap, pretending that she is not home; she feels unworthy of polite society. And loud, imperious bangings would only send her into shivering tears, for police and bill collectors have troubled her in the past.

And should I break down the door? Or should I show my face at the window? Oh, what terrors I'd cause then. These have happened before. She's suffered the rapings of kindless men, and therefore she hangs her head, and *therefore* she sings, "Puss."

I am none of these, to be sure. But if I came the way that they have come, she would not know me different. She would not receive my love, but might likely die of a failed heart.

I've called from the hall. I've sung her name through cracks in the plaster. But I have a bright trumpet of a voice, and she covers her ears and weeps. She thinks each word an accusation.

I could, of course, ignore the doors and walls and windows, simply appearing before her as I am. I have that capability. But she hasn't the strength to see it and would die. She is, you see, her own deepest hiding place, and fear and death are the truest doors against me.

Then what is left? How can I come to my beloved? Where's the entrance that will not frighten nor kill her? By what door can love arrive after all, truly to nurture her, to take the loneliness away, to make her beautiful, as lovely as my moon at night, my sun come morning?

I KNOW WHAT I will do.

I'll make the woman herself my door—and by her body enter in her life.

Ah, I like that. I like that. However could she be afraid of her own flesh, of something lowly underneath her ribs?

I'll be the baby waking in her womb. Hush: she'll have the time, this way, to know my coming first before I come. Hush: time to get ready, to touch her tummy, touching the promise alone, as it were. When she hangs her head, she shall be looking at me, thinking of *me,* loving me while I gather in the deepest place of her being. It is an excellent plan! Hush.

And then, when I come, my voice shall be so dear to her. It shall call the tenderness out of her soul and loveliness into her face. And when I take milk at her breast, she'll sigh and sing another song, a sweet Magnificat, for she shall feel important then, and worthy, seeing that another life depends on hers. My need shall make her rich!

Then what of her loneliness? Gone. Gone in the bond between us, though I shall not have said a word yet. And for my sake she shall wash her face, for she shall have a reason then.

And the sins that she suffered, the hurts at the hands of men, shall be transfigured by my being: I make good come out of evil; I *am* the good come out of evil.

CHRISTMAS

SAINT AUGUSTINE OF HIPPO

In this poem written some fifteen centuries ago, Augustine sought to capture the mystery of the Incarnation.

> Maker of the sun,
> He is made under the sun.
> In the Father he remains,
> From his mother he goes forth.
> Creator of heaven and earth,
> He was born on earth under heaven.
> Unspeakably wise,
> He is wisely speechless.
> Filling the world,
> He lies in a manger.
> Ruler of the stars,
> He nurses at his mother's bosom.
> He is both great in the nature of God,
> and small in the form of a servant.

THE SINGER

CALVIN MILLER

*In my allegory of the Christ, I picture him as a troubadour and singer
of a new song the world has never heard before. This particular section
features the Singer's argument within himself that he really might be
the Singer of such grand music, that is, the Savior.*

FOR DAYS, HE walked. The dust flew up around his feet as he walked home.

At length, he passed the village signpost and there by odd coincidence, his mother at that very time stood by the well.

They met.

He reached to carry her stone jar.

"It's not traditional," she said.

He took it anyway.

Her cares had made her fifty years seem even more.

"You broke your hammer on the vise," she said. "I had it mended for you."

"I'm through with hammers, anyway," he said. "I've just come home to board the shop."

"And then you'll leave?"

"I will," he said.

"Where will you go?" She studied paving stones as on they walked. He moved the heavy jar to ride upon his other shoulder.

"Wherever there are crowds of many people."

"The Great Walled City of the Ancient King?"

"Yes, I suppose."

He feared to talk to her. Yet he must tell her of the River Singer and all about the Star-Song he had so lately sung. He seemed afraid that she would think him mad. He could not bear to hurt her. For besides the Father-Spirit, he loved her most of all. At length he knew he must lay bare his heart.

"You seem so troubled, son," she said.

"Not for myself," he said. Then with the hand that was not needed in balancing the jar, he took her hand and smiled.

"I hate for you to board the shop and leave . . ."

"Am I the tradesman that my father was, while still he was alive?" he asked.

"You both were good, but somehow wood is never kind to your great hands. Your father's hands never paid the pain it cost you, just to love his trade."

She looked down at the gentle, suffering hand that held her own. Somewhere in her swimming recollection, she remembered the same hand with infant fingers that had clutched the ringlets of her hair and reached to feel the leathered face of Eastern Kings. But he could not remember that.

They walked still further without speaking.

"MOTHER, I AM THE SINGER!" He blurted out at once.

"I know," she said.

"I love the Father-Spirit more than life. He has sent me to the crowded ways to sing the Ancient Star-Song."

"I know," she said again. "I heard the Ancient Star-Song only once. It was the very night that you were born. And all these years, my son, I've known that you would come to board the shop someday. Can you sing the Star-Song yet?"

"I can," he answered back.

They neared a house and entered. They shared a simple meal and sat in silence. And the song, which they alone of all the world did know, was lingering all around them in the air.

She had not heard its strains for thirty years but hungered for its music.

He had not sung it for an afternoon but longed to have its fluid meaning coursing through his soul.

Of course the song began.

❧

THE FLIGHT INTO EGYPT

THOMAS MERTON

Through every precinct of the wintry city
Squadroned iron resounds upon the streets;
Herod's police
Make shudder the dark steps of the tenements
At the business about to be done.

Neither look back upon Thy starry country,
Nor hear what rumors crowd across the dark
Where blood runs down those holy walls,
Nor frame a childish blessing with Thy hand
Towards that fiery spiral of exulting souls!

Go, Child of God, upon the singing desert,
Where, with eyes of flame,
The roaming lion keeps thy road from harm.

∾

BETHLEHEM

ALFRED EDERSHEIM

THE SHORT WINTER'S day was probably closing in, as the two travelers from Nazareth, bringing with them the few necessaries of a poor Eastern household, neared their journey's end. If we think of Jesus as the Messiah from heaven, the surroundings of outward poverty, so far from detracting, seem most congruous to His Divine character. Earthly splendor would here seem like tawdry tinsel, and the utmost simplicity like that clothing of the lilies, which far surpassed all the glory of Solomon's court. But only in the East would the most absolute simplicity be possible, and yet neither it, nor the poverty from which it sprang, necessarily imply even the slightest taint of social inferiority. The way had been long and weary—at the very least, three days' journey, whatever route had been taken from Galilee.

• • •

A sense of rest and peace must, almost unconsciously, have crept over the travellers when at last they reached the rich fields that surrounded the ancient "House of Bread," and, passing through the valley which, like an amphitheatre, sweeps up to the twain heights along which Bethlehem stretches (2,704 feet above the sea), ascended through the terraced vine-yards and gardens. Winter though it was, the green and silvery foliage of the olive might, even at that season, mingle with the pale pink of the almond—nature's "early waker"—and with the darker coloring of the opening peach-buds. The chaste beauty and sweet quiet of the place would recall memories of Boaz, of Jesse, and of David. All the more would such thoughts suggest themselves, from the contrast between the past and the present. For, as the travellers reached the heights of Bethlehem, and, indeed, long before, the most prominent object in view must have been the great castle which Herod had built, and called after his own name. Perched on the highest hill south-east of Bethlehem, it was, at the same time, magnificent palace, strongest fortress, and almost courtier-city. With a sense of relief the travellers would turn from this, to mark the undulating outlines of the highland wilderness of Judea, till the horizon was bounded by the mountain-ridges of Tekoa. Through the break of the hills eastward the heavy molten surface of the Sea of Judgment would appear in view; westward wound the road to Hebron; behind them lay the valleys and hills which separated Bethlehem from Jerusalem, and concealed the Holy City.

But for the present such thoughts would give way to the pressing necessity of finding shelter and rest. The little town of Bethlehem was crowded with those who had come from all the outlying district to register their names. Even if the strangers from far-off Galilee had been personally acquainted with any one in Bethlehem, who could have shown them hospitality, they would have found every house fully occupied. The very inn was filled, and the only available space was where ordinarily the cattle were stabled.

• • •

The Christian heart and imagination, indeed, long to be unable to localise the scene of such surpassing importance, and linger with fond reverence over that Cave, which is now covered by "the Church of the Nativity." It may be—nay, it seems likely—that this, to which the most venerable tradition points, was the sacred spot of the world's greatest event. But certainty we have not. It is better, that it should be so. As to all that passed in the seclusion of that "stable"—the circumstances of the "Nativity," even its exact time after the arrival of Mary (brief as it must have been)—the Gospel-narrative is silent. This only is told, that then and there the Virgin-Mother "brought forth her first-born Son, and wrapped Him in swaddling clothes, and laid Him in a manger." Beyond this announcement of the bare fact, Holy Scripture, with indescribable appropriateness and delicacy, draws a veil over that most sacred mystery.

∾

THE LAMB

WILLIAM BLAKE

Little Lamb, who made thee?
Dost thou know who made thee?
Gave thee life, and bid thee feed
By the stream and o'er the mead;
Gave thee clothing of delight,
Softest clothing, wooly, bright;

Gave thee such a tender voice,
Making all the vales rejoice?
   Little Lamb, who made thee?
   Dost thou know who made thee?

   Little Lamb, I'll tell thee,
   Little Lamb, I'll tell thee:
He is callèd by thy name,
For he calls himself a Lamb.
He is meek, and he is mild;
He became a little child.
I am child, and thou a lamb,
We are callèd by his name.
   Little Lamb, God bless thee!
   Little Lamb, God bless thee!

HEROD'S SUSPICIONS

RICHARD CRASHAW

Why art thou troubled, Herod? what vain fear
   Thy blood-revolving breast to rage doth move?
Heaven's King, who doffs himself weak flesh to wear,
   Comes not to rule in wrath, but serve in love;
Nor would he this thy feared crown from thee tear,
   But give thee a better with himself above.
     Poor jealousy! why should he wish to prey
     Upon thy crown, who gives his own away?

Make to thy reason, man, and mock thy doubts;
   Look how below thy fears their causes are;
Thou art a soldier, Herod; send thy scouts,
   See how he's furnished for so feared a war.
What armour does he wear? A few thin clouts.
   His trumpets? tender cries. His men, to dare
     So much? rude shepherds. What his steeds? alas,
     Poor beasts! a slow ox and a simple ass.

DECEMBER 25...OR THEREABOUT

ALFRED EDERSHEIM

IT WAS, THEN, on that "wintry night" of the 25th of December, that shepherds watched the flocks destined for sacrificial services, in the very place consecrated by tradition as that where the Messiah was to be first revealed. Of a sudden came the long-delayed, unthought-of announcement. Heaven and earth seemed to mingle, as suddenly an Angel stood before their dazzled eyes, while the outstreaming glory of the Lord seemed to enwrap them, as in a mantle of light. Surprise, awe, fear would be hushed into calm and expectancy, as from the Angel they heard, that what they saw boded not judgment, but ushered in to waiting Israel the great joy of those good tidings which he brought: that the long-promised Saviour, Messiah, Lord, was born in the City of David, and that they themselves might go and see, and recognize Him by the humbleness of the circumstances surrounding His Nativity.

∽

BEN-HUR: A TALE OF THE CHRIST

LEW WALLACE

Lew Wallace, an agnostic, had set out to write a novel that would prove all of Christ's claims fraudulent. However, in his research of the life of Christ he became a Christian, and his novel, Ben-Hur: A Tale of the Christ, *was the result of his conversion. The novel he intended to write to disprove Christ became the classic that affirmed Christ.*

IT WAS NOW the beginning of the third watch, and at Bethlehem the morning was breaking over the mountains in the east, but so feebly that it was yet night in the valley. The watchman on the roof of the old khan, shivering in the chilly air, was listening for the first distinguishable sounds with which life, awakening, greets the dawn, when a light came moving up the hill towards the house. He thought it a torch in someone's hand; next moment he thought it a meteor; the brilliance grew, however, until it became a star. Sore afraid, he cried out, and brought everybody within the walls to the roof. The phenomenon, in eccentric motion, continued to approach; the rocks, trees, and roadway under it shone as in a glare of lightning; directly its brightness became blinding. The more timid of the beholders fell upon their knees, and prayed, with their faces hidden; the boldest covering their eyes, crouched, and now and then snatched glances fearfully. Afterwhile the khan and everything thereabout lay under the intolerable radiance. Such as dared look beheld the star standing still directly over the house in front of the cave where the Child had been born.

In the height of this scene, the wise men came up, and at the gate dismounted from their camels, and shouted for admission. When the steward so far mastered his terror as to give them heed, he drew the bars and opened to them. The camels looked spectral in the unnatural light, and, besides their outlandishness, there were in the faces and manner of the three visitors an eagerness and exaltation which still further excited the keeper's fears and fancy; he fell back, and for a time could not answer the question they put to him.

"Is not this Bethlehem of Judea?"

But others came, and by their presence gave him assurance.

"No, this is but the khan; the town lies farther on."

"Is there not here a child newly born?"

The bystanders turned to each other marvelling, though some of them answered, "Yes, yes."

"Show us to him!" said the Greek, impatiently.

"Show us to him!" cried Balthasar, breaking through his gravity; "for we have seen his star, even that which ye behold over the house, and are come to worship him."

The Hindoo clasped his hands, exclaiming, "God indeed lives! Make haste, make haste! The Saviour is found. Blessed, blessed are we above men!"

The people from the roof came down and followed the strangers as they were taken through the court and out into the enclosure; at sight of the star yet above the cave, though less candescent than before, some turned back afraid; the greater part went on. As the strangers neared the house, the orb arose; when they were at the door, it was high up overhead vanishing; when they entered, it went out lost to sight. And to the witnesses of what then took place came a conviction that there was a divine relation between the star and the strangers, which extended also to at least some of the occupants of the cave. When the door was opened, they crowded in.

The apartment was lighted by a lantern enough to enable the strangers to find the mother, and the child awake in her lap.

"Is the child thine?" asked Balthasar of Mary.

And she who had kept all the things in the least affecting the little one, and pondered them in her heart, held it up in the light, saying,

"He is my son!"

And they fell down and worshipped him.

They saw the child was as other children: about its head was neither nimbus nor material crown; its lips opened not in speech; if it heard their expressions of joy, their invocations, their prayers, it made no sign whatever, but, baby-like, looked longer at the flame in the lantern than at them.

In a little while they arose, and, returning to the camels, brought gifts of gold, frankincense, and myrrh, and laid them before the child, abating nothing of their worshipful speeches; of which no part is given, for the thoughtful know that the pure worship of the pure heart was then what it is now, and has always been, an inspired song.

And this was the Saviour they had come so far to find!

Yet they worshipped without a doubt.

Why?

Their faith rested upon the signs sent them by him whom we have since come to know as the Father; and they were of the kind to whom his promises were so all-sufficient that they asked nothing about his ways. Few there were who had seen the signs and heard the promises—the Mother and Joseph, the shepherds, and the Three—yet they all believed alike; that is to day, in this period of the plan of salvation, God was all and the Child nothing. But look forward, O reader! A time will come when the signs will all proceed from the Son. Happy they who then believe in him!

Let us wait that period.

∾

JOSEPH'S SONG
Joseph, a Witness

MICHAEL CARD

Michael Card is one of the most respected contemporary Christian composers influencing evangelical work. Joseph's song is but one example of his many popular compositions.

> How could it be
> This baby in my arms
> Sleeping now so peacefully
> The Son of God the angel said
> How could it be?

Lord, I know he's not my own
Not of my flesh, not of my bones
Still Father let this baby be
The son of my love

Father show me where I fit into
This plan of yours
How can a man be father to the Son of God?
Lord, for all my life I've been a simple carpenter
How can I raise a king?
How can I raise a king?

He looks so small
His face and hands so fair
And when he cries the sun just seems to disappear
But when he laughs
It shines again
How could it be?

Father show me where I fit into
This plan of yours
How can a man be father to the Son of God?
Lord, for all my life I've been a simple carpenter
How can I raise a king?
How can I raise a king?

How could it be
This baby in my arms
Sleeping now so peacefully
The Son of God the angel said
How could it be?

GENEALOGY OF JESUS

SAINT MATTHEW

Only two of the four gospel writers, Matthew and Luke, tell us any-thing about the birth of Christ. Oddly, while both of them mention that Joseph is not Jesus' true biological father, both trace the lineage of Jesus not through Mary but Joseph. Most scholars feel that this is done because in Jesus' time the world was masculine oriented and that it would have been inconsistent for any lineage to have been traced through a woman. Most conservative scholars, however, believe that Mary's lineage, like Joseph's, could be traced back through King David, as proof that he was the Messiah, for there existed a widespread biblical teaching that the Messiah would come through the lineage of King David.

THE BOOK OF the generation of Jesus Christ, the son of David, the son of Abraham. Abraham begat Isaac; and Isaac begat Jacob; and Jacob begat Judas and his brethren; And Judas begat Phares and Zara of Thamar; and Phares begat Esrom; and Esrom begat Aram; And Aram begat Aminadab; and Aminadab begat Naasson; and Naasson begat Salmon; And Salmon begat Booz of Rachab; and Booz begat Obed of Ruth; and Obed begat Jesse; And Jesse begat David the king; and David the king begat Solomon of her *that had been the wife* of Urias; And Solomon begat Roboam; and Roboam begat Abia; and Abia begat Asa; And Asa begat Josaphat; and Josaphat begat Joram; and Joram begat Ozias; And Ozias begat Joatham; and Joatham begat Achaz; and Achaz begat Ezekias; And Ezekias begat Manasses; and Manasses begat Amon; and Amon begat Josias; And Josias begat Jechonias and his brethren, about the time they were carried away to Babylon: And after they were brought to Babylon, Jechonias begat Salathiel; and Salathiel begat Zorobabel; And Zorobabel begat Abiud; and Abiud begat Eliakim; and Eliakim begat Azor; And Azor begat Sadoc; and Sadoc begat Achim; and Achim begat Eliud; And Eliud begat Eleazar; and Eleazar begat Matthan; and Matthan begat Jacob; And Jacob begat Joseph the husband of Mary, of whom was born Jesus, who is called Christ. So all the generations from Abraham to David *are* fourteen genera-tions; and from David until the carrying away into Babylon *are* fourteen generations; and from the carrying away into Babylon unto Christ *are* fourteen generations.

BORN TO BE KING

HENRY GARIEPY

HE WAS BORN of earthly parentage. Though He was God, He became a man. He was the Ancient of Days, yet He was born at a point in time. He created worlds and companied with celestial beings, yet He came to live in a family setting on earth.

We all became captivated by the storybook romance of Prince Charles and Princess Diana. Theirs was billed as "the wedding of the century" as a world looked on the enchanting love story of a gallant prince named Charles and his golden-haired Lady Diana. The grand moment came with the arrival of newborn Prince William, heir to the throne of Great Britain who will be bred to carry on the proud traditions of his homeland. Of Prince William, it was said, he was "Born to be king." Jesus, above all others of history, was born to be King.

JOURNEY OF THE MAGI

T. S. ELIOT

"A cold coming we had of it,
Just the worst time of the year
For a journey, and such a long journey:
The ways deep and the weather sharp,
The very dead of winter."
And the camels galled, sore-footed, refractory,
Lying down in the melting snow.
There were times we regretted
The summer palaces on slopes, the terraces,
And the silken girls bringing sherbet.
Then the camel men cursing and grumbling
And running away, and wanting their liquor and women,
And the night-fires going out, and the lack of shelters,
And the cities hostile and the towns unfriendly
And the villages dirty and charging high prices:
A hard time we had of it.
At the end we preferred to travel all night,

Sleeping in snatches,
With the voices singing in our ears, saying
That this was all folly.

   Then at dawn we came down to a temperate valley,
Wet, below the snow line, smelling of vegetation;
With a running stream and a water-mill beating the darkness,
And three trees on the low sky,
And an old white horse galloped away in the meadow.
Then we came to a tavern with vine-leaves over the lintel,
Six hands at an open door dicing for pieces of silver,
And feet kicking the empty wine-skins.
But there was no information, and so we continued
And arrived at evening, not a moment too soon
Finding the place; it was (you may say) satisfactory.

   All this was a long time ago, I remember,
And I would do it again, but set down
This set down
This: were we led all that way for
Birth or Death? There was a Birth, certainly,
We had evidence and no doubt. I had seen birth and death,
But had thought they were different; this Birth was
Hard and bitter agony for us, like Death, our death.
We returned to our places, these Kingdoms,
But no longer at ease here, in the old dispensation,
With an alien people clutching their gods.
I should be glad of another death.

❧

IN THE BLEAK MID-WINTER

CHRISTINA ROSSETTI

What can I give Him,
   Poor as I am?
If I were a shepherd,
   I would bring a lamb,

If I were a Wise Man,
   I would do my part,—
Yet what can I give Him?
   Give my heart.

❧

HOW HEROD ENDED UP

ALFRED EDERSHEIM

I offer this brief section to illustrate that Herod's cruel demeanor matched in many ways that of those heinous emperors of Rome who came later in time. Some have claimed that Herod could never have been cruel enough to have ordered the Bethlehem massacre described in Matthew's gospel. This excerpt demonstrates otherwise.

A MORE TERRIBLE scene is not presented in history than that of the closing days of Herod. Tormented by nameless fears; ever and again a prey to vain remorse, when he would frantically call for his passionately-loved, murdered wife Mariamme, and her sons; even making attempts on his own life; the *delirium* of tyranny, the passion for blood, drove him to the verge of madness. The most loathsome disease, such as can scarcely be described, had fastened on his body, and his sufferings were at times agonizing. By the advice of his physicians, he had himself carried to the baths of Callirhoe (east of the Jordan), trying all remedies with the determination of one who will do hard battle for life. It was in vain. The namelessly horrible distemper, which had seized the old man of seventy, held him fast in its grasp, and, so to speak, played death on the living. He knew it, that his hour was come, and had himself conveyed back to his palace under the palm-trees of Jericho. They had known it also in Jerusalem, and, even before the last stage of his disease, two of the most honored and loved Rabbis—Judas and Matthias—had headed the wild band, which would sweep away all traces of Herod's idolatrous rule. They began by pulling down the immense golden eagle, which hung over the great gate of the Temple. The two ringleaders, and forty of their followers, allowed themselves to be taken by Herod's guards. A mock public trial in the theatre at Jericho followed. Herod, carried out on a couch, was both accuser and judge. The zealots, who had made noble answer to the tyrant, were burnt alive; and the High-Priest, who was suspected of connivance, deposed.

After that the end came rapidly. On his return from Callirhoe, feeling his death approaching, the King had summoned the noblest of Israel throughout the land of Jericho, and shut them up in the Hippodrome, with orders to his sister to have them slain immediately upon his death, in the grim hope that the joy of the people at his decease would thus be changed into mourning.

❧

THE HOLY BIRTH

JIM BISHOP

Jim Bishop wrote in a fictional style, but his heavy research into all he wrote of Christ led to his being regarded as one of the most readable authorities on how Jesus came and lived. In this very popular excerpt, we have a very practical suggestion as to how it might have happened.

JOSEPH HAD RUN out of prayers and promises. His face was sick, his eyes listless. He looked up toward the east, and his dark eyes mirrored a strange thing: three stars, coming over the Mountains of Moab, were fused into one tremendously bright one. His eyes caught the glint of bright blue light, almost like a tiny moon, and he wondered about it and was still vaguely troubled by it when he heard a tiny, thin wail, a sound so slender that one had to listen again for it to make sure.

He wanted to rush inside at once. He got to his feet, and he moved no further. She would call him. He would wait. Joseph paced up and down, not realizing that men had done this thing for centuries before he was born, and would continue it for many centuries after he had gone.

"Joseph." It was a soft call, but he heard it. At once, he picked up the second jar of water and hurried inside. The two lamps still shed a soft glow over the stable, even though it seemed years since they had been lighted.

The first thing he noticed was his wife. Mary was sitting tailor-fashion with her back against a manger wall. Her face was clean; her hair had been brushed. There were blue hollows under her eyes. She smiled at her husband and nodded. Then she stood.

She beckoned him to come closer. Joseph, mouth agape, followed her to a little manger. It had been cleaned but, where the animals had nipped the edges of the wood, the boards were worn and splintered. In the manger were the broad bolts of white swaddling she had brought on the trip. They were doubled underneath and over the top of the baby.

Mary smiled at her husband as he bent far over to look. There, among the cloths, he saw the tiny face of an infant. This, said Joseph to himself, is the one of whom the angel spoke. He dropped to his knees beside the manger. This was the messiah.

❧

THE HYMN

JOHN MILTON

John Milton is often regarded as the finest English writer after Shake-speare. In this poem, we have the marvelous description of the birth of Christ from this master poet. Milton was able to affirm that he had read every book ever printed in English in his day. From this wide range of reading experience and from the encroaching pain of his own blindness, his sensitivity was honed to incisive power.

It was the winter wild,
While the heaven-born child
All meanly wrapped in the rude manger lies;
Nature, in awe to him,
Had doffed her gaudy trim,
With her great Master so to sympathize:
It was no season then for her
To wanton with the Sun, her lusty paramour.

Only with speeches fair
She woos the gentle air
To hide her guilty front with innocent snow,
And on her naked shame,
Pollute with sinful blame,
The saintly veil of maiden white to throw;
Confounded, that her Maker's eyes
Should look so near upon her foul deformities.

But he, her fears to cease,
Sent down the meek-eyed Peace:
She, crowned with olive green, came softly sliding
Down through the turning sphere,

His ready harbinger,
With turtle wing the amorous clouds dividing;
And, waving wide her myrtle wand,
She strikes a universal peace through sea and land.

No wars or battle's sound
Was heard the world around;
The idle spear and shield were high uphung;
The hookéd chariot stood,
Unstained with hostile blood;
The trumpet spake not to the arméd throng;
And kings sat still with awful eye,
As if they surely knew their sovran Lord was by.

But peaceful was the night
Wherein the Prince of light
His reign of peace upon the earth began.
The winds, with wonder whist,
Smoothly the waters kissed,
Whispering new joys to the mild Ocean,
Who now hath quite forgot to rave,
While birds of calm sit brooking on the charméd wave.

The stars, with deep amaze,
Stand fixed, in steadfast gaze,
Bending one way their precious influence,
And will not take their flight,
For all the morning light,
Or Lucifer that often warned them thence;
But in their glimmering orbs did glow,
Until their Lord himself bespake, and bid them go.

And though the shady gloom
Had given day her room,
The Sun himself withheld his wonted speed,
And hid his head for shame,
As his inferior flame
The new-enlightened world no more should need:
He saw a greater Sun appear
Than his bright throne or burning axletree could bear.

The shepherds on the lawn,
Or ere the point of dawn,
Sat simply chatting in a rustic row;
Full little thought they then
That the mighty Pan
Was kindly come to live with them below:
Perhaps their loves, or else their sheep,
Was all that did their silly thoughts so busy keep.

When such music sweet
Their hearts and ears did greet
As never was by mortal finger struck,
Divinely-warbled voice
Answering the stringéd noise,
As all their souls in blissful rapture took:
The air, such pleasure loth to lose,
With thousand echoes still prolongs each heavenly close.

Nature, that heard such sound
Beneath the hollow round
Of Cynthia's seat the airy region thrilling,
Now was almost won
To think her part was done,
And that her reign had here its last fulfilling:
She knew such harmony alone
Could hold all Heaven and Earth in happier union.

At last surrounds their sight
A globe of circular light,
That with long beams the shamefaced Night arrayed;
The helméd cherubim
And sworded seraphim
Are seen in glittering ranks with wings displayed,
Harping loud and solemn choir,
With unexpressive notes, to Heaven's new-born Heir.

Such music (as 'tis said)
Before was never made,
But when of old the sons of morning sung,
While the Creator great
His constellations set,

And the well-balanced world on hinges hung,
And cast the dark foundations deep,
And bid the weltering waves their oozy channel keep.

Ring out, ye crystal spheres,
Once bless our human ears,
If ye have power to touch our senses so;
And let your silver chime
Move in melodious time;
And let the bass of heaven's deep organ blow;
And with your ninefold harmony
Make up full consort to th'angelic symphony.

For, if such holy song
Enwrap our fancy long,
Time will run back and fetch the age of gold;
And speckled vanity
Will sicken soon and die;
And leprous sin will melt from earthly mold;
And Hell itself will pass away,
And leave her dolorous mansions to the peering day.

Yea, Truth and Justice then
Will down return to men,
Orbed in a rainbow; and, like glories wearing,
Mercy will sit between,
Throned in celestial sheen,
With radiant feet the tissued clouds down steering;
And Heaven, as at some festival,
Will open wide the gates of her high palace-hall.

But wisest Fate says no,
This must not yet be so;
The Babe lies yet in smiling infancy
That on the bitter cross
Must redeem our loss,
So both himself and us to glorify:
Yet first, to those enchained in sleep,
The wakeful trump of doom must thunder through the deep

With such a horrid clang
As on Mount Sinai rang,

While the red fire and smoldering clouds outbrake:
The aged Earth, aghast,
With terror of that blast,
Shall from the surface to the center shake,
When, at the world's last session,
The dreadful Judge in middle air shall spread his throne.

And then at last our bliss
Full and perfect is,
But now begins; for from this happy day
The old Dragon under ground,
In straiter limits bound,
Not half so far casts his usurpéd sway,
And, wroth to see his kingdom fail,
Swings the scaly horror of his folded tail.

The Oracles are dumb;
No voice or hideous hum
Runs through the archéd roof in words deceiving.
Apollo from his shrine
Can no more divine,
With hollow shriek the steep of Delphos leaving.
No nightly trance or breathéd spell
Inspires the pale-eyed priest from the prophetic cell.

The lonely mountains o'er,
And the resounding shore,
A voice of weeping heard and loud lament;
From haunted spring, and dale
Edged with poplar pale,
The parting genius is with sighing sent;
With flower-inwoven tresses torn
The Nymphs in twilight shade of tangled thickets mourn.

In consecrated earth,
And on the holy hearth,
The Lars and Lemures moan with midnight plaint;
In urns and altars round,
A drear and dying sound
Affrights the flamens at their service quaint;
And the chill marble seems to sweat,
While each peculiar power forgoes his wonted seat.

Peor and Baalim
Forsake their temples dim,
With that twice-battered God of Palestine;
And moonéd Ashtaroth,
Heaven's queen and mother both,
Now sits not girt with tapers' holy shine:
The Libyc Hammon shrinks his horn;
In vain the Tyrian maids their wounded Thammuz morn.

And sullen Moloch, fled,
Hath left in shadows dread
His burning idol all of blackest hue;
In vain with cymbals' ring
They call the grisly king,
In dismal dance about the furnace blue;
The brutish gods of Nile as fast,
Isis, Orus, and the dog Anubis, haste.

Nor is Osiris seen
In Memphian grove or green,
Trampling the unshowered grass with lowings loud;
Nor can he be at rest
Within his sacred chest;
Naught but profoundest Hell can be his shroud;
In vain, with timbreled anthems dark,
The sable-stoléd sorcerers bear his worshipped ark.

He feels from Judah's land
The dreaded Infant's hand;
The rays of Bethlehem blind his dusky eye;
Nor all the gods beside
Longer dare abide,
Not Typhon huge ending in snaky twine:
Our Babe, to show his Godhead true,
Can in his swaddling bands control the damnéd crew.

So when the sun in bed,
Curtained with cloudy red,
Pillows his chin upon an orient wave,
The flocking shadows pale
Troop to th'infernal jail;

Each fettered ghost slips to his several grave,
And the yellow-skirted fays
Fly after the night-steeds, leaving their moon-loved maze.

But see! the Virgin blest
Hath laid her Babe to rest.
Time is our tedious song should here have ending:
Heaven's youngest-teeméd star
Hath fixed her polished car,
Her sleeping Lord with handmaid lamp attending;
And all about the courtly stable
Bright-harnessed angels sit in order serviceable.

∽

AWAY IN A MANGER

JAMES R. MURRAY

Away in a manger, no crib for a bed,
The little Lord Jesus laid down His sweet head.
The stars in the sky looked down where he lay,
The little Lord Jesus asleep on the hay.

The cattle are lowing, the poor Baby wakes,
But little Lord Jesus no crying He makes.
I love Thee, Lord Jesus, look down from the sky,
And stay by my cradle till morning is nigh.

Be near me, Lord Jesus, I ask Thee to stay
Close by me forever and love me I pray.
Bless all the dear children in Thy tender care,
And take us to heaven to live with Thee there.

A Christmas Prayer for the Home

HENRY VAN DYKE

Jesus was born to a family, and family has always been a key concern of Christian theology. Van Dyke found a way to make the Christ of an ancient Bethlehem home Lord of the contemporary home.

Father of all men, look upon our family,
Kneeling together before thee,
And grant us a true Christmas.

With loving heart we bless Thee:
    For the gift of Thy dear Son Jesus Christ,
    For the peace He brings to human homes,
    For the good-will He teaches to sinful men,
    For the glory of Thy goodness shining in His face.

With joyful voice we praise Thee:
    For His lowly birth and His rest in the manger,
    For the pure tenderness of His mother Mary,
    For the fatherly care that protected Him,
    For the providence that saved the Holy child
    To be the Saviour of the world.

With deep desire we beseech Thee:
    Help us to keep His birthday truly,
    Help us to offer, in His name, our Christmas prayer.

From the sickness of sin and the darkness of doubt,
From the selfish pleasures and sullen pains,
From the frost of pride and the fever of envy,
God save us every one, through the blessing of Jesus.

In the health of purity and the calm of mutual trust,
In the sharing of joy and the bearing of trouble,
In the steady glow of love and the clear light of hope,
God keep us every one, by the blessing of Jesus.

In praying and praising, in giving and receiving,
In eating and drinking, in singing and making merry,
In parents' gladness and in children's mirth,

In dear memories of those who have departed,
In good comradeship with those who are here,
In kind wishes for those who are far away,
In patient waiting, sweet contentment, generous cheer,
God bless us every one, with the blessing of Jesus.

By remembering our kinship with all men,
By well-wishing, friendly speaking and kindly doing,
By cheering the downcast and adding sunshine to daylight.
By welcoming strangers (poor shepherds or wise men),
By keeping the music of the angels' song in this home,
God help us every one to share the blessing of Jesus:

In whose name we keep Christmas,
And whose words we pray together:

Our Father, which art in heaven, hallowed be Thy name,
Thy kingdom come. Thy will be done in earth, as it is in heaven.
Give us this day our daily bread. And forgive us our debts, as we forgive our
    debtors.
And lead us not into temptation, but deliver us from evil:
For Thine is the kingdom, and the power, and the glory, forever. Amen.

∾

THE BIRD OF DAWNING

WILLIAM SHAKESPEARE

The ghost of Hamlet's father has "faded on the crowing of the cock."
Marcellus, a soldier, speaks these lines.

    . . . Some say that ever 'gainst that season comes
Wherein our saviour's birth is celebrated
The bird of dawning singeth all night long;
And then, they say, no spirit can walk abroad,
The nights are wholesome; then no planets strike,
No fairy takes, nor witch hath power to charm,
So hallowed and so gracious is the time.

THE COVENTRY CAROL

AUTHOR UNKOWN

The music of "The Coventry Carol" dates from the sixteenth century and was taken from a pageant put on by shearmen and tailors of Coventry, England, on the steps of the city's cathedral between 1534 and 1584; this in turn was based on a much older morality play that tradesmen mounted for the entertainment of their monarchs and town officials. The song's minor tune and gently lulling words were sung in the play by the women of Bethlehem shortly before King Herod's men came to slaughter their infant sons in an attempt to kill the newborn king of the Jews. In many churches, those children who were killed by Herod are commemorated on December 28, the feast day of the Holy Innocents.

Lul-lay, Thou little tiny Child,
Bye-bye, lul-loo, lul-lay.
Lul-lay, Thou little tiny Child,
Bye-bye, lul-loo, lul-lay.

O sisters, too, how may we do
For to preserve this day?
This poor Youngling for whom we sing,
Bye-bye, lul-loo, lul-lay.

Herod the king in his raging
Chargèd he hath this day
His men of might, in his own sight,
All children young to slay.

Then woe is me, poor Child for Thee,
And ever morn and day,
For thy parting nor say nor sing,
Bye-bye, lul-loo, lul-lay.

MEDITATION

KEN GIRE

FOR THE CENSUS, the royal family has to travel eighty-five miles. Joseph walks, while Mary, nine months pregnant, rides sidesaddle on a donkey, feeling every jolt, every rut, every rock in the road.

By the time they arrive, the small hamlet of Bethlehem is swollen from an influx of travelers. The inn is packed, people feeling lucky if they were able to negotiate even a small space on the floor. Now it is late, everyone is asleep, and there is no room.

But fortunately, the innkeeper is not all shekels and mites. True, his stable is crowded with his guests' animals, but if they could squeeze out a little privacy there, they were welcome to it.

Joseph looks over at Mary, whose attention is concentrated on fighting a contraction. "We'll take it," he tells the innkeeper without hesitation.

The night is still when Joseph creaks open the stable door. As he does, a chorus of barn animals makes discordant note of the intrusion. The stench is pungent and humid, as there have not been enough hours in the day to tend the guests, let alone the livestock. A small oil lamp, lent them by the innkeeper, flickers to dance shadows on the walls. A disquieting place for a woman in the throes of childbirth. Far from home. Far from family. Far from what she had expected for her firstborn.

But Mary makes no complaint. It is a relief just to finally get off the donkey. She leans back against the wall, her feet swollen, back aching, contractions growing stronger and closer together.

Joseph's eyes dart around the stable. Not a minute to lose. Quickly. A feeding trough would have to make do for a crib. Hay would serve as a mattress. Blankets? Blankets? Ah, his robe. That would do. And those rags hung out to dry would help. A gripping contraction doubles Mary over and sends him racing for a bucket of water.

The birth would not be easy, either for the mother or the child. For every royal privilege for this son ended at conception.

A scream from Mary knifes through the calm of that silent night. Joseph returns, breathless, water sloshing from the wooden bucket. The top of the baby's head has already pushed its way into the world. Sweat pours from Mary's contorted face as Joseph, the most unlikely midwife in all Judea, rushes to her side.

The involuntary contractions are not enough, and Mary has to push with all her strength, almost as if God were refusing to come into the world without her help.

Joseph places a garment beneath her, and with a final push and a long sigh her labor is over.

The Messiah has arrived.

Elongated head from the constricting journey through the birth canal. Light skin, as the pigment would take days or even weeks to surface. Mucus in his ears and nostrils. Wet and slippery from the amniotic fluid. The Son of the Most High God umbilically tied to a lowly Jewish girl.

The baby chokes and coughs. Joseph instinctively turns him over and clears his throat.

Then he cries. Mary bares her breast and reaches for the shivering baby. She lays him on her chest, and his helpless cries subside. His tiny head bobs around on the unfamiliar terrain. This will be the first thing the infant-king learns. Mary can feel his racing heartbeat as he gropes to nurse.

Deity nursing from a young maiden's breast. Could anything be more puzzling—or more profound?

Joseph sits exhausted, silent, full of wonder.

The baby finishes and sighs, the divine Word reduced to a few unintelligible sounds. Then, for the first time, his eyes fix on his mother's. Deity straining to focus. The Light of the World, squinting.

Tears pool in her eyes. She touches his tiny hand. And hands that once sculpted mountain ranges cling to her finger.

She looks up at Joseph, and through a watery veil, their souls touch. He crowds closer, cheek to cheek with his betrothed. Together they stare in awe at the baby Jesus, whose heavy eyelids begin to close. It has been a long journey. The King is tired.

And so, with barely a ripple of notice, God stepped into the warm lake of humanity. Without protocol and without pretension.

Where you would have expected angels, there were only flies. Where you would have expected heads of state, there were only donkeys, a few haltered cows, a nervous ball of sheep, a tethered camel, and a furtive scurry of curious barn mice.

Except for Joseph, there was no one to share Mary's pain. Or her joy. Yes, there were angels announcing the Savior's arrival—but only to a band of blue-collar shepherds. And yes, a magnificent star shone in the sky to mark his birthplace—but only three foreigners bothered to look up and follow it.

Thus, in the little town of Bethlehem . . . that one silent night . . . the royal birth of God's Son tiptoed quietly by . . . as the world slept.

WHAT OF THOSE SILENT YEARS BETWEEN BETHLEHEM

AND THE BEGINNING OF HIS PUBLIC MINISTRY?

ALFRED EDERSHEIM

OF THE MANY years spent in Nazareth, during which Jesus passed from infancy to childhood, from childhood to youth, and from youth to manhood, the Evangelic narrative has left us but briefest notice. Of His *childhood:* that "He grew and waxed strong in spirit, filled with wisdom, and the grace of God was upon Him"; of his *youth:* besides the account of His questioning the Rabbis in the Temple, the year before he attained Jewish majority—that "He was subject to His parents," and that "He increased in wisdom and in stature, and in favour with God and man." Considering what loving care watched over Jewish child-life, tenderly marking by not fewer than eight designations the various stages of its development, and the deep interest naturally attaching to the early life of the Messiah, that silence, in contrast to the almost blasphemous absurdities of the Apocryphal Gospels, teaches us once more, and most impressively, that the Gospels furnish a history of the Saviour; not a biography of Jesus of Nazareth.

THE BIRTH OF JESUS

HENRY VAN DYKE

THE BIRTH OF Jesus is the sunrise of the Bible. Towards this point the aspirations of the prophets and the poems of the psalmists were directed as the heads of flowers are turned toward the dawn. From this point a new day began to flow very silently over the world—a day of faith and freedom, a day of hope and love. When we remember the high meaning that has come into human life and the clear light that has flooded softly down from the manger-cradle in Bethlehem of Judea, we do not wonder that mankind has learned to reckon history from the birthday of Jesus, and to date all events by the years before or after the Nativity of Christ.

BRING A TORCH, JEANNETTE, ISABELLA

AUTHOR UNKNOWN

Bring a torch, Jeannette, Isabella;
Bring a torch, come swiftly and run.
Christ is born, tell the folk of the village;
Jesus is sleeping in His cradle.
Ah, ah, beautiful is the Mother;
Ah, ah, beautiful is her Son.

Hasten now, good folk of the village;
Hasten now, the Christ-Child to see.
You will find Him asleep in the manger;
Quietly come and whisper softly,
Hush, hush, peacefully now He slumbers;
Hush, hush, peacefully now He sleeps.

❧

HARK! THE HERALD ANGELS SING

CHARLES WESLEY

Hark! the herald angels sing,
"Glory to the newborn King;
Peace on earth and mercy mild,
God and sinners reconciled!"
Joyful, all ye nations, rise,
Join the triumph of the skies;
With the angelic host proclaim,
"Christ is born in Bethlehem!"
    Hark! the herald angels sing,
    "Glory to the newborn King!"

Christ, by highest heaven adored,
Christ, the Everlasting Lord!
Late in time behold Him come,
Offspring of the virgin's womb.

Veiled in flesh the Godhead see;
Hail the Incarnate Deity!
Pleased as man with men to dwell,
Jesus, our Immanuel.
    Hark! the herald angels sing,
    "Glory to the newborn King!"

Hail, the heavenborn Prince of Peace!
Hail, the Sun of Righteousness!
Light and life to all He brings,
Risen with healing in His wings.
Mild He lays His glory by,
Born that man no more may die,
Born to raise the sons of earth,
Born to give them second birth.
    Hark! the herald angels sing,
    "Glory to the new born King!"

∾

VIRGIL'S STAR

VIRGIL (PUBLIUS VERGILIUS MARO)

VIRGIL'S *FOURTH ECLOGUE* may have been considered by Romans to be a prophecy of a coming star. Although Virgil died in 19 B.C., his words are hauntingly reminiscent of Isaiah and the prophets as he describes the new utopian age.

According to Virgil's prophecy, Romans felt the new star ushered in the *Pax Augusti;* Luke opined that it ushered in the *Pax Christi*. But neither Virgil nor Luke would disagree about the reality of the celestial appearance.

Now is come the last age of the Cumaean prophecy:
The great cycle of periods is born anew,
Now returns the maid, returns the reign of Saturn:
Now from the high heaven of new generation comes down. . . .
Untended shall the she-goats bring home their milk-swol'n udders,
Nor shall the huge lions alarm the herds:

Unbidden thy cradle shall break into wooing blossom.
The snake too shall die, and die the treacherous poison plant;
Assyrian spice shall grow all up and down. . . .
Behold the world swaying her orbed mass,
Lands and spaces of sea and depth of sky;
Behold how all things rejoice in the age to come.

AVE MARIA GRATIA PLENA

OSCAR WILDE

Was this His coming! I had hoped to see
A scene of wondrous glory, as was told
Of some great god who in a rain of gold
Broke open bars and fell on Danaë:
Or a dread vision as when Semele,
Sickening for love and unappeased desire,
Prayed to see God's clear body, and the fire
Caught her brown limbs and slew her utterly.
With such glad dreams I sought this holy place,
And now with wondering eyes and heart I stand
Before this supreme mystery of Love:
Some kneeling girl with passionless pale face,
An angel with a lily in his hand,
And over both the white wings of a Dove.

A HYMN ON THE NATIVITY OF MY SAVIOR

BEN JONSON

I sing the birth, was born tonight,
The Author both of life and light;
The angels so did sound it,

And like the ravished shepherds said,
Who saw the light and were afraid,
   Yet searched, and true they found it.

The Son of God, the Eternal King,
That did us all salvation bring,
   And freed the soul from danger;
He whom the whole world could not take,
The Word, which heaven and earth did make,
   Was now laid in a manger.

The Father's wisdom willed it so,
The son's obedience knew no No,
   Both wills were in one stature;
And as that wisdom had decreed,
The Word was now made flesh indeed,
   And took on Him our nature.

What comfort by Him do we win?
Who made Himself the Prince of sin
   To make us heirs of glory?
To see this Babe, all innocence;
A Martyr born in our defense;
   Can man forget this story?

❧

THE MEANING OF MIRACLE

CALVIN MILLER

THE MIRACLE OF the virgin birth would seem utterly incredible considered alone. But the natural happenings in the narrative make it seem quite real. Mary may have left Nazareth to keep down the talk of the village busybodies (Luke 1:39). She marries Joseph only after his fears of Mary's infidelity have been allayed by an angel of the Lord (Matthew 1:18–25). Inspired by her estate as "highly favored among women" (Luke 1:42), she sings the *Magnificat,* whose captivating poetry would have been beyond a peasant girl such as herself. Some have said the virgin birth was a fabrication of the evangelists, who thought that including the event would serve as a slur on sex in behalf of the puritanical, primitive Christian ethic. But C. S. Lewis has answered the charge classically in saying that the virgin birth is no more a slur on the sexuality of the day than the feeding of the five thousand was a slur on the bakeries of that day.

∿

WHY THE MAGI MIGHT HAVE FOLLOWED THE STAR

ETHELBERT STAUFFER

Ethelbert Stauffer would not claim that the planets in conjunction were the star of Bethlehem. He does offer the sort of logic that the Magi astronomers might have used in seeking Jesus.

As LONG AGO as the seventeenth century, Kepler ascribed the star of Bethlehem to the unique orbit of the planet Jupiter in the year 7 B.C. In the spring of that year there was a conjunction of Jupiter and Venus. In the summer and autumn of that year Jupiter encountered the planet Saturn in the Sign of the Fishes—this being the extremely rare Great Conjunction that takes place in this form only once every 794 years. According to the account in Matthew, the Magi noted only the beginning of the conjunction, only the appearance of Jupiter "out of the east." Upon this they based their astronomical and astrological forecast and thereupon set out for Palestine; when they reached Palestine they witnessed the crucial phenomenon in the heavens. The rarity of that conjunction of Jupiter could not have escaped the astronomers of antiquity. But was astronomical science in the days of Jesus sufficiently developed to forecast the orbits and conjunctions of the planets?

• • •

What opinions did contemporary astrologers hold concerning this phenomenon? Today we can answer this question also. Jupiter was regarded as the star of the ruler of the universe, and the constellation of the Fishes as the sign of the last days. In the East, Saturn was considered to be the planet of Palestine. If Jupiter encountered Saturn in the sign of the Fishes, it could only mean that the ruler of the last days would appear in Palestine. Such were the passages that prompted the Magi of Matthew 2:2, to go to Jerusalem.

ODE ON THE MORNING OF CHRIST'S NATIVITY

JOHN MILTON

This is the month, and this the happy morn,
Wherein the Son of Heaven's eternal King,
Of wedded maid and virgin mother born,
Our great redemption from above did bring;
For so the holy sages once did sing,
That He our deadly forfeit should release,
And, with His Father work us a perpetual peace.

That glorious form, that Light insufferable,
And that far-beaming blaze of Majesty
Wherewith He wont at Heaven's high council-table
To sit the midst of Trinal Unity,
He laid aside; and, here with us to be,
Forsook the courts of everlasting day,
And chose, with us a darksome house of mortal clay.

Say, heavenly Muse, shall not thy sacred vein
Afford a present to the Infant God?
Hast thou no verse, no hymn, or solemn strain
To welcome Him to this His new abode,
Now while the heaven, by the sun's team untrod,
Hath took no print of the approaching light,
And all the spangled host keep watch in squadrons bright?

See how from far, upon the eastern road,
The star-led wizards haste with odours sweet:
Oh, run, prevent them with thy humble ode
And lay it lowly at His blessed feet;
Have thou the honour first, thy Lord to greet,
And join thy voice into the angel choir;
From out His secret altar touch'd with hallow'd fire.

III

JESUS:

~

HIS FRIENDSHIP
WITH US ALL

THE story may be apocryphal, but when Karl Barth was asked what was the most profound theological truth he knew, he replied, "Jesus loves me, this I know." Jesus once said to his disciples, "I don't call you disciples but friends." All of us are defined by our roster of friends. And to have Jesus at the top of the list makes the best statement of identity.

Jesus as an idea is the longing of God. When asked himself who God was, Jesus replied, "God is a Spirit and they who worship him must worship him in Spirit and in truth" (John 4:24). But when Jesus told the reason for his coming, he said, "The Son of man is come to seek and to save that which was lost" (Luke 19:10). Put together, these two verses of scripture seem to indicate that God is a longing Spirit. He yearns after people and longs to have a relationship with them.

Probably the first verse of scripture most Christians encounter is John 3:16, "For God so loved the world he gave his only begotten son. . . ." God seemed to Francis Thompson to be the Hound of Heaven pursuing us as a great and yearning Spirit eager to have a relationship with us. We are so prone to speak of seekers as those who pursue God in search of meaning. But in Jesus we have the yearning God in pursuit of people. In Christ we find that God is not content to let people live and die beyond his circle of love.

On he comes, ever pursuing the friendship of human beings. So much that Paul of Tarsus was overwhelmed in the Syrian desert by the Savior whose religion he had set out to destroy.

Augustine felt he was claimed by his ardent and *severe mercy*.

Luther was so overwhelmed he cried out his friendship in defense of the very studies of his liturgical, traditional faith.

Pascal agreed that this friendship was the answer to longing, that there is a God-shaped vacuum at the heart of all of us. Only God can fill that vacuum.

John Wesley cried out that this pursuing God had strongly warmed his heart.

C. S. Lewis felt this pursuing love and claimed he was "surprised by joy."

Many of the world's most notable Christians have felt the chase of this pursuing lover. Jesus follows after them until at last he catches them and the relationship is firm.

The hymnist wrote, "What a friend we have in Jesus." This simple theme has been established throughout Christendom. Our immense fear of being alone has been answered by the Christ who never demanded the answer to all loneliness. It is this sustaining relationship that Jesus brings to us. The Savior makes our friendship heaven's agenda. Paul confesses freely that this Jesus had stood by him in every trial of life:

> At my preliminary hearing no one stood by me. They all ran like scared rabbits. But it doesn't matter—the Master stood by me and helped me spread the Message loud and clear to those who had never heard it. I was snatched from the jaws of the lion! God's looking after me, keeping me safe in the kingdom of heaven. All praise to him, praise forever!
>
> 2 Timothy 4:16–18, *The Message*

FRIENDS TO THE DEATH

MAX LUCADO

THE MAN THEY mocked wasn't much to look at. His body was whip-torn flesh, yanked away from the bone. His face was a mask of blood and spit; eyes puffy and swollen. "King of the Jews" was painted over his head. A crown of thorns pierced his scalp. His lip was split. Maybe his nose was bleeding or a tooth was loose.

The man they mocked was half-dead. The man they mocked was beaten. But the man they mocked was at peace. "Father, forgive them, because they don't know what they are doing" (Luke 23:34).

After Jesus' prayer, one of the criminals began to shout insults at him: "Aren't you the Christ? Then save yourself and us" (v. 39).

The heart of this thief remains hard. The presence of Christ crucified means nothing to him. Jesus is worthy of ridicule, so the thief ridicules. He expects his chorus to be harmonized from the other cross. It isn't. Instead, it is challenged.

"You should fear God! You are getting the same punishment he is. We are punished justly, getting what we deserve for what we did. But this man has done nothing wrong" (vv. 40–41).

Unbelievable. The same mouth that cursed Christ now defends Christ. What has happened? What has he seen since he has been on the cross? Did he witness a miracle? Did he hear a lecture? Was he read a treatise on the Trinity?

No, of course not. According to Luke, all he heard was a prayer, a prayer of grace. But that was enough. Something happens to a man who stands in the presence of God. And something happened to the thief.

Read again his words. "We are punished justly, getting what we deserve. . . . But this man has done nothing wrong."

The core of the gospel in one sentence. The essence of eternity through the mouth of a crook:

I am wrong; Jesus is right.

I have failed; Jesus has not.

I deserve to die; Jesus deserves to live.

The thief knew precious little about Christ, but what he knew was precious indeed. He knew that an innocent man was dying an unjust death with no complaint on his lips. And if Jesus can do that, he just might be who he says he is.

So the thief asks for help: "Jesus, remember me when you come into your kingdom."

The heavy head of Christ lifts and turns, and the eyes of these two meet. What Jesus sees is a naked man. I don't mean in terms of clothes. I mean in terms of charades. He has no cover. No way to hide.

His title? Scum of the earth. His achievement? Death by crucifixion. His reputation? Criminal. His character? Depraved until the last moment. Until the final hour. Until the last encounter.

Until now.

❦

THE GRAND SECT

ELTON TRUEBLOOD

IT IS NOT easy to be a human being. Human life carries with it marvelous possibilities of joy, but there are, at the same time, untold ways in which it can go wrong. Even after we have learned all that we can of the literature of tragedy, we have but an imperfect sense of the sorrow and frustrations which occur in countless lives. The harm that comes from the ravages of disease is terrible, but the harm that comes from the hatred and ignorance of other men is even more terrible. Often we are shocked when we realize that the persons who are near us are suffering in some serious way without our consciousness either of the fact or of the degree of seriousness. My neighbor kills himself, and I have to admit that I did not even realize that he was particularly troubled. I am ashamed that I did not know, and I wonder why I did not suspect that he was in distress. Would I have known if I had been more sensitive to his need and less occupied with my own troubles? It is sobering to realize that the person next to you on the train, or even in a congregation, may be struggling with problems that seem insoluble. We read in the newspapers of the harm that comes to individuals, but we forget about it because the story appears only one day. The awful fact, however, is that the tragedy does not end with the disappearance of the newspaper story. Many of the people of whom we have read, but soon forget, are living out the rest of their days in quiet desperation. The maimed are still maimed.

The universality of human sorrow and need is one of the reasons for the great attractiveness of the words of Jesus which appear at the end of the eleventh chapter of Matthew. When Jesus says, "Come unto me, all ye who labor and are heavy laden," He is really speaking to all.

• • •

If Christ were speaking to us today, as He spoke earlier to the people of Galilee, and if He were to use parables from contemporary life as He did before, He might easily use the parable of the sonic boom. This He might do, because we know more about jets and their pilots than we know about sheep and their shepherds. The message of the sonic boom is that there is no calm and nonviolent way in which flyers can surpass the speed of sound. The peculiar combination of waves, which occurs at the crucial speed, producing the loud report with which we are increasingly familiar, is something we are not likely to escape or avoid. Some changes are great changes, and what Christ teaches is that Christian discipleship involves such a change. It means entrance into a new kind of experience and organization around a new center.

∽

ON MEETING CHRIST

SAINT AUGUSTINE OF HIPPO

Saint Augustine's conversion, in the fourth century, was to impact the Christian faith as no one else's with the possible exception of St. Paul's. This is the account of his conversion taken from his Confessions.

THE VERY TOYS of toys and vanities of vanities still held me; they plucked at the garment of my flesh and whispered softly, "Will you cast us off for ever? And from that moment shall we no longer be with you—for ever?" and I hesitated, for a strong habit said to me, "Do you think you can live without them?"

But continence said to me, "Why do you rely on yourself and so waver? Cast yourself upon him, fear not, he will not withdraw himself and let you fall; he will receive you and heal you."

So I rose and, throwing myself down under a certain fig tree, wept bitterly in contrition of heart. Suddenly I heard from a neighbouring house the voice of a child, singing over and over again, "Take up and read, take up and read."

Checking my weeping I got up and went back to where I had been sitting, and had laid down the volume of the apostle, and read the first passage which met my eyes: "Not in rioting and drunkenness, not in impurity and wantonness, not in strife and envy; but put on the Lord Jesus Christ, and make no provision for the flesh, to fulfil its lusts."

I needed to read no further, for suddenly, as it were by a light infused into my heart, all darkness vanished away.

~

JESUS TEACHES NICODEMUS

CLARENCE JORDAN

NOW THERE WAS a very prominent churchman by the name of Nicodemus. This man came to Jesus one night and said, "Professor, we are aware that you are an inspired teacher, because nobody could present the marvelous things you're presenting without God's help."

"I want to make it clear," Jesus answered, "that *no one* can be a member of God's family unless he is fathered from above."

Nicodemus asked, "But how can a man be fathered once he is born? He can't return to his mother's womb and be re-fathered, can he?"

Jesus replied, "Except a person be fathered by both semen and Spirit, he can't be a member of God's family. Flesh fathers flesh, and Spirit fathers spirit. Don't be so surprised, then, that I told you that people have to be fathered from above. The wind blows as it will, and you listen to its sound, but you have no idea where it's coming from or where it's going. It's like that when a person is fathered by the Spirit."

"How can this possibly be true?" Nicodemus asked.

"Well, well," Jesus answered. "Here you are, 'the nation's foremost theologian,' and yet you don't grasp these things? I assure you that we speak and testify from firsthand knowledge and experience, but you folks won't accept our evidence. If I have used simple illustrations and you're not convinced, how would I ever persuade you with theological arguments?

"No one has penetrated the spiritual realm except the son of man, who came out of it. And just as Moses put a brass snake on a pole in the wilderness, even so must the son of man be put on a pole, in order that all who trust him might have spiritual life. In the same way, God loved the world so much that he gave his only Son, that whoever trusts him might not die, but might have spiritual life. For God did not send his Son into the world to damn it, but that through him the world might be rescued. He who lives by him is not damned, but he who does not live by him is already damned, because he does not live up to the name of God's only Son. This is the damnation: The Light came into the world, and the people preferred the darkness to the Light, because their ways were wicked. For the person whose life is false shuns the Light and won't go near it, for fear that his ways will be rebuked. But the person whose life is true comes out into the Light, so that it might be clear that his ways are rooted in God."

❧

THE CENTURION

RICHARD CRASHAW

Thy God was making haste into thy roof,
Thy humble faith and fear keeps him aloof:
He'll be thy guest, because he may not be;
He'll come—into thy house? No, into thee.

❧

I HAVE CALLED YOU FRIENDS

ROBERT SOUTH

It is on the basis of this idea that George Fox and John Woolman and the Quakers did not call themselves a church but referred to themselves as the Society of Friends. In John 15:15 Jesus calls his disciples friends and lays down a relational basis for the Kingdom of God. Quakers have always been strong to emphasize that they are bound together in a community of friendship, and friends naturally love and care for one another. Out of all proportion to their size, the Quakers have always taken seriously the fact that they are friends and out to take care of all other needy friends of God whether they are Quakers or not.

IT IS THE excellency of friendship to rectify, or at least to qualify, the malignity of those surmises that would misrepresent a friend and traduce him in our thoughts. Am I told that my friend has done me an injury, or that he has committed an indecent action? Why, the first debt that I both owe to his friendship, and that he may challenge from mine, is rather to question the truth of the report than presently to believe my friend unworthy. Or if matter of fact breaks out and blazes with too great an evidence to be denied or so much as doubted of; why, still there are other lenitives that friendship will apply before it will be brought to the decretory rigours of a condemning sentence. A friend will be sure to act the part of an advocate before he will assume that of a judge. And there are few actions so ill, unless they are of a very deep and black tincture indeed, but will admit of some extenuation, at least from those common topics of human frailty; such as are ignorance or inadvertency, passion or surprise, company or solicitation, with many other such things, which may go a great way towards an excusing of the agent, though they cannot absolutely justify the action. All which apologies for and alleviations of faults, though they are the heights of humanity, yet they are not the favours but the duties of friendship. Charity itself commands us, where we know no ill, to think well of all. But friendship, that always goes a pitch higher, gives a man a peculiar right and claim to the good opinion of his friend. . . .

We have seen here the demeanour of friendship between man and man: but how is it, think we now, between Christ and the soul that depends upon Him? Is He any ways short in these offices of tenderness and mitigation? No, assuredly: but by infinite degrees superior. For where our heart does but relent, His melts; where our eye pities, His bowels yearn. How many forwardnesses of ours does He smother, how many indignities does He pass by, with how many affronts does He put up at our hands, because His love is invincible, and His friendship unchangeable!

~

KEEP OUR COOL BECAUSE

BERNARD BANGLEY

An obscure member of the religious order of Canons Regular, too humble to sign his name, is nevertheless given initial credit for these words about Christ. Thomas à Kempis first wrote these words in his classic Imitation of Christ. *Bernard Bangley formulated this contemporary paraphrase.*

WHEN JESUS IS with us, all is well and nothing seems insurmountable. But when Jesus is absent, everything is difficult. If Jesus does not speak to us inwardly, all other comfort is meaningless. But the slightest communication from him brings consolation.

Life without Jesus is like a dry garden, baking in the sun. It is foolish to want anything that conflicts with Jesus. What can the world give you without Jesus? His absence is hell; his presence, paradise. If Jesus is with you, no enemy can injure you. Whoever finds Jesus has discovered a great treasure, the best of all possible good. The loss of him is a tremendous misfortune, more than the loss of the entire world. Poverty is life without Jesus, but close friendship with him is incalculable wealth.

❧

WHAT IT MEANS TO BE A DISCIPLE

C. S. LEWIS

THE NEW TESTAMENT has lots to say about self-denial, but not about self-denial as an end in itself. We are told to deny ourselves and to take up our crosses in order that we may follow Christ; and nearly every description of what we shall ultimately find if we do so contains an appeal to desire. If there lurks in most modern minds the notion that to desire our own good and earnestly to hope for the enjoyment of it is a bad thing, I submit that this notion has crept in from Kant and the Stoics and is no part of the Christian faith. Indeed, if we consider the unblushing promises of reward and the staggering nature of the rewards promised in the Gospels, it would seem that Our Lord finds our desires, not too strong, but too weak. We are half-hearted creatures, fooling about with drink and sex and ambition when infinite joy is offered us, like an ignorant child who wants to go on making mud pies in a slum because he cannot imagine what is meant by the offer of a holiday at the sea. We are far too easily pleased.

THE CHILDREN'S JESUS

J. C. CARLILE

How GOOD TO know that there is a Friend for little children above the bright blue sky, and that He is not only there, wherever that may be, but is with us among the children wherever we are. He has not changed, He is the same yesterday, to-day and for ever. The love-light in His eye as He took the children into His arms has not dimmed. His attraction for the little people is unabated. He still calls them to Himself and blessed are they who come to His feet. Happy are the mothers who bring their little ones to the Saviour. If it be true that Heaven lies about us in our infancy, it is surely when the unsophisticated eyes look up into the face that never grows old.

Jesus delights to reveal Himself to the child mind. It was not to the worldly wise and prudent He displayed His pearls, but to those who possessed the conscious simplicity, the responsive affection of a little child.

Jesus was a great lover of little people. Did He not say in His prayer: "I thank Thee, O Father, Lord of heaven and earth, because Thou hast hid these things from the wise and prudent, and hast revealed them unto babes"? Did He not say: "Out of the mouth of babes and sucklings Thou hast perfected praise"?

Is it not permissible to think of the days when Jesus was at the carpenter's bench in Joseph's shop and to imagine that the children came to Him with their broken toys to be mended? Did the boy with tearful eyes bring the broken boat that would no longer sail upon the lake? Did the girl bring the camel without a head? What did the Master do with them? It is inconceivable that He sent them away with the sorrow of broken toys in their hearts. It became Him, as the children's Saviour, to add to their pleasures just as surely as He set out to prevent their sorrows.

There is an Old Testament description of the family of Gideon. The smooth-tongued flatterer who described the captives that were at Tabor, some of whom were slain, said: "Each one resembled the children of a king" (Judges viii. 18). There is no mistaking the people of God. It may not be easy to recognise royalty in plain clothing. There is a common humanity belonging to us all so that kings and princes are compelled to wear their labels of distinction in order to be known, but those who become the children of King Jesus have a common resemblance.

• • •

All the children of the Master have the resemblance of the King. They are not exact copies, they are very imperfect, but there is no doubt about the likeness, and as we seek to do His will, becoming His servants who serve Him, we shall share in the promise, "They shall see His face and be like Him."

Let us think of the Lord of Life walking the lowly ways of earth, gladdening the hearts of boys and girls by His smiles and by His gracious words. Some wise people have said that Jesus was always of sad countenance, that laughter did not ripple over His lips. That could never have been so or the children would not have gone near Him. It belongs to the Son of God to reveal the gladness of the Father's heart. Life is meant to be joyous, and little children are normally glad. Theirs is the happiness of irresponsibility; they have not yet felt the burdens of obligations that come with maturity. Theirs is the delight of the carefree, they have not become anxious, they have not yet lost faith. They know the delight of clinging to the one they love, the joy of being owned that finds expression in after years in some such utterance as "My Beloved is mine and I am His." But while childhood lingers there is the delight of dependence, just belonging to father and mother and finding gladness in the simple things of every day and in the dream time when the faraway unseen, the invisible, takes shape and becomes real. There is inspiration in the remembrance that in the long ago the Lord and Master of us all not only lingered by the beds of pain and blessed the lame, the halt and the blind, but that He delighted the hearts of boys and girls.

❧

FRIENDSHIP

GEORGE A. BUTTRICK

THOSE WHO WALKED with Jesus found they could not plumb the depths of His nature. They discovered in His friendship a quality enhanced by death, and a fathomless ocean of love. One word is clear in the testimony of those who walked with Him: "This man speaketh with authority."

UNTO THE HILLS

BILLY GRAHAM

TO BE SURE we must deplore wickedness, evil, and wrongdoing, but our commendable intolerance of sin too often develops into a deplorable intolerance of sinners. Jesus hates sin but loves the sinner.

I am amused and shocked to hear a man of considerable religious background declare on television not long ago that "you didn't catch Jesus associating with questionable people or those whose basic ideas and attitudes were at variance with what Jesus knew to be honorable and right!"

Such a man should have known that Jesus wasn't afraid to associate with anyone! One of the things which the scribes and Pharisees criticized bitterly was His willingness to help and talk to and exchange ideas with anyone, be they publicans, thieves, learned professors or prostitutes, rich or poor! Even His own followers decried some of the people with whom He was seen in public, but this did not lessen the compassion that Jesus felt for all the members of poor, blinded, struggling humanity.

Jesus had the most open and all-encompassing mind that this world has ever seen. His own inner conviction was so strong, so firm, so unswerving that He could afford to mingle with any group secure in the knowledge that he would not be contaminated. It is fear that makes us unwilling to listen to another's point of view, fear that our own ideas may be attacked. Jesus had no such fear, no such pettiness of viewpoint, no need to fence Himself off for His own protection. He knew the difference between graciousness and compromise and we would do well to learn from Him. He set for us the most magnificent and glowing example of truth combined with mercy of all time, and in departing said: "Go ye and do likewise" (Luke 10:37).

IN THE NAME OF JESUS

SØREN KIERKEGAARD

TO PRAY "in the name of Jesus" may perhaps be explained most simply in this way. A magistrate orders this and the other thing *in the name of the King*. What does that mean? In the first place it means: I myself am nothing. I have no power, nothing to say for myself—but it is in the name of the King. Thus to pray in the name of Christ means: I dare not approach God without a mediator; if my prayer is to be heard, then it will be in the name of Jesus; what gives it strength is that name. Next, when a magistrate gives a command in the name of the King it naturally follows that what he commands must be the King's will, he cannot command his own will in the King's name. The same thing is true of praying in the name of Jesus, to pray in such a way that it is in conformity with the will of Jesus. I cannot pray in the name of Jesus to have my own will; the name of Jesus is not a signature of no importance, but the decisive factor; the fact that the name of Jesus comes at the beginning is not prayer in the name of Jesus; but it means to pray in such a manner that I dare name Jesus in it, that is to say think of Him, think His holy will together with whatever I am praying for. Finally, when a magistrate gives an order in the name of the King it means that the King assumes the responsibility. So too with prayer in the name of Jesus, Jesus assumes the responsibility and all the consequences, He steps forward for us, steps into the place of the person praying.

∾

LETTER FROM JESUS

AUTHOR UNKNOWN

DEAR FRIEND:

How are you? I just had to send you this letter and to tell you how much I love and care about you. I saw you yesterday as you were walking with friends. I waited all day hoping you would talk to me also. As evening drew near, I gave you a sunset to close your day, a cool breeze to rest you, and I waited. You never came. Oh, yes, it hurt me, but I still love you, because I am your friend.

I saw you fall asleep last night, and I longed to touch your brow, so I spilled moonlight upon your pillow and face. Again I waited, wanting to rush down so we could talk. I have so many gifts for you.

You awakened late and rushed off for the day—my tears were in the rain. Today you looked so sad, so alone. It makes my heart ache because I understand. My friends let me down and hurt me many times, too, but I love you. I try to tell you in the quiet green grass. I whisper it in the leaves and the trees, and give it in the color of the flowers. I shout it to you in the mountain streams, and give the birds love songs to sing. I clothe you with warm sunshine and perfume the air. My love for you is deeper than the oceans, and bigger than the biggest want or need you have.

We will spend eternity together in heaven. I know how hard it is on this earth, I really know . . . My father wants to help you too . . . He's that way, you know. Just call on me, ask me, talk to me . . . But if you don't call, you'll see . . . I have chosen you and because of this, I will wait . . . because I love you.

Your friend Jesus

☙

JESUS' LOVE OF CHILDREN

HARRY EMERSON FOSDICK

JESUS' HOME IN Nazareth was full of children—"his brothers James and Joseph and Simon and Judas" and "all his sisters"—and Jesus' understanding and appreciation of children are evident. He recalled hungry children, asking for bread or fish. He knew children's capricious moods, happy or sulky at their games. He remembered neighbors disturbing the family at midnight, when all the children were peaceably in bed. When his disciples jealously asked who among them was to be greatest, he set a child before them, saying, "Whoever humbles himself like this child, he is the greatest in the kingdom of heaven." He identified himself with children, declaring that to welcome "one such child" is to welcome him. According to Matthew, when children in the temple shouted "Hosanna" at the sight of him and indignant priests protested, he quoted the Psalmist:

> Out of the mouths of babes and sucklings thou has brought
> perfect praise.

As for his personal affection toward children, Matthew, Mark and Luke all recall how the disciples, trying to prevent parents from bringing their babes for his blessing, were rebuked: "Let the children come unto me; do not hinder them."

IF I HAD A VOICE

LOIS A. CHENEY

If I had a voice,
I'd sing to God.

If I had the hands,
I'd sculpt for God.

If I had the brains,
I'd think for God.

If I had the strength,
I'd fight for God.

If I had the skill,
I'd write for God.

If I had the faith,
I'd build for God.

If I had the heart,
I'd love for God.

If I had the money,
I'd buy for God.

And the most extraordinary thing is,
He still says, "Come."
And the most extraordinary thing is,
He commands, "Come!"
And the most extraordinary thing is,
God
and his awe-ful God-ness.

KNOWING CHRIST IN THE QUIET PLACE

RICHARD BAXTER

Richard Baxter stands among those contemplative pastors who believed that the way to know Christ is through the inner way of the heart.

CONCERNING THE FITTEST place for heavenly meditation it is sufficient to say that the most convenient is some private retirement. Our spirits need every help, and to be freed from every hindrance in the work. If in private prayer, Christ directs us to "enter into our closet and shut the door," that "our Father may see us in secret"; so should we do in this meditation. How often did Christ Himself retire to some mountain, or wilderness, or other solitary place! I give not this advice for occasional meditation, but for that which is set and solemn. Therefore withdraw thyself from all society of godly men, that thou mayest awhile enjoy the society of the Lord. If a student cannot study in a crowd, who exerciseth only his invention and memory, much less shouldst thou be in a crowd, who art to exercise all the powers of thy soul, and upon an object so far above nature. . . .

But observe for thyself what place best agrees with thy spirit; whether within doors, or without. Isaac's example in "going out to meditate in the field" will, I believe, best suit with most. Our Lord so much used a solitary garden that even Judas, when he came to betray Him, knew where to find Him: and though He took His disciples thither with Him, yet He was "withdrawn from them" for more secret devotions. . . . So that Christ had His accustomed place, and consequently accustomed duty, and so must we; He hath a place that is solitary, whither He retireth Himself, even from His own disciples, and so must we; His meditations go farther than His words, they affect and pierce His heart and soul, and so must ours. Only there is a wide difference in the object: Christ meditates on the sufferings that our sins had deserved, so that the wrath of His Father passed through all His soul; but we are to meditate on the glory He hath purchased, that the love of the Father, and the joy of the Spirit, may enter at our thoughts, revive our affections, and overflow our souls.

LONGING TO BE WITH CHRIST

WILLIAM COWPER

To Jesus, the Crown of my Hope,
  My soul is in haste to be gone;
Oh bear me, ye cherubims, up,
  And waft me away to His throne!

My Savior, whom absent I love,
  Whom not having seen I adore,
Whose Name is exalted above
  All glory, dominion, and power,

Dissolve Thou the bond that detains
  My soul from her portion in Thee,
And strike off the adamant chains
  And make me eternally free.

When that happy era begins,
  When arrayed in Thy beauty I shine,
Nor pierce anymore, by my sins,
  The bosom on which I recline,

Oh then shall the veil be removed
  And round me Thy brightness be poured.
I shall meet Him whom absent I loved;
  I shall see whom unseen I adored.

And then never more shall the fears,
  The trials, temptations, and woes,
Which darken this valley of tears,
  Intrude on my blissful repose.

Or, if yet remembered above,
  Remembrance no sadness shall raise;
They will be but new signs of Thy love,
  New themes for my wonder and praise.

Thus the strokes which from sin and from pain
  Shall set me eternally free
Will but strengthen and rivet the chain
  Which binds me, my Savior, to Thee.

LIFE TOGETHER

DIETRICH BONHOEFFER

CHRIST OPENED THE WAY

A Christian comes to others only through Jesus Christ. Among people there is strife. "He is our peace," says Paul of Jesus Christ (Eph. 2:14). Without Christ there is discord between God and man and between man and man. Christ became the Mediator and made peace with God and among men.

Without Christ we should not know God, we could not call upon him, nor come to him. But without Christ we also could not know our brother, nor could we come to him. The way is blocked by our own ego. Christ opened the way to God and to our brother. Now Christians can live with one another in peace; they can love and serve one another; they can become one. But they can continue to do so only by way of Jesus Christ. Only in Jesus Christ are we one, only through him are we bound together. To eternity he remains the one Mediator.

WE ARE IN HIM

When God's Son took on flesh, he truly and bodily took on, out of pure grace, our being, our nature, ourselves. This was the eternal counsel of the triune God. Now we are in him. Where he is, there we are too, in the Incarnation, on the Cross, and in his Resurrection. We belong to him because we are in him. That is why the Scriptures call us the Body of Christ.

But if, before we could know and wish it, we have been chosen and accepted with the whole Church in Jesus Christ, then we also belong to him in eternity with one another. We who live here in fellowship with him will one day be with him in eternal fellowship.

He who looks upon his brother should know that he will be eternally united with him in Jesus Christ. Christian community means community in and through Jesus Christ. On this presupposition rests everything that the scriptures provide in the way of directions and precepts for the communal life of Christians.

NO HURRY

CALVIN MILLER

ONE BARRIER TO full intimacy with the Savior is hurriedness. Intimacy may not be rushed. To meet with the Son of God takes time. We can't dash into his presence and choke down spiritual inwardness before we hurry to our one o'clock appointment. Inwardness is time-consuming, open only to minds willing to sample spirituality in small bites, savoring each one.

Intimacy with Christ comes from entering his presence with inner peace rather than bursting into his presence from the hassles of life. A relaxed contemplation of the indwelling Christ allows for an inner communion impossible to achieve while oppressed by busyness and care.

Holy living is not abrupt living. No one who hurries into the presence of God is content to remain for long. Those who hurry in, hurry out.

∼

HOW THE GREAT GUEST CAME

EDWIN MARKHAM

This poem discusses how Christ came to visit a common cobbler in an unexpected manner. It is more poetic than a Tolstoy selection, "What Men Live By," that tells the same story differently. This very popular retelling of the Tolstoyan truth is based on Jesus' teaching in Matthew 25, that Christ often comes to us disguised as the needy or the poor.

Before the cathedral in grandeur rose
At Ingelburg where the Danube goes;
Before its forest of silver spires
Went airily up to the clouds and fires;
Before the oak had ready a beam,
While yet the arch was stone and dream—
There where the altar was later laid,
Conrad, the cobbler, plied his trade.

• • •

It happened one day at the year's white end—
Two neighbors called on their old-time friend;

And they found the shop, so meager and mean,
Made gay with a hundred boughs of green.
Conrad was stitching with face ashine,
But suddenly stopped as he twitched a twine:
"Old friends, good news! At dawn today,
As the cocks were scaring the night away,
The Lord appeared in a dream to me,
And said, 'I am coming your Guest to be!'
So I've been busy with feet astir,
Strewing the floor with branches of fir.
The wall is washed and the shelf is shined,
And over the rafter the holly twined.
He comes today, and the table is spread
With milk and honey and wheaten bread."

His friends went home; and his face grew still
As he watched for the shadow across the sill.
He lived all the moments o'er and o'er,
When the Lord should enter the lowly door—
The knock, the call, the latch pulled up,
The lighted face, the offered cup.
He would wash the feet where the spikes had been,
He would kiss the hands where the nails went in,
And then at the last would sit with Him
And break the bread as the day grew dim.

While the cobbler mused there passed his pane
A beggar drenched by the driving rain.
He called him in from the stony street
And gave him shoes for his bruisèd feet.
The beggar went and there came a crone,
Her face with wrinkles of sorrow sown.
A bundle of fagots bowed her back,
And she was spent with the wrench and rack.
He gave her his loaf and steadied her load
As she took her way on the weary road.
Then to his door came a little child,
Lost and afraid in the world so wild,
In the big, dark world. Catching it up,
He gave it the milk in the waiting cup,
And led it home to its mother's arms,
Out of the reach of the world's alarms.

The day went down in the crimson west
And with it the hope of the blessed Guest,
And Conrad sighed as the world turned gray:
"Why is it, Lord, that your feet delay?
Did You forget that this was the day?"
Then soft in the silence a Voice he heard:
"Lift up your heart, for I kept my word.
Three times I came to your friendly door;
Three times my shadow was on your floor.
I was the beggar with bruisèd feet;
I was the woman you gave to eat;
I was the child on the homeless street!"

HIS MERCY AND LOVE

CHARLES DICKENS

Charles Dickens was not just a popular novelist, though he was popular. He seemed in some ways determined to make a moral difference in his world. In this brief section we have Dickens's own statement on the mercy of Jesus.

ONE OF THE Pharisees begged Our Saviour to go into his house and eat with him. And while Our Saviour sat eating at the table, there crept into the room a woman of that city who had led a bad and sinful life, and was ashamed that the Son of God should see her; and yet she trusted so much to His goodness and His compassion for all who having done wrong were truly sorry for it in their hearts, that, by little and little, she went behind the seat on which He had sat, and dropped down at His feet, and wetted them with her sorrowful tears; then she kissed them, and dried them on her long hair, and rubbed them with some sweet-smelling ointment she had brought with her in a box. Her name was Mary Magdalene.

When the Pharisee saw that Jesus permitted this woman to touch Him, he said within himself that Jesus did not know how wicked she had been. But Jesus Christ, who knew his thoughts, said to him, "Simon"—for that was his name—"if a man had debtors, one of whom owed him only fifty pence, and he forgave them, both, their debts, which of those two debtors do you think would love him most?" Simon answered, "I suppose that one whom he forgave most." Jesus told him he was right, and said, "As God forgives this woman so much sin, she will love Him, I hope, the more." And He said to her, "God forgives you!" The company who were present wondered that Jesus Christ had power to forgive sins. But God had given it to Him. And the woman, thanking Him for all His mercy, went away.

~

SOMETIMES, PEOPLE ARGUE

LOIS A. CHENEY

There are twenty-seven books in the New Testament, all of them committed to honoring Jesus. Lois A. Cheney customarily reminds us that Jesus was a practical Christ, teaching practical things that worked in practical ways to help people of faith make sense of their world.

"No ONE BORN of God commits sin, for God's nature abides in him, and he cannot sin because he is born of God. By this it may be seen who are the children of God, and who are the children of the devil: whoever does not do right is not of God, nor he who does not love his brother."

Sometimes,
People argue whether there is a God or not,
Or if there is one, they then argue
Whether he's dead or not.

Sometimes,
I argue about the nature of God
Whether he's this way or that;
I wonder about the way of Christ
Whether it's this way or that.

Sometimes,
I wonder if I'll succeed,
Or if I'll do something well enough;
I wonder if I'm doing the right thing.

Sometimes,
I wonder if I'll be strong enough
Or bright enough, or good enough;
I wonder if I'll measure up.

You can't read the Bible for
More than ten minutes,
Anywhere—Old Testament or New—
Without being hit squarely with:

Some are chosen of God;
Some do not sin,
And those who sin are
Of the Devil.

And for those who sin
There is no hope,
And I am frightened
And I am small.

It isn't in keeping with the times,
This being frightened of an angry God,
But I believe in an angry God,
He can reject me . . .
    And then nothing else will matter.
    Nothing at all.

❧

IT ONLY REQUIRES A TOUCH

WATCHMAN NEE

Jesus' last words spoken during his earthly sojourn were a command to his fledgling church to "go into all the world and make disciples" (Matthew 28:18). This strong commandment still stands at the heart of how the church views her role in the world. Whether Catholic or Protestant, Christians believe that helping other people learn of Jesus and thus become Christians is the church's great commission. In this selection, Watchman Nee sounds very much like Mother Teresa of Calcutta. He seems to teach that the physical touch of Christ changed people's lives. The church has become the hands of Jesus to touch the needy and thus tell people about Christ.

LET US TAKE three examples from the Gospels. First, the thief on the cross. When he asked the Lord to remember him when Jesus came into

His kingdom, Jesus did not remind him of his evil life, nor did He explain the plan of redemption—no, the Lord had only one answer: "Today you shall be with me in paradise." The thief recognized who Jesus was, and he believed *in the Lord,* and that was enough.

Consider the woman who was bleeding and was trying to touch Jesus. There were many pressing in on Him, but only one was healed. She was healed because with a special intention she "touched" Him. And it only required a touch; for in her it represented a reaching out in spirit to God for help in her deep need.

Or recall the incident of the Pharisee and the publican at prayer in the temple. The Pharisee understood all about offerings and sacrifices and tithes, but there was from him no cry of the heart to God. But the publican cried out, "Lord have mercy upon me!" Something went out from him to God which met with an immediate response, and the Lord Jesus singles him out as the one whom God reckoned as righteous. For what is it to be reckoned righteous? It is *to touch God.* That is why our first object must be to lead people to meet Him.

~

LORD, LORD, OPEN UNTO ME

HOWARD THURMAN

Open unto me—light for my darkness.
Open unto me—courage for my fear.
Open unto me—hope for my despair.
Open unto me—peace for my turmoil.
Open unto me—joy for my sorrow.
Open unto me—strength for my weakness.
Open unto me—wisdom for my confusion.
Open unto me—forgiveness for my sins.
Open unto me—tenderness for my toughness.
Open unto me—love for my hates.
Open unto me—Thy Self for my self.

Lord, Lord, open unto me!
Amen.

HOLY FELLOWSHIP WITH JESUS

CHARLES H. SPURGEON

Charles H. Spurgeon was one of the greatest and most popular preach-
ers in nineteenth-century England. His sermons could be purchased at
newsstands and railway kiosks all over England.

Contrary to the heavy social gospel preachers of his day, Spurgeon
believed that it was not possible to change the evil on the planet until
you changed the people who lived there. He believed that the easiest
way to change people was to get them acquainted with Christ. Thus,
Jesus was the subject of his sermons. The English saw him as having a
special inner friendship with Jesus, and that friendship Spurgeon re-
ferred to as holy fellowship.

BUT EVEN IF our conduct and conversation were more consistent with our
faith, I would still have this third charge against us: there is *too little real*
communion with Jesus Christ. If, by the grace of God, our conduct and
conversation were consistent and our lives were unblemished, many of us
are still sorely lacking in that area we call holy fellowship with Jesus.

Men and women, let me ask you, How long has it been since you
have had an intimate conversation with Jesus Christ? Some of you may be
able to say, "It was only this morning that I last spoke with him, I beheld
his face with joy." But I fear that the great majority of you will have to
say, "It has been months since I have been with the Lord."

What have you been doing with your life? Is Christ living in your
home and yet you have not spoken to him for months? Do not let me
condemn you or judge; only let your conscience speak: Have we not all
lived too much without Jesus? Have we not grown content with the world
to the neglect of Christ?

❧

ADORE THE SAVIOR

CALVIN MILLER

Most people are concerned about their moral infractions, the things
they do wrong. These actions Jesus called sin. But Jesus would have us
defeat these continual wrongs not by giving them undue focus, which
only leads to keeping them central in our thoughts. Little ever comes

from our attempts to clear up our negative morality by trying to stop being immoral. There is a more positive way to go about this. We can better alter our moral habits by focusing on Jesus and offering him our worship.

THE BEST WAY to deal with sin is not to attempt reform but to adore the Savior. Winning over our lower nature is made positive by adoration. While we worship the enthroned and inner Christ, we cannot be intrigued by negative preoccupations with sin. Rules, instead of limiting our sin, define sin, rivet our attention to it and lead us to desire it. Worship, on the other hand, avoids all interest in sin, pointing our hearts and minds in a totally different direction.

❧

FOOTPRINTS

MARGARET FISHBACK POWERS

This very popular work speaks to the widespread confidence that we never have to pass any crisis by ourselves. Jesus says, "I will never leave you nor forsake you" (Hebrews 13:5).

ONE NIGHT I dreamed a dream. / I was walking along the beach with my Lord. / Across the dark sky flashed scenes from my life. / For each scene, I noticed two sets / of footprints in the sand, / one belonging to me / and one to my Lord. / When the last scene of my life shot before me / I looked back at the footprints in the sand. / There was only one set of footprints. / I realized that this was at the lowest / and saddest times of my life. / This always bothered me / and I questioned the Lord / about my dilemma. / "Lord, you told me when I decided to follow You, / You would walk and talk with me all the way. / But I'm aware that during the most troublesome / times of my life there is only one set of footprints. / I just don't understand why, when I need You most, / You leave me." / He whispered, "My precious child, / I love you and will never leave you, / never, ever, during your trials and testings. / When you saw only one set of footprints, / it was then that I carried you."

HEAVEN IS A PLAYGROUND

WILLIAM GRIFFIN

William Griffin paints clear pictures of the life and teachings of Jesus by letting us see both through the eyes of children. His book Jesus for Children *is a colorful and engaging retelling of Christ's life and teachings.*

"ARE YOU GOING to do a miracle today?"

Wherever Jesus went, children seemed to follow. They wanted to see him heal a cripple or zap a fig tree, to say hello to him, to tell him something special.

"Don't shoo them away!" said Jesus to his friends.

"But you don't have time for this foolishness," said Judas.

"I've got the time."

"You don't have enough time to sleep. You don't have enough time to pray. You don't have enough time to spend with us, your friends," said Judas. "So how come you have enough time to spend with these noisy, runny-nosed children?"

"Because they're so much fun," said Jesus.

The boys and girls crowded around the great man. Jesus asked who they were, did they pray for their mothers and fathers, was Solomon a judge or a prophet or a king, weren't Ruth and Miriam and Deborah the real heroes of the Scriptures, and no, he wasn't going to do any tricks today.

"Heaven is a lot like a playground," Jesus said to Judas later, "and unless you remember what it was like to be a child, you won't get in."

"Does that mean I have to hop, skip, and jump forever?" asked Judas.

"No," said Jesus. "It means you have to be curious and eager and good and honest and fair."

❧

PRACTICE THE PRESENCE OF GOD

BROTHER LAWRENCE

Nicolas Herman was born in Herimesnil, Lorraine, in 1611. After being wounded as a footsoldier in the French army, he became attached to an order of Parisian Carmelites and was renamed Lawrence of the Resurrection. He has become endeared to Christians of all ages as

Brother Lawrence. He spent the last thirty years of his life washing pots and pans in the monastery kitchen. Yet he performed this menial task as unto Jesus alone, and his friendship with Jesus has instructed the church in matters of worship and prayer ever since.

IN A CONVERSATION some days since with a person of piety, he told me the spiritual life was a life of grace, which begins with servile fear, which is increased by hope of eternal life, and which is consummated by pure love; that each of these states had its different stages, by which one arrives at last at that blessed consummation.

I have not followed all these methods. On the contrary, from I know not what instincts, I found they discouraged me. This was the reason why, at my entrance into religion, I took a resolution to give myself up to God, as the best return I could make for His love, and, for the love of Him, to renounce all besides.

For the first year I commonly employed myself during the time set apart for devotion with the thought of death, judgment, heaven, hell, and my sins. Thus I continued some years, applying my mind carefully the rest of the day, and even in the midst of my business, *to the presence of God,* whom I considered always as *with* me, often as *in* me.

At length I came insensibly to do the same thing during my set time of prayer, which caused in me great delight and consolation. This practice produced in me so high an esteem for God that *faith* alone was capable to satisfy me in that point.

Such was my beginning, and yet I must tell you that for the first ten years I suffered much. The apprehension that I was not devoted to God as I wished to be, my past sins always present to my mind, and the great unmerited favors which God did me, were the matter and source of my sufferings. During this time I fell often, and rose again presently. It seemed to me that all creatures, reason, and God Himself were against me, and *faith* alone for me I was troubled sometimes with thoughts that to believe I had received such favors was an effect of my presumption, which pretended to be *at once* where others arrive with difficulty; at other times, that it was a willful delusion, and that there was no salvation for me.

When I thought of nothing but to end my days in these troubles (which did not at all diminish the trust I had in God, and which served only to increase my faith), I found myself changed all at once; and my soul, which till that time was in trouble, felt a profound inward peace, as if she were in her center and place of rest.

Ever since that time I walk before God simply, in faith, with humility and with love, and I apply myself diligently to do nothing and think nothing which may displease Him. I hope that when I have done what I can, He will do with me what He pleases.

As for what passes in me at present, I cannot express it. I have no pain or difficulty about my state, because I have no will but that of God, which I endeavor to accomplish in all things, and to which I am so resigned that I would not take up a straw from the ground against His order, or from any other motive than purely that of love to Him.

I have quitted all forms of devotion and set prayers but those to which my state obliges me. And I make it my business only to persevere in His holy presence, wherein I keep myself by a simple attention, and a general fond regard to God, which I may call an *actual presence* of God; or, to speak better, an habitual, silent, and secret conversation of the soul with God, which often causes me joys and raptures inwardly, and sometimes also outwardly, so great that I am forced to use means to moderate them and prevent their appearance to others.

In short, I am assured beyond all doubt that my soul has been with God above these thirty years. I pass over many things that I may not be tedious to you, yet I think it proper to inform you after what manner I consider myself before God, whom I behold as my King.

I consider myself as the most wretched of men, full of sores and corruption, and who has committed all sorts of crimes against his King. Touched with a sensible regret, I confess to Him all my wickedness, I ask His forgiveness, I abandon myself in His hands that He may do what He pleases with me. The King, full of mercy and goodness, very far from chastising me, embraces me with love, makes me eat at His table, serves me with His own hands, gives me the key of His treasures; He converses and delights Himself with me incessantly, in a thousand and a thousand ways, and treats me in all respects as His favorite. It is thus I consider myself from time to time in His holy presence.

My most useful method is this simple attention, and such a general passionate regard to God, to whom I find myself often attached with greater sweetness and delight than that of an infant at the mother's breast; so that, if I dare use the expression, I should choose to call this state the bosom of God, for the inexpressible sweetness which I taste and experience there.

If sometimes my thoughts wander from it by necessity or infirmity, I am presently recalled by inward motions so charming and delicious that I am ashamed to mention them. I desire your Reverence to reflect rather upon my great wretchedness, of which you are fully informed, than upon the great favors which God does me, all unworthy and ungrateful as I am.

As for my set hours of prayer, they are only a continuation of the same exercise. Sometimes I consider myself there as a stone before a carver, whereof he is to make a statue; presenting myself thus before God, I desire Him to form His perfect image in my soul, and make me entirely like Himself.

At other times, when I apply myself to prayer, I feel all my spirit and all my soul lift itself up without any care or effort of mine, and it continues as if it were suspended and firmly fixed in God, as in its center and place of rest.

I know that some charge this state with inactivity, delusion, and self-love. I confess that it is a holy inactivity, and would be a happy self-love if the soul in that state were capable of it, because, in effect, while she is in this repose, she cannot be disturbed by such acts as she was formerly accustomed to, and which were then her support, but which would now rather hinder than assist her.

Yet I cannot bear that this should be called delusion, because the soul which thus enjoys God desires herein nothing but Him. If this be delusion in me, it belongs to God to remedy it. Let Him do what He pleases with me: I desire only Him, and to be wholly devoted to Him. You will, however, oblige me in sending me your opinion, to which I always pay a great deference, for I have a singular esteem for your Reverence, and am, in our Lord,

Yours, etc.

∾

GOD IS NO FOOL

LOIS A. CHENEY

The Old Testament teaches that obedience to the Ten Commandments will give us favor with God, but Jesus taught it isn't so much what we do that makes us acceptable to God. It is rather what we believe, for in the end, what we believe determines what we do. Good morality will not necessarily lead us to faith, but faith will always lead us to good morality.

They say that God has infinite patience,
And that is a great comfort.

They say God is always there,
And that is a deep satisfaction.

They say that God will always take you back,
And I get lazy in that certitude.

They say that God never gives up,
And I count on that.

They say you can go away for years and years,
And he'll be there, waiting, when you come back.

They say you can make mistake after mistake,
And God will always forgive and forget.

They say lots of things,
These people who never read the Old Testament.

There comes a time,
A definite, for sure time,
When God turns around.

I don't believe God shed his skin
When Christ brought in the New Testament,
Christ showed us a new side of God,
And it is truly wonderful.

But he didn't change God.
God remains forever and ever
And that God
is
no
fool.

❧

CHRIST WITH ME, CHRIST BEFORE ME
Breastplate Prayer of Saint Patrick

Christ to protect me to-day
   against poison, against burning,
   against drowning, against wounding,
   so that there may come abundance of reward.

Christ with me, Christ before me, Christ behind me,
Christ in me, Christ beneath me, Christ above me,
Christ on my right, Christ on my left,
Christ where I lie, Christ where I sit, Christ where I arise,
Christ in the heart of every man who thinks of me,
Christ in the mouth of every man who speaks of me,
Christ in every eye that sees me,
Christ in every ear that hears me.

DEVELOP IN ME A LONGING THAT IS UNRESTRAINED

RICHARD ROLLE

I ask you, Lord Jesus,
to develop in me, your lover,
an immeasurable urge towards you,
an affection that is unbounded,
a longing that is unrestrained,
a fervour that throws discretion to the winds!
The more worthwhile our love for you,
all the more pressing does it become.
Reason cannot hold it in check,
fear does not make it tremble,
wise judgment does not temper it.

MARY THOUGHT SHE KNEW HER SON

LOIS A. CHENEY

THEY WERE MISTAKEN.
Mary thought she knew her son. Mary loved and yearned for him.
She followed and pleaded with him to come home. Mary wanted
to protect him:
Mary was mistaken.

Peter thought he loved him most. Peter felt he knew him truly. Peter thought he would never fail his Master; Peter knew he would remain true to him no matter what happened: Peter was mistaken.

Judas thought he should organize. Judas thought he should live up to his view of the ancient promise and hope, or give it all up. Judas began to be disappointed, and he began to distrust: Judas was mistaken.

Thomas thought they were all very gullible. Thomas loved and revered him, and Thomas missed him; he grieved at his death. Thomas didn't really believe he'd be back: Thomas was mistaken.

Now, we know his ways. Given years of scholarship and prayerful perspective, we are now ready to box and label this man from Galilee. He's ready for the completed file.

We are mistaken.

❧

JESUS PRAYING
Luke 6:12

HARTLEY COLERIDGE

The writers of the New Testament characteristically show us how often Jesus prayed. Often Jesus would withdraw himself to some lonely desert place to pray. Even though Jesus is in heaven now, he continues even there to pray for his church. While Catholic devotion has often focused on Mary as the incessant intercessor (one who prays in behalf of another), Protestantism has been more focused on Jesus as the great intercessor, constantly praying for those in his church (Hebrews 7:25).

He sought the mountain and the loneliest height,
For He would meet His Father all alone,
And there, with many a tear and many a groan,
He strove in prayer throughout the long, long night.
Why need He pray, who held by filial right

O'er all the world alike of thought and sense,
The fulness of His Sire's omnipotence?
Why crave in prayer what was His own by might?
Vain is the question,—Christ was man in need,
And being man His duty was to pray.
The Son of God confess'd the human need,
And doubtless ask'd a blessing every day.
Nor ceases yet for sinful man to plead,
Nor will, till heaven and earth shall pass away.

❧

THE SANCTIFICATION OF EACH STAGE OF LIFE

SAINT IRENAEUS OF LYONS

HE CAME TO save all through his own person; all, that is, who through him are reborn to God; infants, children, boys, young men and old. Therefore he passed through every stage of life. He was made an infant for infants, sanctifying infancy; a child among children, sanctifying childhood, and setting an example of filial affection, of righteousness and of obedience, a young man among young men, becoming an example to them, and sanctifying them to the Lord. So also he was a grown man among the older men, that he might be a perfect teacher for all, not merely in respect to revelation of the truth, but also in respect of this stage of life, sanctifying the older men, and becoming an example to them also. And thus he came even to death, that he might be "the first-born from the dead, having the pre-eminence among all," the Author of Life, who goes before all and shows the way (Col. i. 18).

❧

JESUS, THE RIGHTEOUS HUSBAND

JAMES LONG

Throughout the New Testament, Christ is presented as married to his bride, the church. The marriage relationship is a dominant New

Testament metaphor. Saint Paul said that earthly husbands should love their wives just as Jesus loves his bride (Ephesians 5:25). This marriage will be consummated in heaven when all Christians will be reunited with Jesus, the bridegroom, who is in eternity eagerly anticipating the ultimate union, which is called the marriage supper of the Lamb (Jesus) in Revelation 19:9.

I LOOKED AROUND my living room, seeing reminders of the relationship my wife and I share. I reflected on just how much I love this woman, and I reminded myself of my desire to be all she needs in a husband. That's when this question occurred to me: What kind of husband would Jesus have made?

I flipped through the gospel of Matthew with the image in mind of Jesus as a husband. "He will not quarrel or cry out; no one will hear his voice in the streets. A bruised reed he will not break, and a smoldering wick he will not snuff out" (Matthew 12: 19–20).

It was an image of strong gentleness. I thought of Jesus taking time for the children; patiently instructing his followers, though tired and hungry; touching the rotting skin of outcast lepers; weeping over a city's waywardness; calling even his betrayer "friend."

This Man felt the whole spectrum of emotion, yet always maintained self-control. He experienced success without it degenerating to egotism. He faced reversal without turning bitter. He endured temptation, but did not yield to its pressure. You could freeze any moment of his life in time and he would have no reason for regret or embarrassment.

I realized that, in a sense, every moment of my life is a moment frozen. An expression of who I am, in that instant. And I decided to devote myself to piling up moments and memories that will give my wife some small glimpse of Jesus in my life.

∽

THE HOUND OF HEAVEN

FRANCIS THOMPSON

Francis Thompson, an English poet who lived from 1859 to 1907, expressed his conversion in terms of the Christ who pursued him until he had no choice but to agree that Jesus had every right to be the Lord of his life. In the conversion of St. Paul—and to some extent St. Augustine—came to the surface the idea of "irresistible grace." This powerful tenet, popularized by John Calvin, expressed the notion that Christ pursued those who needed to be converted until they yielded to grace. Francis Thompson's classic poem develops this theme with rare excellence.

I fled Him, down the nights and down the days;
   I fled Him, down the arches of the years;
I fled Him, down the labyrinthine ways
   Of my own mind; and in the mist of tears
I hid from Him, and under running laughter.
        Up vistaed hopes I sped;
        And shot, precipitated
Adown Titanic glooms of chasmèd fears,
  From those strong Feet that followed, followed after.
       But with unhurrying chase,
       And unperturbèd pace,
   Deliberate speed, majestic instancy,
      They beat—and a Voice beat
      More instant than the Feet—
"All things betray thee, who betrayest Me."

      I pleaded, outlaw-wise,
By many a hearted casement, curtained red,
  Trellised with intertwining charities;
(For, though I knew His love Who followèd,
      Yet was I sore adread
Lest, having Him, I must have naught beside);
But, if one little casement parted wide,
  The gust of His approach would clash it to.
Fear wist not to evade, as Love wist to pursue.
Across the margent of the world I fled,
  And troubled the gold gateways of the stars,
  Smiting for shelter on their clangèd bars;
      Fretted to dulcet jars
And silvern chatter the pale ports o' the moon.
I said to dawn, Be sudden; to eve, Be soon;
  With thy young skiey blossoms heap me over
      From this tremendous Lover!
Float thy vague veil about me, lest He see!
  I tempted all His servitors, but to find

My own betrayal in their constancy,
In faith to Him their fickleness to me,
   Their traitorous trueness, and their loyal deceit.
To all swift things for swiftness did I sue;
   Clung to the whistling mane of every wind.
      But whether they swept, smoothly fleet,
   The long savannahs of the blue;
         Or whether, Thunder-driven,
      They clanged his chariot 'thwart a heaven
Plashy with flying lightnings round the spurn o' their feet:—
   Fear wist not to evade as Love wist to pursue.
        Still with unhurrying chase,
        And unperturbèd pace,
    Deliberate speed, majestic instancy,
      Came on the following Feet,
      And a Voice above their beat—
   "Naught shelters thee, who wilt not shelter Me."

I sought no more that after which I strayed
      In face of man or maid;
But still within the little children's eyes
     Seems something, something that replies;
They at least are for me, surely for me!
I turned me to them very wistfully;
But, just as their young eyes grew sudden fair
     With dawning answers there,
Their angel plucked them from me by the hair.
"Come then, ye other children, Nature's—share
With me" (said I) "your delicate fellowship;
    Let me greet you lip to lip,
    Let me twine with you caresses,
       Wantoning
    With our Lady-Mother's vagrant tresses,
       Banqueting
    With her in her wind-walled palace,
    Underneath her azured daïs,
    Quaffing, as your taintless way is,
      From a chalice
Lucent-weeping out of the dayspring."
      So it was done:
I in their delicate fellowship was one—
Drew the bolt of Nature's secrecies.

I knew all the swift importings
  On the wilful face of skies;
  I knew how the clouds arise
  Spumèd of the wild sea-snortings;
   All that's born or dies
  Rose and drooped with——made them shapers
Of mine own moods, or wailful or divine——
  With them joyed and was bereaven.
  I was heavy with the even,
  When she lit her glimmering tapers
  Round the day's dead sanctities.
  I laughed in the morning's eyes.
I triumphed and I saddened with all weather,
  Heaven and I wept together,
And its sweet tears were salt with mortal mine;
Against the red throb of its sunset-heart
   I laid my own to beat,
   And share commingling heat,
But not by that, by that, was eased my human smart.
In vain my tears were wet on Heaven's grey cheek.
For ah! we know not what each other says,
  These things and I; in sound *I* speak——
Their sound is but their stir, they speak by silences.
Nature, poor stepdame, cannot slake my drouth;
  Let her, if she would owe me,
Drop yon blue bosom-veil of sky, and show me
  The breasts o' her tenderness:
Never did any milk of hers once bless
   My thirsting mouth.
   Nigh and nigh draws the chase,
   With unperturbèd pace,
  Deliberate speed, majestic instancy;
   And past those noisèd Feet
   A voice comes yet more fleet——
  "Lo! naught contents thee, who content'st not Me."

Naked I wait Thy love's uplifted stroke!
My harness piece by piece Thou hast hewn from me,
  And smitten me to my knee;
  I am defenseless utterly.
  I slept, methinks, and woke,
And, slowly gazing, find me stripped in sleep.

In the rash lustihead of my young powers,
  I shook the pillaring hours
And pulled my life upon me; grimed with smears,
I stand amid the dust o' the mounded years—
My mangled youth lies dead beneath the heap.
My days have crackled and gone up in smoke,
Have puffed and burst as sun-starts on a stream.
  Yea, faileth now even dream
The dreamer, and the lute the lutanist;
Even the linked fantasies, in whose blossomy twist
I swung the earth a trinket at my wrist,
And yielding; cords of all too weak account
For earth with heavy griefs so overplussed.
  Ah! is Thy love indeed
A weed, albeit an amaranthine weed,
Suffering no flowers except its own to mount?
  Ah! must—
  Designer infinite!—
Ah! must Thou char the wood ere Thou canst limn with it?
My freshness spent its wavering shower i' the dust;
And now my heart is as a broken fount,
Wherein tear-drippings stagnate, spilt down ever
  From the dank thoughts that shiver
Upon the sighful branches of my mind.
  Such is; what is to be?
The pulp so bitter, how shall taste the rind?
I dimly guess what Time in mists confounds;
Yet ever and anon a trumpet sounds
From the hid battlements of Eternity;
Those shaken mists a space unsettle, then
Round the half-glimpsèd turrents slowly wash again.
  But not ere him who summoneth
  I first have seen, enwound
With glooming robes purpureal, cypress-crowned;
His name I know, and what his trumpet saith.
Whether man's heart or life it be which yields
  Thee harvest, must Thy harvest fields
  Be dunged with rotten death?

   Now of that long pursuit
   Comes on at hand the bruit:
  That Voice is round me like a bursting sea:

"And is thy earth so marred,
       Shattered in shard on shard?
   Lo, all things fly thee, for thou fliest Me!
       Strange, piteous, futile thing,
Wherefore should any set thee love apart?
Seeing none but I makes much of naught" (He said),
"And human love needs human meriting:
       How hast thou merited—
Of all man's clotted clay the dingiest clot?
       Alack, thou knowest not
How little worthy of any love thou art!
Whom wilt thou find to love ignoble thee
       Save Me, save only Me?
All which I took from thee I did but take,
       Not for thy harms,
But just that thou might'st seek it in My arms.
       All which thy child's mistake
Fancies as lost, I have stored for thee at home:
       Rise, clasp My hand, and come!"

       Halts by me that footfall:
       Is my gloom, after all,
   Shade of His hand, outstretched caressingly?
       "Ah, fondest, blindest, weakest,
       I am He Whom thou seekest!
Thou dravest love from thee, who dravest Me."

❧

LATE HAVE I LOVED YOU

SAINT AUGUSTINE OF HIPPO

Saint Augustine was grateful he had become a Christian, but regretted he had used so much of his life for his own selfish pursuits before he did.

LATE HAVE I loved you, O beauty so ancient and so new. Late have I loved you! You were within me while I have gone outside to seek you. Unlovely myself, I rushed towards all those lovely things you had made. And always you were with me, and I was not with you.

All these beauties kept me far from you—although they would not have existed at all unless they had their being in you.

You called, you cried, you shattered my deafness.

You sparkled, you blazed, you drove away my blindness.

You shed your fragrance, and I drew in my breath, and I pant for you. I tasted and now I hunger and thirst. You touched me, and now I burn with longing for your peace.

∾

WOMEN DISCIPLES

HARRY EMERSON FOSDICK

THE PROMINENCE OF women among Jesus' first devoted and loyal contemporaries is notable. They were drawn to him alike by their needs and by his masterful personality and message. They came for healing, for forgiveness, for power to lead a new life, and for his benediction on their children. The timid woman who touched the hem of his garment, and when found out "came in fear and trembling" to thank him; the aggressive Canaanite woman, who would not be put off by the fact that she was not of Jewish race and faith; the women who provided for him out of their means; and the mothers whose children he took "in his arms and blessed, . . . laying his hands upon them," are typical. There is no explaining how that first precarious movement of thought and life which Jesus started, with so much against it and, humanly speaking, so little for it, moved out into its world-transforming influence, without taking into account the response of womanhood to Jesus. When they were sunk in sin, he forgave them; when they were humiliated, he stood up for them; when they suffered social wrongs, he defended them; when they had abilities to offer, he used them; and when they became sentimental and effusive in their devotion to him, he stopped them: "A woman in the crowd raised her voice and said to him, 'Blessed is the womb that bore you, and the breasts that you sucked!' But he said, 'Blessed rather are those who hear the word of God and keep it!' "

IV

JESUS:

HIS BECOMING ONE OF US

ACROSS the centuries many men have tried to become God, said the sage, but only once did God try to become man. This is not just a Christmas doctrine; it is the central truth of Christianity. *Incarnation* is the word Christians use to refer to this truth that God, who is Spirit, became a man at Bethlehem. Jesus remained on earth for thirty-three years.

Incarnations are not unique to Christianity alone. In Greco-Roman religion the gods were always coming down to spend time among those they created. Hindu literature and belief have tales of their gods descending into human flesh as well. In all other religions, however, incarnations are seen as miraculous but incidental to the issue of faith. In Christianity the Incarnation is the faith. If this miracle is removed from Christianity the whole system falls. The Christian faith does not gather around this miracle. The Christian faith *is* this miracle.

The miracle of God's becoming a man aims at ending the separation of humankind and God. God has always been viewed by humans as immortal and "safe." Earthly existence, on the other hand, is tenuous and risky and threatening. Heaven is safe. When God became a human being he consciously opted for life at risk. But the big accomplishment was not merely God putting himself at risk; it was the merger of Spirit and human form. In Christ this uneasy separation of flesh and Spirit was over.

Now God could be of real help to humankind. Once a famous American evangelist was walking in the woods with his son. In the course of the stroll the evangelist accidentally stepped on an ant den. His young son saw that a great many of the insects were instantly killed. With a serious demeanor, the little boy knelt down and studied the dying ants. The quivering insects caught in their final struggle evoked a child's special pity. "Isn't there anything we can do for these poor ants?"

"No, nothing," replied the evangelist. After a moment of thought he added, "If only I could somehow shrink myself down to their world and become an ant myself . . ."

It can be no mere coincidence that one of Jesus' chief teachings was that the Kingdom of God is within us (Luke 17:21). The idea is that Christians who accept the truth that God was in Christ (2 Corinthians 5:19) find that the Christ whom God indwelt now indwells them. The Incarnation is not, therefore, a first-century event. Incarnation goes on and on as each new Christian believes. Christ's Incarnation now exists in millions of Christians at once. The Savior currently goes about doing his work as he lives in the lives of these who believe.

> God put the world square with himself through the Messiah, giving the world a fresh start by offering forgiveness of sins. God has given us the task of telling everyone what he is doing.
>
> 2 Corinthians 5:19

> But when the time arrived that was set by God the Father, God sent his Son, born among us of a woman, born under the conditions of the law.
>
> Galatians 4:4

> The angel answered,
> "The Holy Spirit will come upon you,
> The power of the Highest hover over you;
> Therefore, the child you bring to birth
> will be called Holy, Son of God."
>
> Luke 1:35, *The Message*

LIFE OF CHRIST

WILLIAM J. DAWSON

ON THAT STARRY night two fugitives from Nazareth, themselves conscious not only of an awful hope but of an ineluctable force of fate that held their feet in an appointed way, climbed the limestone hill of Bethlehem. It was the season of early spring, probably toward the close of February; for at an earlier date than this it would not have been possible for shepherds to spend the night on the open hillside with their flocks. The country through which these fugitives passed in the last stage of their journey is full of pastoral sweetness and charm. The town of Bethlehem, sitting squarely on its terraced height, surrounded with fig-trees and olive-orchards, still retains unaltered its outstanding features. It is a long grey cluster of houses, with no pretence of architecture, a typical Syrian hill-town. At its base is the tomb of Rachel, the pathetic memorial of a man's love, of a woman's travail and untimely death. Doubly significant would that tomb appear to this woman, whose hour had come; one can fancy the sidelong, tearful look of fear with which she would regard it. But there was more than fear in the heart of Mary that night. Slight as is the memorial of her, yet it is deeply suggestive of the sweetness of her nature, and especially of her devout piety of heart. Perhaps it was Ruth she remembered that night rather than Rachel—Ruth, the Moabitess, driven into Bethlehem by misfortune and calamity, to find herself the unexpected mother of a race of kings. Nor would she forget the ancient prophecy of Micah, that as little as Bethlehem was among the thousands of Judah, yet out of it should come One who should be the "Ruler of Israel, whose goings forth have been from of old, from everlasting." But whatever portents others saw in the Syrian sky that night, Mary saw none. Among the crowd of travelers, driven hither by a strange, almost unintelligible command, she stood alone, confused, unrecognized. It was an unforeseen and painful end of a journey full of sadness and alarm. No door was opened to the weary, suffering woman, not because the fine traditional hospitality of the Jew had failed, but because already every house was crowded to excess. There was no place of refuge for her but a rough chamber, hewn in the limestone rock, and used as a stable. In that last refuge of the destitute there was born a few hours later the Child, who by His poverty was to make many rich.

A Shocking Departure from the Expected

ELTON TRUEBLOOD

IN CALLING THE fishermen as His recruits, Christ was breaking with established religious practice, for these men were unschooled and in no sense professionally religious. The calling of Levi was, however, an even more striking departure. This was because Levi had become, by the very nature of his work, unpopular with his neighbors. The fact that the man was a tax gatherer meant that he, though a Jew, was closely allied to the Roman tyranny. His position was somewhat like that of a collaborator in the language of contemporary struggles. But Christ defied popular opinion in order to secure a man whom He needed.

This boldness was even more pronounced in Christ's social life. Christ shocked the devout by deliberately associating, not only with tax collectors, but with other people who had broken with narrowly sectarian or nationalistic practices. He chose, moreover, to gather with those who were conspicuously careless of the Law. We are not surprised that the Pharisees were outraged when we realize that the idea of maintaining holiness through separation is involved in their name itself. Christ's bold action represented a genuine departure from a received conception of what religion means, in His determination to seek out sinners, rather than to avoid them. His interest was in the welfare of broken and needy men, not in the trivial determination to keep His own skirts clean.

❧

God with Us

HENRY HART MILMAN

When God came down from Heaven—the living God—
    What signs and wonders marked His stately way?
Brake out the winds in music where He trod?
    Shone o'er the heavens a brighter, softer day?

The dumb began to speak, the blind to see,
    And the lame leaped, and pain and paleness fled;
The mourner's sunken eye grew bright with glee,
    And from the tomb awoke the wondering dead!

When God went back to Heaven—the living God—
　　Rode He the heavens upon a fiery car?
Waved seraph-wings along His glorious road?
　　Stood still to wonder each bright wandering star?

Upon the cross He hung, and bowed the head,
　　And prayed for them that smote, and them that cursed;
And, drop by drop, His slow life-blood was shed,
　　And His last hour of suffering was His worst.

∾

WE CAN COMMUNE WITH CHRIST EVERY DAY

LOUIS EVELY

"Oh," we exclaim, "if we'd lived in His day, if we could've heard
　　and seen
　　and touched Him,
how dearly we'd have loved Him,
How gladly we'd have left everything to follow Him!"

Really?
Haven't we ever seen or touched Him?
　　We can commune with Him every day.

∾

CHRIST OUR SCULPTOR

PAUL BILLHEIMER

'Tis the Master who holds the mallet,
　　And day by day
He is chipping whatever environs
　　The form away;
Which, under His skillful cutting,
　　He means shall be

Wrought silently out to beauty
   of such degree
Of faultless and full perfection,
   That angel eyes
Shall look on the finished labor
   With new surprise,
That even His boundless patience
   Could grave His own
Features upon such fractured
   And stubborn stones.

∾

JESUS, FULLY MAN

MAJOR W. IAN THOMAS

JESUS CHRIST HIMSELF is the final exegesis of all truth. He is all that we need to know about God, and He is all that we need to know about man, and if "to live in the land" is to enjoy that quality of life which is made possible only by virtue of allowing Him to live His life in us, we could not do better than to conclude our studies in this book by turning our eyes again upon Him, whose perfect humanity is matched only by His perfect deity.

> Jesus knowing that the Father had given all things into his hands and that he was come from God, and went to God; he riseth from supper, and laid aside his garments; and took a towel, and girded himself. After that, he poureth water into a basin, and began to wash the disciples' feet, and to wipe them with the towel wherewith he was girded (John 13:3–5).

The Lord Jesus knew that the Father had given all things into His hands—that as a Man, all the illimitable resources of deity had been vested in His person. That is the first thing I would like you to notice, for although He was in the beginning with God, and was God, and *is* God— and although as the Creative Word, all things were made by Him—when He came to this earth, in the very fullest sense of the term, He became Man; but He became Man as God intended man to be, and behaved as

God intended man to behave, walking day by day in that relationship to the Father which God had always intended should exist between man and Himself.

> Who, although being essentially one with God *and* in the form of God (possessing the fulness of the attributes which make God God), did not think this equality with God was a thing to be eagerly grasped or retained; but stripped Himself (of all privileges and rightful dignity) so as to assume the guise of a servant (slave), in that He became like men and was born a human being. And after He had appeared in human form He abased *and* humbled Himself (still further) and carried His obedience to the extreme of death, even the death of [the] cross! (Philippians 2:6–8 *Amplified New Testament*).

We shall enlarge upon this as we proceed, but I mention it in particular now, that we may recognize the fact that in all His activities, in all His reactions, in every step He took and in every word He said, in every decision He made, He did so *as man,* even though He was God. He knew that in His perfection *as man,* the Father had vested in Him all that God intended to vest in man—all things! In other words, man in perfection has an unlimited call upon the inexhaustible supplies of deity.

To put it another way, all the inexhaustible supplies of God are *available* to the man who is *available* to all the inexhaustible supplies of God; and Jesus Christ was that Man! He was Man in perfection—totally, unrelentingly, unquestioningly available—and that is why there was available to Him all that to which He was available—all things! Now that is a principle to which we shall need to return on many occasions.

A second thing is this: He knew that He was come from God—that is to say, His divine origin; and He knew that He went to God—that is to say, His divine destination. He came from God and He was going to God. This is reiterated in John 16:27—"The Father himself loveth you, because ye have loved me, and have believed that I came out from God. I came forth from the Father, and am come into the world: again, I leave the world, and go to the Father." *From* the Father *to* the Father, and in between 33 years on earth *in* the world; a parenthesis in time, as it were, with eternity on one side and eternity on the other, and a short limited time space—33 years—on earth. He was in the beginning with God in the past—*of* the Father. He was to be eternally with God in the future—*to* the Father. But in the meantime for 33 years He must play the role of Man in perfection, and as such He knew that the Father had given all things into His hands—that He had come from God and was going to God!

One might imagine that at this stage we are poised upon the threshold of some sensational event or some sensational utterance; but instead it comes almost as an anti-climax to read that He rose from supper, laid aside His garments, took a towel, girded Himself, poured water into a basin, and washed His disciples' feet. With all the illimitable resources of deity—of divine origin and divine destination—He washed His disciples' feet, something which was too lowly even for His own disciples, who felt themselves above such condescension.

Did He need all the illimitable resources of deity to wash His disciples' feet? *God* on His knees!

The Lord Jesus Christ was demonstrating a principle, that it is not the *nature* of what you are doing that determines its spirituality, but the *origin* of what you are doing. Not its nature, but its origin!

There was never a moment in the life of the Lord Jesus that was without divine significance, because there was never anything He did, never anything He said, never any step He took, which did not spring from a divine origin—nothing that was not the activity of the Father in and through the Son. Thirty-three years of availability to the Father, that the Father in and through Him might implement the program that had been established and agreed on between the Father and the Son before ever the world was.

Why did the Father give all things into His hands? Because Jesus Christ was completely Man. And He was completely Man because He was completely available! For the first time since Adam fell into sin, there was on earth a Man as God intended man to be!

Which of His activities were the more spiritual, the Sermon on the Mount, the raising of Lazarus from the dead, or the washing of His disciples' feet? The answer, of course, is that no one activity was more spiritual than another, for *all* had their origin in the Father, who acted through the Son. "I do always those things that please Him" (John 8:29). Spirituality in man is his availability to God for His divine action, and the *form* of this activity is irrelevant. If it pleases you, always and only, to do what pleases God—you can do as you please!

JESUS BECAME A HUMAN BEING

MEISTER ECKHART

JESUS BECAME A human being because God the compassionate One could not suffer and lacked a back to be beaten. God needed a back like our backs on which to receive blows and thereby to perform compassion as well as to preach it.

∾

THE INCARNATION

C. S. LEWIS

IN THE INCARNATION, God the Son takes the body and human soul of Jesus, and, through that, the whole environment of Nature, all the creaturely predicament, into His own being. So that "He came down from Heaven" can almost be transposed into "Heaven drew earth up into it," and locality, limitation, sleep, sweat, footsore weariness, frustration, pain, doubt, and death, are, from before all worlds, known by God from within. The pure light walks the earth; the darkness, received into the heart of Deity, is there swallowed up. Where, except in uncreated light, can the darkness be drowned?

∾

IMMANUEL

MICHAEL CARD

THE IMPLICATIONS OF the name *Immanuel* are both comforting and unsettling. Comforting, because He has come to share the danger as well as the drudgery of our everyday lives. He desires to weep with us and to wipe away our tears. And what seems most bizarre, Jesus Christ, the Son of God, longs to share in and to be the source of the laughter and the joy we all too rarely know.

The implications are unsettling. It is one thing to claim that God looks down upon us, from a safe distance, and speaks to us (via long distance, we hope). But to say that He is right here, is to put ourselves and Him in a totally new situation. He is no longer the calm and benevolent observer in the sky, the kindly old caricature with the beard. His image becomes that of Jesus, who wept and laughed, who fasted and feasted, and who, above all, was fully present to those He loved. He was there with them. He is here with us.

❧

THE WORD BECAME FLESH

MAX LUCADO

HE WAS TOUCHABLE, approachable, reachable. And, what's more, he was ordinary. If he were here today you probably wouldn't notice him as he walked through a shopping mall. He wouldn't turn heads by the clothes he wore or the jewelry he flashed.

"Just call me Jesus," you can almost hear him say.

He was the kind of fellow you'd invite to watch the Rams-Giants game at your house. He'd wrestle on the floor with your kids, doze on your couch, and cook steaks on your grill. He'd laugh at your jokes and tell a few of his own. And when you spoke, he'd listen to you as if he had all the time in eternity.

❧

DID YOU EVER CRY, JESUS?

DONNA SWANSON

Did you ever cry, Jesus?
did the world ever pile up on you
   'til you wanted to quit?

Did you ever cry, Jesus?
Did you ever get so tired of humanity
   you wished you'd never come?

Did life ever throw you too much hate?
Were there more lies and apathy
    than could be borne silently?

Did your back ever ache, Jesus?
Did you sometimes fret at family obligations
    and long to be about your Father's business?

Did the blind eyes, the twisted bodies,
The warped minds and maimed souls get to you?
    Were you ever just plain mad?

Were you ever lonely, Jesus?
When your friends misunderstood and walked out on you,
    did you ever cry, Jesus?

I think you must have,
for you know me so well. So well!
    I think you must have cried a little.

∽

BREAD AND SPIRITUAL HUNGER

MALCOLM MUGGERIDGE

Malcolm Muggeridge saw the Incarnation (Jesus becoming a human being) as a kind of bridge between earth and heaven, between human-kind and God. Without this bridge we would have been forever separate.

Muggeridge had a "conversion" experience after his long and distinguished life as a British magazine editor and journalist. This experience and its impact was the subject of Jesus Rediscovered, *the book in which he describes this experience.*

I GRASPED THAT over it lay, as it were, a cable-bridge, frail, swaying, but passable. And this bridge, this reconciliation between the black despair of lying bound and gagged in the tiny dungeon of ego, and soaring upwards into the white radiance of God's universal love—this bridge was the Incarnation, whose truth expresses that of the desperate need it meets. Because of our physical hunger we know there is bread; because of our spiritual hunger we know there is Christ.

GRACE

JOHN BUNYAN

John Bunyan, an English Baptist, suffered much for his faith in Bedford Gaol. There he wrote the classic Pilgrim's Progress. *In this brief poem, he celebrates God's undeserved love, grace, and states that it is this great love that caused Christ to leave heaven and become a human being in order to save everyone.*

THOU SON OF the Blessed, what grace was manifest in thy condescension! Grace brought thee down from heaven; grace stropped thee of thy glory; grace made thee poor and despicable; grace made thee bear such burdens of sin, such burdens of sorrow, such burdens of God's curse as are unspeakable.

O Son of God, grace was in all thy tears; grace came bubbling out of thy side with thy blood; grace came forth with every word of thy sweet mouth; grace came out where the whip smote thee, where the thorns pricked thee, where the nails and spear pierced thee. O blessed Son of God, here is grace indeed! unsearchable riches of grace! unthought of riches of grace! grace to make angels wonder, grace to make sinners happy, grace to astonish devils!

❧

FOLLOWING JESUS

MICHAEL CARD

ALMOST EVERYONE WHO follows Jesus in the New Testament leaves something behind for His sake. Simon and the other disciples who were fishermen left their nets and boats. James and John, the sons of Zebedee, left their father in the process as well as a prosperous family business. Archaeologists tell us they have uncovered a fish market, a "branch office" in Jerusalem that belonged to Zebedee (perhaps the first store in a chain called "Captain Zee's"?).

Matthew left behind an even more lucrative business, tax gathering. Not only do I see his tax booth abandoned alongside my visionary path, I see a pile of money on it. Once Matthew left his wealth to follow Jesus we never hear him mention money or power again! (Though the other disciples talk about it frequently.)

Others left things behind after they encountered Jesus. The blind beggar, who used his cloak to gather the coins he begged, jumped up and left the cloak lying there after Jesus gave him his sight. The woman at the well ran off and forgot her water jar once she was confronted by this man who told her "everything she had ever done." The woman who suffered from continual bleeding left a long line of doctors behind. The son of the widow of Nain left an empty coffin lying there by the city gate. The sinful woman left behind an empty alabaster perfume jar. Lazarus, perhaps most miraculous of all, left behind a pile of grave clothes and an empty tomb.

THE THINGS WE LEAVE BEHIND

There sits Simon, foolish and wise.
Proudly he's tending his nets.
Jesus calls and the boats drift away.
And all that he owns he forgets.
But more than the nets he abandoned that day,
He found that his pride was soon fading away.
It's hard to imagine the freedom we find
From the things we leave behind.
The sightless beggar; pleading each day,
Catching the coins in his robe.
At finding Jesus he threw it away
And joyfully followed his Lord.
But more than the robe that he left by the way,
The darkness that dwelt in his heart went away.
It's hard to imagine the freedom we find
From the things we leave behind.

Matthew was mindful of taking the tax
And pressing the people to pay.
At hearing the call he responded in faith
And followed the Light and the Way.
And leaving the people so puzzled he found
That the greed in his heart was no longer around.
It's hard to imagine the freedom we find
From the things we leave behind.

BAPTIZING JESUS

H. I. HESTER

I THINK MARY noticed a strange light in the eye of her First-born. There was a far-away air about Him, as if He felt in His soul the call to a new career. He was more than usually reticent. He spent more time out in the hills alone. Each morning He took with Him to the little shop a "roll of the Book." From it He would read a bit, then lay it upon a shelf while He worked and thought; then read again, and turn almost absentmindedly to work again. All this Mary's keen, discerning eye saw. There was nothing for her to say. Then there came an evening when she noted that He carefully put away His tools, swept the shop out all clean and shut the door with a care that spelled finality. He came into the house and laid up His scroll and went out into the solitude of the night.

Mary could not think of sleep. She got together a "change of raiment" and prepared a simple lunch, all of which she made into a neat packet. Then she got ready a simple breakfast. In the morning twilight she saw Him coming in from his night with that Father about whose affairs it is needful for him to be. Mary met Him, very quietly, and led Him to the waiting breakfast. As they sat and He ate she watched Him furtively, lovingly, longingly. They did not talk much. Rather they felt each other and mingled their souls in spiritual converse and questioning. As He finished, Mary went and brought out the packet and handed it to Him. She helped Him adjust it, thus to touch Him with her hands in gentle caress. A moment they gazed into the depths of each other's eyes. Very gently He placed His arm about her, drew her to Him as they stood together there in the doorway, planted a kiss on her upturned face. No word was spoken. He turned about, walked past the little shop, followed the path as it wound eastward and south and then, more than a quarter of a mile below, passed around the point out of sight into the highway leading down to Judea and the Jordan. Mary turned into her house with a great surge of mingled feeling and fell on her face on His bed. She knew that her wonderful Son had gone out into the world to do His work, to attend to the affairs of His Father.

A PSALM FOR PALM SUNDAY

JOSEPH BAYLEY

King Jesus
why did you choose
a lowly ass
to carry you
to ride in your parade?
Had you no friend
who owned a horse
—a royal mount with spirit
fit for a king to ride?
Why choose an ass
small unassuming
beast of burden
trained to plow
not carry kings.

King Jesus
why did you choose
me
a lowly unimportant person
to bear you
in my world today?
I'm poor and unimportant
trained to work
not carry kings
—let alone the King of kings
and yet you've chosen me
to carry you in triumph
in this world's parade.
King Jesus
keep me small
so all may see
how great you are
keep me humble
so all may say
Blessed is he who cometh in the name of the Lord
not what a great ass he rides.

JESUS IN THE TEMPLE

JOHN DONNE

John Donne was the royal dean preaching to the British royal family when he was taken ill during a seige of the Black Death. Thinking he had the plague, he listened to the tolling of the bells and wrote his immortal "No Man Is an Island." What Donne had was not the plague. He recovered. In this sonnet, he celebrates Jesus going into the temple at age twelve. While separated from his parents during the holiday of Passover, Jesus goes into the temple and talks to the scholars, who are amazed at Jesus' understanding of God. This may have been Jesus' Bar Mitzvah. The incident (Luke 2:41–49) is the only biographical inclusion of what is called the silent years; we have no other recorded event in Jesus' life between his second and thirtieth year.

> With His kind mother, who partakes thy woe,
> Joseph, turn back; see where your Child doth sit,
> Blowing, yea blowing out those sparks of wit
> Which Himself on the doctors did I bestow.
> The Word but lately could not speak, and lo!
> It suddenly speaks wonders; whence comes it
> That all which was, and all which should be writ,
> A shallow-seeming child should deeply know?
> His Godhead was not soul to His manhood,
> Nor had time mellow'd Him to this ripeness;
> But as for one which hath a long task, 'tis good,
> With the sun to begin His business,
> He in His age's morning thus began,
> By miracles exceeding power of man.

THE LIFE OF SORROW WHICH JESUS LED FROM HIS BIRTH

SAINT ALPHONSUS MARIA DE LIGUORI

JESUS CHRIST COULD have saved mankind without suffering and dying. Yet, in order to prove to us how much He loved us, He chose for Himself a life full of tribulations. Therefore the prophet Isaiah called Him "a man of sorrows." His whole life was filled with suffering. His Passion began, not merely a few hours before His death, but from the first moment of His birth. He was born in a stable where everything served to torment Him. His sense of sight was hurt by seeing nothing but the rough, black walls of the cave; His sense of smell was hurt by the stench of the dung from the beasts in the stable; His sense of touch was hurt by the prickling straw on which He lay. Shortly after His birth He was forced to flee into Egypt, where He spent several years of His childhood in poverty and misery. His boyhood and early manhood in Nazareth were passed in hard work and obscurity. And finally, in Jerusalem, He died on a cross, exhausted with pain and anguish.

Thus, then, was the life of Jesus but one unbroken series of sufferings, which were doubly painful because He had ever before His eyes all the sufferings He would have to endure till His death. Yet, since our Lord had voluntarily chosen to bear these tribulations for our sake, they did not afflict Him as much as did the sight of our sins, by which we have so ungratefully repaid Him for His love towards us. When the confessor of Saint Margaret of Cortona saw that she never seemed satisfied with all the tears she had already shed for her past sins, he said to her, "Margaret, stop crying and cease your lamenting, for God has surely forgiven you your offences against Him." But she replied, "Father, how can I cease to weep, since I know that my sins kept my Lord Jesus in pain and suffering during all His life?"

∾

KNOWING GOD

J. I. PACKER

THE MOST EXCELLENT study for expanding the soul, is the science of Christ, and Him crucified, and the knowledge of the Godhead in the glorious Trinity. Nothing will so enlarge the intellect, nothing so magnify the whole soul of man, as a devout, earnest, continued investigation of the great subject of the Deity.

And, whilst humbling and expanding, this subject is eminently *consolatory*. Oh, there is, in contemplating Christ, a balm for every wound; in musing on the Father, there is a quietus for every grief; and in the influence of the Holy Ghost, there is a balsam for every sore. Would you lose your sorrow? Would you drown your cares? Then go, plunge yourself in the Godhead's deepest sea; be lost in his immensity; and you shall come forth as from a couch of rest, refreshed and invigorated. I know nothing which can so comfort the soul; so calm the swelling billows of sorrow and grief; so speak peace to the winds of trial, as a devout musing upon the subject of the Godhead.

∾

GOD'S LOVE REVEALED IN HIS BECOMING MAN

SAINT ALPHONSUS MARIA DE LIGUORI

BECAUSE OUR FIRST parent Adam had rebelled against God, he was driven out of paradise and brought on himself and all his descendants the punishment of eternal death. But the Son of God, seeing man thus lost and wishing to save him from death, offered to take upon Himself our human nature and to suffer death Himself, condemned as a criminal on a cross. "But my Son," we may imagine the eternal Father saying to Him, "think of what a life of humiliations and sufferings Thou wilt have to lead on earth. Thou wilt have to be born in a cold stable and laid in a manger, the feeding trough of beasts. While still an infant, Thou wilt have to flee into Egypt, to escape the hands of Herod. After Thy return from Egypt, Thou wilt have to live and work in a shop as a lowly servant, poor and despised. And finally, worn out with sufferings, Thou wilt have to give up Thy life on a cross, put to shame and abandoned by everyone." "Father," replies the Son, "all this matters not. I will gladly bear it all, if only I can save man."

What should we say if a prince, out of compassion for a dead worm, were to choose to become a worm himself and give his own life blood in order to restore the worm to life? But the eternal Word has done infinitely more than this for us. Though He is the sovereign Lord of the world, He chose to become like us, who are immeasurably more beneath Him than a worm is beneath a prince, and He was willing to die for us, in order to win back for us the life of divine grace that we had lost by sin. When He saw that all the other gifts which He had bestowed on us were not sufficient to induce us to repay His love with love, He became man Himself and gave Himself all to us. "The Word was made flesh and dwelt among us"; "He loved us and delivered Himself up for us."

JESUS, THE WORM

ROY HESSION

THOSE WHO HAVE been in tropical lands tell us that there is a big difference between a snake and a worm, when you attempt to strike at them. The snake rears itself up and hisses and tries to strike back—a true picture of self. But a worm offers no resistance, it allows you to do what you like with it, kick it or squash it under your heel—a picture of true brokenness. Jesus was willing to become just that for us—a worm and not man. He did so, because that is what he saw us to be, worms having forfeited all rights by our sins, except to deserve hell. And he now calls us to take our rightful place as worms for him and with him.

RENUNCIATION

WILLIAM SHAKESPEARE

In Richard II's renunciation of royalty, many feel, Shakespeare's images are built on a strong metaphorical understanding of Jesus laying aside his heavenly crown to wear his own redeeming crown of thorns. At Flint Castle, Richard II begins to yield to the usurping Henry Bolingbroke.

KING RICHARD
What must the King do not? Must he submit?
The King shall do it. Must he be deposed?
The King shall be contented. Must he lose
The name of King? A God's name, let it go.
I'll give my jewels for a set of beads,
My gorgeous palace for a hermitage,
My gay apparel for an almsman's gown,
My figured goblets for a dish of wood,
My scepter for a palmer's walking staff,
My subjects for a pair of carvèd saints,
And my large kingdom for a little grave,
A little, little grave, an obscure grave,
Or I'll be buried in the King's highway,
Some way of common trade where subjects' feet

May hourly trample on their sovereign's head,
For on my heart they tread now, whilst I live,
And buried once, why not upon my head?
Aumerle, thou weep'st, my tender-hearted cousin.
We'll make foul weather with despisèd tears.
Our sighs and they shall lodge the summer corn,
And make a dearth in this revolting land.
Or shall we play the wantons with our woes,
And make some pretty match with shedding tears;
As thus to drop them still upon one place
Till they have fretted us a pair of graves
Within the earth, and therein laid? "There lies
Two kinsmen digged their graves with weeping eyes."
Would not this ill do well? Well, well, I see
I talk but idly and you mock at me.
Most mighty prince, my lord Northumberland,
What says King Bolingbroke? Will his majesty
Give Richard leave to live till Richard die?
You make a leg, and Bolingbroke says "Ay."

NORTHUMBERLAND
My lord, in the base court he doth attend
To speak with you. May it please you to come down?

KING RICHARD
Down, down I come like glist'ring Phaëton,
Wanting the manage of unruly jades.
In the base court: base court where kings grow base
To come at traitors' calls, and do them grace.
In the base court, come down: down court, down King,
For night-owls shriek where mounting larks should sing.

❧

THE THEATER OF INCARNATION

HELMUT THIELICKE

JESUS CHRIST DID not remain at base headquarters in heaven, receiving
reports of the world's suffering from below and shouting a few encourag-

ing words to us from a safe distance. No, he left the headquarters and came down to us in the front-line trenches, right down to where we live and worry about what the Bolsheviks may do, where we contend with our anxieties and the feeling of emptiness and futility, where we sin and suffer guilt, and where we must finally die. There is nothing that he did not endure with us. He understands everything.

☙

ONLY BEGOTTEN SON

NATE ADAMS

Nate Adams learned through his son's accident how unpredictable and uncertain life can be at times. His admiration for Christ's becoming one of us is celebrated in his son's near brush with death.

I WAS SHAVING when I heard a crash in the bedroom. The full-length mirror that was leaning against our bedroom wall must have fallen. Then I heard Caleb's scream.

I flew around the corner to see a zillion pieces of broken mirror on the floor—and Caleb, my 19-month-old, lying in the middle of it. Then I saw the blood.

The sight of my son's blood overwhelmed me. I snatched him up and scanned his body. Though the glass had been scattered all around him, the only mark was a small scratch on the inside of his left ear. Only a trickle of blood flowed, so it was apparently more fear than injury that was forcing his tears.

The interesting thing about this little crisis is now I can't read, hear or even think of John 3:16 without remembering Caleb lying in the middle of that broken glass. The most familiar Bible verse had become much too familiar, even trite to me. But now when I hear it I get a lump in my throat, thinking about what kind of determined, redemptive love could be strong enough to let an only Son cry out in pain on a cross.

A few months after Caleb's accident, our second son was born. I no longer had an "only begotten son." But as I experienced the joy of a new life and an expanded family, I realized in a fresh way that it was Jesus' death that made it possible for the Only Begotten Son to have many brothers and sisters.

A PSALM TO THE GOD MAN

JOSEPH BAYLEY

Lord Jesus Christ
I thank you
that you were real
a real man
and before that
a real boy.
It hurt
when you were planing wood
and you got a splinter
under your nail.
You felt it
when a stone got stuck
in your sandal.
You had to shake it out.
You removed the sand
from between your toes
and slept on hard ground
on cold nights
dreaming of foxes
with their warm holes.
You got thirsty
hungry
tired
bone tired
tired of crowds
tired because you walked
too far.
You died.
Lord Jesus Christ
I thank you
that you were real
real God.
You healed people's hurts
even raised their dead.
You said
Come to me
if you're tired
and I will give you rest.

You fed hungry crowds
and said
I am living bread
that came down from heaven.
You rose from deadness
into life bringing life.
Lord Jesus Christ
I thank you
that you are real
real God man.
I worship you
I adore you
because you who bore
my sins
know what it's like
to have a splinter
under your nail
and to die.

∾

MOTHER TERESA AND THE BABY FOUND IN A DUSTBIN

MALCOLM MUGGERIDGE

THOUGH IN OUR time motherhood has been greatly devalued, and the sick phrase "unwanted child" been given currency, it still remains true, as any nurse or gynecologist will confirm, that it is extremely rare for any child at the moment of birth to be other than wanted in its mother's eyes. Once when I was in Calcutta with Mother Teresa she picked up one of the so-called "unwanted" babies which had come into the care of her Missionaries of Charity. It had been salvaged from a dustbin, and was so minute that one wondered it could exist at all. When I remarked on this, a look of exultation came into Mother Teresa's face. "See," she said, "there's life in it!" So there was; and suddenly it was as though I were present at the Bethlehem birth, and the baby Mother Teresa was holding was another Lamb of God sent into the world to lighten our darkness. How could we know? How dare we prognosticate upon what made life worth while for this or that child?

GOD'S LOVE REVEALED IN HIS BEING BORN AN INFANT

SAINT ALPHONSUS MARIA DE LIGUORI

WHEN THE SON of God became man for our sake, He could have come on earth as an adult man from the first moment of His human existence. But since the sight of little children draws us with an especial attraction to love them, Jesus chose to make His first appearance on earth as a little infant. . . . "God wished to be born as a little baby," wrote Saint Peter Chrysologus, "in order that He might teach us to love and not to fear Him." The prophet Isaias had long before foretold that the Son of God was to be born as an infant and thus give Himself to us on account of the love He bore us: "A child is born to us, a son is given to us."

My Jesus, supreme and true God! What has drawn Thee from heaven to be born in a cold stable, if not the love which Thou bearest us men? What has allured thee from the bosom of Thy Father, to place Thee in a hard manger? What has brought Thee from Thy throne above the stars to lay Thee down on a little straw? What has led Thee from the midst of the nine choirs of angels, to set Thee between two animals? Thou, who inflamest the seraphim with holy fire, art now shivering with cold in this stable! Thou, who settest the stars in the sky in motion, canst not now move unless others carry Thee in their arms! Thou, who givest men and beasts their food, hast need now of a little milk to sustain Thy life! Thou, who art the joy of heaven, dost now whimper and cry in suffering! Tell me, who has reduced Thee to such misery? "Love has done it," says Saint Bernard. The love which Thou bearest us men has brought all this on Thee.

❧

THE ANGELS' SONG

JOHN MILTON

"True image of the Father; whether thron'd
In the bosom of bliss, and light of light
Conceiving, or, remote from Heaven, enshrin'd
In fleshly tabernacle, and human form,
Wandering the wilderness; whatever place,

Habit, or state, or motion, still expressing
The Son of God, with godlike force endur'd
Against the attempter of Thy Father's throne,
And thief of Paradise! him long of old
Thou didst debel, and down from Heaven cast
With all his army; now Thou hast aveng'd
Supplanted Adam, and, by vanquishing
Temptation, hast regain'd lost Paradise,
And frustrated the conquest fraudulent.
He never more henceforth will dare set foot
In Paradise to tempt; his snares are broke;
For, though that seat of earthly bliss be fail'd,
A fairer Paradise is founded now
For Adam and his chosen sons, whom Thou,
A Saviour, art come down to reinstall,
Where they shall dwell secure, when time shall be,
Of tempter and temptation without fear.
But thou, infernal Serpent! shalt not long
Rule in the clouds; like an autumnal star,
Or lightning, thou shalt fall from Heaven, trod down
Under His feet: for proof, ere this thou feel'st
Thy wound, yet not thy last and deadliest wound,
By this repulse receiv'd, and hold'st in Hell
No triumph: in all her gates Abaddon rues
Thy bold attempt. Hereafter learn with awe
To dread the Son of God: He, all unarm'd,
Shall chase thee, with the terror of His voice,
From thy demoniac holds, possession foul,
Thee and thy legions; yelling they shall fly,
And beg to hide them in a herd of swine,
Lest He command them down into the deep,
Bound, and to torment sent before their time.
Hail, Son of the Most High, heir of both worlds,
Queller of Satan! on Thy glorious work,
Now enter; and begin to save mankind."
Thus they the Son of God, our Saviour meek,
Sung victor, and, from heavenly feast refresh'd,
Brought on His way with joy; He, unobserv'd,
Home to His mother's house private return'd.

V

JESUS:

~

HIS MIRACLES

C. S. Lewis once said that miracles are the heart of Christianity. While they may lie at its heart, they have a harder time snuggling their way into the gray matter of the twentieth-century mind. Unfortunately, miracles are so much a part of the Hebrew-Christian faith that it is not possible to doubt them and affirm the faith that was created by them. Faith created by miracles? Exactly. It is the Exodus miracle of the parting of the Red Sea around which Jewish faith is gathered. The Seder ritual is a celebration of the final plague by which God does at last convince Pharaoh to let his people go.

In the New Testament the Resurrection is that central miracle around which the Christian faith is gathered. The apostle Paul said that without believing the miracle of the Resurrection, faith was impossible (Romans 10:9; 1 Corinthians 15:17). Still, to the rigid logicians of our times the miracles seem to be scientific monstrosities. Science has made such formidable technicians out of us that we are not as open as earlier people may have been to miracles. We have painted ourselves into an empirical corner and have become the victims of the scientific monster we created.

Miracles in scripture are never random, pointless infringements on natural law. Miracles are not violations of cosmic order. They are not acts of God denying his own natural laws. Miracles occur when God sets natural law aside. When God sets it aside, he does it to say to those who encounter the miracle that people mean more to God than the mere observance of natural law. God split the Red Sea not to amaze the Egyptians but to say to Pharaoh, "I care more for the lives of the poor trapped Israelites than I care for buoyancy and gravitational laws. I therefore make the waters of the Red Sea misbehave that I may prove how much Israel means to me."

In a similar way, when Jesus feeds the five thousand, the miracle plays havoc with the natural law that matter is neither created nor destroyed. Here matter is created. Jesus multiplies the loaves not to wow the Galilean peasantry, but to show how very much God cared for the poor, the hungry, and the dispossessed.

Perhaps one final thing must be said about miracles. They exist that God may be free from his own imprisonment in the system of cosmic laws he established. When God performs any miracle he is saying, "I'm free to act as I will in the natural world." He proved to all at the Red Sea that he could act above the laws he made. By walking on the sea Jesus proved he was indeed the Son of God. He could perform a miracle to prove he was God and not imprisoned within the natural system over which he too took charge.

Miracles are those acts which establish the central beliefs of the Hebrew-Christian tradition. They create the faith.

> From there he went all over Galilee. He used synagogues for meeting places and taught people the truth of God. God's kingdom was his theme—that beginning right now they were under God's government, a good government! He also healed people of their diseases and of the bad effects of their bad lives. Word got around the entire Roman province of Syria. People brought anybody with an ailment, whether mental, emotional, or physical. Jesus healed them, one and all. More and more people came, the momentum gathering. Besides those from Galilee, crowds came from the "Ten Towns" across the lake, others up from Jerusalem and Judea, still others from across the Jordan.
>
> Matthew 4.23–25, *The Message*

THE CONSCIOUS WATER

RICHARD CRASHAW

CRASHAW ONCE WROTE on the Miracle of Cana of Galilee:
"The Conscious Water knew its Lord, and blushed."

∽

THE MAN WHO SCRATCHED

WILLIAM GRIFFIN

"HELLO, I'M A leper." A man popped out from behind a building and stood right in front of Jesus. "Please don't run away."

"What's the matter with your skin?" asked Jesus.

"Can't you see? I'm covered with runny sores and crusty scabs. Nobody wants to look at me, my face is so horrible."

"What do you want me to do?"

"You can make me better. I know you can," said the man, falling on his knees in front of Jesus. "If you don't, I'll scratch myself to death."

Jesus felt sorry for the poor man.

"Don't touch me," said the man. "That's how you get it."

"I'm not afraid to touch you." Jesus reached down, took hold of the man's arms, and pulled him to his feet.

The itching was gone. The sores started to dry. The scabs began to fall off.

"Thank you, thank you, thank you!" shouted the man. "What can I do to thank you?"

"You can go to the temple, show yourself to a priest, and say a prayer of thanks to God."

"Yes, yes, I will, I will," promised the man, hurrying off.

"One more thing," said Jesus.

"Anything, anything," said the man.

"You don't have to tell what I just did."

"I won't tell a soul," agreed the man as he skipped toward Jerusalem.

But the man was so happy and the walk to the temple so long that he forgot. He told everyone he met.

And the lepers along the road began to look for the wonderful man with the healing touch.

THE MIRACLES OF JESUS

MARCUS BORG

MEDIATORS BETWEEN THE two worlds of the primordial tradition often become "people of power," or miracle-workers, especially healers. To be sure, not all do. In the history of Israel and other cultures, some were primarily mediators of the divine will as prophets and law-givers, or of "supernatural" knowledge as diviners or clairvoyants. Others were charismatic military leaders, "spirit warriors." But some became channels through which healing power flowed from the world of Spirit into the visible world. Such figures of power ("men of deeds," as they were called in Judaism) were known in first-century Palestine, both in her ancient tradition (notably, Elijah) and in charismatics contemporary with Jesus such as Hanina ben Dosa and Honi the Circle-Drawer.

JESUS WAS ONE of these "men of deeds." Indeed, to his contemporaries, it was the most remarkable thing about him. During his lifetime he was known primarily as a healer and exorcist. People flocked to him, drawn by his wonder-working reputation, as the gospels report again and again: "They brought to him all who were sick or possessed with demons. And the whole city was gathered together about the door"; as a healer, "His fame spread, and great crowds followed him"; "People came to him from every quarter."

His healings attracted attention in other quarters as well. In prison before his execution by King Herod Antipas, John the Baptist heard of Jesus' mighty deeds and sent messengers to inquire if Jesus might be Elijah *returned,* one of the great charismatic healers of Israel's history. After John's death, Herod himself heard of Jesus' reputation as a miracle-worker and wondered if Jesus' powers might be the powers of John the Baptist "raised from the dead." Not only do the gospel writers report the fame which Jesus' mighty deeds caused, but they devote substantial portions of their narratives to accounts of such deeds.

Despite the difficulty which miracles pose for the modern mind, on historical grounds it is virtually indisputable that Jesus was a healer and exorcist. The reasons for this judgment are threefold. First, there is the widespread attestation in our earliest sources. Second, healings and exorcisms were relatively common in the world around Jesus, both within Judaism and the Hellenistic world. Third, even his opponents did not challenge the claim that powers of healing flowed through him; rather, as we shall see, they claimed that his powers came from the lord of the evil spirits. By admiring followers and skeptical foes alike, he was seen as a holy man with healing powers.

• • •

As an exorcist, Jesus drove evil spirits out of many possessed people. In addition to summaries which mention multiple exorcisms (for example, "And those who were troubled with unclean spirits were cured") and the reference to Mary Magdalene "from whom seven demons had gone out," the synoptic gospels contain several extended accounts of particular exorcisms and a number of sayings referring to the practice. The gospels consistently distinguish between exorcisms and healings; not all healings were exorcisms, and not all maladies were caused by evil spirits. The gospels also speak of exorcists other than Jesus: Pharisaic exorcists, an unnamed exorcist who expelled demons in Jesus' name even though he was not a follower of Jesus, and Jesus' own disciples. Obviously well-attested, exorcisms were not uncommon, even though not everyday occurrences.

More so than extraordinary cures, exorcism is especially alien to us in the modern world. In part, this is because we do not normally see the phenomenon (though are there cases of "possession" which we call by another name?). Even more, it is because the notion of "possession" by a spirit from another level of reality does not fit into our worldview. Rather, possession and exorcism presuppose the reality of a world of spirits which can interact with the visible world; that is, they presuppose the truth of the "primordial tradition."

Cross-cultural studies of the phenomenon indicate a number of typical traits. "Possession" occurs when a person falls under the control of an evil spirit or spirits. Such people are inhabited by a presence which they (and others) experience as "other than themselves." In addition to having two or more "personalities," they exhibit bizarre behavior and are often destructive or self-destructive. Convulsions, sweating, and seizures are common. Unusual strength and uncanny knowledge are sometimes also reported. Exorcism is the expulsion of the evil spirit, driving it out of the person and ending its "ownership." This can be done only with the aid of a superior spirit in order to overpower the evil spirit. Often elaborate rituals are used, involving incantations and "power objects."

The synoptic gospels describe two cases of possession in considerable detail. Inhabited by a legion of demons with supernatural strength, the "Gerasene demoniac" lived howling in a graveyard on the east shore of the Sea of Galilee:

A man with an unclean spirit lived among the tombs; and no one could bind him even with a chain; for he had often been bound with fetters and chains, but the chains he wrenched apart, and the fetters he broke in pieces; and no one had the strength to subdue him. Night and day among the tombs and on the mountains he was always crying out, and bruising himself with stones. [And he said] "My name is Legion; for we are many."

According to Mark's account, the demon also had nonordinary knowledge. It recognized Jesus' "status," even though no human being in Mark's gospel had yet done so: "What have you to do with me, Jesus, Son of the Most High God?"

Jesus' exorcisms not only attracted crowds but controversy. Some of his opponents charged that he performed them with the aid of evil powers: "And the scribes who came down from Jerusalem said, 'He is possessed by Beelzebub, and by the prince of demons he casts out demons.' " The accusation was "witchcraft" or "sorcery." A Jewish source from a few centuries later, referring to Jesus by his name in Aramaic, repeated the charge and connected it to his death: "Yeshu of Nazareth" was executed "because he *practiced sorcery* and led Israel astray." The charge of sorcery is a pejorative characterization of his powers, and attributes them (like the Beelzebub accusation) to the powers of darkness. From his opponents' point of view, he was an unorthodox holy man, a "magician," but his powers were not denied.

• • •

Jesus was also known as a healer. In fact, according to the gospels, his healings outnumbered his exorcisms. They are often referred to in summary statements, as well as in words attributed to Jesus himself. To messengers sent to him by John the Baptist, he said, "Go and tell John what you hear and see: the blind receive their sight and the lame walk, lepers are cleansed and the deaf hear, and the dead are raised up, and the poor have good news preached to them."

In addition to these summaries, the synoptic gospels contain thirteen narratives of healings of particular conditions: fever, leprosy, paralysis, withered hand, bent back, hemorrhage, deafness and dumbness, blindness, dropsy, severed ear, and a sickness near death or paralysis. These thirteen should not be thought of as the sum total of Jesus' healings; rather, they are narrated as "typical" or to make some point or other. Given the nature of the gospel narratives, we shall not treat the question of the precise event behind each account, but will simply note the impression the stories create. Even though we are not dealing with "newspaper account" material, we are at the very least in touch with how Jesus' very early followers, still in contact with the living oral tradition, saw him.

The stories create a vivid impression of a charismatic healer at work. Sometimes Jesus healed by word. He said to the man with the withered hand, "Stretch out your hand," and the hand was restored. Most often touching was also involved. When a leper came to him, Jesus was "moved with pity" and touched him, and immediately the leprosy left him. Sometimes he used physical means in addition to touching, as in the case of a deaf man. Jesus "put his fingers into his ears, and he spat and touched his tongue; and looking up to heaven, he sighed, and said to him, '*Ephphatha*,' that is, 'Be opened.' And his ears were opened, his tongue released, and he spoke plainly." Of special interest here is the Aramaic word *ephphatha*, "Be opened." In context, it clearly refers to the opening of the man's ears, but may also have the connotation of *the heavens* opening up: "Looking up into heaven, he said, 'Be opened.' " Through the opening from heaven, healing power flowed.

Like the contemporary Galilean holy man Hanina ben Dosa, Jesus healed at a distance. A Roman centurion entreated Jesus to heal his servant who was lying paralyzed in the centurion's home some distance away. Seeing the centurion's faith, Jesus said, "Go; be it done for you as you have believed." The text concludes: "And the servant [at home] was healed at that very moment."

To attempt to explain how these happened is beyond our purpose, and probably impossible. There is a tendency to see these as "faith healings," perhaps because doing so makes possible a psychosomatic explanation that stretches but does not break the limits of the moden worldview. But, though faith is involved in some of the stories, clearly in other cases the faith of the healed person was not involved at all.

• • •

In an important sense, neither of the sea stories concerns the public ministry of Jesus; rather, only his inner group of followers is present. In both stories, they are in a boat, at night, distressed and frightened; in both, Jesus comes to them, the winds cease, and the sea is calmed.

Central to these stories is "the sea," an image which reverberates with rich resonances of meaning in the Hebrew Bible. The Hebrew word for "sea," derived from the name of the evil god in the Babylonian creation story, carried connotations of evil, a mysterious and threatening force opposed to God. Accordingly, when the ancient Hebrews wanted to stress God's power and authority, they spoke of the divine mastery over the sea. The authors of the psalms exclaimed, "The sea is his, for he made it!" and "Thou dost rule the raging of the sea; when its waves rise, thou stillest them." According to the book of Job, it was God who "shut in the sea with doors" and said to it, "Thus far shall you come, and no farther, and here shall your proud waves be stayed."

THE CURE OF THE DEAF AND DUMB

MARTIN LUTHER

Martin Luther had an immense skepticism for contemporary miracles,
but very much believed in the biblical miracles. But in this inclusion
he asks whether those who believe in God's corrective miracles of healing
should not much more praise God for all of those who are so miracu-
lously well they need no healing at all.

THE MIRACLE OF the cure of the deaf-and-dumb man is insignificant compared to what God does every day. For every day children are born who
previously had neither ears nor tongues, nor indeed even a soul. In less
than a year they are furnished with soul, body, tongue, and everything
else. But this miracle is so common that no one pays any attention to it.
Scarcely anyone in the world ever says thank you to God for his tongue
and his ears. How many are there who having enjoyed good sight for fifty
years ever give God thanks with all their hearts? How many rejoice over
so great a miracle? They marvel that Christ healed this man, but not that
they themselves are able to hear. By this little miracle God stirs us up to
recognize the great miracles. The whole world is deaf not to hear this.
Pythagoras was considered a heretic because he heard the wonderful song
of the stars. But one who is not blind will see the heavens so wondrous
that one could die for very joy over the sight. If we had eyes and ears, we
would be able to see and hear what the wheat says to us: "Rejoice in God,
eat and drink, use me and serve your neighbors. Soon I will fill the barns."
If I were not deaf, I would hear what the cows say: "Be glad, we bring
butter and cheese. Eat and drink and give to others." So the hens say, "We
lay eggs for you." And the birds, "Be joyful, we are hatching chicks." And
the sows grunt for joy because they bring pork and sausages. So speak all
the animals to us, and everyone should say, "I will use what God has
given, and I will give to others."

But as Christ effected this cure he sighed because he knew that as
soon as the man's tongue was restored he would misuse it.

LOAVES AND FISHES

FULTON OURSLER

Jesus is credited with performing thirty-five miracles. This miracle is one of the nine so-called nature miracles. In these nature miracles Jesus interrupted natural forces by turning the water into wine (John 2:1– 11) or stilling the storm (Matthew 8:23–27) or walking on the water (Matthew 14:22–32). But the most significant of these nature miracles may have been the feeding of the multitudes (Matthew 14:13–21). One must remember that these are not Western people gorged on abundance. These are the poor, the rabble, the destitute. In this famous miracle, Jesus shares a little boy's lunch of five loaves and two fishes with more than five thousand people. In the history of the church, this miracle has always been seen as a symbol of the way that God takes care of his people. The American novelist Fulton Oursler (1893– 1952) describes the miracle as follows.

STORIES OF JESUS' miracles reached King Herod almost daily, causing him great concern about his continued authority. Then Herod . . . heard of something not only incomprehensible, but inconceivable. One could be told that it happened, but how could one think of it as happening?

The scene was on the northeast side of the Lake of Galilee; the time was at the beginning of April, A.D. 29, just when the paschal feast was again coming on. That day a great multitude—at least five thousand people—had follow the Master. Now evening was near and the crowds were hungry. Making a hasty inventory, the disciples found that hardly anyone had brought food on this excursion into the hills.

But Andrew, Peter's brother, said:

"There is a lad here who has five barley loaves and two small fishes. But what are they among so many?"

As the story was carried to Herod, Jesus calmly invited the crowd to sit down on the green hillside. Then He took the loaves, faced the descending sun, and when He had given thanks, He distributed to the disciples, and the disciples to the people, enough to feed the whole five thousand.

How could Herod's mind, or anyone's visualize such a happening? Yet he was informed that there were five thousand witnesses; that the Master had fed Herod's hungry subjects; and that act was enough to unsettle any king.

LAZARUS

ALFRED, LORD TENNYSON

When Lazarus left his charnel-cave,
   And home to Mary's house returned,
   Was this demanded—if he yearned
To hear her weeping by his grave?

"Where wert thou, brother, these four days?"
   There lives no record of reply,
   Which telling what it is to die
Had surely added praise to praise.

From every house the neighbours met,
   The streets were filled with joyful sound
   A solemn gladness even crowned
The purple brows of Olivet.

Behold a man raised up by Christ!
   The rest remaineth unrevealed;
   He told it not; or something sealed
The lips of that Evangelist.

· · ·

Her eyes are homes of silent prayer,
   Nor other thought her mind admits
   But, he was dead, and there he sits,
And he that brought him back is there.

Then one deep love doth supersede
   All other, when her ardent gaze
   Roves from the living brother's face,
And rests upon the Life indeed.

All subtle thought, all curious fears,
   Borne down by gladness so complete,
   She bows, she bathes the Saviour's feet
With costly spikenard and with tears.

THE PRINCE OF PEACE

WILLIAM JENNINGS BRYAN

CHRIST CANNOT BE separated from the miraculous; His birth, His ministrations and His resurrection, all involve the miraculous, and the change which His religion works in the human heart is a continuing miracle. Eliminate the miracles and Christ becomes merely a human being and His gospel is stripped of divine authority.

The miracle raises two questions: "Can God perform a miracle?" and, "Would He want to?" The first is easy to answer. A God who can make a world can do anything He wants to do with it. The power to perform miracles is necessarily implied in the power to create. But would God want to perform a miracle?—this is the question which has given most of the trouble. The more I have considered it the less inclined I am to answer in the negative. To say that God would not perform a miracle is to assume a more intimate knowledge of God's plans and purposes than I can claim to have. I will not deny that God does perform a miracle or may perform one merely because I do not know how or why He does it. The fact that we are constantly learning of the existence of new forces suggests the possibility that God may operate through forces yet unknown to us, and the mysteries with which we deal every day warn me that faith is as necessary as sight. Who would have credited a century ago the stories that are now told of the wonder working electricity? For ages man had known the lightning, but only to fear it; now this invisible current is generated by a man-made machine, imprisoned in a man-made wire and made to do the bidding of man. We are even able to dispense with the wire and hurl words through space, and the X-ray has enabled us to look through substances which were supposed, until recently, to exclude all light. The miracle is not more mysterious than many of the things with which man now deals—it is simply different. The immaculate conception is not more mysterious than any other conception—it is simply unlike; nor is the resurrection of Christ more mysterious than the myriad resurrections which mark each annual seed-time.

It is sometimes said that God could not suspend one of His laws without stopping the universe, but do we not suspend or overcome the law of gravitation every day? Every time we move a foot or lift a weight, we temporarily interfere with the operation of the most universal of natural laws, and yet the world is not disturbed.

THE WOMAN WHO CAME BEHIND HIM

IN THE CROWD

GEORGE MACDONALD

This story is recorded in Luke 8:43–48. It is often used by Christians to demonstrate that we are to be open in acknowledging all good things that Jesus does for us.

Near him she stole, rank after rank;
  She feared approach too loud;
She touched his garment's hem, and shrank,
  Back in the sheltering crowd.

A shame-faced gladness thrills her frame:
  Her twelve years' fainting prayer
Is heard at last! she is the same
  As other women there!

She hears his voice. He looks about,
  Ah! is it kind or good
To drag her secret sorrow out
  Before that multitude?

The eyes of men she dares not meet—
  On her they straight must fall!
Forward she sped, and at his feet
  Fell down, and told him all.

To the one refuge she hath flown,
  The Godhead's burning flame!
Of all earth's women she alone
  Hears there the tenderest name!

"Daughter," he said, "be of good cheer;
  Thy faith hath made thee whole":
With plenteous love, not healing mere,
  He comforteth her soul.

THE SERVANT WHO WAS SICK

WILLIAM GRIFFIN

"EXCUSE ME," SAID the Roman army officer, "but I have a favor to ask."

"What is it?" asked Jesus.

"Well, I have a boy at my house, he's a servant of mine, and he's very sick."

"I'm sorry to hear that," said Jesus.

"He can't move, and the pain is terrible. Is there anything you can do?"

"I could heal him," said Jesus.

"I was hoping you'd say that."

"How far is it to your house?" asked Jesus.

"Oh no," said the officer, "you don't have to go to the house."

"Is it that far?"

"What I mean to say," said the officer, "is that I'm a centurion."

"I can see that," said Jesus.

"I've got a hundred soldiers under me."

"I understand."

"When I give an order, the men carry it out."

"Yes."

"When I say *hop,* they hop."

"What are you trying to say now?" asked Jesus.

"If you just give the order, the disease will march off into the sunset."

"Do you really believe that if I say the word, the boy will be healed?"

"That's exactly what I believe," said the officer, "only I couldn't have put it so well."

"What a surprise this is," said Jesus turning to his followers. "Here in this one man of Rome I have found more faith than in all the people of Israel."

"When you arrive home," said Jesus turning back to the officer, "the boy will be better. Your faith has made him well."

THE STORM

FULTON OURSLER

LATE ONE AFTERNOON Jesus and His group left the west side of the Lake of Galilee and sailed eastward for the desert shore, where there would be no crowds and they could all rest for a while. His resilient nature would always respond to small periods of rest. Now He was tired; soon after they shoved off He fell into a slumber peaceful and deep, as if no harm could possibly overtake Him.

But in those days, as now, the Lake of Galilee was one of the most treacherous of all earth's waters. One moment it ripples in wifely felicity and the next will foam itself into shrewish fury.

On this twilight voyage, while Jesus slept in the hinder part of the ship, His head on a lumpy old pillow, there came out of a sudden dark cloud above them a spit of forked lightning and a peal of thunder. The blow of a high wind rattled the small sails; waves splashed frothing over the bow, and water poured over the side rails.

"Master!" yelled the disciples. "We perish!"

Grabbing Jesus by the shoulders, they shook Him violently awake. As He blinked at them sleepily, the Master did what no ordinary sailor would ever do: He stood up in the rocking boat. More, He spread His hands and commanded the storm to cease, as if expecting immediate compliance—and got it. Instantly the wind fell off and the skies cleared and the little boat rode on over miraculously quieted waters.

But, He asked them, with a mournful shake of the head:

"Where is your faith? Why are you fearful?"

What could they answer? Where *was* their faith? Many times they had seen Him give movement to paralyzed legs; sight to blind eyes; health to the centurion's servant; life to the widow's son. But they had not seen enough to abolish fears for their own skins. Even now Thomas wondered: was not the vanishing storm perhaps just a coincidence?

THE CURE IN THE SYNAGOGUE

EMIL LUDWIG

WITH SWIFT STRIDES, he draws near the sick man, people making room as for a physician. He kneels down beside the invalid, grips him firmly, looks at him fixedly, shakes him, and exclaims: "Hold thy peace, and come out of him!" Thereupon the patient tosses from side to side, screams, rolls his eyes, and is again convulsed. Then, under stress of Jesus' compelling gaze, thrilled to the marrow by the urgency of an unprecedented command and by the awesomeness of the scene in this holy place, he surrenders to the new impressions. His limbs relax, his eyes close, his breathing grows calm. Soon he opens his eyes once more, and looks up quietly at the exorcist. He feels that the devil, in whose existence both of them believe with equal fervor, quits him even as has been ordered. He believes this because the stranger compels him to believe it. The storm has passed, and, assuaged though still rather weak, he rises to his feet—seemingly cured.

Hundreds have witnessed the miracle. The stranger is one of those magicians who can drive out devils, like the prophets of old. Reverently, the crowd divides to let him pass. But Jesus is weary. The joy of preaching, which had increased while he was speaking, the physician's fixity of purpose, which had demanded all his energy to sustain, have vanished; he flees from the multitude, shuns the streets, makes his way out of the town. Not till he has reached the shore of the lake does he sink to the ground, lying on the sand among the reeds, striving to regain his composure.

❧

THE BIRTH

GENE EDWARDS

The Virgin Birth precedes the earthly existence of Christ. The Resurrection and Ascension conclude it. Gene Edwards here argues for the utter necessity of the miracle of the Virgin Birth. The Virgin Birth and the Resurrection are the two grand miracles of Jesus becoming a person. Without the Resurrection and Ascension there is no way to get Jesus back into the presence of the Father. Without the miracle of the Virgin Birth there is no way to get him to earth in the first place.

EVERY SON AND daughter of Adam ever born has been born of the *seed* of man, the mutated chromosome of the male forever passing on to Adam's race the damning legacy of the Fall.

Yet long ago, in the first book of Moses, it had been foretold that once, and only once, a man-child would be born of the seed of a woman (Genesis 3:15). And it would be this son of a woman's seed who would destroy the enemy of God.

And so it came to pass that once, and only once, a man-child was born of the seed of woman.

And the woman's name was Mary.

While Mary slept, the Holy Spirit overshadowed this young maiden, and the seed of woman sprang into germination. And in this wondrous seed there was *none* of the sin-stained DNA of the descendants of the man Adam.

So from Mary's exotic seed there began to form a soul and body unscarred by the history of fallen man.

In that same mysterious moment, an even greater wonder emerged, for the *very DNA of God* joined with this unique seed. And so there joined in this one-cell embryo an unblemished body and soul from the visible realm. And from the invisible realm there was joined to this embryo a living spirit . . . even the very spirit and life of God.

The very essence of all that God is pulsated deep within that man-child embryo. Behold, the genetics of unfallen mankind growing together with the genetics of God.

Residing within these now multiplying cells was a truly *living* human spirit. Surely nothing like this had existed since Adam's spirit flickered out in the garden and Adam died to the spiritual realm.

And thus it came about that there was conceived, once, and only once, One who was wholly Son of Man and wholly Son of God.

Earth had never witnessed such a conception. Sinless man, with the very life of God the Father dwelling within. Heaven had never witnessed such a conception: almighty God . . . become visible in human form, in the physical realm.

What grew in Mary's womb was a being unlike any creature that had ever existed before. Would He remain unique, a glorious one-of-a-kind, or did He portend the beginning of a new species?

Whatever this One was, whatever He would become, His conception was quite simply the greatest single miracle of all time.

For in that hour, God became a man!

CANA

THOMAS MERTON

This first of Jesus' nature miracles may lack the importance and humanitarian impact of Christ's greater miracles of healing, but it does demonstrate that Jesus cares about every area of human need. There was not enough wine, the host was embarrassed, Jesus cared: this is one very primary meaning of the miracle.

"This beginning of miracles did Jesus in Cana of Galilee."

Once when our eyes were clean as noon, our rooms
Filled with the joys of Cana's feast:
For Jesus came, and His disciples, and His Mother,
And after them the singers
And some men with violins.

Once when our minds were Galilees,
And clean as skies our faces,
Our simple rooms were charmed with sun.
Our thoughts went in and out in whiter coats than God's disciples',
In Cana's crowded rooms, at Cana's tables.

Nor did we seem to fear the wine would fail:
For ready, in a row, to fill with water and a miracle,
We saw our earthen vessels, waiting empty.
What wine those humble waterjars foretell!

Wine for the ones who, bended to the dirty earth,
Have feared, since lovely Eden, the sun's fire,
Yet hardly mumbled, in their dusty mouths, one prayer.

Wine for old Adam, digging in the briars!

His Miracles

CHARLES DICKENS

THAT THERE MIGHT be some good men to go about with Him, teaching the people, Jesus Christ chose twelve poor men to be His companions. These twelve are called the Apostles or Disciples, and He chose them from among poor men, in order that the poor might know—always after that, in all years to come—that Heaven was made for them as well as for the rich, and that God makes no difference between those who wear good clothes and those who go barefoot and in rags. The most miserable, the most ugly, deformed, wretched creatures that live, will be bright Angels in Heaven if they are good here on earth. Never forget this, when you are grown up. Never be proud or unkind, my dears, to any poor man, woman, or child. If they are bad, think that they would have been better if they had had kind friends, and good homes, and had been better taught. So, always try to make them better by kind persuading words; and try to teach them and relieve them if you can. And when people speak ill of the poor and miserable, think how Jesus Christ went among them, and taught them, and thought them worthy of His care. And always pity them yourselves, and think as well of them as you can.

The names of the twelve Apostles were, Simon Peter, Andrew, James the son of Zebedee, John, Philip, Bartholomew, Thomas, Matthew, James the son of Alphaeus, Labbaeus, Simon, and Judas Iscariot. This man afterwards betrayed Jesus Christ, as you will hear bye and bye.

The first four of these were poor fishermen, who were sitting in their boats by the seaside, mending their nets, when Christ passed by. He stopped, and went into Simon Peter's boat, and asked him if he had caught many fish. Peter said No; though they had worked all night with their nets, they had caught nothing. Christ said, "Let down the net again." They did so; and it was immediately so full of fish, that it required the strength of many men (who came and helped them) to lift it out of the water, and even then it was very hard to do. This was another of the Miracles of Jesus Christ.

Jesus then said, "Come with me." And they followed Him directly. And from that time the twelve Disciples or Apostles were always with Him.

As great crowds of people followed Him, and wished to be taught, He went up into a mountain, and there preached to them, and gave them, from His own lips, the words of that prayer, beginning, "Our Father which art in Heaven," that you say every night. It is called the Lord's

Prayer, because it was first said by Jesus Christ, and because He commanded His Disciples to pray in those words.

When He was come down from the mountain, there came to Him a man with a dreadful disease called the leprosy. It was common in those times; and those who were ill with it were called lepers. This leper fell at the feet of Jesus Christ, and said, "Lord! If Thou wilt, Thou canst make me well!" Jesus, always full of compassion, stretched out His hand, and said, "I will! Be thou well!" And his disease went away, immediately, and he was cured.

Being followed, wherever He went, by great crowds of people, Jesus went with His Disciples into a house to rest. While He was sitting inside, some men brought upon a bed a man who was very ill of what he called the palsy, so that he trembled all over from head to foot, and could neither stand nor move. But the crowd being all about the doors and windows, and they not being able to get near Jesus Christ, these men climbed up to the roof of the house, which was a low one; and through the tiling at the top, let down the bed, with the sick man upon it, into the room where Jesus sat. When He saw him, Jesus, full of pity, said, "Arise! Take up thy bed, and go to thine own home!" And the man rose up and went away quite well, blessing Him, and thanking God.

There was a centurion too, or officer over the soldiers, who came to him and said, "Lord! My servant lies at home in my house, very ill." Jesus Christ made answer; "I will come and cure him." But the centurion said, "Lord! I am not worthy that Thou shouldst come to my house. Say the word only, and I know he will be cured." Then Jesus Christ, glad that the centurion believed in Him so truly, said, "Be it so!" And the servant became well, from that moment.

But of all the people who came to Him, none was so full of grief and distress, as one man who was a ruler or magistrate over many people, and he wrung his hands, and cried, and said, "O Lord, my daughter—my beautiful, good, innocent little girl, is dead. Oh come to her, come to her, and lay Thy blessed hand upon her, and I know she will revive, and come to life again, and make me and her mother happy. O Lord, we love her so, we love her so! And she is dead!"

Jesus Christ went out with him, and so did His Disciples, and went to his house, where the friends and neighbours were crying in the room where the poor dead little girl lay, and where there was soft music playing; as there used to be, in those days, when people died. Jesus Christ, looking on her sorrowfully, said—to comfort her poor parents—"She is not dead. She is asleep." Then He commanded the room to be cleared of the people that were in it, and going to the dead child, took her by the hand,

and she rose up, quite well, as if she had only been asleep. Oh what a sight it must have been to see her parents clasp her in their arms, and kiss her, and thank God and Jesus Christ, His Son, for such great mercy!

But He was always merciful and tender. And because He did such good, and taught people how to love God and how to hope to go to Heaven after death, he was called *Our Saviour.*

THE GIRL WHO DIED

WILLIAM GRIFFIN

"MY GIRL, MY daughter, she's only twelve years old, and she's dying!"

Jesus was standing by the lakeside with friends when the man ran up to him. His name was Jairus; he was one of the officials of the synagogue.

"Please come and save her. Touch her, and she will get better."

Jesus went with the man.

Halfway to Jairus's house people ran up to them with the bad news. "You're too late! Your daughter is dead. No one can help her now."

Jairus looked at Jesus. "Don't worry," said Jesus. "It's not too late. Trust me."

When the two of them arrived at the house the relatives and neighbors were already crying because the girl was dead.

"Why all the sad noise?" asked Jesus. "The child is not dead. She's only asleep."

Jesus then went into the room where the child lay, approached the bed, and took her hand.

He prayed for a while and then said to her, "Wake up, child."

She began to breathe again.

"It's time to get up."

She got up from the bed and walked slowly around the room.

Her mother and father were astonished.

"She must be hungry," Jesus said to her parents. "Give her something to eat."

As he was leaving, Jesus asked the family not to tell what happened to anyone else. But word got around.

MIRACLES

BILLY GRAHAM

THE GIFT OF performing miracles takes its key term, "miracles," from a Greek word meaning "powers" (2 Corinthians 12:12). A miracle is an event beyond the power of any known physical law to produce; it is a spiritual occurrence produced by the power of God, a marvel, a wonder. In most versions of the Old Testament the word "miracle" is usually translated "a wonder" or "a mighty work." Versions of the New Testament usually refer to miracles as "signs" (John 2:11) or "signs and wonders" (John 4:48; Acts 5:12; 15:12).

Clearly, the wonders performed by Jesus Christ and the apostles authenticated their claim of authority and gave certitude to their message. And we must remember that people did ask Jesus and the apostles this question, "How do we know that you are what you say you are, and that your words are true?" That was not an improper question. And at strategic moments God again and again manifested Himself to men by miracles so they had outward, confirming evidence that the words they heard from God's servants were true.

ᘓ

HEALING

FULTON OURSLER

JESUS AND HIS band of early disciples are met by a crowd near Nazareth. A wealthy nobleman strides forth.

"I have heard," he began without parley, "strange reports of you—a carpenter of Nazareth. There is a tale of a fountain of wine you caused to spring up at Cana. And another tale, which has gone before you, of how you read the mind of a disreputable woman at Jacob's well. Such reports have given me, a despairing man, hope. I need help. I come from Capernaum; my son is there—very ill. Please come down and heal my son, for he is at the point of death."

"Unless you see signs and wonders, you believe not," Jesus replied with a testing glance at the rich man.

"Lord, come down before my son dies," pleaded the father, breaking into sobs.

Jesus closed His eyes; this man's tears were real. Softly He spoke: "Go your way! Your son lives."

As the rich man looked up, there was no doubt, but only hope in his face. His eyes spoke his gratitude as without another word he turned and with outstretched arms flailed a path . . . through the crowd and ran down the open road. . . .

The next day, as the ruler was still making his way down the steep roads to Capernaum, he was met by servants coming up to greet him, and with news. His son lived!

"Praise God! At what hour did he get better?"

"Yesterday, at the seventh hour!" That, as the father knew, was the exact hour when the carpenter from Nazareth had told him: "Your son lives!"

∽

THE TOUCH OF FAITH

PETER MARSHALL

Peter Marshall may well be the most significant Presbyterian preacher of this century. During the 1940s he was pastor of the prestigious New York Avenue Presbyterian Church in Washington, D.C. During those years he was also chaplain of the U.S. Senate. This sermon was broadcast on radio, and his wife, who had been suffering from a long illness, heard the sermon, and as she listened to the description of this ancient miracle found strength to get out of bed and begin her road to full recovery.

"And his disciples said unto him, Thou seest the multitude thronging thee, and sayest thou, Who touched me?"
Mark 5:31

THAT IS AN electrifying question when you realize who asked it, and under what circumstances. You cannot escape the thrill of it—the tingle of excitement that grips you when you think of Christ stopping in response to the touch of a poor nameless woman.

The words of this question are not cold abstract inanimate dead words.

They do not form a hook on which one could hang theories or finely spun philosophies. No, they are too vital for that. They march into the vestibule of your heart and knock on the door.

They suggest all kinds of daring thoughts to your weak faith. They are like sparks falling into dry grass.

The setting of this text is a vivid picture—colorful, appealing, and of absorbing interest.

The incident takes place in a city street. It is a narrow twisted street packed with a crowd of gesticulating, excited people, surging past its bazaars and pavement stalls with all the noise and confusion of an eastern market place.

A murmur of conversation grows louder as the procession pushes its way through the narrow street. There is a sound like the chanting of some mysterious dirge that frequently rises to an excited crescendo. Here and there a voice rises distinctly out of the medley in what might have been a prayer; but it is lost in crackling laughter, rudely interrupted and drowned in the barking of dogs and the argument and discussion of a crowd that loves to talk.

They are caught up in the infection of curiosity, and walking along in their very midst, wedged in the tightly packed procession is Someone. . . .

It is His face that will hold your gaze—and will haunt you long after the sun has gone down, and the purple night, cool and starlit, has stilled every noise in the city, while only the Syrian stars wink unsleeping.

One is aware of that face even in such a crowd. Having once seen it, one sees it everywhere, for it is a haunting face—an expression that will not fade . . . eyes whose fires never die out . . . a face that lingers in memory. Farmers were to see it as they followed the swaying plow, and fishermen were to watch it dancing on the sun-flecked water.

This One who walks like a king is named Jesus. They called Him the Nazarene or the Galilean. He called Himself the Son of man.

The common people speak of Him softly, with deep affection, such as the shepherds know, who carry the little lambs in their bosoms.

The beggars whisper His name in the streets as they pass, and the children may be heard singing about Him. His name has been breathed in prayer and whispered at night under the stars. He is known to the diseased, the human flotsam and jetsam that shuffles in and out of the towns and drifts hopelessly along the dusty highways of human misery.

His fame has trickled down to the streets of forgotten men, has seeped into the shadowed refuges of the unremembered women. It is Jesus of Nazareth.

Any outcast could tell you of Him. There are women whose lives have been changed who could tell you of Him—but not without tears.

There are silent men—walking strangely as if unaccustomed to it—who speak of Him with lights in their eyes.

It is Jesus whom they are crowding to see. They want to look on His face to see the quality of His expression that seems to promise so much to the weary and the heaven-laden; that look that seems to offer healing of mind and soul and body; forgiveness of sin; another chance—a beginning again.

His look seemed to sing of tomorrow—a new tomorrow—in which there should be no more pain, no more suffering, nor persecution, nor cruelty, nor hunger, nor neglect, nor disillusionments, nor broken promises, nor death.

At the request of one Jairus, a ruler of the synagogue, He is on His way to restore to complete health a little girl.

He is on a mission of restoration, and the crowd is following him in order to see Him perform this miracle.

Speculation is rife. Opinion is divided. There is argument and excited discussion.

Some are declaring that He can do it; others are doubtful. Some frankly say the attempt is bound to fail.

However, their curiosity is aroused, and it promises to be an interesting experiment.

There is in the crowd another face—the face of a woman. Strange that it should be so noticeable—yet not strange, for it is a face that portrays great depth of human emotion.

There is so much in it—pale, pinched, and wan. Great lines of suffering mar its beauty and sweetness, and even now her lips are drawn in a thin line of agony. The face is streaked with pain. Her body is racked with acute suffering.

Who is she? Well, some say her name is Martha and some say Veronica. Tradition gives her various names, but I cannot tell who she was.

It does not matter. Is it not enough that she was a woman in pain? Call her Martha . . . or Mary . . . or Margaret . . . or mother . . . or sister . . . or wife.

She is typical of countless cases of endless pain and suffering. For twelve years she had suffered and twelve years is a long time!

Her malady seems to have been a pernicious hemorrhage or a form of bleeding cancer.

She had gone to many physicians and was none better—but rather worse.

She had spent all that she had, and every new day was another hopeless dawn. Every sunset was stained with the blood of her pain.

She is typical of human despair—not only physical despair but spiritual despair as well. For her the world could offer no healing—so she represents all the people who look everywhere for peace of mind and heart—for hope and comfort—and find none. She represents them all—whatever their wants, their fears, their hopes, their pains.

For her apparently, there was no relief, no human aid. Hers was a hopeless case—incurable!

After twelve years of treatment—she was no better. What would *we* do?

We would probably send her to some home for the incurables, and visiting clergymen would be embarrassed to know what to say to her.

Now, this woman had heard of the Great Teacher, of His wonderful works. She had heard the lepers talk and them that had been blind from birth and now had thrown away their sticks, and looked around them with eyes that flashed or filled with tears as they spoke His name.

She had heard what He had done for others. Surely He had power to bring into the haven of health the lost explorers of the vast treasuries of pain!

Surely, He had power to lift from the dust of disease the flowers whose stems had been crushed or withered in the mildews of human misery!

As this thought burned itself into her mind her faith was curiously stirred as it wrestled in the birth-throes of a great resolve.

It was daring—fantastic, perhaps. Her heart thumped, but it was worth trying. It could only fail and she was no stranger to failure.

There came to the woman the assurance that if she could but touch Him—even only the hem of His garment—she would be healed of her awful malady.

Cannot you imagine her nervous reasoning?

"Touch Him . . . yes . . . just to touch Him—there would be no harm in that!

"I do not think He will harm me . . . They say He is so kind and gentle, so full of sympathy.

"Besides, here is my great chance. He is coming this way, soon He will be gone. Why not touch Him as He passes?

"On the head!—no, that would be irreverent! I would not dare! Well, on the hand!—no, that would be too familiar! But there cannot be any harm in touching His robes as He passes. It would be enough—just to touch the border of His robes. I *must* touch Him. I *must* get some of that power."

Thus reasoning, she pushes her way through the crowd and with the pertinacity of despair she struggles in that dense throng nearer and nearer, pushing and crushing. People get in the way—not knowing her need.

Now she is desperate. He must not pass so near and yet so far away. Was she to lose this opportunity? *She* must touch Him.

Now just a little farther. He is drawing nearer. Now she can almost reach Him—another moment—at last just as He passes, she is able to reach out her hand, and with the tip of her finger touch His robe.

It was enough! She had actually touched the Great Doctor!

With a trembling finger she had touched Him with the touch of a mighty faith! Like an electric shock there surged back into the shrunken veins, the panting lungs, the withered muscles, and the bloodless flesh the rich glow of health and vitality. Once again a body had been redeemed and given life.

She had touched Him with secret and trembling haste and thrilled with the change that had come to her, she retreated back into the crowd unnoticed, she thought.

No one had noticed her—no one—but Christ!

Recognizing the one magnetic touch of faith amid the pressure of the crowd, He stopped and asked that *terrific* question: "Who *touched* me?"

The question seemed absurd to those who heard it.

Impatiently, brusquely, almost with sarcasm, the disciples asked: "How should we know? There are hundreds of people here—pushing all about you. Look at the crowd—and yet you ask 'Who touched me?' "

But, looking around Him, Christ stood still—His kind, but searching, glance fell at last on the face of the woman who had done it.

His gaze held hers. Something passed between them, and she told Him her story while His eyes were fixed upon her; His eyes gave her confidence. They seemed to promise all that she desired. Her fear disappeared.

Then He answered her: not in scorn at her action, not in resentment, not in anger at her presumption, not in ridicule at her faith, not in indignation at her audacity, but in the sympathetic tones of understanding love.

"Daughter, thy faith hath made thee whole. Go in peace . . . and be healed of thy plague."

That is the record. These are the facts. *It is a matter of history.*

She had no money—only faith. She did not meet Him in a house of worship. She met Him on the street. She had no private audience with the Lord. She touched Him in a crowd.

She touched Him in faith—in desperate believing faith and He stopped!

The touch of one anonymous woman in a crowd halted the Lord of glory. *That is the glorious truth of this incident. She touched Him. So can we.*

Let us take it into our apathetic hearts, let its glorious significance thrill our jaded souls.

The human touch has the power to arrest God. Yes, to stop Him, to halt Him, to make Him aware of your problems, your pain, your petition.

Oh, you say, "that's impossible. God is not interested in me. What does He care what happens to me—one tiny individual in all this creation? Who am I—or what am I that God should take special notice of me?" Well, there is the record. There you have it in black and white that, stopped by the touch of a sick woman, He turned about—He who conquered death, He who defeated Satan, He whom all the legions of hell cannot stop, He who is King of kings. He stopped just because a sick and nameless woman touched the hem of His garment.

We need to touch Him—O how much we need to touch Him!

Most of us are thronging Him—just like the crowd . . . It is easy to throng the Lord and never touch Him. A great many people in the churches, and perhaps a great many outside the churches, are thronging Jesus, seeking Him, coming close to Him, but never actually touching Him.

In this matter of eternal importance, coming close is not enough. It is like missing a train . . . You may miss it by one minute—and that's pretty close—but you have lost the train . . . It is gone, and you are left behind.

Thronging saves nobody. Coming near to Jesus will not bring healing. We have to touch Him for ourselves.

One can feel close in the crowd without touching the Lord. And that is exactly the trouble with most of us. We are following the crowd, thronging the Lord, but not many of us are actually in touch with the Master.

And because we are not in touch, there is no vitality in our spiritual life. There is no thrill in our prayers, no tingle of contact with the infinite resources, no flush of reality about our religion.

Because we are out of touch with the Lord, we are lost in the crowd, have become separated from the Master.

We preach the Immanence of God. Our creeds set forth our belief that the Lord is with us, near us in this very place. The Old Book records for us some amazing promises, some startling assurances if we would only believe them.

He promised that we should have power, *power*—to do amazing things; *grace*—to do unnatural things, such as to harbor no grudges and to forgive those who hurt us, to love even those who treat us unjustly or unkindly, to pray for those who give us pain and grieve us, to confess our own private and secret sins, to try to make right situations that have been wrong, even if it means humbling ourselves, swallowing our pride, and risking a snub or a slight. We can have grace to do these things, and we know perfectly well that it takes a lot of grace to do them!

He Who made these promises is here with us now.

But you may ask: "How can I touch Christ?" It was one thing for that woman long ago, for she saw Him with her eyes, and could touch Him with her fingers. She heard His voice, saw the sunlight dance on His hair.

He was in the flesh then, and she could touch Him.

How can I, today, touch Him with the same results?

Some of you may seek healing of body or mind or of soul. Some of you may seek guidance on some problem. Some of you need faith to stand up under the tensions and suspenses of life. Some of you seek forgiveness and a new beginning.

All of us need to touch Christ for some reason or other.

As the Church offers this wonderful new life—this peace of mind and heart—this healing of mind and soul and body in Christ's name— perhaps she ought more and more to give instructions with her soul medicine.

You are justified in looking for directions on the lid or some instructions for taking, a manual of operation.

Perhaps I can make some suggestions which will be helpful.

First, give God a chance. Take your problem, whatever it may be, to Him in prayer. Tell Him all about it—just as if He didn't know a thing. In the telling be absolutely honest and sincere. Hold nothing back.

Our minds are sometimes shocked when we permit our hearts to spill over, but it is good for our souls when we do.

If we would only have the courage to take a good look at our motives for doing certain things we might discover something about ourselves that would melt away our pride and soften our hearts so that God could do something with us and for us.

Then the second step is to believe that God will hear you. Remember that He heard the poor woman who only touched the hem of His garment. Believe with all your faith that He cares what happens to you. You must believe that. You can't doubt it when you look at the cross.

Next, you must be willing to wait patiently for the Lord. He does not answer every prayer on Sunday afternoon. You may have to wait until Friday. But wait. God is never in a hurry.

Then when He speaks to you—as He will—do what He tells you.

He may not tell you audibly. You may not hear your voices—as did Joan of Arc. You may not see any writing in the sky and have any unusual experience. God *could,* if He wanted, send you messages in that way, but that is not His usual method.

It generally comes through your own conscience—a sort of growing conviction that such and such a course of action is the one He wants you to take. Or it may be given you in the advice of friends of sound judgment —those who love you most.

God speaks sometimes through our circumstances and guides us, closing doors as well as opening them.

He will let you know what you must do, and what you must be. He is waiting for you to touch Him. The hand of faith is enough. Your trembling fingers can reach Him as He passes. Reach out your faith— touch Him. He will not ask, "who touched me?" He will know.

❧

BARTIMEUS

HENRY WADSWORTH LONGFELLOW

This miracle, recorded in Mark 10:46–52, comes close in time with the raising of Lazarus. Both of these highly publicized miracles would have fueled the grudges of Jesus' enemies, who desperately resented his growing popularity. Those grudges would have precipitated the scheming that produced the crucifixion some six weeks later.

> Blind Bartimeus at the gates
> Of Jericho in darkness waits;
> He hears the crowd—he hears a breath
> Say, "It is Christ of Nazareth!"
> And calls in tones of agony,
> "Jesus, have mercy now on me!"
>
> The thronging multitudes increase;
> Blind Bartimeus, hold thy peace!
> But still, above the noisy crowd,
> The beggar's cry is shrill and loud;
> Until they say, "He calleth thee!"
> "Fear not, arise, He calleth thee!"

Then saith the Christ, as silent stands
The crowd, "What wilt thou at My hands?"
And he replies, "O give me light!
Rabbi, restore the blind man's sight."
And Jesus answers,
                        "Go in peace
Thy faith from blindness gives release!"

Ye that have eyes yet cannot see,
In darkness and in misery,
Recall those mighty Voices Three,
"Jesus, have mercy now on me!
Fear not, arise, and go in peace!
Thy faith from blindness gives release!"

                          ∽

LIGHT SNOW

WILLIAM GRIFFIN

"FEAST YOUR EYES on that!"

Peter, James, and John had climbed a mountain with Jesus. When they reached the top, they began to pray with their arms outstretched. After a few minutes, Peter looked toward Jesus.

"Look at that! He's filling up with light!"

The three of them saw Jesus growing white with light so bright they had to cover their eyes.

When they peeked through their fingers, they saw him talking with two other people who also were filled to overflowing with light.

"One of them is saying something about the law," said John.

"I can't get every word the other one is saying," said James, "but it's something about the prophets."

"Lord," said Peter stepping forward. "It's a good thing you brought us along today. We can get some branches and build a shelter for you and your friends."

Light changed to cloud. A voice boomed out. The men fell to the ground.

"This is my beloved son," they heard the voice say. "Whatever he does gives me great pleasure. Listen to him."

The men began to shiver and shake.

"Don't be afraid, my friends." The three looked up. The cloud was gone. The two light persons were gone. "It's only me," said Jesus gently.

"Who was the person talking about the law?" asked Peter as they began the long walk down the mountainside.

"That was Moses," said Jesus.

"Who was the other person?" asked James, "the one who said something about the prophets?"

"Micah," said Peter. "No, it was Isaiah. Wait a minute. It had to be Jeremiah."

"It was Elijah," said Jesus.

"That's just what I was going to say," said Peter.

"Can I run ahead to tell the others?" asked John.

"No," said Jesus.

"Why not?"

"Because I want to keep it a secret," said Jesus.

"Keeping secrets is hard," said John.

"When I rise from the dead," said Jesus, "then you can tell the story."

Peter, James, and John looked at each other. They each had the same question.

"Are you going to rise from the dead?"

VI

JESUS:

❧

HIS TEACHINGS

THE teachings of Christianity are substantial, but the teachings alone cannot be considered the basis of the Christian faith. Christ's teachings, like those of the Old Testament, came packaged in stories of his miracles. His teachings and miracles are so Siamese that the philosophical surgery that might separate them would kill them both.

The Old Testament (Hebrew) word *dabar* is the term for *word*. The power of *dabar* lies in its seeing the speech of God as action rather than talk. When God speaks, his words are never abstractions, only to be heard or defined or fit into an ongoing conversation with mortals. God's *word* is, rather, an event, a happening. The moment God says anything, the event it evokes is already in the process of happening.

Jesus' teaching was sometimes a code of ethics, but never merely a series of rules governing human behavior. His teachings centered on the nature of his true reality. True reality to Christ was what was everlasting.

In remembering that his name means *Jehovah saves,* it is not difficult to see that his teaching had to do with humanity's desperation. He taught that people were prisoners of their own tendencies to do wrong. If anyone refuses to deal with these inclinations, such a one would be forever condemned by those wrongs.

So it was not the nature of Jesus' teachings merely to instruct us about behavior. His teaching intended to deal with desperation, not to provide subjects of philosophical discussion.

The religion that grew from the thought of Jesus was early

referred to as "the Way," not "the Code." These accumulative teachings were given to provide an enduring relationship with God. *The Way* indeed was the early name of Christianity (Acts 9:2). Still, the precepts that comprise his teachings were seen to be words that held in themselves a kind of power. His words were not an *abracadabra* of magic formulas. They held power as the Hebrews' *dabar* also did.

The words held power to save, to heal, and to give hope. They were always to be delivered with respect and authority. In Jesus' day, the remarkable quality of any teacher's tenets were to be delivered with due respect to their spiritual force. In fact, Jesus' listeners marveled at his words in the Sermon on the Mount. They commented that unlike the weak religious leaders of his day, Jesus taught in a very forceful manner (Matthew 7:29).

At the center of his teachings was the Kingdom of God. Under the oppression of the Roman Empire, Jesus championed a utopian kingdom where morality would reign. In this monarchy of the Messiah, the dispossessed would have an eternal inheritance, and racial oppression would end. Peace would characterize both his kingdom and his glorious, eternal reign.

> They sent their disciples, with a few of Herod's followers mixed in, to ask, "Teacher, we know you have integrity, teach the way of God accurately, are indifferent to popular opinion, and don't pander to your students."
>
> Matthew 22:16

> He taught by using stories, many stories.
>
> Mark 4:2

> All Jesus did that day was tell stories—a long storytelling afternoon. His storytelling fulfilled the prophecy:
> "I will open my mouth and tell stories;
> I will bring out into the open things hidden since the world's
>   first day."
>
> Matthew 13:34–35, *The Message*

THE GRACE THAT IS COSTLY AND YET IS FREE

DIETRICH BONHOEFFER

Dietrich Bonhoeffer was executed by officials in the Third Reich for his complicity in the attempted assassination of Adolf Hitler. He paid dearly for his faith in Christ, and referred to those who wanted to be Christians without any real cost as pursuers of cheap grace. Bonhoeffer believed that when Jesus said, "Take up your cross and follow me" (Luke 9:23), he was really saying, "Come with me and die!" Any attempt to follow Christ on the basis of partial commitment is trying to buy heaven with only casual discipleship.

CHEAP GRACE IS the preaching of forgiveness without requiring repentance, baptism without church discipline, Communion without confession, absolution without personal confession. Cheap grace is grace without discipleship, grace without the cross, grace without Jesus Christ, living and incarnate.

Costly grace is the treasure hidden in the field; for the sake of it a man will gladly go and sell all that he has. It is the pearl of great price to buy which the merchant will sell all his goods. It is the kingly rule of Christ, for whose sake a man will pluck out the eye which causes him to stumble, it is the call of Jesus Christ at which the disciple leaves his nets and follows him.

Costly grace is the gospel which must be *sought* again and again, the gift which must be *asked* for, the door at which a man must *knock*.

Such grace is *costly* because it calls us to follow, and it is *grace* because it calls us to follow *Jesus Christ*. It is costly because it costs a man his life, and it is grace because it gives a man the only true life. It is costly because it condemns sin, and grace because it justifies the sinner. Above all, it is *costly* because it cost God the life of his Son: "ye were bought at a price," and what has cost God much cannot be cheap for us. Above all it is *grace* because God did not reckon his Son too dear a price to pay for our life, but delivered him up for us. Costly grace is the Incarnation of God.

Costly grace is the sanctuary of God; it has to be protected from the world, and not thrown to the dogs. It is therefore the living word, the Word of God, which he speaks as it pleases him. Costly grace confronts us as a gracious call to follow Jesus, it comes as a word of forgiveness to the broken spirit and the contrite heart. Grace is costly because it compels a man to submit to the yoke of Christ and follow him; it is grace because Jesus says: "My yoke is easy and my burden is light."

On two separate occasions Peter received the call, "Follow me." It was the first and last word Jesus spoke to his disciple (Mark 1.17; John 21.22). A whole life lies between these two calls. The first occasion was by the lake of Gennesareth, when Peter left his nets and his craft and followed Jesus at his word. The second occasion is when the Risen Lord finds him back again at his old trade. Once again it is by the lake of Gennesareth, and once again the call is: "Follow me." Between the two calls lay a whole life of discipleship in the following of Christ. Half-way between them comes Peter's confession, when he acknowledged Jesus as the Christ of God. Three times Peter hears the same proclamation that Christ is his Lord and God—at the beginning, at the end, and at Caesarea Philippi. Each time it is the same grace of Christ which calls to him "Follow me" and which reveals itself to him in his confession of the Son of God. Three times on Peter's way did grace arrest him, the one grace proclaimed in three different ways.

This grace was certainly not self-bestowed. It was the grace of Christ himself, now prevailing upon the disciple to leave all and follow him, now working in him that confession which to the world must sound like the ultimate blasphemy, now inviting Peter to the supreme fellowship of martyrdom for the Lord he had denied, and thereby forgiving him all his sins. In the life of Peter grace and discipleship are inseparable. He had received the grace which costs.

∿

The Laborers in the Vineyard

ROBERT FARRAR CAPON

SINCE YOU HAVE all read the assignment . . . (much eye-rolling, some guilty looks) . . . I shall tell you the story anyway.

There was a man who owned a vineyard. His operation was not on the scale of E & J Gallo, but it was quite respectable: let us put him in the Robert Mondavi class. We first see this gentleman on the evening of the second Sunday in October. September has been a perfect month—hot and dry, bringing the grapes to 20° brix—but his meteorological service tells him that the weather is about to turn into cold soup. So what does our friend Robert do? He gets up first thing Monday morning, goes down to what passes for the local hiring hall and contracts for as much day labor as he can pick up. Unfortunately, every other grower in the neighborhood uses the same weather reports, so he has to promise higher pay to attract the workers he needs: $120 for the day is the figure that finally guarantees him a crew.

I see a hand up. Yes, Virginia?

No, Virginia, $120 is not a ridiculous figure. A *denarius* was a day's pay; I have simply taken the liberty of making it a good day's pay. A penny a day may have been alright for the translators of the KJV, but this is 1989.

Anyway, Robert loads his crew into a couple of old school buses and puts them to work, chop-chop. Just before nine A.M., though, he gets another weather bulletin. They have moved the start of the three weeks of rain from Wednesday back to Tuesday: he has one day, not two, to get the harvest in. Out he goes at nine, therefore—and with increasing panic at noon and at three—to hire on still more hands. Each time he succeeds in rounding up all the available help, giving them the by now practiced line that he is Robert Mondavi, the famous payer of top dollar who is also Mr. Fairness himself: whatever is right, they will get.

It's a huge harvest, though, and with only one hour left before dark, Robert realizes he won't get it in on time without still more help. So out he goes again, but the hiring hall is closed by now and the village square has only its usual crowd of up-to-the-minute losers hanging out in a haze of smoke. You know the types: lots of leather, some girls (and their boyfriends) with more mousse than brains, six-packs everywhere, and music that ruptures eardrums. What the hell, Robert thinks in desperation: it's worth at least a try. So he walks up to the group, ostentatiously switches off the offending ghetto-blaster, and goes into his spiel: he's Robert Mondavi; he's famous and he's fair; they could probably use a buck; so what do they think? What they think, of course, is also What the hell: whatever he wants them to do, it won't take long; and whatever he pays, at least it's a couple more six-packs for the night. Off they go.

Now then: run your mind over the story so far. I'm sure you know exactly what happens each time one of those new batches of workers gets dropped off at the vineyard. Before they pick even a single grape, they make sure they find out from the workers already on the job the exact per diem amount on which Robert Mondavi is basing his chances at the Guinness Book of World Records. And since they are—like the rest of the human race—inveterate bookkeepers, they take the $120 figure, divide it by twelve and multiply it by the number of hours they'll be working. Then and only then do they lay hand to grape, secure in the knowledge that they will be getting, respectively, $100, $70, $40, and $10.

Robert, however, has a surprise for them. At the end of the day, he is a happy man. With his best and biggest harvest on its way to the stemmer-crusher, he feels expansive—and a little frisky. So he says to his foreman, "I have a wild idea. I'm going to fill the pay envelopes myself; but when you give them out, I want you to do it backwards, beginning with the last ones hired."

Once again, I'm sure, you know what happens. When the first girl with purple hair gets her envelope and walks away opening it, she finds six crisp, new twenties inside. What does she do?

No, Virginia, put your hand down. She does *not* go back and report the overage; she just keeps on walking—fast.

But when her shirt-open-to-the-waist boyfriends catch up with her and tell her they got $120, too . . . well, dear old human nature triumphs again: they cannot resist going back and telling everybody else what jerks they were for sweating a whole day in the hot sun when they could have made the same money for just an hour's work.

The entail of Adam's transgression being what it is, however, the workers who were on the job longer come up with yet another example of totally unoriginal sin. On hearing that Robert Mondavi is now famous for paying $120 *an hour,* they put their mental bookkeeping machinery into reverse and floor the pedal. And what do they then come up with? O frabjous joy! They conclude that they are now about to become the proud possessors of, in order, $480, or $840, or even—bless you, Robert Mondavi—$1,440.

But Robert, like God, is only crazy, not stupid. Like God, he has arranged for their recompense to be based only on the weird goodness he is most famous for, not on the just deserts they have infamously imagined for themselves: every last envelope, they find, has six (6) twenties in it; no more for those who worked all day, and no less for those who didn't.

Which, of course, goes down like Gatorade for the last bunch hired, like dishwater for the next-to-the-last, like vinegar for the almost-first, and like hot sulfuric acid for the first-of-all. Predictably, therefore—on the lamebrained principle that those who are most outraged should argue the case for those who are less so (wisdom would have whispered to them, "Reply in anger and you'll make the best speech you'll ever regret")— the sweatiest and the most exhausted decide to give Robert a hard time. "Hey, man," they say; "you call this a claim to fame? Those punks over there only worked one hour and we knocked ourselves out all day. How come you made them equal to us?"

Robert, however, has his speech in his pocket. "Look, Pal," he says. (Incidentally, the Greek word in the parable is *hetaíre,* which is a distinctly unfriendly word for "friend." In three of its four uses in the New Testament—here, and to the man without the wedding garment in the King's

Son's Wedding, and to Judas at the betrayal—it comes off sounding approximately like "Buster.") "Look, Pal," he tells the spokesman for all the bookkeepers who have gagged on this parable for two thousand years, "Don't give me *agita*. You agreed to $120 a day, I gave you $120 a day. Take it and get out of here before I call the cops. If I want to give some pot-head in Gucci loafers the same pay as you, so what? You're telling me I can't do what I want with my own money? I'm supposed to be a stinker because you got your nose out of joint? All I did was have a fun idea. I decided to put the last first and the first last to show you there are no insiders or outsiders here: when I'm happy, everybody's happy, no matter what they did or didn't do. I'm not asking you to like me, Buster; I'm telling you to enjoy me. If you want to mope, that's your business. But since the only thing it'll get you is a lousy disposition, why don't you just shut up and go into the tasting room and have yourself a free glass of Chardonnay? The choice is up to you, Friend: drink up, or get out; compliments of the house, or go to hell. Take your pick."

∾

LET CHRIST TAKE THE SIN OUT OF YOUR LIFE

BILLY SUNDAY

Billy Sunday was one of the colorful evangelists in the early decades of the twentieth century. His sermons against booze became central in his effort to enforce prohibition in Chicago. But the simple people of America appreciated his singular devotion to Christ. He preached colorful if simple sermons on the teachings of Jesus.

LET US TALK with Jesus a minute. "Jesus, how many disciples have you?" "I had twelve. I have but eleven now." "Where is the missing one?" "He has gone to betray Me." "And yet with eleven left you are praying all alone?" Just like many a minister with hundreds of members, and bearing the burden all alone.

Judas bought a ticket for hell for thirty pieces of silver, and it wasn't a round-trip ticket either. Let us go talk with the eight:

"Where is Jesus?" "We don't know." "Where are Peter, James and John?" "Don't know; haven't seen them." "Where is Judas?" "Why, he just went past not long ago, with the scribes and Pharisees and a great company." "Where was he going?" "Why, he was looking for Jesus, to betray Him." "Why do you think that?" "Because tonight at the feast Jesus said, 'One of you shall betray Me, and it is he to whom I give the sop,' and after dipping it in the dish He handed it to Judas." "Didn't you try to stop him in his dastardly work of betrayal?" "No." "Well, don't you suppose Judas thought he would find Jesus here with you men?"

No, he never suspected that Jesus was near that bunch. Judas knew that crowd. He knew that first group out near the edge of the garden through and through. Why do I think so? I will tell you. Jesus had gone up on the mount of transfiguration, taking with him Peter, James and John, members of the second group, and while He was away a father whose boy was possessed with a devil came to the disciples who composed the first group, out near the edge of the garden, and besought them to cast the devil out of his boy.

Jesus had given His disciples power against unclean spirits, to drive them out, but instead of doing the work He gave them to do, they spent the time chewing the rag about who would be greatest in the kingdom.

I wonder if there is a father in this world who never had trouble with his boy. This father was weighted down with trouble all caused by the devil. The devil is the cause of every saloon, every drunkard, every murder, every theft, every lie, every heartache, every house of shame. All of the deception, envy, malice, filthy communications that come out of your mouth are prompted by the devil, and yet some people think I am throwing stones at them when I preach against the devil.

Some say, "Well, the devil pays, so let him stay. We need the license from the saloons to pave our streets and light our city." Yes, and you need your saloons in order to keep your jails, penitentiaries, poorhouses and insane asylums filled. Every saloon gives the devil that much better chance to get your boy.

If you want the world to be better after a while, keep the devil out of the boys and girls. If you want to drive the devil out of the world, hit him with a cradle, not a crutch.

When Jesus returned from the mount the sorrowing father ran to Him with his boy, crying, "If Thou canst do anything, have compassion on us, and help us. I brought my son to Thy disciples, and they could not cast the devil out!"

That "if" implies a doubt. Failure on the part of those disciples to keep in touch with Jesus, so they could have power to cast out devils, led the poor old father to doubt the power of Jesus. The divine philosophy, as demonstrated by thousands of church members, breeds more infidels than all the Paines, Parkers and Ingersolls combined.

As a principle increases in its meaning, it decreases in the number that should adhere to that principle. Suppose by education I mean every one who can read and write; then there are about eighty-five millions of educated people in the United States. But, suppose that by education I mean every one who has graduated from high school; about one-fifth of the population would be classified as educated. On the other hand, if by education I mean every one who has graduated from a university or a college; one-half of one per cent would come under that heading.

Suppose by your friends you mean all who shake your hand, smile and say, "How are you? I am glad to see you." You have scores of friends of that sort; but suppose by friends you mean all who will stand by you through thick and thin, and defend you when they hear your name defamed, I fear they are lamentably few. Suppose by a Christian I mean every one who has his name on a church record; there are about twenty-six million in the United States, about equally divided between the Catholics and Protestants. On the other hand, suppose I mean every man and woman who is willing to do God's will; I question whether there are ten million that would die for Jesus.

I said to a minister one time, "How many members have you?" He said, "Eight hundred and seventy-two; but there are two hundred and seventy-eight I do not count." I asked: "Out of the number you do count, how many are helping in the meetings: singing in the choir, ushering or doing personal work?" Tears flowed down his cheeks as he said, "The largest number I have been able to muster any one night was twenty-eight, and if my life depended on my making the number fifty, I would die!"

There we were wearing out our lives, trying to bring that God-forsaken, whisky-soaked, gambling-cursed, harlot-blighted town to her knees, and the church calmly looking on. I sometimes doubt whether the church needs new members one-half as much as she needs the old bunch made over. Judging by the way multitudes in the church live, you would think they imagined they had a through ticket to heaven in a Pullman palace car, and had left orders for the porter to wake them up when they head into the yards of the New Jerusalem. If that's the case you will be doomed to disappointment, for you will be side-tracked with a hot box.

If I had a hundred tongues, and every tongue speaking a different language, in a different key at the same time, I could not do justice to the splendid chaos that the world-loving, dancing, card-playing, whisky-guzzling, gin-fizzling, wine-sizzling, novel-reading crowd in the church brings to the cause of Christ.

THE BEATITUDES THAT ARE

J. B. PHILLIPS

The Beatitudes of scripture are some of the most famous of Jesus' words. Here J. B. Phillips suggests a parody on those beatitudes and seems to speak of the way things are rather than the way Christ would have them be.

MOST PEOPLE THINK:

Happy are the pushers: for they get on in the world.
Happy are the hard-boiled: for they never let life hurt them.
Happy are they who complain: for they get their own way in the end.
Happy are the blasé: for they never worry over their sins.
Happy are the slave-drivers: for they get results.
Happy are the knowledgeable men of the world: for they know their way around.
Happy are the trouble-makers: for people have to take notice of them.

Jesus Christ said:

Happy are those who realize their spiritual poverty: they have already entered the kingdom of Reality.
Happy are they who bear their share of the world's pain: in the long run they will know more happiness than those who avoid it.
Happy are those who accept life and their own limitations: they will find more in life than anybody.
Happy are those who long to be truly "good": they will fully realize their ambition.
Happy are those who are ready to make allowances and to forgive: they will know the love of God.
Happy are those who are real in their thoughts and feelings: in the end they will see the ultimate Reality, God.
Happy are those who help others to live together: they will be known to be doing God's work.

THE MARTYR WATCHERS

DR. DAVID YONGGI CHO

When we consider the martyrs who have given their lives for Jesus we tend to visualize flaming stakes and medieval times. The actual truth is that more martyrs have been slain in the twentieth century than in any other era. Dr. Cho is pastor of the largest church in the world. It is in Seoul, Korea. Many of the members of his church have suffered through very hard times and have witnessed many martyrdoms. This is one account.

THE COMMUNISTS WERE vicious to the ministers. One minister's family was captured in Inchon, Korea, and the Communist leaders put them on what they called a "People's Trial." The accusers would say, "One man is guilty of causing this kind of sin, and for that kind of sin it is proper that he be punished."

The only response then given would be a chorus of voices agreeing, "Yah, Yah!"

This time they dug a large hole, putting the pastor, his wife, and several of his children in. The leader then spoke, "Mister, all these years you misled the people with the superstition of the Bible. Now if you will publicly disclaim it before these people, and repent of this misdemeanor, then you, your wife, and your children will be freed. But if you persist in your superstitions, all of your family is going to be buried alive. Make a decision!"

All of his children then blurted, "Oh Daddy! Daddy! Think of us! Daddy!"

Think of it. If you were in his place, what would you do? I am the father of three children, and would almost feel like going to hell rather than see my children killed.

This father was shaken. He lifted up his hand and said, "Yes, yes, I'll do it. I am going to denounce . . . my . . ."

But before he could finish his sentence his wife nudged him, saying, "Daddy! Say NO!"

"Hush children," she said. "Tonight we are going to have supper with the King of kings, the Lord of lords!"

She led them in singing "In the Sweet By and By," her husband and children following, while the Communists began to bury them. Soon the children were buried, but until the soil came up to their necks they sang, and all the people watched. God did not deliver them, but almost all of those people who watched this execution became Christians, many now members of my church.

Through their suffering the grace of redemption flowed. God gave His only begotten Son to be crucified on the cross so that this world could be saved and redeemed. That is God's uppermost goal—the redemption of souls. So when you desire divine healing, or an answer from above, always focus through the lenses of the uppermost goal, the redeeming of souls. If you see that your suffering brings about more redemption than your healing, then do not ask for deliverance, but ask God to give you strength to persevere.

∾

THIS THING IS FROM ME
1 Kings 12:24

LAURA A. BARTER SNOW

MY CHILD, I have a message for you today; let Me whisper it in your ear, that it may gild with glory any storm clouds that may arise, and smooth the rough places upon which you may have to tread. It is short, only five words, but let them sink into your inmost soul; use them as a pillow upon which to rest your weary head: *"This thing is from me."*

Have you ever thought of it, that all that concerns you concerns Me too? For, "He that toucheth you toucheth the apple of mine eye" (Zech. 2:8). "You are very precious in my sight" (Isa. 43:4). Therefore, it is My special delight to educate you.

I would have you learn when temptations assail you, and the "enemy comes in like a flood," that this thing is from Me, that your weakness needs My might, and your safety lies in letting Me fight for you.

Are you in difficult circumstances, surrounded by people who do not understand you, who never consult your taste, who put you in the background? This thing is from Me. I am the God of circumstances. Thou camest not to thy place by accident, it is the very place God meant for thee.

Have you not asked to be made humble? See then, I have placed you in the very school where the lesson is taught; your surroundings and companions are only working out My will.

Are you in money difficulties? Is it hard to make both ends meet? This thing is from Me, for I am your purse-bearer and would have you draw from and depend upon Me. My supplies are limitless (Phil. 4:19). I would have you prove My promises. Let it not be said of you, "In this thing you did not believe the Lord your God" (Deut. 1:32).

Are you passing through a night of sorrow? This thing is from Me. I am the "Man of sorrows and acquainted with grief." I have let earthly comforters fail you, that by turning to Me you may obtain everlasting consolation (2 Thess. 2:16–17). Have you longed to do some great work for Me and instead been laid aside on a bed of pain and weakness? This thing is from Me. I could not get your attention in your busy days and I want to teach you some of My deepest lessons. "They also serve who only stand and wait." Some of My greatest workers are those shut out from active service, that they may learn to wield the weapon of all prayer.

This day I place in your hand this pot of holy oil. Make use of it freely, my child. Let every circumstance that arises, every word that pains you, every interruption that would make you impatient, every revelation of your weakness be anointed with it. The sting will go as you learn to see *Me* in all things.

∾

The Golden Rule

A. E. GARVIE

EFFORTS HAVE BEEN made to discredit the originality of Jesus by showing that many of His characteristic sayings can be paralleled elsewhere. For instance, it is said that the Golden Rule is found in a negative form in Confucius, but in a positive in Lao-tsze. There is a likeness between the kind of life enjoined by Gautama the Buddha and that presented in the moral teaching of Jesus. In the Jewish fathers there are sayings about forgiveness which very closely resemble what He taught. It is assumed that in His teaching about the last things He reproduced the apocalyptic ideas of His own age. Regarding this argument it may be said that it would be very strange if Jesus had never said what had been said before Him. God had not been without witness in other lands and former times, speaking not through the succession of Hebrew prophets alone "by divers portions and in divers manners." To be saying what nobody else has ever thought of saying is proof of folly and vanity rather than of wisdom and virtue. Jesus came, not to startle the world with unheard-of novelties, but to carry the moral and religious development of mankind to a new stage, transcending and yet fulfilling the previous stages, continuous with them as well as contrasted to them.

∿

THE HOSPITAL

CHARLES H. SPURGEON

"Ask and it will be given to you."
Matthew 7:7

WE KNOW A place in England where bread is served to everyone who asks. All you have to do is knock on the door of St. Cross Hospital and bread is offered.

Jesus Christ so loves sinners that He has built His own St. Cross Hospital, where all hungry sinners have to do is knock. No, even better, Jesus has attached a bath to this Hospital of the Cross. Whenever souls are dirty and filthy, all they need to do is go there and be washed. The fountain is always full and effectual. Every sinner who ever came found that this bath washed away their stains. Sins that were scarlet and crimson disappeared and the sinner became whiter than snow.

As if this were not enough, a wardrobe is also attached to this Hospital of the Cross. Simply by asking, sinners may be clothed from head to foot. If they want to be soldiers, they are not given ordinary garments, but armor to cover them fully, and a sword and a shield.

Nothing good will be denied. They will have spending money as long as they live, and they will find an eternal heritage of glorious treasure when they enter into the joy of the Lord.

If all these things are to be had by merely knocking at mercy's door, Oh my soul, knock hard this morning, and ask large things of your generous Lord. Do not leave the throne of grace until all your wants have been spread before the Lord and until by faith you are persuaded that they will be supplied.

Do not be bashful when Jesus invites. No unbelief should hinder when Jesus promises. No cold heart should restrain when such blessings are to be obtained.

THE CANAANITE WOMAN

MARTIN LUTHER

THE WOMAN SAID, "Lord, help me," and if he didn't give her a death blow when he told her to her face she was a dog and not worthy to share the children's bread! What could she say to that? He told her she was one of the damned and lost and could not be counted among the elect. That was a final irrevocable answer, and nobody could get away from it. But she did not give up. She agreed with him that she was a dog and asked no more than a dog, that she should eat the crumbs that fell from the master's table. Was that not tremendous! She caught Christ in his own words. What could he do now? He opened his heart and answered her wish and made her not a dog, but a child of Israel.

This is written for our comfort and instruction that we may know how deeply God hides his grace from us and that we must not think of him according to our ideas and feeling, but only according to his Word. Here we see that though Christ speaks harshly he does not give a final judgment, an absolute "no." All his answers sound like "no," but are not exactly, but hang in the air. He did not say she was not of the house of Israel but only that he was not sent save to the house of Israel. His answer wavered between "yes" and "no." He did not say she was a dog but only that it is not proper to take the children's food and give it to the dogs. Again he left it hanging whether or not she was a dog. The "no" sounds stronger than the "yes," but nevertheless there was more there of "yes" than of "no," a pure "yes," deep and secret.

This shows the state of our heart when sore pressed. Christ in this story behaves the way the heart feels, for it thinks the answer is "no" when in reality it is not. Therefore the heart must turn away from its feeling and lay hold of the deep, secret "yes" under the "no," with firm faith in God's Word, as did this woman.

THE SEVEN LAST WORDS

LEHMAN STRAUSS

*The seven last words of Christ on the cross are usually considered to be
in this order:*

"Father, forgive them; for they know not what they do." Luke 23:34
KJV
"Today shalt thou be with me in paradise." Luke 23:43 KJV *(to the
thief)*
"Woman, behold thy son! . . . Behold thy mother!" John 19:26–27
KJV *(to his mother and to John the beloved)*
"My God, my God, why hast thou forsaken me?" Matthew 27:46 KJV
"I thirst." John 19:28 KJV
"Tetelestai (it is finished)." John 19:30 KJV
"Father, into thy hands I commend my spirit." Luke 23:46 KJV

FOR THE MOST part, people die much in the same way they lived. If the
favor of God is to shine on our death-bed, we must know Him and
fellowship with Him in life. He who dies the death of the righteous must
live the life of the righteous. If it is unnatural for a man to commune with
God when he is in good health and well-provided for in this life, it is not
likely that he will turn to God at the hour of his death.

∾

TEACHINGS

CHARLES DICKENS

AND HE TOLD His Disciples this story: He said, "There was once a servant
who owed his master a great deal of money, and could not pay it, at which
the master, being very angry, was going to have this servant sold for a
slave. But the servant kneeling down and begging his master's pardon with
great sorrow, the master forgave him. Now this same servant had a
fellow-servant who owed him a hundred pence, and instead of being kind
and forgiving to this poor man, as his master had been to him, he put him
in prison for the debt. His master, hearing of it, went to him, and
said, 'O wicked servant, I forgave you. Why did you not forgive your

fellow-servant?' And because he had not done so, his master turned him away with great misery. So," said Our Saviour, "how can you expect God to forgive you, if you do not forgive others?" This is the meaning of that part of the Lord's Prayer, where we say "Forgive us our trespasses"—that word means faults—"as we forgive them that trespass against us."

And He told them another story, and said: "There was a certain farmer once, who had a yard, and he went out early in the morning, and agreed with some labourers to work there, all day, for a penny. And bye and bye, when it was later, he went out again and engaged some more labourers on the same terms; and bye and bye went out again; and so on, several times, until the afternoon. When the day was over, and they all came to be paid, those who had worked since morning complained that those who had not begun to work until late in the day had the same money as themselves, and they said it was not fair. But the master said, 'Friend, I agreed with you for a penny; and is it less money to you, because I give the same money to another man?' " Our Savior meant to teach them by this, that people who have done good all their lives long will go to Heaven after they are dead. But that people who have been wicked, because of their being miserable, or not having parents and friends to take care of them when young, and who are truly sorry for it, however late in their lives, and pray God to forgive them, will be forgiven and will go to Heaven too. He taught His Disciples in these stories, because He knew the people liked to hear them, and would remember what He said better, if He said it in that way.

HOW TO PRAY

WILLIAM GRIFFIN

"LORD, TEACH us how to pray."

The men had prayed with Jesus many times and in many places, but he had never told them how to pray and what to say.

"Don't shout on a street corner as some people do. That's the first thing.

"Don't pray in a crowd. It is better to pray alone.

"Remember, God knows what you need before you ask, but he wants you to ask anyway."

"What's the best prayer?" asked Peter.

"Would you like to know my favorite prayer?" asked Jesus, not expecting an answer.

"Our father, who art in heaven, hallowed be thy name, thy kingdom come, thy will be done on earth as it is in heaven.

"Give us this day our daily bread, and forgive us our trespasses as we forgive those who trespass against us. And lead us not into temptation but deliver us from evil."

∾

THE PARABLE OF THE UNMERCIFUL SERVANT

CLARENCE JORDAN

THEN ROCK SIDLED up and asked, "Sir, how often should I forgive my brother when he keeps doing me wrong? Seven times?"

"I wouldn't say seven times," Jesus replied, "but *seventy times seven!* That's why the God Movement is like a big businessman who wanted to settle the accounts of his customers. As he started to do so, one customer came in who owed a bill of more than ten thousand dollars. He had nothing to pay on the account, so the businessman told the sheriff to put up for sale everything the guy had and apply it to the debt. But the fellow did a song and dance. 'Please give me some more time and I'll pay every cent!' he begged. The businessman was touched by the guy's pitiful pleas, so he let him go and marked off the debt. Then that same guy went out and found a man who owed him a hundred dollars. Grabbing him around the neck, he choked him and said, 'Pay me that money you owe.'

" 'Please give me a little more time,' the man begged, 'and I'll pay every cent.' But he refused and, instead, he swore out a warrant for him. When the little man's friends found out about it, they were really upset, so they went and told the big businessman all that had happened. Then the big businessman sent for the guy who had owed him the huge debt and said to him, 'You low-down bum! I marked off all that debt for you because you begged me to. Shouldn't you, then, have been kind to that little man just as I was kind to you?' Still hot under the collar, he turned the fellow over to the law to be thrown into the clink until every last dime of the debt had been paid. And my spiritual Father will treat you along the same lines unless every single one of you forgives your brother from your heart."

THE SEVENTH BEATITUDE

CHARLES H. SPURGEON

"Blessed are the peacemakers, for they shall be called sons of God."
Matthew 5:9

THIS IS THE seventh beatitude, and seven was the number of perfection among the Hebrews. Perhaps the Savior placed the peacemaker seventh on the list because the peacemaker most closely resembles the perfect man Christ Jesus. If you want perfect blessedness, so far as it can be enjoyed on earth, become a peacemaker.

There is a significance in the position of this text. The verse which precedes it speaks of the blessedness of "the pure in heart, for they shall see God." It is well to understand that our wisdom is to be "first pure, then peaceful" (James 3:17). Our peace is never to be a compact with sin or toleration with evil. We must set ourselves like steel against everything that is contrary to God and His holiness. Once purity is established in our hearts we can proceed to peace.

The verse that follows our text is also appropriately placed. Regardless of how peaceful we may be, in this world we will be misrepresented and misunderstood. Even the Prince of Peace by His very peacefulness brought fire on the earth. Although He loved mankind and did no harm, "He was despised and rejected by men, a man of sorrows and acquainted with grief" (Isaiah 53:3).

Peaceful one, don't be surprised when you meet with enemies for the beatitudes continue with, "Blessed are those who are persecuted for righteousness' sake, for theirs is the kingdom of heaven." The peacemakers are more than blessed, they are encircled with blessings.

Lord, give us grace to climb to this seventh beatitude! Purify our minds that we may be first pure, then peaceful. Fortify our souls that our peace may not make us cowards when for Your sake we are persecuted.

❧

CHRIST'S TEACHINGS IN ETERNITY

MARTIN LUTHER

THE CONVERSATION OF Christ with His disciples, when He took His leave of them at His last supper, was most sweet, loving and friendly, talking with them lovingly, as a father with his children when he must depart from them. He took their weakness in good part and bore with them, though now and then their discourse was very full of simplicity, as when Philip said, "Shew us the Father," and Thomas, "We know not the way," and Peter, "I will go with Thee unto death"; each freely showing the thoughts of his heart. Never since the world began was a more precious, sweet and amiable conversation!

• • •

Is it not a shame that we are always afraid of Christ, whereas there was never in heaven or earth a more loving, familiar, or milder man, in words, works and demeanour, especially towards poor, sorrowful and tormented consciences?

• • •

I expect more goodness from Kate my wife, from Philip Melanchthon, and from other friends, than from my sweet and blessed Saviour Christ Jesus; and yet I know for certain that neither she nor any other person on earth will or can suffer that for me which He has suffered. Why then should I be afraid of Him? This my foolish weakness grieves me very much. We plainly see in the Gospel how mild and gentle He showed Himself towards His disciples; how kindly He passed over their weakness, their presumption, yea, their foolishness. He checked their unbelief and in all gentleness admonished them. . . . Fie on our unbelieving hearts that we should be afraid of this man who is more loving, friendly, gentle, and compassionate towards us than are our own kindred, our brothers and sisters—yea, than parents towards their own children.

❧

FOLLOWING CHRIST

ELIJAH P. BROWN

A rich ruler once came to Christ and asked what he must do to have eternal life (Matthew 19:16–22). Jesus asked him how he was doing at keeping the Ten Commandments. He agreed that he was keeping them as well as could be expected. Then he asked Jesus if there was anything else he could do to be sure that he had eternal life. Jesus told him that just being good wasn't good enough. He must not only live a moral life; he must use his life and his money in serving God. The young man went away sadly, because he just felt the cost of following Christ was too great a price to pay.

GOD HAS EVERY right to demand our very best. It would have been no harder for the young man to give up all he had than for Abraham to give up his friends, his home and his native land. Peter left his boat and fishing nets—all he had—to follow Christ, and every Christian worth his salt does the same, and so must you and I.

[Billy Sunday said]

"Matthew left his place of business as a tax collector to follow Jesus, and he didn't have to be told the second time. All the disciples gave up their business, their homes—everything—to follow the Master. There were no regrets, and they made no excuses. Even Christ gave up his place in heaven, and all the glory he had there, to suffer for our sakes, and certainly we should not hesitate to give up everything for him.

"The thing that wrecked the young man was his unwillingness to surrender the thing that held him to the earth. He wanted to go to heaven, but didn't want to give up the world, and this, I fear, is just as true of some of you. It is a noble thing to seek to know God's will, as this young man did, but an awful sin to refuse to obey it."

One day when Sunday was at home between meetings, his little daughter Helen, who had but recently commenced going to school, said to him:

"Papa, let's go to bed and tell stories."

"I can't do it, Helen, for I have to go away," said he.

"Where are you going to, papa?"

"Well, I've got to go to Urbana, Ohio, and then to Troy, and then to Evansville, and after that to Richmond, and then to Indianapolis."

"Papa, you're the best friend I've got, and I don't want you to go away. Let's go to bed and tell stories."

"But I must go away, my dear, and if you will be a nice little girl and not cry, I will get you a present," her father said, trying to console her.

"Will you get me a ring?"

"Yes, I'll get you a ring."

"With a set in it?"

"Yes, I'll get you a ring with a little blue set in it." And he did. He got her a very pretty ring with a little turquoise set.

"But maybe I'd like to have a new dress, papa."

"All right. You shall have a new dress. What kind of a dress do you want?"

"I believe I would like to have a dress with some blue in it."

"All right. You shall have it; if you will be a good girl, and not cry."

And he afterward did that very thing. He went to Carson, Pirie & Scott, and got her a very pretty silk dress with a blue stripe in it, that made her dance with delight when she saw it. She wore it for a long time, and then gave it to a poor little girl, who wore it till it looked like a battleflag.

But as soon as she had her father's promise for the ring and the dress, little Helen looked very sober and said:

"Papa, I don't want a ring; I don't want a dress. I just want you. You're the best friend I've got. Stay at home with me, papa, and I won't never want anything but you!"

"And that is the way it should be with the Christian," says Mr. Sunday, when he tells this touching incident. "The greatest desire of our hearts should be for a constant sense of the presence of Him whom having not seen we love."

∾

THE GOTTA-BE-ALIVE GOD

J. B. PHILLIPS

IF THE RESURRECTION DID NOT HAPPEN, WHO WAS CHRIST?

Many people, who have not read the Gospels since childhood, imagine that they can quite easily detach the "miraculous" element of the Resurrection and still retain Christ as an Ideal, as the best Moral Teacher the world has ever known—and all the rest. But the Gospels, all four of them, bristle with supernatural claims on the part of Christ, and unless each man is going to constitute himself a judge of what Christ said and what He did not say (which is not far from every man being his own evangelist), it is impossible to avoid the conclusion that He believed Himself to be God and spoke therefore with quite unique authority. Now if He believed thus and spoke thus and failed to rise from the dead, He was, without question, a lunatic. He was quite plainly a young idealist suffering from *folie de grandeur* on the biggest possible scale, and cannot on that account be regarded as the World's Greatest Teacher. No Mahomet or Buddha or other great teacher ever came within miles of making such a shocking boast about himself. Familiarity has blinded many people to the outrageousness of Christ's claim and traditional reverence inhibits them from properly assessing it. If He did not in fact rise, His claim was false, and He was a very dangerous personality indeed.

WHY ARE SO MANY CHRISTIANS SURE THAT CHRIST NOT ONLY ROSE, BUT IS ALIVE TODAY?

Though this question may enrage the critic it is a fair one. The common experience of Christians of all kinds of temperaments and of a great many nationalities for nineteen centuries cannot be airily dismissed. Men and women by the thousands today are convinced that the One whom they serve is not a heroic figure of the past, but a living Personality with spiritual resources upon which they can draw. A man may find difficulty in writing a poem, but if he cries, "Oh, William Shakespeare, help me!" nothing whatever happens. A man may be terribly afraid, but if he cries, "Oh, Horatio Nelson, help me!" there is no sort of reply. But if he is at the end of his moral resources or cannot by effort of will muster up sufficient positive love and goodness and he cries, "Oh, Christ, help me!" something happens at once. The sense of spiritual reinforcement, of drawing spiritual vitality from a living source, is so marked that Christians cannot help being convinced that their Hero is far more than an outstanding figure of the past.

∽

THE IMITATION OF CHRIST

THOMAS À KEMPIS

OF THE INWARD SPEAKING OF CHRIST TO A FAITHFUL SOUL

I shall take heed, says a devout soul, and I shall hear what my Lord Jesus will say to me.

Blessed is that man who hears Jesus speaking in his soul, and who takes from His mouth some word of comfort. Blessed are those ears which hear the secret whisperings of Jesus, and give no heed to the deceitful whisperings of this world, and blessed are the good plain ears which heed not outward speech but what God speaks and teaches inwardly in the soul. Blessed are those eyes which are shut to the sight of outward vanities and give heed to the inward movings of God. Blessed are they, too, who win virtue and prepare themselves by good bodily and spiritual works to receive daily more and more the secret inspirations and inward teachings of God. And blessed are they who set themselves wholly to serve God and who for His service put away all worldly hindrances.

O my soul take heed to what has been said before and shut the doors of your sensuality, which are your five senses, so that you may hear inwardly what our Lord Jesus speaks within your soul. Thus says your beloved: I am your health, I am your peace, I am your life. Keep yourself in Me and you will find peace in Me. Forsake the love of transitory things and seek things that are everlasting. What are all temporal things but deceptive? And what help can any creature be to you if your Lord Jesus forsake you? Therefore, forsaking and leaving all creatures and all worldly things, do what lies in you to make yourself pleasing in His sight, so that you may after this life come to everlasting life in the kingdom of heaven.

OF THE OBLATION OF CHRIST ON THE CROSS, AND OF A FULL FORSAKING OF OURSELVES

Our Lord Jesus says to His servant: As I offered Myself to God the Father for your sins, hanging all naked with My arms spread wide upon the cross, so that nothing remained in Me, but all went in sacrifice to please My Father and to appease His wrath against mankind, so in the Mass you daily ought to offer yourself freely to God as much as you can, as a pure and holy oblation.

What more do I ask of you than that you should study to resign yourself wholly to Me? I do not regard whatever you give Me besides yourself, for I do not look for your gifts, but for you. For, as it should not be sufficient for you to have all things else besides Me, so it will not please Me unless you give Me yourself, whatever else you give. Offer yourself to Me and give yourself all for God, and your oblation will be acceptable.

Lo, I offered Myself wholly to My Father for you, and I gave my Body and Blood to be your meat, so that I should be wholly yours and you wholly Mine. But if you have trust in yourself and do not freely offer yourself to My will, your oblation is not pleasing and there will not be between us a perfect union. A free offering of yourself into the hands of God must precede all your works if you will obtain grace and true liberty. And so it happens that so few are inwardly illuminated and free, because they cannot wholly forsake themselves. My words are true: Unless a man renounce himself, he cannot be My disciple. Therefore, if you desire to be My disciple, offer yourself fully to Me, with all your affection and love.

THAT WE OUGHT TO FORSAKE OURSELVES AND FOLLOW CHRIST BY BEARING HIS CROSS

My son, as much as you can abandon yourself and your own will, so much will you enter into Me. And as to desire nothing outwardly brings peace to a man's soul, so a man, by an inward forsaking of himself, joins himself to God. It is My will, therefore, that you learn to have a perfect abandonment of yourself and a full resignation of yourself into My hands, without contradicting or complaining, and follow Me, for I am the Way, I am the Truth, and I am the Life. Without a way, no man can go; without the truth, no man can know; and without life no man can live. I am the Way by which you ought to go, the Truth you ought to believe, and the Life you ought to hope to have. I am the Way that cannot be made foul, the Truth that cannot be deceived, and the Life that will never have an end. I am the Way most straight, the Truth most perfect and the Life most certain, a blessed Life and an uncreated Life that created all things. If you dwell and abide in My way, you will know the truth, and the truth will deliver you and you will come to everlasting life.

If you would come to that life, keep My commandments; if you would know the truth, believe My teaching; if you would be perfect, sell all that you have. If you would be My disciple, forsake yourself; if you would possess the blessed life, despise this present life; if you would be exalted in heaven, humble yourself here on earth; and if you would reign with Me, bear the Cross with Me, for, truly, only the servants of the Cross will find the life of blessedness and of everlasting light.

O Lord Jesus, inasmuch as Your way is narrow and straight and is, as well, much despised by the world, give me grace gladly to bear the contempt of the world. There is no servant greater than his lord, and no disciple who is above his master. Let Your servant, therefore, be exercised in Your ways, for in them is the health and the very perfection of life. Whatever I read or hear, beside that way, does not refresh me or fully delight me.

My son, inasmuch as you know these things and have read them all, you will be blessed if you fulfill them. He who has My commandments and keeps them is the one who loves Me, and I will love him and show Myself to him, and make him sit with Me in the kingdom of My Father. Lord, be it done to me as You have said and promised. I have taken the Cross of penance from Your hands and I will bear it unto death as You have directed me to do. The life of every good man is the Cross, and it is also the way and guide to paradise. And now that it has begun, it is not lawful for me to turn my back upon it or proper for me to abandon it.

Have done, therefore, my well-beloved brethren; let us go forth together. Jesus will be with us; for Jesus we have taken this Cross, for Jesus let us persevere, and He who is our Guide and Leader will be our help. Lo, our King who fights for us will go before us. Let us follow Him boldly, let us fear no perils, but be ready to die for Him manfully in battle, so that we place no blot upon our glory, or diminish our reward by fleeing like cowards away from the Cross.

❧

A SYMPOSIUM: JESUS ON TEACHING

JOHN BLANCHARD

Christ's statements are either cosmic or comic.

How is it that nobody has dreamed up any moral advances since Christ's teaching? What was there in his heredity and his environment to account for this unique teacher, and the remarkable fact that no greater has ever looked like emerging?

Michael Green

Certainly, no revolution that has ever taken place in society can be compared to that which has been produced by the words of Jesus Christ.

Mark Hopkins

The discrepancy between the depth, sincerity and, may I say, shrewdness of Christ's moral teaching and the rampant megalomania which must lie behind his theological teaching unless he is indeed God, has never been got over.

C. S. Lewis

Jesus was the greatest religious genius that ever lived. His beauty is eternal and his reign will never end. He is in every respect unique and nothing can be compared with him.

Ernest Renan

He is not the Great—he is the Only!

Carnegie Simpson

Christ is the most unique person in history. No man can write a history of the human race without giving first and formost place to the penniless teacher of Nazareth.

H. G. Wells

THE PARABLE OF THE TENANTS

CLARENCE JORDAN

"LISTEN TO ANOTHER Comparison. Once there was a farmer who set out a peach orchard, built a fence around it, bought some equipment, and put up a packing shed. Then he rented it to some sharecroppers and left. When peach-picking time came he sent his workers to the croppers to get his share of the fruit. But the croppers took his workers and beat one of them, killed another, and stoned the other. So he tried again, this time sending more important workers than before, but the croppers treated them the same way. Finally he sent his son, thinking that surely they would respect *him*. But when the croppers saw the son they got together and said, 'Hey, there's the old man's boy. Let's kill this cat and take over his estate!' So they grabbed him and dragged him out of the orchard and murdered him. Now, when the owner of the orchard comes, what will he do to those croppers?"

They answered, "Why, he'll tear those bastards to bits, and let out the orchard to croppers who'll give him his share of the fruit at harvesttime."

Jesus asked them, "Haven't you ever read in the Bible: 'The stone which the craftsmen rejected was selected as the cornerstone. This was done by the owner, and is an amazing sight for us'? Now that's why I'm telling you that the God Movement will be taken out of your hands and turned over to people who will be productive. (And the person who falls on this stone will be splattered, but whoever it falls on will be pulverized.)" The ministers and church people listened to his Comparisons, and were aware that they were aimed at them. They were dying to arrest him, but feared the crowd, who regarded him as a man of God.

∽

JESUS' TEACHING ON PRAYER

MARTIN LUTHER

JESUS HIMSELF HAS said, "Therefore I say unto you, What things soever ye desire, when ye pray, believe that ye receive them, and ye shall have them" (Mark 11, KJV). And in Luke 11 (editor's trans.) he said, "Ask, and it shall be given; seek, and you shall find; knock, and it shall be opened unto you. For everyone that asks receives, everyone who seeks finds, and to everyone who knocks it shall be opened. For what father among you, if his son asks for bread, will give him a stone? or if he asks for an egg, will give him a scorpion? If you know how to give good gifts to your children, how much more shall your Father who is in heaven give the Holy Spirit to all them that ask Him!"

Are we so hard of heart that these words of Jesus do not move us to pray with confidence, joyfully and gladly? So many of our prayers must be reformed if we are to pray according to these words. To be sure, all of the churches across the land are filled with people praying and singing, but why is it that there is so little improvement, so few results from so many prayers? The reason is none other than the one which James speaks of when he says, "You ask and do not receive because you ask amiss" (James 4:3). For where this faith and confidence is not in the prayer, the prayer is dead.

∿

THE GREAT STIRRER-UP

FRANK C. LAUBACH

HAS GOD EVER struck you as the *Great Stirrer-Up?* One thing He seems to have determined is that we shall not fall asleep. We make or discover paradises for ourselves, and these paradises begin to lull us into sleepy satisfaction. Then God comes with His awakening hand, takes us by the shoulders and gives us a thorough awakening.

And God knows we need it. If our destiny is to *grow* on and on and on, into some far more beautiful creatures than we are now, with more of the ideals of Christ, that means that we need to have the shells broken quite frequently so that we can grow.

My confidence that this earth is but a brief school grows into certainty as my fellowship with God grows more tender. As a discipline this world is admirable.

Jesus and Buddha had almost the same message about this life. Buddha said, "Abolish all desire." Jesus said, "Fix not your desires upon this earth, but lay up all the desires you can for a fuller life, which begins within you now, and is endless." Many people seek other escapes. Some in prodigious work, some in reckless play, some in drugs, some in insanity —for insanity is but an escape from pitiless, crushing failure. But I wish to tell all the world that needs a better way, that God on Signal Hill satisfies, and sends through me a glow of glory which makes me sure that this is the pathway of true intuition.

∾

WHO CAN BE SAVED?

CHARLES KINGSLEY

TRUE, THERE WERE excuses for him; for whom are there none? He was poor and struggling; and it is much more difficult (as Becky Sharp, I think, pathetically observed) to be good when one is poor than when one is rich. It is (and all rich people should consider the fact) much more easy, if not to go to heaven, at least to think one is going thither, on three thousand a year than on three hundred. Not only is respectability more easy, as is proved by the broad fact that it is the poor people who fill the jails, and not the rich ones; but virtue and religion—of the popular sort. It is undeniably more easy to be resigned to the will of heaven, when that will seems tending just as we would have it; much more easy to have faith in the goodness of providence, when that goodness seems safe in one's pocket in the form of bank-notes; and to believe that one's children are under the protection of omnipotence, when one can hire for them in half an hour the best medical advice in London. One need only look into one's own heart to understand the disciples' astonishment at the news that "How hardly shall they that have riches enter into the kingdom of heaven."

"Who then can be saved?" asked they, being poor men, accustomed to see the wealthy Pharisees in possession of "the highest religious privileges and means of grace." Who indeed, if not the rich? If the noblemen, and the bankers, and the dowagers, and the young ladies who go to church, and read good books, and have been supplied from youth with the very best religious articles which money can procure, and have time for all manner of good works, and give their hundreds to charities, and head reformatory movements, and build churches, and work altar-cloths, and can taste all the preachers and father-confessors round London, one after another, as you would taste wines, till they find the spiritual panacea which exactly suits their complaint—if they are not sure of salvation, who can be saved?

My Neighbor

CHARLES H. SPURGEON

"You shall love your neighbor."
Matthew 5:43

PERHAPS YOUR NEIGHBOR rolls in riches and you are poor. Your little house is close to a fine mansion and occasionally you look at that great estate where banquets are held. God has given your neighbor these gifts, so do not envy such wealth. Be content with what you have if you cannot better it. Do not wish for your neighbor to be like you are. Love him, and then you will not envy him.

On the other hand perhaps you are rich and near to you reside the poor. Call them *neighbor,* and remember that you are to love them. The world may call the poor inferior, but they are not. They are far more your equal than your inferiors, for "God has made from one blood every nation of men to dwell on all the face of the earth, and has determined their preappointed times and the boundaries of their dwellings" (Acts 17:26).

It is your clothing that is better, not you. The poor one is a *person,* and what are you more than that? Make sure you love your neighbors, even if they are in rags or sunk in the depths of poverty.

You may say, "I cannot love my neighbors. Anything I do for them is returned with ingratitude and contempt." All the more room for the heroism of love. Would you be a feather bed warrior rather than bearing the rough fight of love? Those who dare the most will win the most. If your path of love is rough, tread it fearlessly. Love your neighbor through thick as well as thin, "for in so doing you will heap coals of fire on his head" (Romans 12:20).

If your neighbors are hard to please, don't seek their praise, please your Master. If they reject your love, your Master still loves you and your deed is as acceptable to Him as if it had been accepted by them.

Love your neighbor, for in doing this you are following in the footsteps of Christ.

PARABLE OF THE BANQUET

CLARENCE JORDAN

JESUS CONTINUED THE conversation by speaking to them with Comparisons. "The God Movement is like a governor who gave a big dinner for his party chairman. He told his secretaries to invite the prominent dignitaries, but they refused to accept. So he told his secretaries to try again. 'Tell them,' he said, ' "The banquet is all arranged for—the steer has been butchered and the hogs barbecued. Y'all come on to the dinner." ' But they couldn't have cared less. One left to go out to his farm; another went to his store. The rest of them taunted and insulted the secretaries. At that, the governor had a duck fit, and ordered the names of the scoundrels to be struck from the list of his friends. Then he said to his secretaries, 'Plans for the banquet are all made, but the people I invited aren't fit to come. So go to the various precincts, and whoever you find there, invite them to the banquet.' Well, they went to the precincts and brought in everybody they could find, good and bad. The banquet hall was filled with guests, and the governor went in to greet them. There he saw a guy sitting at the table who looked and smelled like he had just come in from his farm. The governor said to him, 'Hey, buddy, how did you get in here, looking and smelling like that?' He just clammed up. Then the governor said to the waiters, 'Tie the bum up and throw him in the back alley.' Outside there'll be yelling and screaming, for the big ones were invited but the little ones got in."

❧

WASHING OF THE DISCIPLES' FEET

MARTIN LUTHER

CHRIST SENT THE disciples into the city to prepare the Passover supper for him. And when they were gathered, he took "a basin, and began to wash the disciples' feet." In this, one sees what a person he was; how inconceivably friendly. "Ye call me Master and Lord," he said, "and ye say well; for so I am. If I then, your Lord and Master, have washed your feet; ye also ought to wash one another's feet."

There was no need that Christ should have done this. He could have said to Peter, "You go and wash Judas' feet; I am the Master." But instead he subjected himself and emptied himself of his majesty and behaved as a servant. Then Peter undertook to instruct him and said, "You are the Master, and I am the servant," but Christ rebuffed him and went on to explain the meaning of the foot washing. . . .

If you really want to wash the feet of the poor, take them into your house, feed them, and clothe them, and do it the whole year through.

In washing the feet of the disciples, Christ gave an example of love, for this is the nature of love—to serve and to be subject to another. If one esteems another more highly than himself, then love and all good works are there. Jesus said, "Ye also ought to wash one another's feet." Thus Christ made himself the lowliest. One sees here genuine love, for the heart is with the loved one and desires to do his pleasure. In this, one finds sympathy, mercy, brotherliness, and a helping hand, but then the devil breaks in and says through the pope that these are not enough; that they are just ordinary commands; that one should go farther, become a monk, put on a cowl, and fast for six days. Even faith is called an ordinary thing, and we are told to do something extraordinary. Faith is merely for the heathen, but Christians must be urged to do something more, to take a cowl and the like. As for myself, I have scarcely made a beginning in faith. To the very grave, I shall have to go on learning. I am not concerned about works. I pray simply, "Help me that I may firmly believe." If that happens, then bring on all the cowls and everything else the pope has commanded. So, then, love your neighbor and esteem him higher than yourself. But then again they come and say that this is only an ordinary command. I reply: "Where are those who have kept it? Have you? You have not."

It is a mighty love that puts us all to confusion that the divine majesty should so humble himself. Fie, how shameful if we do not take it to heart! But who knows whether his heart is pure. Look at Judas. There he sits like a lord full of the devil. And the Lord God goes down on his knees as a servant in front of him. If the kaiser should kiss a beggar's feet, that would be a stinking humility and not worthy to be named in comparison with what was done by the divine majesty. These examples are too deep for us to think of imitating.

DISCIPLESHIP THEN

DALLAS WILLARD

Dallas Willard teaches philosophy in southern California. He has asked not merely what Jesus taught, but how we can incorporate those teachings and make them inwardly a part of our service to humanity.

WHEN JESUS WALKED among humankind there was a certain simplicity to being a disciple. Primarily it meant to go with him, in an attitude of study, obedience, and imitation. There were no correspondence courses. One knew what to do and what it would cost. Simon Peter exclaimed: "Look, we've left everything and followed you!" (Mark 10:28). Family and occupations were deserted for long periods to go with Jesus as he walked from place to place announcing, showing, and explaining the governance of God. Disciples had to be with him to learn how to do what he did.

Imagine doing that today. How would family members, employers, and coworkers react to such abandonment? Probably they would conclude that we did not much care for them, or even for ourselves. Did not Zebedee think this as he watched his two sons desert the family business to keep company with Jesus (Mark 1:20)? Ask any father in a similar situation. So when Jesus observed that one must forsake the dearest things —family, "all that he hath," and "his own life also" (Luke 14)—insofar as that was necessary to accompany him, he stated a simple fact: it was the only possible doorway to discipleship.

❧

LET THE LITTLE CHILDREN COME UNTO ME

HORACE BUSHNELL

LET EVERY CHRISTIAN father and mother understand, when their child is three years old, that they have done more than half of all they will ever do for his character. What can be more strangely wide of all just apprehension than the immense efficacy imputed by most parents to the Christian ministry, compared with what they take to be the almost insignificant power conferred on them in their parental charge and duties? Why, if all preachers of Christ could have their hearers for whole months and years in their own will, as parents do their children, so as to move them by a look, a motion, a smile, a frown, and act their own sentiments over in them at pleasure; if also, a little further on, they had them in authority to command, direct, tell them whither to go, what to learn, what to do, regulate their hours, their books, their pleasures, their company, and call them to prayer over their own knees every night and morning, who could think it impossible, in the use of such a power, to produce almost any result? Should not such a ministry be expected to fashion all who come under it to newness of life? Let no parent, shifting off his duties to his children, in this manner think to have his defects made up, and the consequent damages mended afterwards, when they have come to their maturity, by the comparatively slender, always doubtful, efficacy of preaching and pulpit harangue.

❦

JESUS: THE CATCHY STORYTELLER

LOIS A. CHENEY

WHO WAS JESUS?

He was a storyteller.

He told stories. He was the world's greatest storyteller. Ask him a question; he'd answer with a story. Give him a crowd of people listening intently; he told them stories. Give him an argument; he'd give you a story. Give him a real tricky, catchy question; he'd give you a real tricky, catchy story.

Have you ever watched a seven-year-old listening—inhaling—a story? Eyes wide, mouth slung open, mind churning, he lives, accepts, and believes. He is totally absorbed.

This man-God Jesus. He was a good storyteller. He knew what he was doing.

THE SINNER WHO WAS SORRY

WILLIAM GRIFFIN

"WHAT HAPPENS WHEN a sinner is sorry for his or her sins?" people often asked Jesus.

"Let me answer you question," Jesus would say, "by telling you a story."

A young man was walking the long road home. His father ran to meet him.

"Where have you been?" asked the father.

"A long, long way from home," said the young man.

"Where's the money I gave you?"

"I spent it."

"What have you got to show for it?"

"Nothing."

"No clothes?"

"Just the rags I've got on."

"You look thin."

"I haven't eaten for days."

"How come you're so dirty?"

"My last job was taking care of pigs."

"You look it," said the father.

"Father, I've been thinking."

"That's a good start."

"I've sinned against God. I've sinned against you. I'm sorry," said the young man. "Well, aren't you going to slug me?"

"No."

"Why not?"

"I'm going to give you a party," said the father.

"But I don't deserve it."

"And I'm inviting everybody to come."

The father threw his arms around the young man's neck. The young man kissed his father. And they headed down the road toward home.

"But I don't want to go to his party," said the father's other son.

"Why not?" asked the father.

"It's not fair. You never gave me a party."

"Why should I?"

"I didn't run away from home," said the other son. "I stayed home and worked."

"May I tell you something?" the father asked his son. "Just between you and me?"

"What?"

"When your brother left home, your mother and I never heard from him. We thought he was dead. Seeing him again is like having him brought back from the dead."

"I never thought of it like that," said the other son.

"When you and I are together," said the father, "it's always good times. Let's go into the party," said the father, putting his arm around his son's shoulder, "and get something to eat. A little singing. A little dancing. It will be our party too."

❧

THE SPIRIT OF LOVE THAT MAKES EVERYTHING EASY

FRANÇOIS FÉNELON

JESUS CHRIST SAID to all Christians without exception, "Let him who would be my disciple carry his cross, and follow me." The broad way leads to perdition. We must follow the narrow way which few enter. We must be born again, renounce ourselves, hate ourselves, become a child, be poor in spirit, weep to be comforted, and not be of the world which is cursed because of its scandals.

These truths frighten many people, and this is because they only know what religion exacts without knowing what it offers, and they ignore the spirit of love which makes everything easy. They do not know that it leads to the highest perfection by a feeling of peace and love which sweetens all the struggle.

Those who are wholly God's are always happy. They know by experience that the yoke of the Lord is "easy and light," that we find in him "rest for the soul," and that he comforts those who are weary and overburdened, as he himself has said.

CONFLICT, NOT COZINESS

BILLY GRAHAM

JESUS CHRIST SPOKE frankly to His disciples about the future. He hid nothing from them. No one could ever accuse Him of deception or making false promises.

In unmistakable language, He told them that discipleship meant a life of self-denial and the bearing of a cross. He asked them to count the cost carefully, lest they should turn back when they met with suffering and privation.

Jesus told His followers that the world would hate them. They would be arrested, scourged, and brought before governors and kings. Even their loved ones would persecute them. As the world hated Him, so it would treat His servants. He also warned, "a time is coming when anyone who kills you will think he is offering a service to God" (John 16:2).

The Christian therefore must expect conflict, not an easy, cozy life. He is a soldier, and as it has been said, his captain never promised him immunity from the hazards of battle.

Many of Christ's early followers were disappointed in Him, for, in spite of His warnings, they expected Him to subdue their enemies and set up a world political kingdom. When they came face to face with reality, they "turned back and no longer followed him" (John 6:66). But the true disciples of Jesus all suffered for their faith.

We are told that the early Christians went rejoicing to their deaths, as if they were going to a marriage feast. They bathed their hands in the blaze kindled for them and shouted with gladness. One early historian, witnessing their heroism, wrote, "When the day of victory dawned, the Christians marched in procession from the prison to the arena as if they were marching to Heaven, with joyous countenances agitated by gladness rather than fear."

❧

BY BREAD ALONE

PHILLIPS BROOKS

"IT IS WRITTEN, Man shall not live by bread alone." What a man finds in his own consciousness, he is strengthened by being able to recognize in the whole history of his race. "It is written" long ago, this which he is doing now. He is only tracing over with his blood the unfaded characters which other men have written in theirs. It is not a mere whim of his, this conviction that it is better to serve God than to eat bread. It is the corporate conviction of mankind. That is a very mysterious support, but it is a very real one. It plants the weak tree of your will or mine into the rich soil of humanity. Do not lose that strength. Do not so misread history that it shall seem to you when you try to do right as if you were the first man that ever tried it. Put yourself with your weak little struggle into the company of all the strugglers in all time. Recognize in your little fight against your avarice, or your untruthfulness, or your laziness, only one skirmish in that battle whose field covers the earth, and whose clamour rises and falls from age to age, but never wholly dies. See in the perpetual struggle of good and evil that the impulse after good is eternal, and the higher needs are always asserting their necessity. In their persistent assertion read the prophecy of their final success and take courage.

∾

Doctor to the Sick

DAVID WENHAM

HUMAN REVOLUTIONS ARE usually good news for some people and bad news for others. Jesus' announcement of the coming of God's revolution also cut two ways. But it was first and foremost good news. We saw this . . . in the saying about the children in the marketplace, which contrasted John the Baptist's sombre ministry with its focus on judgement and Jesus' ministry with its focus on God's mercy. That saying was a comment on the accusation that Jesus was "a friend of tax-collectors and sinners."

• • •

God's revolution, proclaimed and brought by Jesus, was a revolution bringing deliverance. That idea of the kingdom was, of course, well understood by Jesus' contemporaries, but whereas they thought in terms of national deliverance from foreign oppression and of personal deliverance for the righteous, Jesus had a bigger concept; God's revolution meant deliverance for the needy, the oppressed and the depressed, for the sick, the demon-possessed and the sinners. Jesus' opponents expected sinners to be judged in the coming kingdom, and, although they subscribed in theory to the desirability of getting sinners to repent, in practice they tended to keep away from evildoers and they expected God to endorse their condemnation of the unclean and ungodly. When Jesus mixed with such people and announced the coming of God's kingdom to them, this contradicted what his opponents stood for and was very uncomfortable to them. Jesus seemed to be undermining their high standards, and they protested vocally.

∾

JESUS' VIEW OF SCRIPTURE

JOHN R. W. STOTT

LOOKING BACK OVER the chapter which we have surveyed, the sequence of thought is plain. Jesus was advancing great claims when He said He had authority to quicken and to judge, for these are activities of God. When challenged, He said He had testimony enough to substantiate His claims, neither self-testimony, nor human testimony, but divine. And this divine testimony was borne to Him partly through the mighty works which the Father had given Him to do, but especially through the written word of Scripture.

This, then, was Jesus Christ's view of the Scriptures. Their witness is God's witness. The testimony of the Bible is the testimony of God. And the chief reason why the Christian believes in the divine origin of the Bible is that Jesus Christ Himself taught it.

Moreover, He taught it consistently. He adopted towards the Scriptures of the Old Testament an attitude of reverent assent and submission, and He maintained this position throughout His life and ministry, including the post-resurrection period. According to John He said "scripture cannot be broken" (John 10:35), and according to Matthew "not an iota, not a dot, will pass from the law until all is accomplished" (Matthew 5:18). He accepted the statements of Scripture without question, believing them to be true. He predicted with confidence His rejection by His own people, His sufferings, death and resurrection, because thus it was written. He obeyed the requirements and applied the principles of Scripture in His everyday life. He voluntarily accepted a position of humble subordination to what Scripture said. The word *gegraptai* ("it stands written") was enough to settle any issue for Him (*e.g.*, Matthew 4:4, 7, 10). He understood His mission in the light of Old Testament prophecy, recognizing and declaring Himself to be both Daniel's Son of man and Isaiah's suffering Servant of the Lord. At least from the age of 12 He felt the compulsion of Scripture upon His soul, an inner constraint to fulfil the role which Scripture portrayed for Him. Thus, "Did you not know that I must be in my Father's House?" "He began to teach them that the Son of man must suffer many things, and be rejected . . . , and be killed, and after three days rise again." "The Son of man goes as it is written of him." "Behold, we are going up to Jerusalem, and everything that is written of the Son of man by the prophets will be accomplished." (Luke 2:49; Mark 8:31; 14:21; Luke 18:31.) No wonder the apostle Paul could later write that He "became obedient unto death" (Philippians 2:8). When Peter tried to avert His arrest in the garden, Jesus rebuked him: "Do you think that I cannot appeal to my Father, and he will at once send me more than twelve legions of angels? But how then should the scriptures be fulfilled, that it must be so?" (Matthew 26:53, 54).

Further, what He Himself believed and practised with regard to the authority of Scripture He expected others to believe and practise also. In debate with religious leaders, as we have seen, it was to Him axiomatic that Scripture must be the court of appeal. His great complaint against the Jews was, "Have you not read?" Ignorance of Scripture had caused the Sadducees to err, and disregard for Scripture the Pharisees; while to some of His own disciples after the resurrection He had to say: "O foolish men, and slow of heart to believe all that the prophets have spoken! Was it not necessary that the Christ should suffer these things and enter into his glory?" Then, Luke adds, "beginning with Moses and all the prophets, he interpreted to them in all the scriptures the things concerning himself" (Luke 24:25–27; *cf.* vv. 44–47).

$\backsim$

DO NOT WORRY ABOUT YOUR LIFE

DIETRICH BONHOEFFER

WE USED TO think that one of the inalienable rights of man was that he should be able to plan both his professional and his private life. That is a thing of the past. The force of circumstances has brought us into a situation where we have to give up being "anxious about tomorrow" (Matt. 6:34).

But it makes all the difference whether we accept this willingly and in faith (as the Sermon on the Mount intends), or under continual constraint. For most people, the compulsory abandonment of planning for the future means that they are forced back into living just for the moment, irresponsibly, frivolously, or resignedly; some few dream longingly of better times to come, and try to forget the present. We find both these courses equally impossible, and there remains for us only the very narrow way, often extremely difficult to find, of living every day as if it were our last, and yet living in faith and responsibility as though there were to be a great future: "Houses and fields and vineyards shall again be bought in this land," proclaims Jeremiah (32:15), in paradoxical contrast to his prophecies of woe, just before the destruction of the holy city. It is a sign from God and a pledge of a fresh start and a great future, just when all seems black. Thinking and acting for the sake of the coming generation, but being ready to go any day without fear or anxiety—that, in practice, is the spirit in which we are forced to live. It is not easy to be brave and keep the spirit alive, but it is imperative.

∼

To Teach His Teachings

HORACE BUSHNELL

Horace Bushnell, a nineteenth-century Congregational clergyman, was concerned with how to nurture children in the process of educating them so that they didn't become fixated on the horrible and the negative in religion. He was concerned that parents should avoid presenting an image of God that was harsh and condemning. Religion has often been severe, and images of Jesus as a severe judge too much abound and tend to create neuroses in young children.

THE OSTRICH, IT will be observed, is nature's type of all unmotherhood. She hatches her young without incubation, depositing her eggs in the sand to be quickened by the solar heat. Her office as a mother bird is there ended. . . .

Probably enough there may be some of you that, without being Christians yourselves, are yet careful to teach your children all the saving truths of religion, and who thus may take it as undue severity to be charged with only giving your children this unnatural ostrich nurture. But how poor a teacher of Christ is anyone who is not in the light of Christ, and does not know the inward power of His truth, as a gospel of life to the soul. You press your child in this manner with duties you do not practise and promises you do not embrace; and if you do not succeed, it only means that you cannot impose on him to that high extent. A mother teaches by words only? No! But more, a great deal more by the atmosphere of love and patience she breathes. Besides, how easy it is for her to make everything she teaches legal and repulsive, just because she has no liberty or joy in it herself. What is wanted, therefore, is not merely to give a child the law, telling him this is duty, this is right, this God requires, this He will punish, but a much greater want is to have the spirit of all duty lived and breathed around him; to see, and feel, and breathe himself the living atmosphere of grace. Therefore it is vain, let all parents so understand, to imagine that you can really fulfil the true fatherhood and motherhood unless you are true Christians yourselves. I am sorry to discourage you in any good attempts. Rightly taken, what I say will not discourage you, but will only prompt you by all that is dearest to you on earth to become truly qualified for your office. By these dear pledges God has given you to call you to Himself, I beseech you to turn yourselves to the true life of religion. Have it first in yourselves, then teach it as you live it; teach it by living it; for you can do it in no other manner. Be Christians yourselves, and then it will not be difficult for you to do your true duties to your children. Until then it is really impossible.

∾

TEACHINGS ON FORGIVENESS

RICHARD ROLLE

IN MEAT AND drink be thou scarce and wise. Whiles thou eatest or drinkest let not the memory of thy God that feeds thee pass from thy mind; but praise, bless, and glorify Him in like morsel, so that thy heart be more in God's praising than in thy meat, that thy soul be not parted from God at any hour. This doing, before Christ Jesu thou shalt be worthy a crown, and the temptations of the fiend that in meat and drink await most men and beguile them thou shalt eschew. Either soothly by unmannerly taking of food they are cast down from the heights of virtue, or by too much abstinence they break down that virtue. . . .

But truly abstinence by itself is not holiness, but if it be discreet it helps us to be holy. If it is indiscreet it lets holiness, because it destroys discipline, without which virtues are turned to vices. If a man would be singular in abstinence, he ought to eschew the sight of men and their praising, that he be not proud for nought and so lose all: for men truly when they be holiest that they see most abstinent, when in truth ofttimes they are the worst.

He certain that has truly tasted the sweetness of endless love shall never deem himself to pass any man in abstinence, but the lower he supposes himself in abstinence anent himself, the more he shall be held marvellous among men. The best thing, and as I suppose pleasing to God, is to conform theyself in meat and drink to the time and place and estate of them with whom thou art; so that thou seem not to be wilful nor a feigner of religion. . . .

Truly the virtue of others is the ore in that it is not seen of men. Who may know how much love a man has anent God, how great compassion anent his neighbour? And doubtless the virtue of charity surpasses without comparison all fasting or abstinence, and all other works that may be seen; and oft it happens that he that before men is seen least to fast, within, before Christ, is most fervent in love.

∾

JESUS' SELF-CENTERED TEACHING

JOHN R. W. STOTT

THE MOST STRIKING feature of the teaching of Jesus is that he was constantly talking about himself. It is true that he spoke much about the fatherhood of God and the kingdom of God. But then he added that he was the Father's "Son," and that he had come to inaugurate the kingdom. Entry into the kingdom depended on men's response to him. He even did not hesitate to call the kingdom of God "my kingdom."

This self-centeredness of the teaching of Jesus immediately sets him apart from the other great religious teachers of the world. They were self-effacing. He was self-advancing. They pointed men away from themselves, saying, "That is the truth, so far as I perceive it; follow that." Jesus said, "I am the truth; follow me." The founder of none of the ethnic religions ever dared to say such a thing. The personal pronoun forces itself repeatedly on our attention as we read his words. For example:

I am the bread of life; he who comes to me shall not hunger, and he who believes in me shall never thirst.

I am the light of the world; he who follows me will not walk in darkness, but will have the light of life.

I am the resurrection and the life; he who believes in me, though he die, yet shall he live, and whoever lives and believes in me shall never die.

I am the way, and the truth, and the life; no one comes to the Father, but by me.

Come to me, all who labour and are heavy laden, and I will give you rest. Take my yoke upon you, and learn from me. . . .

John 6:35; 8:12; 11:25, 26; 14:6; Matthew 11:28, 29

The great question to which the first part of his teaching led was, "Who do you say that I am?" He affirmed that Abraham had rejoiced to see his day, that Moses had written of him, that the Scriptures bore witness to him, and that indeed in the three great divisions of the Old Testament—the law, the prophets and the writings—there were "things concerning himself" (Mark 8:29; John 8:56; 5:46; 5:39; Luke 24:27, 44).

Luke describes in some detail the dramatic visit which Jesus paid to the synagogue of his home village, Nazareth. He was given a scroll of the Old Testament Scriptures and he stood up to read. The passage was Isaiah 61:1–2:

The Spirit of the Lord is upon me,
because he has anointed me to preach good news to the poor.
He has sent me to proclaim release to the captives
and recovering of sight to the blind,
to set at liberty those who are oppressed,
to proclaim the acceptable year of the Lord.

He closed the book, returned it to the synagogue attendant and sat down, while the eyes of all the congregation were fastened on him. He then broke the silence with the amazing words, "Today this scripture has been fulfilled in your hearing." In other words, "Isaiah was writing about me."

With such an opinion of himself, it is not surprising that he called people to himself. Indeed, he did more than issue an invitation; he uttered a command. "Come to me," he said, and "Follow me." If men would only come to him, he promised to lift the burdens of the weary, to satisfy the hungry, and to quench the thirst of the parched soul (Matthew 11:28–30; John 6:35; 7:37). Further, his followers were to obey him and to confess him before men. His disciples came to recognize the right of Jesus to make these totalitarian claims, and in their letters Paul, Peter, James and Jude delight to call themselves his "slaves."

More than that, he offered himself to his contemporaries as the proper object of their faith and love. It is for man to believe in God; yet Jesus appealed to men to believe in himself. "This is the work of God," he declared, "that you believe in him whom he has sent." "He who believes in the Son has eternal life." If to believe in him was man's first duty, not to believe in him was his chief sin (John 6:29; 3:36; 8:24; 16:8, 9).

∾

SMILING AT THE SPOUSE

MOTHER TERESA OF CALCUTTA

Most orders of nuns, while practicing celibacy, see Jesus as their husband, and their commitment to him as marriage to the divine spouse. Mother Teresa of Calcutta is but enlarging on her vow to her divine spouse as she speaks about marriage.

ONE DAY AT a meeting, I was asked to give a message. So I told the people, "Husbands smile at your wives; wives smile at your husbands and your children." They could not understand how I was able to tell them this sort of thing. "Are you married?" one of them asked. "Yes," I replied, "and sometimes I find it difficult to smile at Jesus because He can be so demanding." And it is true. By our vow of chastity we are married to Jesus.

THE LITTLE FLOWERS OF SAINT FRANCIS

SAINT FRANCIS OF ASSISI

Francis of Assisi was born Giovanni di Pietro di Bernardone in 1182. While he came from a wealthy family, at his conversion he rejected the lifestyle of his rich parents, and after 1209 he lived out the teachings of Jesus and strove to imitate Christ. He preferred being rich in godliness.

GREAT AGONY OF DOUBT

The humble servant of Christ, St. Francis, at the beginning of his conversion when he had already gathered many companions and received them in the Order, was placed in great agony of doubt as to what he should do: whether to give himself only to continual prayer or to preach sometimes.

He wanted very much to know which of these would please our Lord Jesus Christ most. And as the holy humility that was in him did not allow him to trust in himself or in his own prayers, he humbly turned to others in order to know God's will in this matter.

SHOW ME WHAT IS BEST

So he called Brother Masseo and said to him: "Dear Brother, go to Sister Clare and tell her on my behalf to pray devoutly to God, with one of her more spiritual companions, that he may deign to show me what is best: either that I preach sometimes or that I devote myself only to prayer. And then go also to Brother Silvester, who is staying on Mount Subasio, and tell him the same thing."

This was that Lord Silvester who had seen a cross of gold issuing from the mouth of St. Francis which extended in length to heaven and in width to the ends of the world. And this Brother Silvester was so devout and holy that God immediately granted or revealed to him whatever he asked in prayer.

The Holy Spirit had made him remarkably deserving of divine communications, and he had conversed with God many times. And, therefore, St. Francis was very devoted to him and had great faith in him.

A HARVEST OF SOULS

Brother Masseo went and, as St. Francis had ordered him, gave the message first to St. Clare and then to Brother Silvester. When the latter received it, he immediately set himself to praying. And while praying he quickly had God's answer.

He went out at once to Brother Masseo and said: "The Lord says you are to tell Brother Francis this: that God has not called him to this state only on his own account, but that he may reap a harvest of souls and that many may be saved through him."

After this Brother Masseo went back to St. Clare to know what she had received from God. And she answered that both she and her companion had had the very same answer from God as Brother Silvester.

AFLAME WITH DIVINE POWER

Brother Masseo therefore returned to St. Francis. And the saint received him with great charity: he washed his feet and prepared a meal for him. And after he had eaten, St. Francis called Brother Masseo into the woods. And there he knelt down before Brother Masseo, and baring his head and crossing his arms, St. Francis asked him: "What does my Lord Jesus Christ order me to do?"

Brother Masseo replied that Christ had answered both Brother Silvester and Sister Clare and her companion and revealed that "He wants you to go about the world preaching, because God did not call you for yourself alone but also for the salvation of others."

And then the hand of the Lord came over St. Francis. As soon as he heard this answer and thereby knew the will of Christ, he got to his feet, all aflame with divine power and said to Brother Masseo with great fervor: "So let's go—in the name of the Lord!"

LIKE A BOLT OF LIGHTNING

And he took as companions Brother Masseo and Brother Angelo, holy men. And he set out like a bolt of lightning in this spiritual ardor, not paying any attention to the road or path.

They arrived at a village called Cannara. And St. Francis began to preach, first ordering the swallows who were twittering to keep quiet until he had finished preaching. And the swallows obeyed him. He preached there so fervently that all the men and women of that village, as a result of his sermon and the miracle of the swallows, in their great devotion wanted to follow him and abandon the village.

But St. Francis did not let them, saying to them: "Don't be in a hurry and don't leave, for I will arrange what you should do for the salvation of your souls." And from that time he planned to organize the Third Order of the Continent for the salvation of all people everywhere.

THE MULTITUDE OF BIRDS

And leaving them much consoled and disposed to penance, he left there and came between Cannara and Bevagna. And while going with the same fervor through that district with his companions, he looked up and saw near the road some trees on which there was such a countless throng of different birds as he had never seen before in that area. And also a very great crowd of birds was in a field near those trees. While he gazed and marveled at the multitude of birds, the Spirit of God came over him and he said to his companions: "Wait for me here on the road. I am going to preach to our sisters, the birds."

And he went into the field toward the birds that were on the ground. And as soon as he began to preach, all the birds that were on the trees came down toward him. And all of them stayed motionless with the others in the field, even though he went among them, touching many of them with his habit. But not a single one of them made the slightest move, and later they did not leave until he had given them his blessing, as Brother James of Massa, a holy man, said, and he had all the above facts from Brother Masseo, who was one of those who were the companions of the holy Father at that time.

STRIVE ALWAYS TO PRAISE GOD

The substance of St. Francis' sermon to those birds was this: "My little bird sisters, you owe much to God your Creator, and you must always and everywhere praise him, because he has given you a double and triple covering, and your colorful and pretty clothing, and your food is ready without your working for it, and your singing was taught to you by the Creator, and your numbers that have been multiplied by the blessing of God—and because he preserved your species in Noah's ark so that your race should not disappear from the earth.

"And you are also indebted to him for the realm of the air which he assigned to you. Moreover, you neither sow nor reap, yet God nourishes you, and he gives you the rivers and springs to drink from. He gives you high mountains and hills, rocks and crags as refuges, and lofty trees in which to make your nests. And although you do not know how to spin or sew, God gives you and your little ones the clothing which you need. So the Creator loves you very much since he gives you so many good things. Therefore, my little bird sisters, be careful not to be ungrateful, but strive always to praise God."

THEY SANG A WONDERFUL SONG

Now at these words of St. Francis, all those birds began to open their beaks, stretch out their necks, spread their wings, and reverently bow their heads to the ground, showing by their movements and their songs that the words which St. Francis was saying gave them great pleasure. And when St. Francis noticed this, he likewise rejoiced greatly in spirit with them, and he marveled at such a great throng of birds and at their very beautiful variety and also at their attention and familiarity and affection. And therefore he devoutly praised the wonderful Creator in them and gently urged them to praise the Creator.

Finally, when he had finished preaching to them and urging them to praise God, St. Francis made the Sign of the Cross over all those birds and gave them permission to leave. Then all the birds rose up unto the air simultaneously, and in the air they sang a wonderful song. And when they had finished singing, according to the form of the Cross which St. Francis had made over them, they separated in an orderly way and formed four groups. And each group rose high into the air and flew off in a different direction: one toward the east, another toward the west, the third toward the south, and the fourth toward the north. And each group sang marvelously as it flew away.

To the Four Quarters of the World

Thereby they signified that, just as St. Francis—who was later to bear the marks of Christ's Cross—had preached to them and made the Sign of the Cross over them, so they had separated in the form of a cross and had flown away, singing, toward the four quarters of the world, thus suggesting that the preaching of the Cross of Christ, which had been renewed by St. Francis, was to be carried throughout the world by him and by his friars, who, like birds, possess nothing of their own in this world and commit themselves entirely to the Providence of God.

And so they were called eagles by Christ when he said, "Wherever the body shall be, there eagles will gather." For the saints who place their hope in the Lord will take on wings like eagles and will fly up to the Lord and will not die for all eternity.

To the praise of Christ. Amen.

❧

Absolute Truthfulness

DIETRICH BONHOEFFER

The commandment of absolute truthfulness is really only another name for the fullness of discipleship. Only those who follow Jesus and cleave to

Him are living in absolute truthfulness. Such men have nothing to hide from their Lord. He knows them and has placed them in a state where truth prevails. They cannot hide their sinfulness from Jesus; for they have not revealed themselves to Jesus, but He has revealed Himself to them by calling them to follow Him. At the moment of their call Jesus showed up their sin and made them aware of it. Absolute truthfulness is possible only where sin has been uncovered, that is to say, where it has been forgiven by Jesus. Only those who are in a state of truthfulness through the confession of their sin to Jesus are not ashamed to tell the truth wherever it must be told. The truthfulness which Jesus demands from His followers is the self-abnegation which does not hide sin. Nothing is then hidden, everything is brought forth to the light of day.

In this question of truthfulness, what matters first and last is that a man's whole condition should be exposed, his whole evil laid bare in the sight of God. But sinful men do not like this sort of truthfulness, and they resist it with their might. That is why they persecute it and crucify it. It is only because we follow Jesus that we can be genuinely truthful, for then He reveals to us our sin upon the cross. The cross is God's truth about us, and therefore it is the only power which can make us truthful. When we know the cross we are no longer afraid of the truth.

~

THE GREAT COMMISSION

BILLY GRAHAM

IT IS HARD to imagine what must have been passing through the minds of that little band of eleven disciples as they clustered around the risen Lord Jesus Christ on a mountain somewhere in Galilee. They recently had gone through the misery of apparent defeat, watching helplessly as Jesus was nailed to a cross. Their dreams of a world kingdom under Christ's rule were shattered. Then came the reports from the women who had visited the tomb early on that first Easter morning—reports that He was alive! At first they doubted; but as time went on, they knew the reports to be true, for Jesus Himself appeared to them many times. Finally, He comes to them and issues the greatest challenge they—or we—could ever hear: "All power is given unto me in heaven and in earth. Go ye therefore, and teach all nations, baptizing them in the name of the Father, and of the Son, and of the Holy Ghost: Teaching them to observe all things whatsoever I have commanded you: and, lo, I am with you always, even unto the end of the world" (Matthew 28:18–20).

∾

JESUS THE WANDERER

LOIS A. CHENEY

WHO WAS JESUS?
He was a wanderer.

Foxes have holes, and the birds of the air have nests; but the Son of Man hath not where to lay his head.

He knows the loneliness that has its own completeness. He wandered from his parents at the age of twelve, and they were irritated with him and were worried about him. He wandered from his home and never returned. What did his mother think? What did she think of this son who left her and her home? He wandered up and down the land, and neighbors brought her stories of his strange behavior. Did his eyes ever meet hers—hers full of quiet confusion, maybe pain? He wandered purposefully and directly to the cross, and there she had to stand quietly and watch her wandering son die.

DID SHE KNOW that the cross would splinter into a million shafts that would wander through the centuries? When I wander from the good, the right, and the true; when I become discordant with my purpose; when I wander down roads of self-pity, busyness, weakness, and pride, it is good to know that my Savior is a wanderer too. There's no place toward which I can drift, but what I'll find him there. The wanderer quietly looks at me with tired eyes filled with welcoming love.

SAY THANK YOU

ALBERT SCHWEITZER

WHEN I LOOK back upon my early days I am stirred by the thought of the number of people whom I have to thank for what they gave me or for what they were to me. At the same time I am haunted by an oppressive consciousness of the little gratitude I really showed them when I was young. . . . For all that, I think I can say with truth that I am not ungrateful. I did occasionally wake up out of that youthful thoughtlessness. . . . But down to my twentieth year, and even later still, I did not exert myself sufficiently to express the gratitude which was really in my heart. I valued too low the pleasure felt at receiving real proofs of gratitude. Often, too, shyness prevented me from expressing the gratitude I felt.

As a result of this experience with myself I refuse to think that there is so much ingratitude in the world as is commonly maintained. I have never interpreted the parable of the Ten Lepers to mean that only one was grateful. All the ten, surely, were grateful, but nine of them hurried home first . . . One of them, however, had a disposition which made him act at once as his feelings bade him; he sought out the person who had helped him, and refreshed his soul with the assurance of his gratitude.

❧

THE SEVEN GREAT "I AM'S" OF JESUS

CALVIN MILLER

There are fourteen unique metaphors in the gospel of John that appear nowhere else in the gospels. A very prominent one, common among Christians, is the powerful metaphor of being born again; this metaphor sees Christian conversion as a new kind of spiritual life, just as birth is a new kind of physical being (John 3:3,5). In John 3:14, Jesus sees his saving purpose like that of the bronze serpent of Moses, as Moses once used it to save the camp of Israel. When Jesus met the woman at the well he used the metaphor of living water to illustrate the refreshing nature of his salvation (John 4:10ff). He sees his plan to save all of humanity as the great harvesting of souls (John 4:35). A fifth unique metaphor, taken by a large segment of the church to mean Communion, is that of commitment as the drinking of Christ's blood and the eating of his flesh (John 6:53). Jesus used a sixth metaphor when he taught that the Holy Spirit was the great, indwelling human counselor (John 14:17; 20:22). But the most powerful of all his metaphors appear in the seven "I am" statements. It is to these all-powerful "I am" metaphors that the church has so often turned to understand how Jesus defined himself. All of these inclusions are taken from the Contemporary English Version of the Bible.

THE BREAD OF LIFE
JOHN 6:35, 49–51

I am the bread that gives life! No one who comes to me will ever be hungry. No one who has faith in me will ever be thirsty. . . . Your ancestors ate manna in the desert, and later they died. But the bread from heaven has come down, so that no one who eats it will ever die. I am that bread from heaven!

THE LIGHT OF THE WORLD
JOHN 8:12

I am the light of the world! Follow me, and you won't be walking in the dark. You will have the light that gives life.

THE GATE OF THE SHEEP
JOHN 10:7–10

This rural metaphor would have been readily understood by shepherds of that day. Once a sheep was inside the sheepfold, it was safe from wild animals or thieves. Jesus, like other shepherds, guarded the safety of those who believed in him and protected them forever. This I am *was meant to assure his followers that he would guarantee their lives from every threat of eternal loss.*

I TELL YOU for certain that I am the gate of the sheep. Everyone who came before me was a thief or a robber, and the sheep did not listen to any of them. I am the gate. All who come in through me will be saved. Through me they will come and go and find pasture. A thief comes only to rob, kill, and destroy. I came so that everyone would have life, and have it in its fullest.

THE GOOD SHEPHERD
JOHN 10:11–13, 27–30

I am the good shepherd, and the good shepherd gives up his life for his sheep. Hired workers are not like the shepherd. They don't own the sheep, and when they see a wolf coming, they run off and leave the sheep.

Then the wolf attacks and scatters the flock. Hired workers run away because they don't care for the sheep. . . . My sheep know my voice and I know them. They follow me, and I give them eternal life, so that they will never be lost. No one can snatch them out of my hand. My Father gave them to me, and he is greater than all others. No one can snatch them from his hands, and I am one with the Father.

THE TEACHER AND LORD
JOHN 13:13−17

You call me your teacher and Lord, and you should, because that is who I am. And if your Lord and teacher has washed your feet, you should do the same for each other. I have set the example, and you should do for each other exactly what I have done for you. I tell you for certain that servants are not greater than their master, and messengers are not greater than the one who sent them. You know these things, and God will bless you, if you do them.

THE WAY, THE TRUTH, AND THE LIFE
JOHN 14:6−7

I am the way, the truth, and the life! Without me, no one can go to the Father. If you had known me, you would have known the Father. But from now on, you do know him, and you have seen him.

THE VINE
JOHN 15:1−8

I am the true vine, and my Father is the gardener. He cuts away every branch of mine that doesn't produce fruit. But he trims clean every branch that does produce fruit, so that it will produce even more fruit. You are already clean because of what I have said to you.

Stay joined to me and I will stay joined to you. Just as a branch cannot produce fruit unless it stays joined to the vine, you cannot produce fruit unless you stay joined to me. I am the vine, and you are the branches. If you stay joined to me, and I stay joined to you, then you will produce lots of fruit. But you cannot do anything without me. If you don't stay joined to me, you will be thrown away. You will be like dry branches that are gathered up and burned in a fire.

Stay joined to me and let my teachings become part of you. Then you can pray for whatever you want, and your prayer will be answered. When you become fruitful disciples of mine, my Father will be honored.

THE TEACHINGS
Matthew 11:28

PAUL TILLICH

WHEN I WAS of the age to receive confirmation and full membership of the Church, I was told to choose a passage from the Bible as the expression of my personal approach to the Biblical message and to the Christian Church. Every confirmand was obliged to do so, and to recite the passage before the congregation. When I chose the words, "Come unto me, all ye that labour and are heavy laden," I was asked with a kind of astonishment and even irony why I had chosen that particular passage. For I was living under happy conditions and, being only fifteen years old, was without any apparent labour and burden. I could not answer at that time; I felt a little embarrassed, but basically right. And I was right, indeed; every child is right in responding immediately to those words; every adult is right in responding to them in all periods of his life, and under all the conditions of his internal and external history. These words of Jesus are universal, and fit every human being and every human situation. They are simple; they grasp the heart of the primitive as well as that of the profound, disturbing the mind of the wise. Practically every word of Jesus had this character, sharing the difference between Him as the originator and the dependent interpreters, disciples and theologians, saints and preachers. Returning for the first time in my life to the passage of my early choice, I feel just as grasped by it as at that time, but infinitely more embarrassed by its majesty, profundity, and inexhaustible meaning.

❧

THE SERMON ON THE MOUNT
Matthew 4:23–7:29 KJV

The Sermon on the Mount is the best-known sermon in the world. It contains the best-known prayer ever prayed, the Lord's Prayer. It also contains the golden rule, perhaps the best-known of all English proverbs. It can be preached in less than eighteen minutes and yet is the most profound gathering of all of Jesus' teachings. Most scholars believe that while it may have been preached exactly in this form, it is doubtless a gathering of Jesus' finest teachings.

AND JESUS WENT about all Galilee, teaching in their synagogues, and preaching the gospel of the kingdom, and healing all manner of sickness and all manner of disease among the people. And his fame went throughout all Syria; and they brought unto him all sick people that were taken with diverse diseases and torments, and those who were possessed with demons, and those who were epileptics, and those who had the palsy; and he healed them. And there followed him great multitudes of people from Galilee, and from Decapolis, and from Jerusalem, and from Judaea, and from beyond the Jordan. And seeing the multitude, he went up into a mountain: and when he was seated, his disciples came unto him. And he opened his mouth, and taught them, saying, "Blessed are the poor in spirit; for theirs is the kingdom of heaven. Blessed are they that mourn; for they shall be comforted. Blessed are the meek; for they shall inherit the earth. Blessed are they who do hunger and thirst after righteousness; for they shall be filled. Blessed are the merciful; for they shall obtain mercy. Blessed are the pure in heart; for they shall see God. Blessed are the peacemakers; for they shall be called the sons of God. Blessed are they who are persecuted for righteousness' sake; for theirs is the kingdom of heaven. Blessed are ye, when men shall revile you, and persecute you, and shall say all manner of evil against you falsely, for my sake. Rejoice, and be exceedingly glad; for great is your reward in heaven; for so persecuted they the prophets who were before you.

"Ye are the salt of the earth, but if the salt have lost its savor, with what shall it be salted? It is thereafter good for nothing, but to be cast out, and to be trodden under foot of men. Ye are the light of the world. A city that is set on an hill cannot be hidden. Neither do men light a lamp, and put it under a bushel, but on a lampstand, and it giveth light unto all that are in the house. Let your light so shine before men, that they may see your good works, and glorify your Father, who is in heaven.

"Think not that I am come to destroy the law, or the prophets; I am not come to destroy, but to fulfill. For verily I say unto you, till heaven and earth pass, one jot or one tittle shall in no way pass from the law, till all be fulfilled. Whosoever, therefore shall break one of these least commandments, and shall teach men so, he shall be called the least in the kingdom of heaven; but whosoever shall do and teach them, the same shall be called great in the kingdom of heaven. For I say unto you that except your righteousness shall exceed the righteousness of the scribes and Pharisees, ye shall in no case enter into the kingdom of heaven.

"Ye have heard that is was said by them of old, 'Thou shalt not kill and whosoever shall kill shall be in danger of judgment'; but I say unto you that whosoever is angry with his brother without a cause shall be in danger of judgment; and whosoever shall say to his brother, 'Raca,' shall be in danger of the council; but whosoever shall say, 'Thou fool,' shall be in danger of hell fire. Therefore, if thou bring thy gift to the altar, and there rememberest that thy brother hath anything against thee, leave there thy gift before the altar, and go thy way; first be reconciled to thy brother, and then come and offer thy gift. Agree with thine adversary quickly, while thou art in the way with him, lest at any time the adversary deliver thee to the judge, and the judge deliver thee to the officer, and thou be cast into prison. Verily I say unto thee, thou shalt by no means come out from there, till thou hast paid the uttermost farthing.

"Ye have heard that it was said by them of old, 'Thou shalt not commit adultery'; but I say unto you that whosoever looketh on a woman to lust after her hath committed adultery with her already in his heart. And if thy right eye offend thee, pluck it out, and cast it from thee; for it is profitable for thee that one of thy members should perish, and not that thy whole body should be cast into hell. And if thy right hand offend thee, cut it off, and cast it from thee; for it is profitable for thee that one of thy members should perish, and not that thy whole body should be cast into hell. It hath been said, 'Whosoever shall put away his wife, let him give her a writing of divorcement'; but I say unto you that whosoever shall put away his wife, except for the cause of fornication, causeth her to commit adultery; and whosoever shall marry her that is divorced committeth adultery.

"Again, ye have heard that it hath been said by them of old, 'Thou shalt not perjure thyself, but shalt perform unto the Lord thine oaths'; but I say unto you, swear not at all; neither by heaven, for it is God's throne; nor by the earth, for it is his footstool; neither by Jerusalem, for it is the city of the great King. Neither shalt thou swear by thy head, because thou canst not make one hair white or black. But let your communication be, Yea, yea; Nay, nay; for whatever is more than these cometh of evil.

"Ye have heard that it hath been said, 'An eye for an eye, and a tooth for a tooth'; but I say unto you that ye resist not evil, but whosoever shall smite thee on thy right cheek, turn to him the other also. And if any man will sue thee at the law, and take away thy coat, let him have thy cloak also. And whosoever shall compel thee to go a mile, go with him two. Give to him that asketh thee, and from him that would borrow of thee turn not thou away.

"Ye have heard that it hath been said, 'Thou shalt love thy neighbor, and hate thine enemy'; but I say unto you, love your enemies, bless them that curse you, do good to them that hate you, and pray for them who despitefully use you and persecute you, that ye may be the sons of your Father, who is in heaven; for he maketh his sun to rise on the evil and on the good, and sendeth rain on the just and on the unjust. For if ye love them who love you, what reward have ye? Do not even the tax collectors the same? And if ye greet your brethren only, what do ye more than others? Do not even the heathen so? Be ye, therefore perfect, even as your Father, who is in heaven, is perfect.

"Take heed that ye do not your alms before men, to be seen by them; otherwise ye have no reward of your Father, who is in heaven. Therefore, when thou doest thine alms, do not sound a trumpet before thee, as the hypocrites do in the synagogues and in the streets, that they may have glory from men. Verily I say unto you, they have their reward. But when thou doest alms, let not thy left hand know what thy right hand doeth, that thine alms may be in secret; and thy Father, who seeth in secret, shall reward thee openly.

"And when thou prayest, thou shalt not be as the hypocrites are; for they love to pray standing in the synagogues and at the corners of the streets, that they may be seen by men. Verily I say unto you, they have their reward. But thou, when thou prayest, enter into thy room, and when thou hast shut thy door, pray to thy Father, who is in secret; and thy Father, who seeth in secret, shall reward thee openly. But when ye pray, use not vain repetitions, as the pagans do; for they think that they shall be heard for their much speaking. Be not ye, therefore, like unto them; for your Father knoweth what things ye have need of, before ye ask him. After this manner, therefore, pray ye: Our Father, who art in heaven, hallowed be thy name. Thy kingdom come. Thy will be done in earth, as it is in heaven. Give us this day our daily bread. And forgive us our debts, as we forgive our debtors. And lead us not into temptation, but deliver us from evil. For thine is the kingdom, and the power, and the glory, forever. Amen. For if ye forgive men their trespasses, your heavenly Father will also forgive you; but if ye forgive not men their trespasses, neither will your Father forgive your trespasses.

"Moreover, when ye fast, be not, as the hypocrites, of a sad countenance; for they disfigure their faces, that they may appear unto men to fast. Verily I say unto you, they have their reward. But thou, when thou fastest, anoint thine head, and wash thy face, that thou appear not unto men to fast, but unto thy Father, who is in secret; and thy Father, who seeth in secret, shall reward thee openly.

"Lay not up for yourselves treasures upon earth, where moth and rust doth corrupt, and where thieves break through and steal, but lay up for yourselves treasures in heaven, where neither moth nor rust doth corrupt, and where thieves do not break through nor steal; for where your treasure is, there will your heart be also. The lamp of the body is the eye; if, therefore, thine eye be healthy, thy whole body shall be full of light. But if thine eye be evil, thy whole body shall be full of darkness. If, therefore, the light that is in thee be darkness, how great is that darkness!

"No man can serve two masters; for either he will hate the one, and love the other; or else he will hold to the one, and despise the other. Ye cannot serve God and money. Therefore, I say unto you, be not anxious for your life, what ye shall eat, or what ye shall drink; nor yet for your body, what ye shall put on. Is not the life more than food and the body than raiment? Behold the fowls of the air; for they sow not, neither do they reap, nor gather into barns, yet your heavenly Father feedeth them. Are ye not much better than they? Which of you by being anxious can add one cubit unto his stature? And why are ye anxious for raiment? Consider the lilies of the field, how they grow; they toil not, neither do they spin, and yet I say unto you that even Solomon, in all his glory, was not arrayed like one of these. Wherefore, if God so clothe the grass of the field, which today is, and tomorrow is cast into the oven, shall he not much more clothe you, O ye of little faith? Therefore, be not anxious saying, 'What shall we eat?' or, 'What shall we drink?' or, 'With what shall we be clothed?' For after all these things do the Gentiles seek. For your heavenly Father knoweth that ye have need of all these things. But seek ye first the kingdom of God, and his righteousness, and all these things shall be added unto you. Be, therefore, not anxious about tomorrow; for tomorrow will be anxious for the things of itself. Sufficient unto the day is its own evil.

"Judge not, that ye be not judged. For with what judgment ye judge, ye shall be judged; and with what measure ye measure, it shall be measured to you again. And why beholdest thou the mote that is in thy brother's eye, but considerest not the beam that is in thine own eye? Or how wilt thou say to thy brother, 'Let me pull the mote out of thine eye'; and, behold a beam is in thine own eye? Thou hypocrite, first cast the beam out of thine own eye, and then shalt thou see clearly to cast the mote out of thy brother's eye.

"Give not that which is holy unto the dogs, neither cast your pearls before swine, lest they trample them under their feet, and turn again and lacerate you.

"Ask, and it shall be given you; seek, and ye shall find; knock, and it shall be opened unto you; for every one that asketh receiveth; and he that seeketh findeth; and to him that knocketh it shall be opened. Or what man is there of you whom, if his son ask bread, will he give him a stone? Or if he ask a fish, will he give him a serpent? If ye then, being evil, know how to give good gifts unto your children, how much more shall your Father, who is in heaven, give good things to them that ask him? Therefore, all things whatever ye would that men should do to you, do ye even so to them; for this is the law and the prophets.

"Enter in at the narrow gate; for wide is the gate, and broad is the way, that leadeth to destruction, and many there be who go in that way; because narrow is the gate, and hard is the way, which leadeth unto life, and few there be that find it.

"Beware of false prophets, who come to you in sheep's clothing, but inwardly they are ravening wolves. Ye shall know them by their fruits. Do men gather grapes of thorns, or figs of thistles? Even so, every good tree bringeth forth good fruit, but a corrupt tree bringeth forth bad fruit. A good tree cannot bring forth bad fruit, neither can a corrupt tree bring forth good fruit. Every tree that bringeth not forth good fruit is hewn down, and cast into the fire. Wherefore, by their fruits ye shall know them.

"Not every one that saith unto me, Lord, Lord, shall enter into the kingdom of heaven, but he that doeth the will of my Father, who is in heaven. Many will say to me in that day, 'Lord, Lord, have we not prophesied in thy name? And in thy name have cast out demons? And in thy name done many wonderful works?' And then will I profess unto them, I never knew you; depart from me, ye that work iniquity.

"Therefore, whosoever heareth these sayings of mine, and doeth them, I will liken him unto a wise man, who built his house upon a rock. And the rain descended, and the floods came, and the winds blew and beat upon that house and it fell not; for it was founded upon a rock. And every one that heareth these sayings of mine, and doeth them not, shall be likened unto a foolish man, who built his house upon the sand. And the rain descended, and the floods came, and the winds blew and beat upon the house, and it fell; and great was the fall of it." And it came to pass, when Jesus had ended these sayings, the people were astonished at his doctrine; for he taught them as one having authority, and not as the scribes.

WHOEVER WOULD BE GREAT

J. C. AND AUGUSTUS HARE

YOUNG MEN ARE perpetually told that the first of duties is to render oneself independent. But the phrase, unless it mean that the first of duties is to avoid hanging, is unhappily chosen; saying what it ought not to say, and leaving unsaid what it ought to say.

It is true that, in a certain sense, the first of duties is to become free; because freedom is the antecedent condition for the fulfilment of every other duty, the only element in which a reasonable soul can exist. Until the umbilical cord is severed, the child can hardly be said to have a separate life. So long as the heart and mind continue in slavery, it is impossible for a man to offer up a voluntary and reasonable sacrifice of himself. Now in slavery, since the Fall, we are all born; from which slavery we have to emancipate ourselves by some act of our own, half-conscious it may be, or almost unconscious. By some act of our own, I say; not indeed unassisted; for every parent, every friend, every teacher is a minister ordained to help us in this act. But though we cannot by our own act lift ourselves out of the pit, we must by an act of our own take hold of the hand which offers to lift us out of it. . . .

Hence we perceive that the true motive for our striving to set ourselves free is to manifest our freedom by resigning it through an act to be renewed every moment, ever resuming and ever resigning it; to the end that our service may be entire, that the service of the hands may likewise be the service of the will; even as the Apostle, *being free from all, made himself servant to all.* This is the accomplishment of the great Christian paradox, *Whosoever will be great, let him be a minister; and whosoever will be chief, let him be a servant.*

～

REVOLUTIONARY NEIGHBOR RELATIONS

DAVID WENHAM

THE REVOLUTION THAT Jesus proclaimed was, as we have seen, good news of God's love to the needy and bad news of God's judgement to the comfortable and complacent. But what did joining the Jesus revolution mean in practice? We have already had many hints of this, for example in the parable of the sower with its picture of fruitful crops, in the parables about the end with their call for faithful service to the absent master, and in the parables on wealth with their warnings about a selfish this-worldly lifestyle. But a number of other parables spell out more of what is involved.

Several of Jesus' parables make it clear that joining the revolution means active commitment to the exciting work of the revolution. It means, in other words, living out and spreading the love and healing work that characterized Jesus' ministry.

❧

THE STORIES OF JESUS

CALVIN MILLER

If we consider all four gospels—Matthew, Mark, Luke, and John— the illustrated teachings of Christ fall into three categories. First, there are the eighteen major stories for which Jesus' teachings are most remembered. There are sixty-seven analogies where Jesus does quick comparisons of his truths to ordinary, understandable images. And finally, in a category all to themselves, there are sixteen metaphors in the gospel of John, where Jesus refers to himself as bread, light, water, or the Good Shepherd. Matthew, Mark, and Luke are called the synoptic gospels (from the Greek common eye) because these three writers tell the story of Jesus in the same way. In fact, nearly every verse in the gospel of Mark is contained in the gospel of Matthew. Both Matthew and Luke, however, have a great many illustrated teachings of Christ found in neither of the other gospels. John's gospel contains none of the parables of Christ so common in Matthew, Mark, and Luke, but John's teachings are held together by—and group themselves around—the sixteen powerful metaphors of Christ. Besides these illustrated teachings there are a great many precept-centered teachings of Christ (found in places like the Sermon on the Mount or in those passages where Jesus states his views of the end of the world). The King James Version of the Sermon on the Mount is included in this chapter on the teachings of Christ, in part so that you can examine the less-illustrated, more precept-centered teachings of Christ. All of the following stories are from the Living Bible.

1. The Story of the Soils

This parable, the story of a farmer planting grain by casting it broadly by hand, is often called the parable of the sower. But the emphasis of the story is not so much on how the farmer planted the grain as on how the soil received it. Jesus told this tale to illustrate that the gospel is received differently by different people. Only a few —in this parable about a fourth of the hearers—believe it to the extent that its truths become productive in their lives.

One day he gave this illustration to a large crowd that was gathering to hear him—while many others were still on the way, coming from other towns.

"A farmer went out to his field to sow grain. As he scattered the seed on the ground, some of it fell on a footpath and was trampled on; and the birds came and ate it as it lay exposed. Other seed fell on shallow soil with rock beneath. This seed began to grow but soon withered and died for lack of moisture. Other seed landed in thistle patches, and the young grain stocks were soon choked out. Still others fell on fertile soil; this seed grew and produced a crop one-hundred times as large as he had planted." (As he was giving this illustration he said, "If anyone has listening ears, use them now!")

His apostles asked him what the story meant.

He replied, "God has granted you to know the meaning of these parables, for they tell a great deal about the Kingdom of God. But these crowds hear the words and do not understand, just at the ancient prophets predicted.

"This is the meaning: The seed is God's message to men. The hard path where some seed fell represents the hard hearts of those who hear the words of God, but then the devil comes and steals the words away and prevents people from believing and being saved. The stony ground represents those who enjoy listening to sermons, but somehow the message never gets through to them and doesn't take root and grow. They know the message is true and sort of believe for a while, but when the hot winds of persecution blow, they lose interest. The seed among the thorns represents those who listen and believe God's words but whose faith afterwards is choked out by worry and riches and the responsibilities and pleasures of life. And so they are never able to help anyone else believe the Good News.

"But the good soil represents honest, good-hearted people. They listen to God's words and cling to them and steadily spread them to others who also soon believe."

Luke 8:4—15

2. THE STORY OF THE GOOD SAMARITAN

The point of this teaching was not so much that the Samaritan was a good man, but that he was a Samaritan. Samaritans were Jews who were racially mixed. Their tainted bloodlines and errant teachings had left them odious to the purebred and orthodox Jews of Palestine in the time of Christ. In this story Jesus quickened the interest of Jews by telling them that mercy was an attribute for whoever performed it. The blue-ribbon Jews in this tale turn out to be wintry institutional professionals when compared to the kind Samaritan whom their prejudice scorned.

One day an expert on Moses' laws came to test Jesus' orthodoxy by asking him this question: "Teacher, what does a man need to do to live forever in heaven?"

Jesus replied, "What does Moses' law say about it?"

"It says," he replied, "that you must love the Lord your God with all your heart, and with all your soul, and with all your strength, and with all your mind. And you must love your neighbor just as much as you love yourself."

"Right!" Jesus told him. "Do this and you shall live!"

The man wanted to justify (his lack of love for some kinds of people), so he asked, "Which neighbors?"

Jesus replied with an illustration: "A Jew going on a trip from Jerusalem to Jericho was attacked by bandits. They stripped him of his clothes and money and beat him up and left him lying half dead beside the road.

"By chance a Jewish priest came along: and when he saw the man lying there, he crossed to the other side of the road and passed him by. A Jewish Temple-assistant walked over and looked at him there, but went on.

"But a despised Samaritan came along, and when he saw him, he felt deep pity. Kneeling beside him, the Samaritan soothed his wounds with medicine and bandaged them. Then he put the man on his donkey and walked along beside him till they came to an inn, where he nursed him through the night. The next day he handed the innkeeper two twenty dollar bills and told him to take care of the man. 'If his bill runs any higher than that,' he said, 'I'll pay the difference the next time I am here.'

"Now which of these three would you say was a neighbor to the bandit's victim?"

The man replied, "The one who showed him some pity."

Then Jesus said, "Yes, now go and do the same."

Luke 10:25–37

3. THE STORY OF THE BIG BARNS

This parable is alternately called the story of the rich fool. Like many of Jesus' stories, this one is severely set against crass materialism. You will notice that this story—like many of Jesus' tales—did not come from a sermon but from a happenstance encounter along the edges of his travel and experience.

Then someone called from the crowd, "Sir, please tell my brother to divide my father's estate with me."

But Jesus replied, "Who made me a judge over you to decide such things as that? Beware! Don't always be wishing for what you don't have. For real life and real living are not related to how rich we are."

Then he gave an illustration: "A rich man had a fertile farm that produced rich crops. In fact, his barns were full to overflowing—he couldn't get everything in. He thought about his problem, and finally exclaimed, 'I know—I'll tear down my barns and build bigger ones! Then I'll have room enough. And I'll set back and say to myself, "Friend, you have enough stored away for years to come. Now take it easy! Wine, women and song for you!'

"But God said to him, 'Fool! Tonight you die! Then who will get it all?'

"Yes, every man is a fool who gets rich on earth but not in heaven."

Luke 12:13–21

4. THE UNPRODUCTIVE FIG TREE

Jesus' teachings focused on the importance of living productive, fruitful lives. This story indicates a great truth, that the personal meaning we find in life comes from our feelings of productive living. But more than that, the story seems to say that God as well has an expectation that Christ's followers will lead productive lives.

"A man planted a fig tree in his garden and came again and again to see if he could find any fruit on it, but he was always disappointed. Finally, he told his gardener to cut it down. 'I've waited three years and there hasn't been a single fig!' he said. 'Why bother with it any longer? It's taking up space we can use for something else.'

" 'Give it one more chance,' the gardener answered. 'Leave it another year, and I'll give it special attention and plenty of fertilizer. If we get figs next year, fine; if not, I'll cut it down.' "

Luke 13:6–9

5. THE GREAT FEAST

This story seems to indicate that Jesus' own people would likely not be as responsive to the Christian faith as Gentiles would be. In Matthew's gospel (22:1ff) this story is told in the context of a wedding feast, but here in Luke, the feast becomes a symbol of God's love for all people. Outcasts are welcome in the Kingdom of God, especially as those who do not prize the Kingdom of God reject their favored status.

"A man prepared a great feast and sent out many invitations. When he was ready, he sent his servant around to notify the guests that it was time for them to arrive. But they all began to make excuses. One said he had just bought a field and wanted to inspect it, and asked to be excused. Another said that he had just bought five pair of oxen and wanted to try them out. Another had just been married and for that reason couldn't come. The servant returned and reported to his master what they had said. His master was angry and told him to go quickly into the streets and alleys of the city and to invite the beggars, crippled, lame and blind. But even then there was still room.

" 'Well, then,' said his master, 'go out into the country lanes and out behind the hedges and urge anyone you find to come so that the house will be full. For none of those that I invited first will get even the smallest taste of what I had prepared for them.' "

Luke 14:16–24

6. THE LOST SHEEP

The entire fifteenth chapter of Luke's gospel is occupied with three stories—all about things that are lost. Jesus tells these stories to illustrate how valuable even errant and wandering people are to God. In each tale what is lost might seem insignificant, and yet while it is lost, those who desire it to be found are in anguish over the missing article. It has been pointed out that in the first story one sheep out of a hundred is lost—or 1 percent of the shepherd's valuable flock. In the second tale, one of a woman's ten coins is lost—or 10 percent of her valuable purse. In the final tale, of a lost boy, otherwise known as the prodigal son, one of the two boys is lost—or 50 percent of an old man's family. In each of the stories, as the lost object is found, there is great rejoicing. Jesus says this is how God feels every time one of his lost children is found.

Dishonest tax collectors and other notorious sinners often came to listen to Jesus' sermons; but this caused complaints from the Jewish religious leaders and the experts on Jewish law, because he was associating with such despicable people—even eating with them! So Jesus used this illustration: "If you had a hundred sheep and one of them strayed away and was lost in the wilderness, wouldn't you leave the ninety-nine others to go and search for the lost one until you found it? And then you would joyfully carry it home on your shoulders. When you arrived you would call together your friends and neighbors to rejoice with you because your lost sheep was found.

"Well in the same way heaven will be happier over one lost sinner who returns to God than over the ninety-nine others who haven't strayed away!"

Luke 15:1–7

7. THE LOST COIN

"Or take another illustration: A woman has ten valuable silver coins and loses one. Won't she light a lamp and look in every corner of the house and sweep every nook and cranny until she finds it? And then won't she call in her friends and neighbors to rejoice with her? In the same way there is joy in the presence of the angels of God when one sinner repents."

Luke 15:8–10

8. THE PRODIGAL SON

To further illustrate the point, he told them this story: "A man had two sons. When the younger told his father, 'I want my share of the estate now, instead of waiting till you die!' his father agreed to divide his wealth between his sons.

"A few days later this younger son packed all his belongings and took a trip to a distant land, and there wasted all his money on parties and prostitutes. About the time his money was gone a great famine swept over the land, and he began to starve. He persuaded a local farmer to hire him to feed his pigs. The boy became so hungry that even the pods he was feeding the swine looked good to him. And no one gave him anything.

"When he finally came to his senses, he said to himself, 'At home even the hired men have food enough and to spare, and here I am, dying of hunger! I will go home to my father and say, "Father, I have sinned against both heaven and you, and am no longer worthy of being called your son. Please, take me as a hired man." '

"So he returned home to his father. And while he was still a long distance away, his father saw him coming, and was filled with loving pity and ran and embraced him and kissed him.

"His son said to him, 'Father, I have sinned against heaven and you, and am not worthy of being called your son—'

"But his father said to the slaves, 'Quick! Bring the finest robe in the house and put it on him. And a jeweled ring for his finger; and shoes! And kill the calf we have in the fattening pen. We must celebrate with a feast, for this son of mine was dead and has returned to life. He was lost and is found.' So the party began.

"Meanwhile, the older son was in the fields working; when he returned home, he heard dance music coming from the house, and he asked one of the servants what was going on.

" 'Your brother is back,' he was told, 'and your father has killed the calf we were fattening and has prepared a great feast to celebrate his coming home again unharmed.'

"The older brother was angry and wouldn't go in. His father came out and begged him, but he replied, 'All these years I've worked hard for you and never once refused to do a single thing you told me to; and in all that time you never gave me even one young goat for a feast with my friends. Yet when this son of your comes back after spending your money on prostitutes, you celebrate by killing the finest calf we have on the place.'

" 'Look, dear son,' his father said to him, 'you and I are very close, and everything I have is yours. But it is right to celebrate. For he is your brother; and he was dead and has come back to life! He was lost and is found!' "

Luke 15:11–32

9. THE DISHONEST STEWARD

This is one of the most enigmatic of all of Jesus' stories. Why Jesus praises a rogue intrigues scholars. It must be remembered that Jesus does not praise his dishonest business tactics—only his shrewd way of looking out for his own future. Jesus makes it clear that to fail to provide for our own future is foolhardy indeed. To live this brief life as though this were all there is, is irresponsible.

Jesus now told this story to his disciples: "A rich man hired an accountant to handle his affairs, but soon the rumor went around that the accountant was thoroughly dishonest.

"So his employer called him in and said, 'What's this I hear about your stealing from me? Get your report in order for you are to be dismissed.'

"The accountant thought to himself, 'Now what? I'm through here, and I haven't got the strength to go out and dig ditches, and I'm too proud to beg. I know just the thing! And then I'll have plenty of friends to take care of me when I leave!'

"So he invited each one who owed money to his employer to come and discuss the situation. He asked the first one, 'How much do you owe him?' 'My debt is 850 gallons of olive oil,' the man replied. 'Yes, here is the contract you signed,' the accountant told him. 'Tear it up and write another one for half that much!'

" 'And how much do you owe him?' he asked the next man. 'A thousand bushels of wheat,' was the reply. 'Here,' the accountant said, 'take your note and replace it with one for only 800 bushels!'

"The rich man had to admire the rascal for being so shrewd. And it is true that the citizens of this world are more clever (in dishonesty) than the godly are. But shall I tell you to act that way to buy friendship through cheating? Will this assure you entry into an everlasting home in heaven? No! For unless you are honest in small matters, you won't be in large ones. If you cheat even a little, you won't be honest with greater responsibilities. And if you are untrustworthy about worldly wealth, who will trust you with the true riches of heaven."

Luke 16:1–11

10. The Rich Man and the Beggar

This parable is set against that crass, unfeeling materialism which does not see the poor and misfortunate around us on the outskirts of our lives. It is another of Jesus' frequent comments on the nonspiritual wealthy, who may in the end be judged by the poor they have wronged for not showing mercy.

"There was a certain rich man," Jesus said, "who was splendidly clothed and lived each day in mirth and luxury. One day Lazarus, a diseased beggar, was laid at his door. As he lay there longing for scraps from the rich man's table, the dogs would come and lick his open sores. Finally the beggar died and was carried by the angels to be with Abraham in the place of the righteous dead. The rich man also died and was buried, and his soul went into hell. There in torment, he saw Lazarus in the far distance with Abraham.

" 'Father Abraham,' he shouted, 'have some pity! Send Lazarus over here if only to dip the tip of his finger in water and cool my tongue, for I am in anguish in these flames.'

"But Abraham said to him, 'Son, remember that during your lifetime you had everything you wanted, and Lazarus had nothing. So now he is here being comforted and you are in anguish. And besides, there is a great chasm separating us, and anyone wanting to come to you from here is stopped at its edge; and no one over there can cross to us.'

"Then the rich man said, 'O Father Abraham, then please send him to my father's home—for I have five brothers—to warn them about this place of torment lest they come here when they die.'

"But Abraham said, 'The Scriptures have warned them again and again. Your brothers can read them anytime they want to.'

"The rich man replied, 'No, Father Abraham, they won't bother to read them. But if someone is sent to them from the dead, they will turn from their sins.'

"But Abraham said, 'If they won't listen to Moses and the prophets, they won't listen even though someone rises from the dead.' "

Luke 16:19–31

11. THE IMPORTUNATE WIDOW

The idea of praying continually in this parable is attached to God's answer. Many scholars, including the late C. S. Lewis, turned from the very idea that prayer could change God's mind about our circumstances. Such a notion makes God appear fickle and somewhat at the mercy of human demand. But Jesus seems to teach here that the continued earnestness of prayer will eventually get God to answer our prayers. In this case, the city judge decides to give the poor woman what she wants just to get her off his back. The parable is not given to entice Christians to vex God into giving them their way. Rather, the parable is a kind of evidence that praying without giving up is the kind of petition that God eventually hears.

One day Jesus told his disciples a story to illustrate their need for constant prayer and to show them that they must keep praying until the answer comes.

"There was a city judge," he said, "a very godless man who had great contempt for everyone. A widow of that city came to him frequently to appeal for justice against a man who had harmed her. The judge ignored her for a while, but eventually she got on his nerves.

" 'I fear neither God nor man,' he said to himself, 'but this woman bothers me. I'm going to see that she gets justice, for she is wearing me out with her constant coming!' "

Then the Lord said, "If even an evil judge can be worn down like that, don't you think that God will surely give justice to his people who plead with him day and night? Yes! He will answer them quickly!"

Luke 18:1–8

12. THE TALENTS

This parable, told in a slightly different way in Matthew's gospel, holds at its heart the notion that while all people have different gifts and talents, no talent—no matter how seemingly insignificant—is unimportant to God. All that we are is to be developed and used to further God's purposes in the world. Those who decry their service on the premise that their gift was insignificant will face an unpleasant reckoning.

And because Jesus was nearing Jerusalem, he told a story to correct the impression that the Kingdom of God would begin right away.

"A nobleman living in a certain province was called away to the distant capital of the empire to be crowned king of his province. Before he left he called together ten assistants and gave them each $2,000 to invest while he was gone. But some of his people hated him and sent him their declaration of independence, stating that they had rebelled and would not acknowledge him as their king.

"Upon his return he called in the men to whom he had given the money, to find out what they had done with it, and what their profits were.

"The first man reported a tremendous gain—ten times as much as the original amount!

" 'Fine!' the king exclaimed. 'You are a good man. You have been faithful with the little I entrusted to you, and as your reward, you shall be governor of ten cities.'

"The next also reported a splendid gain—five times the original amount.

" 'All right!' his master said. 'You can be governor over five cities.'

"But the third man brought back only the money he had started with. 'I've kept it safe,' he said, 'because I was afraid (you would demand my profits), for you are a hard man to deal with, taking what isn't yours, and even confiscating the crops that others plant.' 'You vile and wicked slave,' the king roared. 'Hard am I? That's exactly how I'll be toward you! If you knew so much about me and how tough I am, then why didn't you deposit the money in the bank so that I could at least get some interest on it?'

"Then turning to the others standing by he ordered, 'Take the money away from him and give it to the man who earned the most.'

" 'But sir,' they said, 'he has enough already!'

" 'Yes,' the king replied, 'but it is always true that those who have, get more, and those who have little, soon lose even that. And now about these enemies of mine who revolted—bring them in and execute them before me.' "

After telling this story, Jesus went on towards Jerusalem, walking ahead of his disciples.

Luke 19:11–28

13. THE VINEYARD OWNER'S SON

This story Jesus told to illustrate the sin of rejecting him as the Messiah. In the gospel of John there is a somber line—that in his own land and among his own countrymen he was not accepted as the Messiah (1:11). Jesus in other passages of the New Testament made it clear that he came so that all men might discover through him the true nature of God (John 10:30). Therefore eternal life was to be found only in him (John 14:6). This parable states the consequence of rejecting Jesus as the Christ. Those tenants who mistreated the owner's son must have been quickly seen by institutional officials to be themselves. Those previous envoys who had come to collect the rent they would clearly have understood to be the prophets, whom their forebears had earlier persecuted and killed.

"A man planted a vineyard and rented it out to some farmers, and went away to a distant land to live for several years. When harvest time came, he sent one of his men to the farm to collect his share of the crops. But the tenants sent him back empty-handed. Then he sent another, but the same thing happened; he was beaten up and insulted without collecting. A third man was sent and the same thing happened. He, too, was wounded and chased away.

" 'What shall I do?' the owner asked himself. 'I know! I'll send my cherished son. Surely they will show respect for him.'

"But when the tenants saw his son, they said, 'This is our chance! This fellow will inherit all the land when his father dies. Come on. Let's kill him, and then it will be ours.' So they dragged him out of the vineyard and killed him.

"What do you think the owner will do? I'll tell you—he will come and kill them and rent the vineyard to others."

"But they would never do a thing like that," his listeners protested.

Jesus looked at them and said, "Then what does the scripture mean when it says, 'The stone rejected by the builders was made the cornerstone'?" And he added, "Whoever stumbles over that Stone shall be broken; and those on whom it falls will be crushed to dust."

Luke 20:9–18

14. THE PARABLE OF THE WEEDS

This parable has traditionally been called the parable of the tares (an old English word for weeds). The parable explains the presence of evil persons within the church. They are not really Christians, but should not be thrown out too quickly, because of the disruption that dismissal would bring upon the church. With this parable we shift to those five major stories of Christ not found in the gospel of Luke. Luke, likewise, contains stories not found in the gospel of Matthew—for instance, all three of the stories found in Luke, chapter fifteen.

"The Kingdom of Heaven is like a farmer sowing good seed in his field; but one night as he slept, his enemy came and sowed thistles among the wheat. When the crop began to grow, the thistles grew too.

"The farmer's men came and told him, 'Sir, the field where you planted choice seed is full of thistles!'

" 'An enemy has done it,' he exclaimed.

" 'Shall we pull out the thistles?' they asked.

" 'No,' he replied. 'You'll hurt the wheat if you do. Let both grow together until the harvest, and I will tell the reapers to sort out the thistles and burn them and put the wheat in the barn.' "

Matthew 13:24–30

15. THE UNFORGIVING STEWARD

This parable focuses on the truth from the Lord's Prayer that Christians have been forgiven for all of their trespasses. Therefore, they should freely extend forgiveness toward others who wrong them personally.

Then Peter came to him and asked, "Sir, how often should I forgive a brother who sins against me? Seven times?"

"No!" Jesus replied, "seventy times seven!

"The Kingdom of heaven can be compared to a king who decided to bring his accounts up to date. In the process one of his debtors was brought in who owed him $10,000,000! He couldn't pay, so the king ordered him sold for the debt, also his wife and children and everything he had.

"But the man fell down before the king, his face in the dust, and said, 'Oh, sir, be patient with me and I will pay it all.'

"Then the king was filled with pity for him, and released him and forgave his debt.

"But when the man left the king, he went to a man who owed him $2,000 and grabbed him by the throat and demanded instant payment.

"The man fell down before him and begged him to give him a little time. 'Be patient with me and I will pay it,' he pled.

"But his creditor wouldn't wait. He had the man arrested and jailed until the debt would be paid in full.

"Then the man's friends sent to the king and told him what had happened. And the king called before him the man he had forgiven and said, 'You evil-hearted wretch! Here I forgave you all that tremendous debt, just as you asked me to—shouldn't you have mercy on others, just as I had mercy on you?'

"Then the angry king sent the man to the torture chamber until he had paid every last penny due. So shall my heavenly Father do to you if you refuse to truly forgive your brothers."

Matthew 18:21–35

16. THE PARABLE OF PAYDAY

In this parable Jesus makes a powerful statement that the level of rewards in heaven is not so significant as the joy of going there. Heaven is not a place where those who died after years of service should be able to gloat over those who came to Christianity later in life. All should rejoice that they were visited by grace and are able to be there at all. All are to accept the eternal provisions of a God who welcomes all into heaven with the same joy, never measuring how long or how short a time they may have served Christ in getting there.

"The owner of an estate went out early one morning to hire workers for his harvest field. He agreed to pay them $20 a day and sent them out to work.

"A couple of hours later he was passing a hiring hall and saw some men standing around waiting for jobs, so he sent them also into his fields, telling them he would pay them what was right at the end of the day. At noon and around three o'clock in the afternoon he did the same thing.

"At five o'clock that evening he was in town again and saw some more men standing around and asked them, 'Why haven't you been working today?'

" 'Because no one hired us,' they replied.

" 'Then go out and join the others in my fields,' he told them.

"That evening he told the paymaster to call the men in and pay them, beginning with the last men first. When the men hired at five o'clock were paid, each received $20. So when the men hired earlier came to get theirs, the assumed they would receive much more. But they, too, were paid $20.

"They protested, 'Those fellows worked only one hour, and yet you've paid them just as much as the rest of us who worked all day long in the scorching heat.'

" 'Friend,' he answered one of them, 'didn't you agree to work all day for $20? Take it and go. It is my desire to pay all the same; is it against the law to give away my money if I want to? Should you be angry because I am kind?' And so it is that the last shall be first, and the first, last."

Matthew 20:1–16

17. THE TEN BRIDESMAIDS

This is one of the key parables relating to Jesus' Second Coming. The point of this story is that since no one knows exactly when Jesus will come again, everyone should always be spiritually prepared for the day.

"The Kingdom of Heaven can be illustrated by the story of ten bridesmaids who took their lamps and went to meet the bridegroom. But only five of them were wise enough to fill their lamps with oil, while the other five were foolish and forgot.

"So, when the bridegroom was delayed, they lay down to rest until midnight, when they were roused by shout, 'The bridegroom is coming! Come out and welcome him!'

"All the girls jumped up and trimmed their lamps. Then the five who hadn't any oil begged the others to share with them, for their lamps were going out.

"But the others replied, 'We haven't enough. Go instead to the shops and buy some for yourselves.'

"But while they were gone the bridegroom came, and those who were ready went in with him to the marriage feast, and the door was locked.

"Later, when the other five returned, they stood outside, calling, 'Sir, open the door for us!'

"But he called back, 'Go away! It is too late!'

"So stay awake and be prepared, for you do not know the date or the moment of my return."

Matthew 25:1–13

18. THE FINAL JUDGMENT

This parable depicts the final judgment of all people, both the true followers of Christ and those who were only followers in pretense. More than any other of Christ's parables, this one makes getting into heaven a matter of social conscience. The great criterion for entering heaven in this parable is how well those who claim to be followers of Christ actually serve the downtrodden souls in society. Those who rightly call themselves Christians—the sheep in this parable—are welcomed into heaven for they have helped the needy around them. False Christians, who have not helped the hurting of this world—the goats—are sentenced to everlasting punishment.

"But when I, the Messiah, shall come in my glory, and all the angels with me, then I shall sit upon my throne of glory. And all the nations shall be gathered before me. And I will separate the people as a shepherd separates the sheep from the goats, and place the sheep at my right hand, and the goats at my left.

"Then I, the King, shall say to those at my right, 'Come, blessed of my Father, into the Kingdom prepared for you from the founding of the world. For I was hungry and you fed me; I was thirsty and you gave me water; I was a stranger and you invited me into your homes; naked and you clothed me; sick and in prison, and you visited me.'

"Then the righteous ones will reply, 'Sir, when did we ever see you hungry and feed you? Or thirsty and give you anything to drink? Or a stranger and help you? Or naked, and clothe you? When did we ever see you sick or in prison, and visit you?'

"And I, the King, will tell them, 'When you did it to these my brothers you were doing it to me!' Then I will turn to those on my left and say, 'Away with you, you cursed ones, into eternal fire prepared for the devil and his demons. For I was hungry and you wouldn't feed me; thirsty, and you wouldn't give me anything to drink; a stranger, and you refused me hospitality; naked, and you wouldn't clothe me; sick, and in prison, and you didn't visit me.'

"Then they will reply, 'Lord, when did we ever see you hungry or thirsty or a stranger or naked or sick or in prison, and not help you?'

"And I will answer, 'When you refused to help the least of these my brothers, you were refusing to help me.'

"And they shall go away into eternal punishment; but the righteous into everlasting life."

Matthew 25:31–46

WHO WAS JESUS?

LOIS A. CHENEY

WHO WAS JESUS?

He was a very brave person.

Mark, who deals mainly with the actions of Jesus, tells us that one day Jesus walked through the temple. He didn't say anything, "and when he had looked round at everything, as it was already late, he went out to Bethany with the twelve." I don't know what they did there, but I think Jesus just sort of sat around and thought a lot, and kind of got worked up. The next time he came to the temple, he "began to cast out them that sold and bought in the temple, and overthrew the tables of the money-changers and the seats of them that sold doves. And would not suffer that any man should carry any vessel through the temple." What did they do when he began to toss things around? I like the picture of birds flapping everywhere; money spinning and disappearing; robes flopping around hustling ankles.

HE KNEW WHAT was coming. He walked up and into Jerusalem—just like that. A couple of nights before, he sat on a hill and looked and looked at that city. I expect he prayed too. He saw the whole thing coming, and he walked right into it—just like that.

THE HIGH PRIEST asked him "and he said unto him, Art thou the Christ, the Son of the Blessed?" And Jesus said, "I am." And when he said that, he set in motion his trial and death. According to Mark, this is the only time he actually said it. And saying it, he set up his death. He knew what he was doing.

And he did it.

And he chose to do it.

Of his own will.

MEDITATION TEACHINGS
Matthew 5:23–25

DIETRICH BONHOEFFER

THERE IS ONLY one way of following Jesus and of worshipping God, and that is to be reconciled with our brethren. If we come to hear the word of God and receive the sacrament without first being reconciled with our neighbors, we shall come to our own damnation. In the sight of God we are murderers. Therefore "go thy way, first be reconciled with thy brother, and then come and offer thy gift." This is a hard way, but it is the way Jesus requires if we are to follow Him. It is a way which brings much personal humiliation and insult, but it is indeed the way to Him, our crucified Brother, and therefore a way of grace abounding. In Jesus the service of God and the service of the least of the brethren were one. He went His way and became reconciled with His brother and offered Himself as the one true sacrifice to His father.

We are still living in the age of grace, for each of us still has a brother, we are still "with him in the way." The court of judgement lies ahead, and there is still a chance for us to be reconciled with our brother and pay our debt to him. The hour is coming when we shall meet the judge face to face, and then it will be too late. We shall then receive our sentence and be made to pay the last farthing. But do we realize that at this point our brother comes to us in the guise not of law, but of grace? It is grace that we are allowed to find favour with our brother, and pay our debt to him; it is grace that we are allowed to become reconciled with him. In our brother we find grace before the seat of judgement.

VII

JESUS:

❧

HIS CROSS

THE cross is the central symbol of Christianity. Many cathedrals have been built in the shape of the cross. Their towers are crowned with the symbol. Every Mass is a reenactment of the sacrificial death of Christ. One can hardly turn in any direction without seeing a cross on a hill, on a church, or as a piece of jewelry. This universal symbol is understood by virtually everyone. Its very sight calls to mind Christ's first-century execution. It is his salvation symbol.

Crucifixion was the method of execution widely used by the Romans. It was a horribly degrading form of capital punishment. According to Jewish law (Deuteronomy 21:22–23) it was the just recompense of evildoers. This law was not sympathetic to those whose deeds were so vile that this sentence turned out to be their form of justice. Judaism judged those to be justly executed who died in this manner. Jesus was not the first person to die on the cross. The practice was widespread. Alexander Janneus, king and high priest of Judea, crucified eight hundred Pharisees in 76 B.C. The rebellion of Spartacus lined Rome's Appian Way with crosses. Many of the Seleucids, who ruled in Palestine after the death of Alexander the Great, crucified their captives with vast fields of crosses.

Still the custom was despised by first-century Jews. Herod the Great, while fiendish enough to massacre the infants of Bethlehem, refused to allow the distasteful crucifixion of his own enemies.

Crucified victims in Jesus' day (like Jesus himself) were

crucified with the same gruesome, savage rituals. They were usually beaten with a flog consisting of leather thongs laced with sharp bone or metal fragments. After being nearly flayed alive, the bloody criminal would be forced to carry his own gallows —at least the cross beam—to the place of his execution. Some sort of sign would be posted on that cross listing the crimes for which he was being put to death. Roped or nailed to the cross, the victim died slowly. Death usually resulted from suffocation, loss of blood, and finally coronary failure.

Most scholars agree that the four gospels give their account of the cross from four separate vantage points. Mark and Matthew seem to concern themselves with a look at the betrayal and the cruel horror of the cross. Mark clearly focused on the cross as one more evidence that Jesus really was the Messiah for whom the Jews so long had waited (Mark 1:7–8). Matthew on the other hand is fascinated by the idea that the cross stood in time at the changing of the ages. The new age of Christianity begins as the cross (coupled with the resurrection) destroys the power of death. Luke, not mentioning the negative aspects of crucifixion (like earthquakes and Jesus' cry of abandonment), focuses on Christ the glorious and merciful martyr who forgave all his crucifiers. John shows Jesus in the hands of temporal rulers but never allows Jesus to appear as a whipped criminal at the mercy of either Jerusalem or Rome. In John, Jesus lays down his life, which none can take from him. He gives his judges the very power to crucify him. The crucifixion, in John's eyes, is all part of the ancient plan of God and is possible only because God has ordained it and Jesus is willing to endure it.

The cross is seen as the saving act of Christ (Romans 3:24– 25), but even more than this, it is seen as the final place of reconciliation between God and humanity (Ephesians 2:14–15). Because there is a cross, all hate has been judged and the world has been forgiven. As the old proverb has it, *"The ground at the foot of the cross is level."* Here in the presence of God's greatest act of love there is no room for smaller, bitter prejudice.

> They took Jesus away. Carrying his cross, Jesus went out to the place called Skull Hill (the name in Hebrew is *Golgotha*), where they crucified him, and with him two others, one on each side, Jesus in the middle. Pilate wrote a sign and had it placed on the cross. It read:
>
> JESUS THE NAZARENE
> THE KING OF THE JEWS
>
> Many of the Jews read the sign because the place where Jesus was crucified was right next to the city. It was written in Hebrew, Latin, and Greek. The Jewish high priests objected. "Don't write," they said to Pilate, "The King of the Jews." Make it, "This man said, 'I am the King of the Jews.' "
> Pilate said, "What I've written, I've written."
>
> John 19:16–22, *The Message*

❦

ASLAN'S REDEMPTION

C. S. LEWIS

Lewis's image of Christ as the great lion at the center of his children's stories demonstrates the power that metaphors have with children. In this section of The Lion, the Witch and the Wardrobe—*the killing of the lion, Aslan—Jesus is never mentioned, but all children sooner or later in their process of maturity would realize the connection.*

"SOMETHING ABOUT ASLAN," said Lucy. "Either some dreadful thing that is going to happen to him, or something dreadful that he's going to do."

"There's been something wrong with him all afternoon," said Susan. "Lucy! What was that he said about not being with us at the battle? You don't think he could be stealing away and leaving us to-night, do you?"

"Where is he now?" said Lucy. "Is he here in the pavilion?"

"I don't think so."

"Susan! Let's go outside and have a look round. We might see him."

"All right. Let's," said Susan, "we might just as well be doing that as lying awake here."

Very quietly the two girls groped their way among the other sleepers and crept out of the tent. The moonlight was bright and everything was quite still except for the noise of the river chattering over the stones. Then Susan suddenly caught Lucy's arm and said, "Look!" On the far side of the camping ground, just where the trees began, they saw the Lion slowly walking away from them into the wood. Without a word they both followed him.

He led them up the steep slope out of the river valley and then slightly to the left—apparently by the very same route which they had used that afternoon in coming from the Hill of the Stone Table. On and on he led them, into dark shadows and out into pale moonlight, getting their feet wet with the heavy dew. He looked somehow different from the Aslan they knew. His tail and his head hung low and he walked slowly as if he were very, very tired. Then, when they were crossing a wide open place where there were no shadows for them to hide in, he stopped and looked round. It was no good trying to run away so they came towards him. When they were closer he said,

"Oh, children, children, why are you following me?"

"We couldn't sleep," said Lucy—and then felt sure that she need say no more and that Aslan knew all they had been thinking.

"Please, may we come with you—wherever you're going?" said Susan.

"Well—" said Aslan and seemed to be thinking. Then he said, "I should be glad of company to-night. Yes, you may come, if you will promise to stop when I tell you, and after that leave me to go on alone."

"Oh thank you, thank you. And we will," said the two girls.

Forward they went again and one of the girls walked on each side of the Lion. But how slowly he walked! And his great, royal head drooped so that his nose nearly touched the grass. Presently he stumbled and gave a low moan.

"Aslan! Dear Aslan!" said Lucy, "what is wrong? Can't you tell us?"

"Are you ill, dear Aslan?" asked Susan.

"No," said Aslan. "I am sad and lonely. Lay your hands on my mane so that I can feel you are there and let us walk like that."

And so the girls did what they would never have dared to do without his permission but what they had longed to do ever since they first saw him—buried their cold hands in the beautiful sea of fur and stroked it and, so doing, walked with him. And presently they saw that they were going with him up the slope of the hill on which the Stone Table stood. They went up at the side where the trees came furthest up, and when they got to the last tree (it was one that had some bushes about it) Aslan stopped and said,

"Oh children, children. Here you must stop. And whatever happens, do not let yourselves be seen. Farewell."

And both the girls cried bitterly (though they hardly knew why) and clung to the Lion and kissed his mane and his nose and his paws and his great, sad eyes. Then he turned from them and walked out onto the top of the hill. And Lucy and Susan, crouching in the bushes, looked after him and this is what they saw.

A great crowd of people were standing all round the Stone Table and though the moon was shining many of them carried torches which burned with evil-looking red flames and black smoke. But such people! Ogres with monstrous teeth, and wolves, and bull-headed men; spirits of evil trees and poisonous plants; and other creatures whom I won't describe because if I did the grown-ups would probably not let you read this book —Cruels and Hags and Incubuses, Wraiths, Horrors, Efreets, Sprites, Orknies, Wooses, and Ettins. In fact here were all those who were on the Witch's side and whom the Wolf had summoned at her command. And right in the middle, standing by the Table, was the Witch herself.

A howl and a gibber of dismay went up from the creatures when they first saw the great Lion pacing towards them, and for a moment the Witch herself seemed to be struck with fear. Then she recovered herself and gave a wild, fierce laugh.

"The fool!" she cried. "The fool has come. Bind him fast."

Lucy and Susan held their breaths waiting for Aslan's roar and his spring upon his enemies. But it never came. Four hags, grinning and leering, yet also (at first) hanging back and half afraid of what they had to do, had approached him. "Bind him, I say!" repeated the White Witch. The hags made a dart at him and shrieked with triumph when they found that he made no resistance at all. Then others—evil dwarfs and apes— rushed in to help them and between them they rolled the huge Lion round on his back and tied all his four paws together, shouting and cheering as if they had done something brave, though, had the Lion chosen, one of those paws could have been the death of them all. But he made no noise, even when the enemies, straining and tugging, pulled the cords so tight that they cut into his flesh. Then they began to drag him towards the Stone Table.

"Stop!" said the Witch. "Let him first be shaved."

Another roar of mean laughter went up from her followers as an ogre with a pair of shears came forward and squatted down by Aslan's head. Snip-snip-snip went the shears and masses of curling gold began to fall to the ground. Then the ogre stood back and the children, watching from their hiding-place, could see the face of Aslan looking all small and different without its mane. The enemies also saw the difference.

"Why, he's only a great cat after all!" cried one.

"Is *that* what we were afraid of?" said another.

And they surged round Aslan jeering at him, saying things like "Puss, Puss! Poor Pussy," and "How many mice have you caught to-day, Cat?" and "Would you like a saucer of milk, Pussums?"

"Oh how *can* they?" said Lucy, tears streaming down her cheeks. "The brutes, the brutes!" for now that the first shock was over, the shorn face of Aslan looked to her braver, and more beautiful, and more patient than ever.

"Muzzle him!" said the Witch. And even now, as they worked about his face putting on the muzzle, one bite from his jaws would have cost two or three of them their hands. But he never moved. And this seemed to enrage all that rabble. Everyone was at him now. Those who had been afraid to come near him even after he was bound began to find their courage, and for a few minutes the two girls could not even see him—so thickly was he surrounded by the whole crowd of creatures kicking him, hitting him, spitting on him, jeering at him.

At last the rabble had had enough of this. They began to drag the bound and muzzled Lion to the Stone Table, some pulling and some pushing. He was so huge that even when they got him there it took all their efforts to hoist him onto the surface of it. Then there was more tying and tightening of cords.

"The cowards! The cowards!" sobbed Susan. "Are they *still* afraid of him, even now?"

When once Aslan had been tied (and tied so that he was really a mass of cords) on the flat stone, a hush fell on the crowd. Four Hags, holding four torches, stood at the corners of the Table. The Witch bared her arms as she had bared them the previous night when it had been Edmund instead of Aslan. Then she began to whet her knife. It looked to the children, when the gleam of the torchlight fell on it, as if the knife were made of stone not of steel and it was of a strange and evil shape.

At last she drew near. She stood by Aslan's head. Her face was working and twitching with passion, but he looked up at the sky, still quiet, neither angry nor afraid, but a little sad. Then, just before she gave the blow, she stooped down and said in a quivering voice,

"And now, who has won? Fool, did you think that by all this you would save the human traitor? Now I will kill you instead of him as our pact was and so the Deep Magic will be appeased. But when you are dead what will prevent me from killing him as well? And who will take him out of my hand *then*? Understand that you have given me Narnia forever, you have lost your own life and you have not saved his. In that knowledge, despair and die."

The children did not see the actual moment of the killing. They couldn't bear to look and had covered their eyes.

∾

CHRIST THE LAMB

ROBERT E. COLEMAN

Christ is often symbolized as a lamb in Christian thought and literature. The symbol derives from the Old Testament sacrificial system, in which lambs were slaughtered as a sacrifice for sin. Jesus became the Lamb of God who was offered as a sacrifice to take away the sin of all the world (John 1:36).

THE STORY IS told of a traveler who looked for unusual things in the cities he visited. During a tour of a town one day, he was attracted by a remarkable spire over a public building. Turning to see it better, he noticed, about two-thirds of the way up, a stone figure of a lamb on the wall.

The man stopped a passerby, to ask if there was some significance to the lamb's stone replica. Told that it marked the place from which a workman lost his balance and fell while the building was under construction, the traveler inquired, "Was he killed?"

"No," said the local resident, "it was a miracle. When his friends hurried down, expecting to find the mangled body on the pavement, there he was, shaken and badly bruised, but with hardly a bone broken. It happened that several lambs were on their way to slaughter, and as the mason fell, he landed on the back of one of them. The lamb was killed, of course, but his soft body broke the mason's fall and saved his life. The builder was so impressed with the miracle that he had the stone lamb placed there, as a lasting tribute."

∽

THE CELTIC TRADITION

AUTHOR UNKNOWN

CHRIST'S CROSS OVER this face, and thus over my ear. Christ's cross over this eye. Christ's cross over this nose.

Christ's cross to accompany me before. Christ's cross to accompany me behind me. Christ's cross to meet every difficulty both on hollow and hill.

Christ's cross eastwards facing me. Christ's cross back towards the sunset. In the north, in the south, increasingly may Christ's cross straightway be.

Christ's cross up to broad Heaven. Christ's cross down to earth. Let no evil or hurt come to my body or my soul.

Christ's cross over me as I sit. Christ's cross over me as I lie. Christ's cross be all my strength until we reach the King of Heaven.

From the top of my head to the nail of my foot, O Christ, against every danger I trust in the protection of the cross.

Till the day of my death, going into this clay, I shall draw without— Christ's cross over this face.

∽

CROSS CARRYING

CHARLES H. SPURGEON

Following Christ is often referred to, especially by Protestants, as discipleship. Jesus taught that to be one of his disciples was to participate in his sacrificial way of life. Since Jesus knew the cross was central in his life, he did not want his followers to assume that they could live lives free of trial. Hence, the chief metaphor for following Christ is cross carrying. Luke 9:23 carries the strength of this metaphor: "If anyone would come after me, he must deny himself and take up his cross daily and follow me."

"Take up your cross and follow me."
Mark 10:21

You CANNOT MAKE your own cross, but unbelief is a master carpenter at cross-making. You do not choose your own cross, but self-will would try to be your lord and master. Your cross is prepared and appointed by divine love. Accept it cheerfully. You are to carry your cross without raising trivial objections. This evening Jesus asks you to submit to His easy yoke (Matthew 11:30). Do not be insolent, or trample it in vain glory, or fall under it in despair, or run away from it in fear. Take up your cross as a true follower of Jesus.

Jesus was a cross-bearer. He leads the way along the path of sorrow, and you could not have a better guide! If He carried a cross, what nobler burden could you carry? The *Via Crucis* is the way of safety. Do not be afraid to walk its thorny path.

The cross is not made of feathers or covered with velvet. It is heavy and cuts disobedient shoulders. But the cross is not made of iron, although your fears may have painted it the color of iron. It is a wooden cross, and you can carry it because the Man of Sorrows knows its weight. Take up your cross, and by the power of the Spirit of God you will soon be in love with it. Like Moses, you would not exchange the reproach of Christ for all the treasures of Egypt (Hebrews 11:26).

Remember, Jesus carried the cross, and so its fragrance is sweet. Remember, the cross will soon be exchanged for the crown. Remember the coming glory, and it will greatly lighten the present heaviness of trouble.

Before you fall asleep tonight, ask the Lord to help you submit your will to His. When you wake tomorrow, may you be able to carry your cross with a holy and submissive spirit as is appropriate for a follower of the Crucified.

MEDITATIONS ON THE CROSS

AUTHOR UNKNOWN

JESUS, POOR AND abject, unknown and despised, have mercy upon me, and let me not be ashamed to follow thee.

O Jesus, hated, calumniated, and persecuted, have mercy upon me, and make me content to be as my master.

O Jesus, blasphemed, accused, and wrongfully condemned, have mercy upon me, and teach me to endure the contradiction of sinners.

O Jesus, clothed with a habit of reproach and shame, have mercy upon me, and let me not seek my own glory.

O Jesus, insulted, mocked, and spit upon, have mercy upon me, and let me not faint in the fiery trial.

O Jesus, crowned with thorns and hailed in derision;

O Jesus, burdened with our sins and the curses of the people;

O Jesus, affronted, outraged, buffeted, overwhelmed with injuries, griefs and humiliations;

O Jesus, hanging on the accursed tree, bowing the head, giving up the ghost, have mercy upon me, and conform my whole soul to be thy holy, humble, suffering Spirit.

THE PASSION

JOHN MILTON

Erewhile of music, and ethereal mirth,
Wherewith the stage of air and earth did ring,
And joyous news of heavenly Infant's birth,
My muse with angels did divide to sing;
But headlong joy is ever on the wing,
   In wintry solstice, like the shorten'd light,
Soon swallow'd up in dark, and long outliving night.

For now to sorrow must I tune my song,
And set my harp to notes of saddest woe,
Which on our dearest Lord did seize, ere long,

Dangers, and snares, and wrongs, and worse than so,
Which He, for us, did freely undergo:
   Most perfect Hero, tried in heaviest plight
Of labours huge and hard, too hard for human wight!

He, Sovereign Priest, stooping His regal head,
That dropt with adorous oil down His fair eyes,
Poor fleshly tabernacle enter'd,
His starry front low-roof'd, beneath the skies;
Oh, what a mask was there, what a disguise!
   Yet more; the stroke of death He must abide,
Then lies Him meekly down, fast by His brethren's side.

∾

HE CAME AS A MAN

SAINT ATHANASIUS

Saint Athanasius, like most Christian scholars and thinkers, strove to show us that to redeem death, Jesus had to experience it and so conquer it. Since all life ends with dying, the cross shows us that Jesus did not shrink back from doing even that. Never, therefore, can anyone ever point to Jesus and say he knew how it felt to live on earth but not to die there. Jesus came to live as a human being to say, "I am in this harsh existence with you!" And when he died on the cross, he said, "I am in this harsh existence with you, regardless of the cost!!"

Now IF THEY ask, Why then did He not appear by means of other and nobler parts of creation, and use some nobler instrument, as the sun, or moon, or stars, or fire, or air, instead of man merely? let them know that the Lord came not to make a display, but to heal and teach those who were suffering. For the way for one aiming at display would be just to appear and to dazzle the beholders; but for one seeking to heal and teach the way is, not simply to sojourn here, but to give himself to the aid of those in want, and to appear as they who need him can bear it; that he may not, by exceeding the requirements of the sufferers, trouble the very persons that need him, rendering God's appearance useless to them. Now nothing in God's creation had gone astray with regard to their notions of

God save man only. Why, neither sun nor moon nor heaven nor the stars nor water nor air had swerved from their order: but knowing their Artificer and Sovereign, the Word, they remain as they were made. But men alone, having rejected what was good, then devised things of nought instead of the truth and have ascribed the honour due to God and their knowledge of Him to demons and men in the shape of stones.

With reason, then, since it were unworthy of the Divine Goodness to overlook so grave a matter, while yet men were not able to recognize Him as ordering and guiding the whole, He takes to Himself as an instrument a part of the whole, the human body, and unites Himself with that, in order that since men could not recognize Him in the whole, they should not fail to know Him in the part; and since they could not look up to His invisible power, might be able at any rate, from what resembled themselves to reason to Him and to contemplate Him.

❧

THE PASSION NOT PASSIVE

H. H. FARMER

IF WE LOOK at the Gospel story of the Passion as a whole and do not isolate the Cross from its context, one of the most impressive and revealing things in it is the air of strong deliberation and mastery which characterizes Jesus throughout those last days. He is so manifestly not in the least a straw on the stream of events. His enemies are not manipulating Him so much as He is manipulating them, not in any wrong way, but in the way in which God does lay hold of the wrath and sin of man and make them subserve His infinite purpose of love. To the end He could have escaped the Cross by the simple expedient of going somewhere else; but He did not do so. He deliberately directs His steps to it. There is an atmosphere of mastery all about Him as He steadfastly sets His face towards Jerusalem. Standing before the council, or before Pilate, there is no suggestion of fumbling or hesitancy. Nor on the other hand is there any suggestion of a merely excited and fanatical confidence. It is the other people who are excited, not He. And it is always the excited people who are the weak people. He says almost regally, "No man taketh my life from me; I lay it down of myself." He says—very plainly, quietly, with the direct steadiness of clear-sighted conviction—"Hereafter ye shall see the Son of man seated at the right hand of power." The hereafter refers to their seeing. He

Himself sees now. He is conscious of being in a very real sense at the right hand of power now. He is with God now; the victory is His now.

∾

THE CRUCIFIED CHRIST

SAINT ANSELM

Saint Anselm was one of those Christian writers who exalted the crucifix almost more than the cross. This distinction in worship has at various times been a source of conflict between the traditional church and the Reformation church. All Christians appreciate and adore the cross. But Protestants and Evangelicals have displayed only empty crosses in their churches, while Catholic and Orthodox churches display the crucifix, the cross containing the dying Christ. In recent years, however, all Christians are more prone to celebrate the actual descriptions of Christ's ordeal. In this inclusion, Saint Anselm, who was archbishop of Canterbury, draws for us the actual picture of horror.

AWAKE NOW, O my soul, shake thyself from the dust, and with deeper attention contemplate this wondrous Man whom, in the glass of the gospel story, thou, as it were, gazest upon, present before thee. Consider, O my soul, who He is, who walketh with the fashion as it were of a king; and nevertheless is filled with the confusion of a most despised slave. He goeth crowned: but His very crown is a torture to Him and woundeth with a thousand punctures His most glorious head. He is clothed in royal purple: yet more is He despised than honoured in it. He beareth a sceptre in His hand: but with it His reverend head is beaten. They worship before Him with bowed knee; they hail Him king: but forthwith they leap up to spit upon His cheeks lovely to look upon, they smite His jaws with the palms of their hands and dishonour His honourable neck. See further how in all things He is constrained, spit upon, despised. He is bid to bend His neck beneath the burden of His Cross, and He Himself to bear His own ignominy. Brought to the place of punishment, He is given to drink myrrh and gall. He is lifted up upon the Cross and He saith, "Father, forgive them, they know not what they do." What manner of man is this, who in all His afflictions never once opened His mouth to utter a word of complaint or pleading, or of threatening or cursing against those accursed dogs, and last of all poured forth over His enemies a word of blessing such as hath not been heard from the beginning? What more gentle than this man, what more kind, O my soul, hast thou seen? Gaze on Him, however, yet more intently, for He seemeth worthy both of great admiration and of most tender compassion. See Him stripped naked, and torn with stripes, between thieves ignominiously fixed with nails of iron to the Cross, given vinegar to drink upon the Cross, and after death pierced in His side with the spear, and pouring forth plentiful streams of blood from the five wounds of His hands and feet and side. Pour down your tears, mine eyes; melt, O my soul, with the fire of compassion at the sufferings of that Man of love, whom in the midst of such gentleness thou seest afflicted with so bitter griefs.

∽

A SYMPOSIUM ON THE CREDIBILITY OF THE CROSS

JOHN BLANCHARD

Christ's blood is heaven's key.

Thomas Brooks

There is no tribunal so magnificent, no throne so stately, no show of triumph so distinguished, no chariot so elevated, as is the gibbet on which Christ hath subdued death and the devil.

John Calvin

The doctrine of the death of Christ is the substance of the gospel.

Stephen Charnock

When Jesus bowed his head,
And dying took our place,
The veil was rent, a way was found
To that pure home of grace.

John Elias

Though God loved Christ as a Son he frowned upon him as a Surety.

Matthew Henry

The cross is the key. If I lose this key I fumble. The universe will not open to me. But with the key in my hand I know I hold its secret.

E. Stanley Jones

The dying of the Lord Jesus rescues us from eternal death, whilst the doing of the Lord Jesus obtains for us eternal life.

J. M. Killen

The whole world in comparison with the cross of Christ is one grand impertinence.

Robert Leighton

One drop of Christ's blood is worth more than heaven and earth.

Martin Luther

The wounds of Christ were the greatest outlets of his glory that ever were. The divine glory shone more out of his wounds than out of all his life before.

Robert Murray M'Cheyne

If I would appreciate the blood of Christ I must accept God's valuation of it, for the blood is not primarily for me but for God.

Watchman Nee

This precious Lamb of God gave up his precious fleece for us.

Christopher Nesse

He suffered not as God, but he who suffered was God.

John Owen

The death of Christ was the most dreadful blow ever given to the empire of darkness.

William S. Plumer

Death stung himself to death when he stung Christ.

William Romaine

If we would live aright it must be by the contemplation of Christ's death.

Charles H. Spurgeon

Christ assumed every consequence of sin which was not itself sinful.

S. P. Tregelles

THE DEAL

WILLIAM GRIFFIN

JUDAS LOOKED NERVOUS.

"What seems to be the trouble?" asked the high priest.

"Jesus says one thing, but he does another."

"What do you mean?" asked the high priest.

"He says 'give to the poor' but he himself keeps some of the gifts."

"All the time?"

"Just some of the time."

"Perhaps we should look into this," said the priest.

"It's so discouraging," said Judas.

"We have been wanting to talk to him for some time now."

"I think you should," said Judas.

"But how can we talk to him privately?" asked the priest. "Crowds follow him everywhere he goes."

"I could tell you when he's by himself," said Judas.

"That would be so good," said the priest.

"What's in it for me?" asked Judas.

"What do you have in mind?" asked the priest.

"I was thinking of money."

"How much?"

"Sixty pieces of silver."

"Ten pieces of silver was what we had in mind."

"Fifty, not a piece less."

"I suppose we could offer you twenty, but not a piece more."

"Forty is as low as I'll go."

"Thirty will buy a lot of bread for the poor."

"Sold," said Judas.

"Good," said the priest.

"And have the money ready when I come back," said Judas as he went out to find Jesus.

JESUS' UNANSWERED APPEAL

C. S. LEWIS

Perhaps the most puzzling of all of Jesus' cries from the cross is "Eloi, Eloi, lama sabachthani?" *which means,* "My God my God, why have you forsaken me?" *(Matthew 27:46). The answer most often given by theologians is that when Jesus died, all of the sins of the world were laid upon his shoulders, and all sin is so repulsive to the holiness of God that, for one brief moment, God turned his back on Jesus, refusing to look upon the horror of all human sin. Other theologians say that God loved Jesus so much he would never have turned his back in his Son's hour of need, and that Jesus was merely praying the Twenty-second Psalm in his hour of utter need. C. S. Lewis uses the cry from the cross to point out that institutions generally sin by stamping out the very confession they were founded to proclaim. Thus this cross cry is the last cry of the unwelcome Messiah, for which his people had so long waited.*

WE ALL TRY to accept with some sort of submission our afflictions when they actually arrive. But the prayer in Gethsemane shows that the preceding anxiety is equally God's will and equally part of our human destiny. The perfect Man experienced it. And the servant is not greater than the master. We are Christians, not Stoics.

Does not every movement in the Passion write large some common element in the sufferings of our race? First, the prayer of anguish; not granted. Then He turns to His friends. They are asleep—as ours, or we, are so often, or busy, or away, or preoccupied. Then He faces the Church; the very Church that He brought into existence. It condemns Him. This also is characteristic. In every Church, in every institution, there is something which sooner or later works against the very purpose for which it came into existence. But there seems to be another chance. There is the State; in this case, the Roman state. Its pretensions are far lower than those of the Jewish church, but for that very reason it may be free from local fanaticisms. It claims to be just on a rough, worldly level. Yes, but only so far as is consistent with political expediency and *raison d'état*. One becomes a counter in a complicated game. But even now all is not lost. There is still an appeal to the People—the poor and simple whom He had blessed, whom He had healed and fed and taught, to whom He Himself belongs. But they have become over-night (it is nothing unusual) a murderous rabble shouting for His blood. There is, then, nothing left but God. And to God, God's last words are "Why hast thou forsaken me?"

RELIGION IN SHAKESPEARE

WILLIAM SHAKESPEARE

Shakespeare's remains lie at Holy Trinity Church in Stratford-upon-Avon. It is said that he was faithful in his attendance at church. If his plays bear any credible witness to the fact, it must certainly be so, for they abound with references to God and Christ. This citation renders Shakespeare almost devout in making such a devotional object of the cross.

> Those holy fields
> Over whose acres walk'd those blessed feet
> Which, fourteen hundred years ago, were nail'd
> For our advantage on the bitter cross.

∾

THE BOGUS DEATH WARRANT OF JESUS CHRIST

EDGAR JOHNSON GOODSPEED

For the past couple of centuries, a bogus death warrant of Jesus Christ has circulated in the West. The document, if authentic, would answer many questions as to the exact descriptions of Jesus' sentence of death and of those who officiated at his crucifixion. Goodspeed, however, makes it clear that the warrant can in no way be considered authentic, and the exact legalities surrounding the cross must remain somewhat obscure.

FOR MANY YEARS a leaflet claiming to be the "Death Warrant" or "Death Sentence" of Jesus Christ has been circulating in the United States, sometimes finding a place in a printed book, along with similar pieces. In its fullest form, it begins with an explanation of its source:

In 1810, some workmen while excavating in the ancient city of Amitorum (now Aguila) in the Kingdom of Naples, found an antique marble vase in which lay concealed a copper plate, bearing on the obverse side a long inscription in Hebrew tongue.

This, when translated, proved to be the death warrant of Jesus Christ. On the reverse side of the plate was found the words: "A similar plate is sent to each tribe." After its excavation it was enclosed in an ebony box and preserved in the sacristy of the Carthusians. This relic, if genuine, is to Christians the most impressive and interesting legal document in existence. It has been faithfully transcribed, and reads as follows:

Sentence rendered by Pontius Pilate, acting governor of lower Galilee, stating that Jesus of Nazareth shall suffer death on the cross. In the seventeenth year of the reign of the Emperor Tiberius and on the twenty-seventh day of March, in the most holy city of Jerusalem, during the pontificate of Annas and Caiaphas, Pontius Pilate, governor of lower Galilee, sitting in the presidential chair of the praetory, condemns Jesus of Nazareth to die on the cross between thieves, the great and notorious evidence of the people saying:

1. Jesus is a seducer.
2. He is seditious.
3. He is the enemy of the Law.
4. He calls himself falsely the Son of God.
5. He calls himself falsely the King of Israel.
6. He entered into the Temple followed by a multitude bearing palm branches in their hands.

Orders the first centurion, Quintus Cornelius, to lead him to the place of execution. Forbids any person whomsoever, either rich or poor, to oppose the death of Jesus Christ.

The witnesses who signed the condemnation of Jesus are

1. Daniel Robani, a Pharisee
2. Joannus Robani
3. Raphael Robani
4. Capet, a citizen

Jesus shall go out of the city of Jerusalem by the Gate of Struenus.

Another form adds: "French translation was literal."

It is not difficult to find a number of flaws in this brief document. It must be recognized at the outset that no such copper plate is known to archeology or learning. Such a plate, if it existed and were genuine, would be one of the prime documents of the New Testament. Archeologists and scholars are eager for the slightest bit of such material, and go to great expense and exertion to find inscriptions or manuscripts about the Christian beginnings. But no competent scholar has ever reported seeing such a plate or published his transcription of one. Nor has any museum or institution claimed to possess such a plate.

The notion that such a proclamation would be engraved upon a brass or copper plate and distributed among the twelve tribes of Israel is groundless. The tribal organization of the Jews had broken down 750 years earlier. Moreover, the Roman officials would never have thought of justifying their actions to the Jewish public.

❧

CRUCIFY HIM

CHARLES DICKENS

THAT YOU MAY know what the people meant when they said, "Crucify Him!" I must tell you that in those times, which were very cruel times indeed (let us thank God and Jesus Christ that they are past!) it was the custom to kill people who were sentenced to death, by nailing them alive on a great wooden cross, planted upright in the ground, and leaving them there, exposed to the sun and wind, and day and night, until they died of pain and thirst. It was the custom too, to make them walk to the place of execution, carrying the cross-piece of wood to which their hands were to be afterwards nailed, that their shame and suffering might be the greater.

Bearing His cross upon His shoulder, like the commonest and most wicked criminal, Our Blessed Saviour, Jesus Christ, surrounded by the persecuting crowd, went out of Jerusalem to a place called, in the Hebrew language, Golgotha; that is, the place of a skull. And being come to a hill called Mount Calvary, they hammered cruel nails through His hands and feet, and nailed Him on the cross, between two other crosses, on each of which a common thief was nailed in agony. Over His head they fastened this writing: "Jesus of Nazareth, the King of the Jews"—in three languages: in Hebrew, in Greek, and in Latin.

Meantime, a guard of four soldiers, sitting on the ground, divided His clothes (which they had taken off) into four parcels for themselves, and cast lots for His coat, and sat there, gambling and talking, while He suffered. They offered Him vinegar to drink, mixed with gall; and wine, mixed with myrrh; but He took none. And the wicked people who passed that way mocked Him, and said, "If Thou be the Son of God, come down from the cross." The chief priests also mocked Him, and said, "He came to save sinners. Let Him save Himself!" One of the thieves, too, railed at Him, in His torture, and said, "If Thou be Christ, save Thyself, and us." But the other thief, who was penitent, said, "Lord! Remember me when Thou comest into Thy Kingdom!" And Jesus answered, "To-day thou shalt be with me in Paradise."

THE DIALOGUE

SAINT CATHERINE OF SIENA

Caterina di Giacomo di Benincasa, born in 1347, came from a poor but pious Catholic family. She was the twenty-fourth of twenty-five children. While still a child she gave her chastity to her Savior. During her service as a nurse and succourer of the poor, she became a model of the inner life in Christ. Much of her writing came as metaphors, as is this story of the bridge.

THE BRIDGE

(Then God the eternal one responded to her soul): I want to describe the Bridge for you. It stretches from heaven to earth by reason of my having joined myself with your humanity which I formed in the earth's clay. The bridge has three stairs. Two of them were built by my Son on the wood of the most holy cross, and the third even as he tasted the bitterness of the gall and vinegar they gave him to drink. You will recognize in these three stairs three spiritual stages.

THE FEET OF AFFECTION

The first stair is the feet which symbolize the affections. For just as the feet carry the body, the affections carry the soul. My Son's nailed feet are a stair by which you can climb to his side where you will see revealed his inmost heart. For when the soul has climbed up on the feet of affection and looked with her mind's eye into my Son's open heart, she begins to feel the love of her own heart in his consummate and unspeakable love. (I say consummate because it is not for his own good that he loves you; you cannot do him any good since he is one with me.)

Then the soul, seeing how much she is loved, is herself filled to overflowing with love. So, having climbed the second stair, she reaches the third. This is his mouth where she finds peace from the terrible war she has had to wage because of her sins.

DIVINITY KNEADED INTO THE CLAY OF HUMANITY

At the first stair, lifting the feet of her affections from the earth, she stripped herself of sin. At the second she dressed herself in love for virtue. And at the third stage she tasted peace.

So the bridge has three stairs, and you can reach the last by climbing the first two. The last stair is so high that the flooding waters cannot strike it—for the venom of sin never touched my Son.

But though the bridge has been raised up so high, it still is joined to the earth. Do you know when it was raised up? When my Son was lifted up on the wood of the most holy cross he did not cut off his divinity from the lowly earth of your humanity. So though he was raised so high, he was not raised off the earth. In fact, his divinity is kneaded in the clay of your humanity like one bread. Nor could anyone walk on that bridge until my Son was raised up. This is why he said, "If I am lifted up high I will draw everything to myself" (John 12:32).

DRAWN BY LOVE

When my goodness saw that you could be drawn in no other way, I sent him to be lifted onto the wood of the cross. I made of that cross an anvil where this child of humankind could be hammered into an instrument to release humankind from death and restore it to the life of grace. In this way he drew everything to himself: for he proved his inspeakable love, and the human heart is always drawn by love. He could not have shown you greater love than by giving his life for you (John 15:13). You can hardly resist being drawn by love, then, unless you foolishly refuse to be drawn.

I said that, having been raised up, he would draw everything to himself. This is true in two ways: First, the human heart is drawn by love as I said, and with all its powers: memory, understanding, and will. If these three powers are harmoniously united in my name, everything else you do, in fact or intention, will be drawn to union with me in peace through the movement of love, because all will be lifted up in the pursuit of crucified love. So my Truth indeed spoke truly when he said, "If I am lifted up high, I will draw everything to myself." For everything you do will be drawn to him when he draws your heart and its powers.

What he said is true also in the sense that everything was created for your use to serve your needs. But you who have the gift of reason were made not for yourselves but for me, to serve me with all your heart and all your love. So when you are drawn to me, everything is drawn with you because everything was made for you. It was necessary, then, that this bridge be raised high. And it had to have stairs so that you would be able mount to it more easily.

THE STONES OF TRUE VIRTUE

This bridge has walls of stone so that travelers will not be hindered when it rains. Do you know what stones these are? They are the stones of true solid virtue. These stones were not, however, built into walls before my Son's passion. So no one could get to the final destination even though they walked along the pathway of virtue. For heaven had not yet been unlocked with the key of my Son's blood, and the rain of justice kept anyone from crossing over.

But after these stones were hewn on the body of the Word, my gentle Son (I have told you that he is the bridge), he built them into walls, tempering the mortar with his own blood. That is, his blood was mixed into the mortar of his divinity with the strong heat of burning love.

By my power the stones of virtue were built into walls on no less a foundation than himself, for all virtue draws life from him, nor is there any virtue that has not been tested in him. So no one can have any life-giving virtue but from him, that is, by following his example and his teaching. He perfected the virtues and planted them as living stones built into walls with his blood. So now all the faithful can walk without hindrance and with no cringing fear of the rain of divine justice because they are sheltered by the mercy that came down from heaven through the incarnation of this Son of mine.

THE KEY OF HIS BLOOD

And how was heaven opened? With the key of his blood. So, you see, the bridge has walls and a roof of mercy. And the hostelry of holy Church is there to serve the bread of life and blood lest the journeying pilgrims, my creatures, grow weary and faint on the way. So has my love ordained that the blood and body of my only-begotten Son, wholly God and wholly human, be administered.

At the end of the bridge is the gate (which is, in fact, one with the bridge), which is the only way you can enter. This is why he said, "I am the light of the world; whoever walks with me walks not in darkness but in light" (John 8:12). And in another place my Truth said that no one could come to me except through him, and such is the truth (John 14:6).

FROM THE IMITATION OF CHRIST
That Temporal Miseries Must Be Borne Patiently,
After the Example of Christ

THOMAS À KEMPIS

The cross provides for us the picture of how we are to behave in extreme adversity. We are often prone to phrase the woes that come upon us in terms of the cross. We are likely to say, "This particular season of pain is my cross to bear." Thomas à Kempis instructs us not to moan and complain about our various hurts or too quickly to label them as a cross to be borne. Christians are not to whimper about any adversity, but to use the cross even as Jesus did to bless their persecutors.

MY SON, I descended from Heaven for thy salvation; I took upon Me thy miseries, not necessity but charity drawing Me thereto; that thou thyself mightest learn patience, and bear temporal miseries without grudging.

For from the hour of my birth, even until my death on the cross, I was not without suffering or grief.

I suffered great want of things temporal, I often heard many complaints against me, I endured meekly disgraces and revilings; in return for benefits I received ingratitude, for miracles, blasphemies, for [heavenly] doctrine, reproofs.

∾

THE LESSON OF THE CROSS

CHARLES H. SPURGEON

HE STRIPPED OFF first one robe of honor and then another until, naked, He was fastened to the cross. There He emptied His inmost self, pouring out His lifeblood, giving Himself for all of us. Finally, they laid Him in a borrowed grave. How low was our dear Redeemer brought! How then, can we be proud? Stand at the foot of the cross and count the scarlet drops by which you have been cleansed. See the thorny crown and His scourged shoulders still gushing with the crimson flow of blood. See His hands and feet given up to the rough iron, and His whole self mocked and scorned. See the bitterness, the pangs, and the throes of inward grief show themselves in His outward frame. Hear the chilling shriek, "My God, my God, why hast thou forsaken me?" (Matthew 27:46). If you are not humbled in the presence of Jesus, you do not know Him. You were so lost that nothing could save you but the sacrifice of God's only begotten Son. As Jesus stooped for you, bow in humility at His feet. A realization of Christ's amazing love has a greater tendency to humble us than even a consciousness of our own guilt. Pride cannot live beneath the cross. Let us sit there and learn our lesson. Then let us rise and carry it into practice.

∾

THE FAITH OF JESUS

D. S. CAIRNS

Many contemporary dramatists, poets, and musicians have visualized the cross as a place where Jesus struggled with his identity. Kazantzakis's Last Temptation of Christ, *while generally offensive to Christians, does show the dying Jesus focused on the question of his identity. Common clichés say that at the moment of death, sometimes, our whole lives pass before us. On the cross, Jesus knows who he is and is certain of his destiny. Still, the issue of who we are comes sharply into focus at the moment of our passing. It is not until we come to the place of our dying that others ask who we are and we ask who we were.*

IT IS QUITE clear that the whole teaching of Jesus Christ about God, expressed alike in His words and in the whole fashion and mould of His character, implies that God is always nearer, mightier, more loving, and more free to help every one of us than any one of us ever realizes. This alone is what makes His incessant summons to faith, and to more faith, coherent and reasonable. This again seems to me to imply that mankind generally is under a kind of hypnotic spell about God, which is always contracting and chilling their thoughts of Him, and leading to all kinds of depressing and terrifying illusions about Him. The story of the growth of the disciples' faith is the story of the breaking of that evil spell. If we transport ourselves in imagination into the little company of His disciples, it is not difficult to imagine what the effect upon them of His continual demand for faith in God must have been. Taken along with His own unbroken confidence of God's presence, power, and love, He must have seemed like one holding a continued dialogue with the Unseen One. Yet a doubt must have sometimes crept in. Was it not rather a monologue? No man but He heard the other Voice. . . . Was He mad? . . . The issue, as He meant that it should, gradually became inevitable. Either He was a dreamer, or they and all other men were dreamers, walking in the darkness and deeming it to be light. . . .

Such, I doubt not, was the early struggle of faith. The issue does not seem to me vitally different today. . . . We are all alike wrapped up in the great earth-dream, and He alone was fully awake of all the sons of men; or we men and women of the twentieth century are broad awake to the reality, and He was dreaming His solitary dream.

❧

THE CROSS

LOIS A. CHENEY

I stand before the cross
and wonder.

I stand before the cross
and fear.

I kneel before the cross
and weep.

I pray before the cross
and rejoice.

To know the cross
Is to know Christ.

To feel the cross
Is to feel Christ.

To gaze at the cross
Is to gaze at Christ.

To carry the cross
Is to be a Christian,
And not until then.

God, forgive us.

LUTHER AND THE DEVIL

MARTIN LUTHER

OUR SONGS AND psalms sorely vex and grieve the devil, whereas our passions and impatiences, our complainings and cryings, our "Alas!" and "Woe is me!" please him well, so that he laughs in his fist. He takes delight in tormenting us, especially when we confess, praise, preach, and laud Christ. For, seeing the devil is a prince of this world and our utter enemy, we must be content to let him pass through his own country. He must needs have imposts and customs duties of us, striking our bodies with manifold plagues.

• • •

I am a great enemy to flies; *quia sunt imagines diaboli et haereticorum.* When I have a good book, they flock upon it and parade up and down upon it, and soil it. 'Tis just the same with the devil. When our hearts are purest, he comes and soils them.

• • •

When I am assailed with heavy tribulations, I rush out among my pigs rather than remain alone by myself. The human heart is like a millstone in a mill: when you put wheat under it, it turns and grinds and bruises the wheat to flour; if you put no wheat, it still grinds on, but then 'tis itself it grinds and wears away. So the human heart, unless it be occupied with some employment, leaves space for the devil, who wriggles himself in and brings with him a whole host of evil thoughts, temptations, and tribulations, which grind out the heart.

• • •

The devil seduces us at first by all the allurements of sin in order thereafter to plunge us into despair. He pampers up the flesh that he may by and by prostrate the spirit. We feel no pain in the act of sin, but the soul after it is sad and the conscience disturbed.

CALVARY AND THE FORESHADOWED CROSS

JESSIE PENN-LEWIS

Most Christians believe that the cross was predestined to come at the precise place that it did with a kind of historical finality that is fixed in time. People of faith, such as Jessie Penn-Lewis, take very seriously the Old Testament prophecies that seem to predict Jesus' death and the New Testament affirmations that the cross is as much a part of history as Washington crossing the Delaware. Neither of them is less likely than the other, but the cross is the ultimate saving human event. It is that pivotal point of understanding that helps all other history make sense.

THE HOUR HAD come! The Lamb slain from the foundation of the world was now to be slain before the eyes of the world. "Herod and Pontius Pilate, with the Gentiles and the peoples of Israel, were gathered together, to do" what had been "foreordained to come to pass" (Acts iv. 27,28).

By picture lessons and prophetic voices, for centuries before, God had been foretelling this dread hour; and He has been directing the world back to it for nearly two thousand years.

Calvary is the very pivot of the world's history. All prior things pointed forward to it; and all subsequent things point back to it. Even the future rests upon it, for the redeemed in heaven find it the centre of heaven as they behold a Lamb in the midst of the throne, "standing as though it had been slain."

Seven hundred years before the Man Christ Jesus was led to the place called Calvary, a prophet inspired of God foreshadowed the Cross; and gave such a word-picture of the Saviour of the world, that none but blinded hearts could fail to recognize Him when He came to earth—God manifest in the flesh.

Through the prophet Isaiah the Spirit of God poured a flood of light upon Calvary; depicting the pathway to the Cross, its atoning sacrifice, its sufferings and its fruit; so that all who knew the Scripture of the prophets, were without excuse as they crucified the Lord of glory.

• • •

How marred must have been the face of the Holy One of God from His crown of thorns! How lacerated the form of His sacred body from the scourging of the soldiers, for the scourges were made from hundreds of leathern thongs, each armed at the point with an angular bony hook, or a sharp sided cube.

"Look at yonder pillar, black with the blood of murderers and rebels. . . . Look at the rude and barbarous beings who busily surround their victim." See them "tear off His clothes, bind those hands . . . press His gracious visage firmly against the shameful pillar," binding Him, "with ropes in such a manner that He cannot move or stir." See! The scourging lasts a full quarter of an hour! The scourges cut ever deeper into the wounds already made, and penetrate almost to the marrow until "His whole back appears an enormous wound." A purple robe is then thrown over the form of the agonized Sufferer, and the twigs of a long-spiked thorn bush are twisted into a circle, and pressed upon His brow.

It was thus that His face was marred, and His form more than the sons of men. The prophet Isaiah had even foretold the words of the Man of sorrows, saying in His hour of agony, "I was not rebellious, neither turned away backward. I gave my back to the smiters, and My cheeks to them that plucked off the hair: I hid not My face from shame and spitting. For the Lord God will help Me . . . therefore have I set My face like a flint" (Isaiah l. 5—7).

Men hid their faces from Him, but "He hid as it were His face from us" is the marginal reading of the R.V. Did the group who had seen His face shine as the sun on the Mount of Transfiguration, remember the hidden glory in that marred frame? Nay, even they "esteemed Him not" and forsook Him in His hour of shame.

• • •

Thus briefly we have portrayed for us the result of the Fall in Eden, and the cause and purpose of the Cross.

Independence of God is the very essence of sin. To every man "his own way" ends in transgression and iniquity. The first ALL includes every human being brought into the world, and the second ALL proclaims the atoning sacrifice of Christ for every one under the curse of sin.

THE DEATH OF THE CROSS

"He humbled Himself, and opened not His mouth. . . ."
"A lamb that is led to the slaughter. . . ."
"A sheep that before her shearers is dumb. . . ."
"He was cut off out of the land of the living. . . ."
"They made His grave with the wicked. . . ."

Isaiah now depicts the obedience unto death of the suffering one. He sees Him as a sheep in the hands of the shearers, dumb and passive; as a lamb being led to the slaughter, innocent and powerless. He Who was equal with God, counted it not a thing to be grasped, but emptied Himself, and came in the likeness of men. As man He humbled Himself yet more, even unto death, consenting to be "led to the slaughter" as a victim in the hands of men. How literally the prophecy was fulfilled in every detail the gospels unfold.

The Christ standing before Pilate "when He was accused" "answering nothing" (Matthew xxvii. 12), so that even the Governor marvelled. From "oppression and judgment He was taken away" outside the city wall to the place called Calvary, and "as for His generation"—the people of His own nation and time—"who among them considered" the tragedy that was being enacted in their midst?

"Cut off out of the land of the living" in the very prime of life, how few realized that it was for the transgression of His people "to whom the stroke was due" (Isaiah liii. 8, *margin*).

How many in Jerusalem during that awful time "considered," and pondered over, the Scripture of the prophets, which gave them the portrait of the Man they crucified?

But the Man of sorrows knew! He said every step of His path must needs be "as it is written of Him." As He set His face to go on His last journey to Jerusalem it was with the words "All the things that are written through the prophets shall be accomplished unto the Son of Man. For He shall be delivered up," "mocked," "shamefully entreated," "spit upon," "and they shall scourge and kill Him" (Luke xviii. 31–33, *margin*).

He said, "It is written," when Judas betrayed Him, and when His disciples forsook Him, and again, after He was risen from the dead, He reminded them that when He was yet with them, He had sought to prepare them for His Cross, by telling them that "all things that must needs be fulfilled" which were written in "the law of Moses, and the prophets, and the Psalms" concerning Him (Luke xxiv. 44).

Moreover Isaiah not only foretold the sufferings and death of the Christ, but the very way of His burial. His grave would be with the wicked, and He Who had been despised and rejected of men, would be with the "rich in His death."

This was literally fulfilled; and the instrument prepared of God to carry out His counsels was found in "Joseph of Arimathea, a counselor of honourable estate," who was one "looking for the kingdom of God" (Mark xv. 43), and said to be a secret disciple of the Lord Jesus.

Joseph had sat in the council that condemned the Righteous One, but "he had not consented to their counsel and deed." He must have marvelled with the Governor at the extraordinary silence of the Divine Sufferer, and in his heart reechoed the verdict of Pilate that there was no cause worthy of death found in Him.

Unable to save the victim from His accusers, Joseph did what he could as soon as the sentence of death had been carried out, by going boldly to Pilate, and asking for the body of the Lord, afterwards reverently laying it in his own new tomb.

CHRIST THE SON OF MAN

C. F. ANDREWS

SINCE I HAVE learnt to know Christ afresh in this Eastern setting, it has been easy for me to point out the weakness of the portraiture when His character has been depicted with only Western ideals to draw from, as though these comprehended the "fullness of the Christ." For in such pictures the true proportion has not been kept. Some of the marked traits of His character have not appeared at all. Much has been lost. Some day I would like to draw His likeness anew, with the colour of the Eastern sky added to the scene.

In the same way, no doubt, the proportion would have been lost in due time, if Christianity had spread only in Asia in the first century, instead of passing on into Europe. Then, after many generations of Christian culture, we should have had an Oriental Christ, whom the West would rightly recognize as inadequate, and wish to draw over again.

For the supreme miracle of Christ's character lies in this: that He combines within Himself, as no other figure in human history has ever done, the qualities of every race. His very birthplace and home in childhood were near the concourse of the two great streams of human life in the ancient world, that flowed East and West. Time and place conspired, but the divine spark came down from above to mould for all time the human character of the Christ, the Son of Man.

This is a tremendous claim to set forward. In all other ages of mankind verification would have been impossible, because the world of men had not yet been fully explored. But in our own generation the claim may at last be made, and may be seen to correspond with the salient facts of human history. For those who, through intimate contact with other races, have gained the right to be heard, have borne witness that each race and region of the earth responds to His appeal, finding in the Gospel record that which applies specially to themselves. His sovereign character has become the one golden thread running through mankind, binding the ages and the races together.

THE CRUCIFIXION

MARTIN LUTHER

Luther makes the point that the cross used as a charm or amulet has little value. Only when its presence symbolizes the price that Jesus paid so that all can enter heaven does the cross have value. When the cross is only a piece of jewelry, it has nothing to offer, but when it is inner light, it is victorious in its power.

LET US NOW meditate a moment on the Passion of Christ. Some do so falsely in that they merely rail against Judas and the Jews. Some carry crucifixes to protect themselves from water, fire, and sword, and turn the suffering of Christ into an amulet against suffering. Some weep and that is the end of it. The true contemplation is that in which the heart is crushed and the conscience smitten. You must be overwhelmed by the frightful wrath of God who so hated sin that he spared not his only-begotten Son. What can the sinner expect if the beloved Son was so afflicted? It must be an inexpressible and unendurable yearning that causes God's Son himself so to suffer. Ponder this and you will tremble, and the more you ponder, the deeper will you tremble.

Take this to heart and doubt not that you are the one who killed Christ. Your sins certainly did, and when you see the nails driven through his hands, be sure that you are pounding, and when the thorns pierce his brow, know that they are your evil thoughts. Consider that if one thorn pierced Christ you deserve a hundred thousand.

The whole value of the meditation of the suffering of Christ lies in this, that man should come to the knowledge of himself and sink and tremble. If you are so hardened that you do not tremble, then you have reason to tremble. Pray to God that he may soften your heart and make fruitful your meditation upon the suffering of Christ, for we of ourselves are incapable of proper reflection unless God instill it.

But if one does meditate rightly on the suffering of Christ for a day, an hour, or even a quarter of an hour, this we may confidently say is better than a whole year of fasting, days of psalm singing, yes, than even one hundred Masses, because this reflection changes the whole man and makes him new, as once he was in baptism.

If, then, Christ is so firmly planted in your heart, and if you are become an enemy to sin out of love and not fear, then henceforth, the suffering of Christ, which began as a sacrament, may continue lifelong as an example. When tribulation and sickness assail you, think how slight these are compared to the thorns and the nails of Christ. If you are thwarted, remember how he was bound and dragged. If pride besets you, see how the Lord was mocked and with robbers despised. If unchastity incites your flesh, recall how his flesh was scourged, pierced, and smitten. If hate, envy, and vengeance tempt you, think how Christ for you and all his enemies interceded with tears, though he might rather have avenged himself. If you are afflicted and cannot have your way, take heart and say, "Why should I not suffer when my Lord sweat blood for very anguish?"

Astounding it is that the cross of Christ has so fallen into forgetfulness, for is it not forgetfulness of the cross when no one wishes to suffer but rather to enjoy himself and evade the cross? You must personally experience suffering with Christ. He suffered for your sake and should you not suffer for his sake, as well as for your own?

Two texts in the Old Testament apply to Christ. The first is, "Thou art fairer than the children of men" (Ps. 45:2), and the second is, "He hath no form nor comeliness" (Isa. 53:2). Evidently these passages must be understood in differing senses. To the eyes of the flesh, he was the lowest among the sons of men, a derision, and to the eyes of the spirit there was none fairer than he. The eyes of the flesh cannot see this. What, then, is the nature of this beauty? It is wisdom and love, light for the understanding, and power for the soul, for in suffering and dying Christ displayed all the wisdom and truth with which the understanding can be adorned. All the treasures of wisdom and knowledge are hidden in him, and they are hidden because they are visible only to the eye of the spirit.

The greater and the more wonderful is the excellence of his love by contrast with the lowliness of his form, the hate and pain of his Passion. Herein we come to know both God and ourselves. His beauty is his own and through it we learn to know him. His uncomeliness and Passion are ours, and in them we know ourselves, for what he suffered in the flesh, we must inwardly, suffer in the spirit. He has in truth borne our stripes. Here, then, in an unspeakably clear mirror you see yourself. You must know that through your sins you are as uncomely and mangled as you see him here.

If we consider the persons, we ought to suffer a thousand and again a thousand times more than Christ because he is God and we are dust and ashes, yet it is the reverse. He, who had a thousand and again a thousand times less need, has taken upon himself a thousand and again a thousand times more than we. No understanding can fathom nor tongue can express, no writing can record, but only the inward feeling can grasp, what is involved in the suffering of Christ.

DESIRE FOR THE CROSS

ELISABETH ELLIOT

Jim Elliot has become a martyr-missionary of near-legend status among American Evangelicals. This gentle mystic and evangelist was killed by Indians in South America in the mid-1950s. While he never published many of his own writings, his journals were brought to the world through the devoted efforts of his wife in the years following his death.

"OH THAT CHRIST were All and Enough for me. He is supposed to be, . . . but oh, to be swept away in a flood of consuming passion for Jesus, that all desire must be sublimated to him.

"Copied out a few lines from Maxwell's *Born Crucified* yesterday, which I must learn:

> " 'The Cross falls like a two-edged sword
> Of heavenly temper keen
> And double were the wounds it made
> Where'er it glanced between.
> 'Twas death to sin, 'twas life
> To all who mourned for sin.
> It kindled and it silenced strife,
> Made war and peace within.' "

MOTHERS

RUTH BELL GRAHAM

Ruth Bell Graham, the wife of the famed evangelist Billy Graham, is a poet and writer of excellence. In a subtle and less obvious way her writing has long been celebrated.

> Had I been Joseph's mother
> I'd have prayed
> protection from his brothers:
> "God keep him safe;
> he is so young,
> so different from

the others."
Mercifully
she never knew
there would be slavery
and prison, too.

Had I been Moses' mother
I'd have wept
to keep my little son;
praying she might forget
the babe drawn from the water
of the Nile,
had I not kept
him for her
nursing him the while?
Was he not mine
and she
but Pharaoh's daughter?

Had I been Daniel's mother
I should have pled
"Give victory!
This Babylonian horde—
godless and cruel—
don't let them take him captive
—better dead,
Almighty Lord!"

Had I been Mary—
Oh, had I been she,
I would have cried
as never mother cried,
". . . Anything, O God,
anything . . .
but crucified!"

With such prayers
importunate
my finite wisdom
would assail
Infinite Wisdom;

God, how fortunate
Infinite Wisdom
should prevail!

⌇

THE CORONET

ANDREW MARVELL

The crown of thorns holds the mystery of both triumph and loss. In every life there is a bit of both. In becoming a person, Christians believe Jesus left his royal crown in heaven and took up a more victorious, if painful, crown of thorns on earth. Andrew Marvell celebrates this mysterious symbol of conquest and shame, victory and humility that is the crown of thorns.

When for the thorns with which I long, too long,
With many a piercing wound,
My Saviour's head have crown'd,
I seek with garlands to redress that wrong:
Through every garden, every mead,
I gather flow'rs (my fruits are only flow'rs),
Dismantling all the fragrant towers
That once adorn'd my shepherdesse's head:
And now, when I have summ'd up all my store,
Thinking (so I my self deceive)
So rich a chaplet thence to weave
As never yet the King of Glory wore:
Alas! I find the Serpent old,
That, twining in his speckled breast,
About the flowers disguis'd, does fold
With wreaths of fame and interest.

Ah! foolish man, that would'st debase with them,
And mortal glory, Heaven's diadem!
But Thou who only could'st the Serpent tame,
Either his slipp'ry knots at once untie,
And disentangle all his winding snare;
Or shatter too with him my curious frame
And let these wither—so that he may die—

Though set with skill, and chosen out with care:
That they, while Thou on both their spoils dost tread,
May crown Thy feet, that could not crown Thy head.

∾

THE LOOK

ELIZABETH BARRETT BROWNING

Three of the evangelists, Matthew, Mark, and Luke, mention Peter's denial of Christ just before his crucifixion. Still, Luke is the only one who mentions that after Peter's third denial, Jesus looked him directly in the eye. That look has long been the subject of art and poetry. In two of her sonnets Elizabeth Barrett Browning takes the look and tries to answer what must have passed between Jesus and Peter on that occasion. The cross is not just a gallows. It is a sequence of betrayal and disappointment and alienations, all of which Jesus must have felt. Let us not therefore suppose that Jesus' worst pain was in the nails or thorns. Elizabeth Barrett Browning explores other kinds of pain Jesus felt: the anguish and betrayal of so many of his close friends. In the following two sonnets, we find both the arch sin and arch betrayal of Simon Peter as Jesus is in the process of trial and crucifixion.

THE LOOK

The Savior looked on Peter. Ay, no word,
No gesture of reproach: the heavens serene,
Though heavy with armed justice, did not lean
Their thunders that way: the forsaken Lord
Looked only on the traitor. None record
What that look was, none guess; for those who have seen
Wronged lovers loving through a death-pang keen,
Or pale-cheeked martyrs smiling to a sword,
Have missed Jehovah at the judgment-call.
And Peter, from the height of blasphemy—
"I never knew this man"—did quail and fall,
As knowing straight *that* God, and turnéd free,
And went out speechless from the face of all,
And filled the silence, weeping bitterly.

THE MEANING OF THE LOOK

I think that look on Christ might seem to say,
"Thou Peter! art thou, then, a common stone
Which I at last must break my heart upon,
For all God's charge to His high angels may
Guard my foot better? Did I yesterday
Wash *thy* feet, my beloved, that they should run
Quick to deny me 'neath the morning sun?
And do thy kisses, like the rest, betray?
The cock crows coldly, Go, and manifest
A late contrition, but no bootless fear;
For, when thy final need is dreariest,
Thou shalt not be denied, as I am here:
My voice to God and angels shall attest,
'Because *I know* this man, let him be clear.' "

∽

THE CROSS

CALVIN MILLER

*I have often wondered how God must have felt in watching his Son die
on the cross. Who could ever objectify the Almighty or define his
emotions at such a moment? But I found this experience from Thomas
Dooley somewhat a help in clarifying how I think God might have felt.*

DR. THOMAS DOOLEY, in his book *The Night They Burned the Mountain,* tells
a correlating story that well illustrates the grief of God when we endure
hopelessness or pain. One of the Laotians had given him a tiny Himalayan
moonbear. It was a cuddly ball of brown fur, full of interesting antics, and
Dr. Dooley set to building a cage for the animal. An old Chinese man
happened upon him as he worked on the cage and stared at him in
disbelief. The old man began to sob as he looked at the cage, and when
Dr. Dooley sought to discover the reason for his tears, he told him that
the cage was reminiscent of the greatest tragedy he had ever experienced.
The old Chinese and his son had once worked together on a commune in
Red China. He reminded the good doctor that laborers on the communes
at harvest time were not to have one grain of rice for themselves, for it
was all the property of the Republic. The son of this old man had dis-

obeyed the harvest mandate. Since his mother was sick with beriberi and malnutrition, the son had concealed a few handfuls of rice in his clothing to take to this starving mother. He was, of course, discovered, and the authorities made a public whipping post out of the boy. They imprisoned him in a cage, not unlike the one that Dr. Dooley had made for his pet bear, and had put the caged youth in the center of the city. The cage was so small that the boy could not move or even sit up straight. The old man's testimony went like this:

> His mother and I were forced to watch, she from one side of the square and I from the other. But the guards would not allow us to go near him. Day after day, as we looked on, my boy died slowly, under the broiling sun with nothing to eat or drink, covered with filth, flies and ants. It was good when the guards pronounced him dead.

The man had since escaped from China, but the very sign of cages aroused his torturous memory once more.

❧

ADORO TE DEVOTE

SAINT THOMAS AQUINAS

Saint Thomas Aquinas was not merely a great theologian and definer of the faith; he was also a great writer. His works are voluminous and make us fear his writing by virtue of the amount of writing that he did, but his words are warm and poetic. They are captivating, literary, and never to be feared. This poem on the cross is not only excellent in form; it is high worship.

Godhead here in hiding, whom I do adore
Masked by these bare shadows, shape and nothing more,
See, Lord, at thy service low lies here a heart
Lost, all lost in wonder at the God thou art.

Seeing, touching, tasting are in thee deceived;
How says trusty hearing? that shall be believed;
What God's Son has told me, take for true I do;
Truth himself speaks truly or there's nothing true,

On the cross thy godhead made no sign to men;
Here thy very manhood steals from human ken:
Both are my confession, both are my belief,
And I pray the prayer of the dying thief.

I am not like Thomas, wounds I cannot see,
But can plainly call thee God and Lord as he:
This faith each day deeper be my holding of,
Daily make me harder hope and dearer love.

O Thou our reminder of Christ crucified,
Living Bread the life of us for whom he died,
Lend this life to me then: feed and feast my mind,
There be thou the sweetness man was meant to find.

Bring the tender tale true of the Pelican;
Bathe me, Jesu Lord, in what thy bosom ran—
Blood that but one drop of has the world to win
All the world forgiveness of its world of sin.

Jesu, whom I look at shrouded here below,
I beseech thee send me what I thirst for so,
Some day to gaze on thee face to face in light,
And be blest for ever with thy glory's sight.

❧

THE ENTRY INTO JERUSALEM

AUTHOR UNKNOWN

*The following is from an anonymous record, of about A.D. 54, suppos-
edly by a member of the council who voted for the death of Jesus.*

IT WAS TWENTY-ONE years ago, but I can remember as if it were yesterday
the excitement in Jerusalem when the news came that Jesus of Nazareth
had arrived in the neighborhood and was spending his Sabbath at the
village of Bethany. All those who were disaffected against the Romans

cried out, "A leader! a leader!" All those who were halt, sick, or blind, cried out, "A healer! a healer!" Wherever we went, there was no talk but of the coming deliverance.

The next day being the first of the week, which the Romans call the day of the Sun, I was pondering the words of the Law in my little study chamber . . . when suddenly I heard the patter of many feet in the street beneath me, and looking out, I saw them all hurrying, as it seemed, to the Temple. I put on my sandals, and, taking my staff in my hand and drawing my mantle over my head, hurried out after the passersby. But when they came to the Broad Place before the Water Gate, they turned sharp at the right, and went down the Tyropoeon as far as the Fountain Gate, where I overtook them.

It is but three hundred paces from the Fountain Gate to En Rogel, and the Nazarene and his friends had advanced somewhat to meet us, but in that short space the enthusiasm of the crowd had arisen to a very fever, and as we neared him one cried out, and all joined in the cry, "Hosanna Barabba! Hosanna Barabba!" and then they shouted our usual cry of welcome, "Blessed be he that cometh in the name of the Lord!" and one bolder than his fellows called out, "Blessed be the coming of the kingdom!" At that there was the wildest joy among the people. Some tore off branches of palms, and stood by the way and waved them in front of Jesus; others took off each his *talith* and threw it down in front of the young ass on which Jesus rode, as if to pave the way into the Holy City with choice linen. But when I looked upon the face of Jesus, there were no signs there of the coming triumph; he sat with his head bent forward, his eyes downcast, and his face all sad. And a chill somehow came over me.

❧

CHRISTIAN REACHES THE CROSS

JOHN BUNYAN

This selection is taken from Bunyan's classic, Pilgrim's Progress, *a post-Reformation allegory that has stood at the center of esteem among Reformed and Protestant Christians. Much of it is believed to have been written in Bedford Gaol, where Bunyan was imprisoned for his straightforward, nonliturgical sermons.*

Now I saw in my dream that the highway which Christian was to go was fenced on either side with a wall, and that wall was called Salvation (Isa. 26:1). Up this way therefore did burdened Christian run, but not without great difficulty, because of the load on his back.

He ran thus till he came to a place somewhat ascending; and upon the place stood a cross, and a little below, in the bottom, a sepulcher. So I saw in my dream that just as Christian came up with the cross, his burden loosed from off his shoulders, and fell from off his back, and began to tumble, and so continued to do till it came to the mouth of the sepulcher, where it fell in, and I saw it no more.

❦

THERE ARE NO LADDERS

JUDITH DEEM DUPREE

There are no ladders
    at the cross,
Ascending or descending.
You do not choose the hill,
The day, the angle of the sun
    against your eyes,
Nor any of the likeliest
    antagonists.
You simply yield,
Because the gaunt necessity
    confronts you . . .
Because there is no stamina
    in the unbroken flesh;
Nothing to forgive,
    until the nails.

ALAS! AND DID MY SAVIOR BLEED

ISAAC WATTS

Many of the poems of Isaac Watts became the texts of hymns that furnished public worship of Anglicans and other Protestants. This is one of his most famous.

Alas! and did my Savior bleed,
And did my Sovereign die?
Would He devote that sacred head
For such a worm as I?

Was it for crimes that I have done
He groaned upon the tree?
Amazing pity, grace unknown,
And love beyond degree!

Well might the sun in darkness hide,
And shut his glories in,
When Christ, the mighty Maker, died
For man the creature's sin.

Thus might I hide my blushing face
While His dear cross appears;
Dissolve, my heart, in thankfulness!
And melt, mine eyes, to tears!

❧

CHRIST DIED QUICKLY ON THE CROSS

WILLIAM D. EDWARDS

Several physicians have commented on the actual physiological aspects of dying by crucifixion. While crucified criminals could last for days during extenuated times of dying, Jesus' crucifixion was over in a matter of hours. William D. Edwards surmised that in Jesus' case, his death may have been hastened by those factors that were evident even without an autopsy.

SCOURGING

Flogging was a legal preliminary to every Roman execution, and only women and Roman senators or soldiers (except in cases of desertion) were exempt. The usual instrument was a short whip (*flagrum* or *flagellum*) with several single or braided leather thongs of variable lengths, in which small iron balls or sharp pieces of sheep bones were tied at intervals. Occasionally, staves also were used. For scourging, the man was stripped of his clothing, and his hands were tied to an upright post. The back, buttocks, and legs were flogged either by two soldiers *(lictors)* or by one who alternated positions. The severity of the scourging depended on the disposition of the lictors and was intended to weaken the victim to a state just short of collapse or death. After the scourging, the soldiers often taunted their victims.

MEDICAL ASPECTS OF SCOURGING

As the Roman soldiers repeatedly struck the victim's back with full force, the iron balls would cause deep contusions, and the leather thongs and sheep bones would cut into the skin and subcutaneous tissues. Then, as the flogging continued, the lacerations would tear into the underlying skeletal muscles and produce quivering ribbons of bleeding flesh. Pain and blood loss generally set the stage for circulatory shock. The extent of blood loss may well have determined how long the victim would survive on the cross.

• • •

The severe scourging, with its intense pain and appreciable blood loss, most probably left Jesus in a preshock state. Moreover, hematidrosis had rendered his skin particularly tender. The physical and mental abuse meted out by the Jews and the Romans, as well as the lack of food, water, and sleep, also contributed to his generally weakened state. Therefore, even before the actual crucifixion, Jesus' physical condition was at least serious and possibly critical.

CRUCIFIXION PRACTICES

Crucifixion probably first began among the Persians. Alexander the Great introduced the practice to Egypt and Carthage, and the Romans appear to have learned of it from the Carthaginians. Although the Romans did not invent crucifixion, they perfected it as a form of torture and capital punishment that was designed to produce a slow death with maximum pain and suffering. It was one of the most disgraceful and cruel methods of execution and usually was reserved only for slaves, foreigners, revolutionaries, and the vilest of criminals. Roman law usually protected

Roman citizens from crucifixion, except perhaps in the case of desertion by soldiers.

In its earliest form in Persia, the victim was either tied to a tree or was tied to or impaled on an upright post, usually to keep the guilty victim's feet from touching holy ground. Only later was a true cross used; it was characterized by an upright post *(stipes)* and a horizontal crossbar *(patibulum),* and it had several variations. Although archaeological and historical evidence strongly indicates that the low Tau cross was preferred by the Romans in Palestine at the time of Christ, crucifixion practices often varied in a given geographic region and in accordance with the imagination of the executioners, and the Latin cross and other forms also may have been used.

• • •

With a knowledge of both anatomy and ancient crucifixion practices, one may reconstruct the probable medical aspects of this form of slow execution. Each wound apparently was intended to produce intense agony, and the contributing causes of death were numerous.

• • •

Death by crucifixion was, in every sense of the word, excruciating (Latin, *excruciatus,* or "out of the cross").

DEATH OF JESUS

Two aspects of Jesus' death have been the source of great controversy, namely, the nature of the wound in his side and the cause of his death after only several hours on the cross.

The gospel of John describes the piercing of Jesus' side and emphasizes the sudden flow of blood and water. Some authors have interpreted the flow of water to be ascites or urine, from an abdominal midline perforation of the bladder. However, the Greek word (πλευρά, or pleura) used by John clearly denoted laterality and often implied the ribs. Therefore, it seems probable that the wound was in the thorax and well away from the abdominal midline.

Although the side of the wound was not designated by John, it traditionally has been depicted on the right side. Supporting this tradition is the fact that a large flow of blood would be more likely with a perforation of the distended and thin-walled right atrium or ventricle than the thick-walled and contracted left ventricle. Although the side of the wound may never be established with certainty, the right seems more probable than the left.

Some of the skepticism in accepting John's description has arisen from the difficulty in explaining, with medical accuracy, the flow of both blood and water. Part of this difficulty has been based on the assumption that the blood appeared first, then the water. However, in the ancient Greek, the order of words generally denoted prominence and not necessarily a time sequence. Therefore, it seems likely that John was emphasizing the prominence of blood rather than its appearance preceding the water.

Therefore, the water probably represented serous pleural and pericardial fluid, and would have preceded the flow of blood and been smaller in volume than the blood. Perhaps in the setting of hypovolemia and impending acute heart failure, pleural and pericardial effusions may have developed and would have added to the volume of apparent water. The blood, in contrast, may have originated from the right atrium or the right ventricle or perhaps from a humopericardium.

Jesus' death after only three to six hours on the cross surprised even Pontius Pilate. The fact that Jesus cried out in a loud voice and then bowed his head and died suggests the possibility of a catastrophic terminal event. One popular explanation has been that Jesus died of cardiac rupture.

• • •

However, another explanation may be more likely. Jesus' death may have been hastened simply by his state of exhaustion and by the severity of the scourging, with its resultant blood loss and preshock state. The fact that he could not carry his *patibulum* supports this interpretation. The actual cause of Jesus' death, like that of other crucified victims, may have been multifactorial and related primarily to hypovolemic shock, exhaustion asphyxia, and perhaps acute heart failure. A fatal cardiac arrhythmia may have accounted for the apparent catastrophic terminal event.

Thus, it remains unsettled whether Jesus died of cardiac rupture or of cardiorespiratory failure. However, the important feature may be not *how* he died but rather *whether* he died. Clearly, the weight of historical and medical evidence indicates that Jesus was dead before the wound to his side was inflicted and supports the traditional view that the spear, thrust between his right ribs, probably perforated not only the right lung but also the pericardium and heart and thereby ensured his death. Accordingly, interpretations based on the assumption that Jesus did not die on the cross appear to be at odds with modern medical knowledge.

A BALLAD OF TREES AND THE MASTER

SIDNEY LANIER

Into the woods my Master went,
Clean forspent, forspent.
Into the woods my Master came,
Forspent with love and shame.
But the olives they were not blind to Him;
The little gray leaves were kind to Him;
The thorn-tree had a mind to Him
When into the woods He came.

Out of the woods my Master went,
And He was well content.
Out of the woods my Master came,
Content with death and shame.
When Death and Shame would woo Him last,
From under the trees they drew Him last:
'Twas on a tree they slew Him—last
When out of the woods He came.

WHEN I SURVEY THE WONDROUS CROSS

ISAAC WATTS

When I survey the wondrous cross
On which the Prince of Glory died,
My richest gain I count but loss,
And pour contempt on all my pride.

Forbid it, Lord, that I should boast,
Save in the death of Christ, my God!
All the vain things that charm me most,
I sacrifice them through His blood.

See from His head, His hands, His feet,
Sorrow and love flow mingled down;

Did e'er such love and sorrow meet,
Or thorns compose so rich a crown?

Were the whole realm of nature mine,
That were a present far too small;
Love so amazing, so divine,
Demands my soul, my life, my all.

∾

IN GETHSEMANE

ELIZABETH GOUDGE

ONLY TWICE IN the Gospels is it recorded that Our Lord wept, for only the most intense grief could have wrung tears from so strong a man. He wept at the grave of Lazarus over the grief of the world and the hatefulness of death, and he wept now over the terror and agony of war and destruction; and we can believe that he wept not only over this particular war that would destroy the beloved city of Jerusalem, but over the passion of the whole world until the end of time. "For nation shall rise against nation, and kingdom against kingdom," he said to his disciples, "and there shall be famines, and pestilences, and earthquakes. All these are the beginning of sorrows. . . . And because iniquity shall abound, the love of many shall wax cold."

And then his thought came back for one brief moment from the passion of his people, of the world, and of his saints, to his own, and like every true man he shrank from the thought of death.

"Now is my soul troubled," he said, "and what shall I say? Father, save me from this hour? But for this cause came I into the world. Father, glorify thy name."

There came a peal of thunder then and those who stood near Our Lord thought that they heard words in the thunder. "I have glorified it, and will glorify thy name."

THE APOCRYPHAL JESUS

JOSEPH CAMPBELL

Joseph Campbell, an authority in world myths, came across this legend of Gethsemane. I include it not because it is accepted as the truth, but because it exists as an example of the apocryphal stories of Jesus that exist in many legendary and less authentic sources.

THERE IS AN equivalent scene described in the apocryphal Christian Acts of John immediately before Jesus goes to be crucified. This is one of the most moving passages in Christian literature. In the Matthew, Mark, Luke and John gospels, it is simply mentioned that, at the conclusion of the celebration of the Last Supper, Jesus and his disciples sang a hymn before he went forth. But in the Acts of John, we have a word-for-word account of the whole singing of the hymn. Just before going out into the garden at the end of the Last Supper, Jesus says to the company, "Let us dance!" And they all hold hands in a circle, and as they circle around him, Jesus sings, "Glory be to thee, Father!"

To which the circling company responds, "Amen."

"Glory be to thee, Word!"

And again, "Amen."

"I would be born and I would bear!"

"Amen."

"I would eat and I would be eaten!"

"Amen."

"Thou that dancest, see what I do, for thine is this passion of the manhood, which I am about to suffer!"

"Amen."

"I would flee and I would stay!"

"Amen."

"I would be united and I would unite!"

"Amen."

"A door am I to thee that knocketh at me. . . . A way am I to thee, a wayfarer." And when the dance is ended, he walks out into the garden to be taken and crucified.

THE FORM OF A SERVANT

CALVIN MILLER

The hands of Christ have been a matter of fascination for Christians across the centuries. They were marked by the stigmata, the scars. But the marks in the hands of Christ are not just old scars. Throughout Christian history they have been seen as fresh wounds, and several saints have been blessed by living stigmata. At certain times of the church year, mostly on Good Friday, these wounds have broken into fresh bleeding. Saint Francis of Assisi is believed by some to have been marked with the stigmata, as well as Padre Pio in our own time. But whether the bleeding stigmata are actually a gift given to some, the hands of Christ are considered to have been the place where redemption was paid for. It was doubting Thomas who said he would not believe unless he saw those hands (John 20:25). The two Christians on the way to Emmaus do not believe that Jesus is risen until he breaks the bread and they see his hands as proof that he is the Christ (Luke 24:31)

It was His hands I noticed first. Big, tough,
And weathered, hammer-gripping, sweating fists,
Quite used to driving nails into the rough
And bronze, blue bruised where once the iron missed.
A hand's a thing of beauty, in the eye
Of those whose vision trained can pierce the skin
To see the steel of sturdy bones laid white
And fragile tendons, filament and thin.
I understand the riddle of the hand
How leathered callouses breeds tougher skin,
Hides tiny porcelain machines within.
Yet love defies my wit to understand
How hands that swung the crushing iron grow frail,
And beckon to each palm a killing nail.

❧

ALONE INTO THE MOUNTAIN

KATHARINE LEE BATES

The scriptures make it clear that Jesus spent a lot of time alone praying. Following his baptism, the bath qol, or loud voice, over the river announces that Jesus is the Son of God (Luke 3:22). From this point on in his final three years of life, Jesus spends a lot of time praying, perhaps to fortify his inner spirit so that he will not swerve from his path of dying for all mankind. Katharine Lee Bates captures the importance that Jesus found in his time alone praying to God.

All day from that deep well of life within
Himself has He drawn healing for the press
Of folk, restoring strength, forgiving sin,
Quieting frenzy, comforting distress.
Shadows of evening fall, yet wildly still
They throng Him, touch Him, clutch His garment's hem,
Fall down and clasp His feet, cry on Him, till
The Master, spent, slips from the midst of them
And climbs the mountain for a cup of peace,
Taking a sheer and rugged track untrod
Save by a poor lost sheep with thorn-torn fleece
That follows on and hears Him talk with God.

A HYMN TO GOD THE FATHER

BEN JONSON

This hymn celebrates the adoration Christians have felt across the centuries for the forgiveness of sins bought by Christ when he died on the cross. The idea of the atonement derives directly from the Old Testament idea that without the shedding of blood there is no remission of sin (Hebrews 9:22). As the Levites once offered the blood of bulls and goats for Israel's cleansing (Hebrews 9:16–21), in Christ's blood, God once for all offered forgiveness for all sin for every person in every age.

Hear me, O God!
A broken heart
Is my best part:
Use still Thy rod,
That I may prove,
Therein, Thy love.

If Thou hadst not
　　Been stern to me,
　　But left me free,
I had forgot
　　Myself and Thee.

For sin's so sweet,
　　As minds ill bent
　　Rarely repent
Until they meet
　　Their punishment.

Who more can crave
　　Than Thou hast done:
　　That gav'st a Son
To free a slave?
　　First made of nought,
　　Withal since bought.

Sin, Death, and Hell
　　His glorious Name
　　Quite overcame,
Yet I rebel
　　And slight the same.

But I'll come in
　　Before my loss
　　Me farther toss,
As sure to win
　　Under His Cross.

❧

SMOKE ON THE MOUNTAIN

JOY DAVIDMAN

Joy Davidman, the wife of C. S. Lewis, was an impressive writer whose
stature was often dwarfed by the reputation of her all-too-famous

husband. Smoke on the Mountain *was her compelling examination of the Ten Commandments for midcentury American and British cultures.*

OUR GENERATION HAS never seen a man crucified except in sugary religious art; but it was not a sweet sight, and few of us would dare to have a real picture of a crucifixion on our bedroom walls. A crucified slave beside the Roman road screamed until his voice died and then hung, a filthy, festering clot of flies, sometimes for days—a living man whose hands and feet were swollen masses of gangrenous meat. That is what our Lord took upon himself, "that through death he might destroy him that had the power of death, that is, the devil; and deliver them, who through fear of death were all their lifetime subject to bondage."

"Thou shalt not" is the beginning of wisdom. But the end of wisdom, the new law, is "Thou shalt." To be Christian is to be old? Not a bit of it. To be Christian is to be reborn, and free, and unafraid, and immortally young.

❧

THE CROSS

CALVIN MILLER

A FABLE IS told of Jesus and Gabriel the archangel. It concerns the Son as he leaves the immaculate state of God's presence to hurl himself into history. Gabriel, at the last of the seven gates, arrests Christ and asks him where he is going. "To Bethlehem of Judah," answers Jesus. Gabriel seems annoyed that anyone would voluntarily leave the Crystal City for any reason, so he asks "Why?" Jesus replies that the Father loves the world and is sending him to redeem it.

Unable to turn him from his mission, Gabriel watches from the outer portal of the estate, while Jesus folds himself into flesh and is laid by a happy young mother in a manger, among the bleating of sheep and lowing of cattle. Gabriel soon loses sight of it all, but he waits patiently while the months become decades. Eagerly he scans the approaches to the Father's House, joyfully anticipating the sight of Jesus again. Then, finally, after thirty-three years of faithful vigilance, Gabriel meets Jesus returning through the celestial pillars. He is horrified as he greets Christ: "Lord, what happened to you down there? Whence came these scars? What fiend would so mistreat the Father's Son? And the world you went to save? Did you save it, Lord?"

Then Jesus speaks, "No, Gabriel, I did not save humanity. I saved only a few and I saved them by these scars."

"But, Lord," protests the archangel, "what about the rest of humanity? Will they never be redeemed?"

"Gabriel, if the rest are ever saved, they will all be saved by these same wounds—there is no other way!"

❧

AM I A SOLDIER OF THE CROSS?

ISAAC WATTS

Isaac Watts wrote many poems, each celebrating some truth about Jesus. In the year 1724, he wrote this classic hymn text. By the end of the eighteenth century it had already become a favorite hymn in the church.

> Am I a soldier of the cross,
> A follower of the Lamb?
> And shall I fear to own His cause
> Or blush to speak His Name?
>
> Must I be carried to the skies
> On flowery beds of ease
> While others fought to win the prize
> And sailed through bloody seas?
>
> Are there no foes for me to face?
> Must I not stem the flood?
> Is this vile world a friend to grace
> To help me on to God?
>
> Since I might fight if I would reign,
> Increase my courage, Lord;
> I'll bear the toil, endure the pain,
> Supported by Thy Word.

CALVARY

EDWIN ARLINGTON ROBINSON

The poetry of Robinson has always been popular for its clear portrayal of Christian truths. This poem, along with "How the Great Guest Came," may be among his most popular.

Friendless and faint, with martyred steps and slow,
Faint for the flesh, but for the spirit free,
Stung by the mob that came to see the show,
The Master toiled along to Calvary;
We gibed him, as he went, with houndish glee,
Till his dim eyes for us did overflow;
We cursed his vengeless hands thrice wretchedly,—
And this was nineteen hundred years ago.

But after nineteen hundred years the shame
Still clings, and we have not made good the loss
That outraged faith has entered in his name.
Ah, when shall come love's courage to be strong!
Tell me, O Lord—tell me, O Lord, how long
Are we to keep Christ writhing on the cross!

THE CROSS

CALVIN MILLER

IT IS IN *following* that our Christianity becomes vital for individuals within the community. Groups do not follow Christ; individuals follow Christ. It is not "they" or "we" who follow, but "I." The kingdom of God is never a pluralized call. We each embrace it alone or not at all. It is said that the Galileans followed, but they followed individually. Regardless of what the rest of the community does, each of us must singularly follow Christ. We need to adopt for ourselves the resolution of Jonathan Edwards:

Resolved: that every man should live to the glory of God.
Resolved Second: That whether others do this or not, I will.

With this endeavor let us follow Christ, exactly as did the Galilean women in Luke 23. They are the real heroines of that chapter. They do not question Jesus' right to be King! They are not bound to him because they seek a sign! They follow him because of love. All they hold in life is bound up in this man Jesus. When he breathed out his last on Golgotha, something vital in their breasts shriveled into nonexistence. Yet they are our teachers.

These women had followed from Galilee. It is such a long way from Galilee to Calvary. Maybe not in miles or furlongs or kilometers, but it is a long way. Between Galilee and Calvary there were tears, humiliation, heartbreak, and "the thousand natural shocks that flesh is heir to." Somewhere between the two, the kingdom of God splintered and fragmented into little groups of fearful believers. For those who followed, God died between Galilee and Calvary. But they followed! Who were these women? They were part of that small but newborn growing community of the cross.

~

A PSALM FOR MAUNDY THURSDAY

JOSEPH BAYLEY

Tonight
Lord Jesus Christ
You sat at supper
with Your friends.
It was a simple meal
that final one
of lamb
unleavened bread
and wine.
Afterward
You went out to die.
How many other meals you shared
beside the lake
fried fish and toasted bread
at Simon's banquet hall a feast
at Lazarus' home in Bethany

the meal that Martha cooked
on mountain slope
where You fed hungry crowd
at close of tiring day.
Please sit with us tonight
at our small meal
of soup and rolls and tea.
Then go with us
to feast of bread and wine
that You provide
because afterward
You went out to die.

❧

FRIDAY

CALVIN MILLER

On with Friday's grisly business!
Let the broad arm raise the sledge!
Let the hammer ring out upon the nails.
I must not flinch with the crimson flows—
He's only a carpenter—a craftsman who claimed too much.
"I need a black nail, soldier."
Give me your hand, carpenter. What a strange man you are!
You stretch forth your hand too eagerly—too willingly, as though I was
        going to shake it, not nail it to a tree.
Steady, man. The first stroke of the hammer is easiest for me and hardest
        for you.
For me the first blow meets only the resistance of soft flesh.
The hardwood beneath drives much slower.
For you the first blow is the worse.
It brings the ripping pain and the bright gore.
The wood beneath your wrist does not feel and bleed as you do.

JESUS

FREDERICK BUECHNER

Frederick Buechner finds the focus of the meaning of Christ's life in his final hours. It is clear from reading the following passage that he believes these are the most important hours of Christ's life for all others as well.

ACCORDING TO JOHN, the last words Jesus spoke from the cross were "It is finished." Whether he meant "finished" as brought to an end, in the sense of finality, or "finished" as brought to completion, in the sense of fulfillment, nobody knows. Maybe he meant both.

What was brought to an end was of course nothing less than his life. The Gospels make no bones about that. He died as dead as any man. All the days of his life led him to this day, and beyond this day there would be no other days, and he knew it. It was finished now, he said. He was finished. He had come to the last of all his moments, and because he was conscious still—alive to his death—maybe, as they say the dying do, he caught one final glimpse of the life he had all but finished living.

Who knows what he glimpsed as that life passed before him. Maybe here and there a fragment preserved for no good reason like old snapshots in a desk drawer: the play of sunlight on a wall, a half-remembered face, something somebody said. A growing sense perhaps of destiny: the holy man in the river, a gift for prayer, a gift for moving simple hearts. One hopes he remembered good times, although the Gospels record few— how he once fell asleep in a boat as a storm was coming up and how he went to a wedding where water was the least of what was turned into wine. Then the failures of the last days, when only a handful gathered to watch him enter the city on the foal of an ass—and those very likely for the wrong reasons. The terror that he himself had known for a few moments in the garden, and that finally drove even the handful away. *Shalom* then, the God in him moving his swollen lips to forgive them all, to forgive maybe even God. Finished.

What was brought to completion by such a life and such a death only he can know now wherever he is, if he is anywhere. The *Christ* of it is beyond our imagining. All we can know is the flesh and blood of it, the *Jesus* of it. In that sense what was completed was at the very least a hope to live by, a mystery to hide our faces before, a shame to haunt us, a dream of holiness to help make bearable our night.

COMMUNION

RUTH BELL GRAHAM

"This is My body
broken like bread for you;
this is My blood
like water shed for you."
Drink it—and wonder.
Marvel—and eat.
God torn asunder,
man made complete!
Stagger the mind
at Truth here revealed:
kneel—and be broken,
rise—and be healed.
Go out and die,
die 'live, and live!
Take all He offers,
take all and give.
Here's a remembering
to scorch and to bless:
sinners partaking
God's righteousness.

• • •

Lord,
this is my body . . .

THE DYING LIFE

CALVIN MILLER

JOSEPH WITTIG ONCE said, "A man's biography ought really to begin not with his birth but with his death; it can be written only from the point of view of its end, because only from there can the whole of his life in its fulfillment be seen." So it is that when we tell anyone of Jesus we must begin with his death. One cannot even begin to understand the life of Christ without understanding his death. It is here at the cross that his biography begins.

Self-sacrifice is the fearsome way to say "self-denial." But neither word should be seen as making us grander than we really are. Both words really refer to the way we use our days, how we spend the small coins with which we buy the years of our lives. Anticipating our dying times keeps us remembering that life is inherently serious. Since, as the wag reminds us, "We cannot get out of life alive," we must let our impending death teach us how to spend the currency of our days.

And how are we to do it? Well, the apostle Paul said that he was "being poured out as a drink offering" (Phil. 2:17a). Indeed, all human life is being poured out, either in self-concern or in service. But it is the judgment of the cross that we should give our lives as a sacrifice to our Lord, who gave his life as a sacrifice for us.

∾

THE BLOOD OF CHRIST

WILLIAM COWPER

William Cowper provided many hymns for Christianity. He was a man whose bouts with psychological depression caused him to be very emotionally needy. Still, out of his dark and needy life issued many victorious hymns on the accomplishments of Jesus. Many of those poems reflect Christ's work on the cross.

> There is a fountain fill'd with Blood,
> Drawn from Emmanuel's veins,
> And sinners plunged beneath that flood
> Lose all their guilty stains.
>
> The dying thief rejoiced to see
> That fountain in his day;
> And there may I, as vile as he,
> Wash all my sins away.
>
> Dear dying Lamb, Thy precious Blood
> Shall never lose its power,
> Till all the ransom'd Church of God
> Be saved to sin no more.

E'er since by faith I saw the stream
Thy flowing wounds supply,
Redeeming love has been my theme,
And shall be till I die.

Then in a nobler, sweeter song,
I'll sing Thy power to save,
When this poor lisping, stammering tongue
Lies silent in the grave.

Lord, I believe Thou hast prepared,
Unworthy though I be,
For me a blood-bought free reward,
A golden harp for me.

'Tis strung and tuned for endless years,
And form'd by power divine,
To sound in God the Father's ears.
No other name but Thine.

VIII

JESUS:

❦

HIS RESURRECTION

$\mathcal{T}$HE Resurrection of Jesus Christ is the epicenter of Christianity. The Resurrection is the faith requirement through which seekers become followers. It is so central to the Christian faith that Paul taught it was impossible to become a Christian without believing it (Romans 10:9). Paul was the first person in the Bible, chronologically, to write of the Resurrection. The apostle wrote that after Jesus' burial, he returned to life and appeared first to Peter, then the Twelve, then to five hundred at once, then to his half brother James, then to the apostles again, and then finally (two years later) to Paul himself (1 Corinthians 15:3–8).

The various gospel writers reported these first appearances of Christ in different ways. John said Jesus appeared first to Mary Magdalene alone (John 20:11). Matthew said that Jesus' empty tomb was revealed on the first Easter Morning to Mary Magdalene, the other Mary (Matthew 28:1–2). Mark (Mark 16:1) says that three women came to the tomb. Luke seems to imply that an even larger company of women came to the tomb (Luke 24:1ff.).

Jesus, during his three-year ministry, raised at least three people from the dead. But these resurrections really amount to little more than resuscitations. These whom Jesus raised, at some later point died again. But with Jesus' Resurrection, his restored life does not end in a second death. Rather, it is precedent to his own Ascension into heaven. The idea that Jesus is now corporeally in heaven lies at the heart of all the great creeds of the church. Further, the Resurrection stands for this truth: death, which could not hold Jesus in the grave, will also not hold those who believe in him.

The Resurrection, said Paul, was symbolized by baptism (Romans 6:4–6). When believers went into the water, baptism was a reenactment of Christ being laid in the ground. When baptism was complete and the believer left the water, it was a symbol that Christ rose from the grave. Christ's central miracle is his Resurrection. In the early church, one of the first doctrinal concerns to frustrate his church was the question of what happened to those Christians who died. The Resurrection of Christ became the great answer of victory for all those who had died.

Paul grew rapturous when he considered the power of the Resurrection over death. "O death where is your sting?" he asked (1 Corinthians 15:55). Since Jesus had come, his Resurrection provided ultimate hope. Jesus himself seems to allude to this when he says at the resurrection of Lazarus, "I am the resurrection and the Life" (John 11:25). The ultimate fear of humankind has always been death. The Easter celebration, therefore, is not a mere exaltation of what Jesus was able to achieve in walking out of the tomb. The Easter story is the message of hope.

The hymns of the church have long expressed this hope. One very popular Protestant hymn says,

> Death could not keep its prey,
> Jesus my Saviour!
> He tore the bars away,
> Jesus my Lord!
> Up from the grave he arose,
> With a mighty triumph o'er his foes;
> He arose a victor from the dark domain,
> And he lives forever with his saints to reign.
> He arose! He arose! Hallelujah! Christ arose!
>
> Robert Lowry

But the reply to this unprovable event knows only one answer for Christians—the reply of Faith. A second hymn we sing exults:

> He lives, he lives, salvation to impart!
> You ask me how I know he lives:
> he lives within my heart.
>
> Alfred H. Ackley

The popular Christian composers Bill and Gloria Gaither have written a hymn that not only states the imperative of the resurrection but tells why it is important.

> Because He lives I can face tomorrow,
> Because He lives all fear is gone;
> Because I know He holds the future,
> And life is worth the living just because He lives.
>
> William J. and Gloria Gaither

When the Sabbath was over, Mary Magdalene, Mary the mother of James, and Salome bought spices so they could embalm him. Very early on Sunday morning, as the sun rose, they went to the tomb. They worried out loud to each other, "Who will roll back the stone from the tomb for us?"

Then they looked up, saw that it had been rolled back— it was a huge stone—and walked right in. They saw a young man sitting on the right side, dressed all in white. They were completely taken aback, astonished.

He said, "Don't be afraid. I know you're looking for Jesus the Nazarene, the one they nailed on the cross. He's been raised up; he's here no longer. You can see for yourselves that the place is empty. Now—on your way. Tell his disciples and Peter that he is going on ahead of you to Galilee. You'll see him there, exactly as he said."

> Mark 16:1–7, *The Message*

JESUS: THE COMPASSIONATE GOD

HENRI J. M. NOUWEN

*The Resurrection is quite probably the most painted, sculpted theme in
the art history of the West. Henri Nouwen is quite possibly the Catholic
priest most read by Protestants and Evangelicals. In this selection is the
moving encounter of Grünewald and the writer.*

Monday, 17th February

MY DEAR MARC,

Yesterday I went with some friends to Colmar, a French town in
Alsace an hour from Freiburg by car. We went there to take a look at the
Isenheimer Altar. You've probably heard about it already. You may even
have seen it. For me it proved to be a very profound experience.

The Isenheimer Altar was painted between 1513 and 1515 for the
chapel at the hospital for plague victims in the small village of Isenheim,
not far from Colmar. The artist was a man of such a retiring disposition,
some say very melancholic as well, that historians are still unable to agree
who he actually was. According to most authorities, Matthias Grünewald
was the creator of this masterpiece. In it the whole pictorial art of the late
Middle Ages is summed up and brought to its highest point. This work is
not only the most spectacular altarpiece ever made, but also the most
moving.

The altarpiece is a multiple series of panels. The front panel depicts
Jesus' death on the cross. On the second, Grünewald has painted the
Annunciation, the birth of Jesus, and his resurrection. On the third, which
actually consists of two panels on each side of a group of sculpted figures, you can see the temptations of St. Anthony and his visit to the
hermit Paul.

Although I had read two booklets by Wilhelm Nyssen before visiting
this altar, the reality surpassed any description or reproduction. When I
saw the body of Jesus on the cross, tortured, emaciated, and covered with
abscesses, I had an inkling of the reaction of the plague-stricken and dying
sufferers in the sixteenth century. On this altar they saw their God, with
the same suppurating ulcers as their own, and it made them realize with a
shock what the Incarnation really meant. They saw solidarity, compassion,
forgiveness, and unending love brought together in this one suffering
figure. They saw that, in their mortal anguish, they had not been left on
their own.

But they saw too, when the front panel was opened out, that the tortured body of Jesus, born of Mary, had not only died for them, but—also for them—had risen gloriously from death. The same ulcerated body they saw hanging dead on the cross exudes a dazzling light and rises upward in divine splendor—a splendor which is also in store for us.

The two Anthony panels on both sides of the dramatic statuary reminded the plague-ridden sufferers that sharing in the divine glory of Jesus demands a readiness to share in his temptations as well. Anthony was the patron of the monastic order that nursed the plague victims, and his life showed, without any cheap sentimentality, that those who would follow Jesus are bound to have a narrow and frequently rocky road to tread.

I remained at the Isenheimer Altar for more than three hours. During that time I learned more about suffering and resurrection than from many days of reading. The crucified and risen Christ of Matthias Grünewald is carved so deeply into my memory and imagination now that wherever I go or stay I can call him to mind. I know now in a completely new way that if I am to succeed in fully living my life, in all its painful yet glorious moments, I must remain united to Jesus.

∽

ASLAN'S RESURRECTION

C. S. LEWIS

Once again the best of truth comes through clearest in metaphor. In helping children understand how Jesus rose from the dead, Lewis has helped us all.

THE RISING OF the sun had made everything look so different—all the colours and shadows were changed—that for a moment they didn't see the important thing. Then they did. The Stone Table was broken into two pieces by a great crack that ran down it from end to end; and there was no Aslan.

"Oh, oh, oh!" cried the two girls rushing back to the Table.

"Oh, it's *too* bad," sobbed Lucy; "they might have left the body alone."

"Who's done it?" cried Susan. "What does it mean? Is it more magic?"

"Yes!" said a great voice behind their backs. "It is more magic." They looked round. There, shining in the sunrise, larger than they had seen him before, shaking his mane (for it had apparently grown again) stood Aslan himself.

"Oh, Aslan!" cried both the children, staring up at him, almost as much frightened as they were glad.

"Aren't you dead then, dear Aslan?" said Lucy.

"Not now," said Aslan.

"You're not—not a—?" asked Susan in a shaky voice. She couldn't bring herself to say the word *ghost*.

Aslan stooped his golden head and licked her forehead. The warmth of his breath and a rich sort of smell that seemed to hang about his hair came all over her.

"Do I look it?" he said.

"Oh, you're real, you're real! Oh, Aslan!" cried Lucy and both girls flung themselves upon him and covered him with kisses.

"But what does it all mean?" asked Susan when they were somewhat calmer.

"It means," said Aslan, "that though the Witch knew the Deep Magic, there is a magic deeper still which she did not know. Her knowledge goes back only to the dawn of Time. But if she could have looked a little further back, into the stillness and the darkness before Time dawned, she would have read there a different incantation. She would have known that when a willing victim who had committed no treachery was killed in a traitor's stead, the Table would crack and Death itself would start working backwards. And now—"

"Oh yes. Now?" said Lucy jumping up and clapping her hands.

"Oh, children," said the Lion, "I feel my strength coming back to me. Oh, children, catch me if you can!" He stood for a second, his eyes very bright, his limbs quivering, lashing himself with his tail. Then he made a leap high over their heads and landed on the other side of the Table. Laughing, though she didn't know why, Lucy scrambled over it to reach him. Aslan leaped again. A mad chase began. Round and round the hill-top he led them, now hopelessly out of their reach, now letting them almost catch his tail, now diving between them, now tossing them in the air with his huge and beautifully velveted paws and catching them again, and now stopping unexpectedly so that all three of them rolled over together in a happy laughing heap of fur and arms and legs. It was such a romp as no one has ever had except in Narnia; and whether it was more like playing with a thunderstorm or playing with a kitten Lucy could never make up her mind. And the funny thing was that when all three finally lay together panting in the sun the girls no longer felt in the least tired or hungry or thirsty.

SATURDAY: JESUS' DAY TO BE DEAD

ROBERT FARRAR CAPON

ITEM: THE PERSONAL significance of the Christian celebration of Holy Saturday —of the Holy Sabbath. What we celebrate is precisely *death,* not dying. *Dying,* if you think about it, is simply the world's worst way of *living:* it is tag-end living, minimal living, hardly living. And dying, besides being no fun, is also totally unfruitful: nothing grows out of it because the common reaction to it is a continuous attempt, physically and mentally, to *reverse* it —to go counter to the direction that the universe in this particular instance wants to take. But death, precisely because it is an arrival at an accomplished fact, and above all because Jesus rises gloriously out of that fact, is the most fruitful thing there is. Death, therefore—nothingness, *no thing*—is the *only thing* we need.

Item: *Nothingness.* On Holy Saturday, the Holy Sabbath, the Easter Vigil begins in a darkened church. The symbolism is obvious: we are dead in Christ's death. But then, in honor of the resurrection, the new fire is struck, the paschal candle is lit, and we begin the celebration of a new creation out of the nothingness of death. People often say they are afraid of death—about, as they sometimes put it, having to be *nothing* after all these lovely years of being *something.* When they tell me that, I try to focus the problem more tightly. "Let me see if I understand you," I say. "You're bothered by the thought that you will be non-existent in, say, the year 2075. But tell me something. Has it ever occurred to you to worry about the fact that you were likewise non-existent in 1875? Of course it hasn't: for the simple reason that, by the forces of nature alone, you got bravely over that first attack of nothingness and were born. Well, all the Gospel is telling you is that your death—your second bout of nothingness —is going to be even less of a problem than your first. By the power of Jesus' death and resurrection, you will get bravely over that too, and be reborn. In fact, you already have been; so go find something more danger-ous to worry about."

BUSINESS OF LIFE

MORTON KELSEY

Morton Kelsey points to the real value of the resurrection life. It has power in times of our own deep discouragement or dark depressions to lift us to life in the moment. The Resurrection is not some attempt of God to pull a resurrection rabbit out of a showbiz hat for the world's applause. If the Resurrection were only a place for Christians to ooh and ahh over some great cosmic trick of God, it would not hold our interest for long. Merely pulling a living Christ out of a dead man's shroud is interesting but not vital. The vitality of the Resurrection comes in how it serves us from day to day by pulling something living and vital out of our dead depressive circumstances.

As WILLIAM JAMES pointed out, if we are indeed part and parcel of a meaningless universe, the kind in which Jesus could be murdered on a cross with no resurrection, then being depressed only makes good sense. Under these conditions the sensitive and sensible person will be depressed. I have discovered only one event in history that redeemed all this evil for me and gave me hope: the resurrection of Jesus. Allowing the resurrected One to be constantly present, I can deal with all the evil suffered by Jesus, by my friends, and by me. I can face all the rape, pillage, war and hatred that I hear about daily, and still have hope. The resurrection reveals the ultimate nature of the universe, and the risen Christ continues to give victory over the power of evil.

There is still another kind of depression that does not seem to be triggered by any known outer pain or crisis. Sometimes it is as if the darkness seizes me and I have no power of my own to tear myself away from it. Sometimes I feel as though I have fallen into the pit of hell and demons of hell are using their most exquisite tortures to force me to give myself up to them. Many of us seem to live on the edge of the abyss and the cliffs are constantly crumbling away even when our outer life tells us that we should feel fine. I have discovered that those souls which, like mine, have been worn thin by misery and lack of love as children are open to the direct intrusion of that destructive, down-pulling, befouling spirit which has caused so much misery in our broken and suffering world.

These inner experiences of evil can often trigger the physical symptoms of depression as completely as brain disease, hormonal imbalance or outer tragedy. I believe that this destructive reality is one factor in most kinds of depression. The good news is that we are given a particular way to be released from this kind of inner agony. When I engage my depression rather than trying to run away from it, allow it to be expressed in imaginative pictures or images, and then ask the risen Christ to enter and free me from my inner tormentors, usually I am soon free of the depression. The gruesome darkness retreats and I am accepted and loved by the Christ. Many friends who are attacked in the same way have been lifted out of the pit by this method and enabled to go about the business of life again.

~

CHRIST IS ARISEN

JOHANN WOLFGANG VON GOETHE

The German master, like other literary greats, found the genius he gave to Faust, breaking forth into this literary anthem to the Resurrection.

Christ is arisen,
    Joy to thee, mortal!
Out of His prison,
    Forth from its portal!
Christ is not sleeping,
    Seek Him no longer;
Strong was His keeping,
    Jesus was stronger.

Christ is arisen,
    Seek Him not here;
Lonely His prison,
    Empty His bier;
Vain His entombing,
    Spices and lawn,
Vain the perfuming,
    Jesus is gone.

Christ is arisen,
    Joy to thee, mortal!
Empty His prison,
    Broken its portal

Rising, He giveth
   His shroud to the sod;
Risen, He liveth,
   And liveth to God.

∽

TALLEYRAND'S ADVICE

C. H. ROBINSON

Some more liberal scholars have asked the question whether miracles create faith or faith creates miracles. Did the apostles love Jesus so much they claimed for him things like the Resurrection, which might never have happened? Or did the miracle create the faith? The overwhelming majority of Christian scholars have agreed that the Resurrection so surprised and overwhelmed the church that it became delirious in the wake of this event. You cannot get Christianity back beyond this ecstatic beginning. Something motivated ordinary fishermen and converted prostitutes to become the spokespersons for a new order. I would believe in the Resurrection if only because Jesus' rather rural and uneducated disciples died hundreds of miles from their homeland and were martyred preaching their ecstatic faith with real vitality. The Resurrection starts the faith; it is not the first miracle Christ did, but it is the genesis miracle of Christendom.

M. LEPEAUX ON one occasion confided to Talleyrand his disappointment at the ill success with which he had met in his attempt to bring into vogue a new religion which he regarded as an improvement on Christianity. He explained that despite all the efforts of himself and his supporters his propaganda made no way. He asked Talleyrand's advice as to what he was to do. Talleyrand replied that it was indeed difficult to found a new religion, more difficult indeed than could be imagined, so difficult that he hardly knew what to advise. "Still," he said after a moment's reflection, "there is one plan which you might at least try. I should recommend you to be crucified and to rise again on the third day." . . .

Whether we are prepared or not to accept the occurrence of the Resurrection as a fact of history, we cannot deny the influence which a belief in it has exercised in the world. We cannot deny that it has brought life and immortality to light as no other belief could conceivably have done; that it has substituted for the fear of death, for a large portion of the human race, that sure and certain knowledge of God which is eternal life; that it has permeated our customs, our literature, and our language with a glory and a hope which could have been derived from no other source.

❧

THE ELEVEN RESURRECTION APPEARANCES

A. T. ROBERTSON

While there is no comprehensive list of Resurrection appearances (and these appearances are likely only partially recorded in the scriptures), the following list has been composed by adding the appearances cited by Saint Paul (1 Corinthians 15:5–8) and the material in the four evangelists.

1. MARY MAGDALENE

After Peter and John had left the empty tomb, Mary arrived, for they had been too swift for her. Another interesting item is the fact that the angels did not appear to Peter and John, but reappeared to Mary. One might argue that this proves that the women started it all out of their excited imaginations, but no one believed the women till their testimony was confirmed. . . . Mary was standing without, weeping in inconsolable grief. It was bad enough before, but now it is far worse. To have dishonored his body was to go to the last extremity of shame. She stooped and looked into the tomb. The angels are surprised at her grief and she at their joy. She gave the angels the same answer of perplexity concerning what had been done with the body of Jesus, and then turned and saw one whom she took to be the gardener. Here, perhaps, was a ray of light. Possibly he had removed the body of Jesus to another part of the garden. The very soul of Mary went out in her reply when she said: "Sir, if thou hast borne him hence, tell me where thou hast laid him, and I will take him away" (John 20:15). It was a pathetic appeal. The answer was the first word that Jesus is known to have spoken to a human being since his resurrection and it was simply "Mary." But it was the old accent and tone of voice. She had not been thinking it possible that Jesus was alive and did not recognize him. . . . now there was no doubt. By the open grave Mary saw Jesus. She could only say, "Rabboni." She ventured to lay her hand tenderly upon him, but he restrained her. . . . Mary is all ablaze with the wondrous reality and comes running to the disciples with the tremendous words, "I have seen the Lord" (John 20:18). But no one believed her. . . . It simply could not be true. It was some new delusion that had seized Mary. Perhaps the demons had her again.

2. THE OTHER WOMEN

He met the women on the way from the tomb. . . . Jesus repeats the message of the angels to them that he would meet them in Galilee. . . . No more did the apostles believe the testimony of the group of women. It was to them as idle talk (Luke 24:11).

3. ANNAS AND CLEOPAS

Cleopas and a friend lived at Emmaus, some eight miles west of Jerusalem. They had come into town this first day of the week to see if there were any developments among the disciples on the situation. It was late afternoon and they were plodding their way home with heavy hearts. It was still all dark in Jerusalem. They were talking it all over as they went along. It was a time for reviewing the whole career of Jesus of Nazareth. Each sought to explain the work of this marvelous man and asked the other questions on difficult points. Why was there so much promise if it was all to end thus?

A stranger joined them and listened to their talk. Finally he asked what it was all about. "They stood still, looking sad" (Luke 24:17). Where had he been these days not to have heard of Jesus of Nazareth? Had he lived all alone in Jerusalem? There was but one theme on people's lips in these days and that was Jesus. They briefly recounted the story of the Nazarene, his works, his character, and his end. They added what had been their own hope about him, a hope now buried in the tomb. "We were hoping that it was he that should redeem Israel." The nation's hope had risen fast around him. It did look once as though he were the long-looked-for Messiah. But now it is all over, for he had been dead three days. . . . Only upon their urgent invitation did he stop for the evening meal. Across the table they now sat and he took the bread and said grace. It was the old voice and the old charm. They looked at each other and he was gone! It was Jesus, and they had seen him. The women were right after all. Christ had risen from the dead and was alive. They must tell the brethren in Jerusalem and bring joy to their hearts.

4. SIMON PETER

It was in the same upper room where they had assembled on that fateful night when Jesus had foretold all that had come to pass. Probably

Simon Peter was the cause of the meeting. The women had brought a special message from the angels for him from the Master. But to crown it all Jesus himself had appeared to Simon Peter (I Cor. 15:5, Luke 24:32). The news created the utmost excitement among the apostles. He was the leader and surely he would not be deceived, even if the women had been. It was a crisis of Christianity, the crisis of all crises.

5. All the Apostles Except Thomas

If Jesus was indeed risen from the dead, then all was not lost: in truth, all was won. There would still be a future, a glorious future, for Christianity. It was important that the apostles do not disband. They must meet at once with those disciples that could be reached and confer on the next step. . . . This last was the salient point to the disciples. . . . the doors had been shut for fear of the Jews, for they must take no chances.

As they talked of Jesus all at once he stood in the midst of them. He had risen from the dead! But were they now convinced? A strange reaction set in, for they were now terrified and supposed that they saw a spirit or ghost, just what some modern critics now allege. This entire appearance as recorded by Luke and John opposes the idea that it was only the spirit of Jesus that was seen by the disciples. He showed them his hands and his side and expressly alleged that he was not mere spirit, but even had "flesh and bones" (Luke 24:39). . . . They are to announce to men the terms of forgiveness. Their task is now to convince others. Can they prove to others that Jesus is alive, that Christianity is alive also and destined to conquer the world? They have at least one qualification; they believe it themselves. They have hope and faith, but they lack experience and power.

6. All of the Apostles with Thomas

They soon meet Thomas, who was absent on the Sunday night when Jesus appeared to the company in the upper room. They try to convince him by saying: "We have seen the Lord" (John 20:25), and fail utterly to move his unbelief. He was still as skeptical as they had been before Peter's experience and before they had seen the prints of the nails in Christ's hands and feet. I will not believe, Thomas bluntly said, till I see what you claim to have seen. After all Thomas was not much more skeptical than the rest had been even after they had Jesus right before their eyes. It is true that he had their testimony added to all the rest. There is an honest doubt which is the foe of all credulity. Christianity is the foe of idle superstition as well as of blatant infidelity. Christianity wishes its adherents to look the facts in the face. Still the disciples had all carried their doubt too far and were openly rebuked by Jesus for it. Thomas is not a comfort to the man who prides himself on his skepticism. Jesus was good to Thomas. On the next Sunday the disciples meet again in the same upper room where Jesus had appeared to them just a week before. They have not seen him during the week, for Christ does not remain with them bodily now though he is with them in spirit. Will he come to-night? Who can tell? They have not yet gone to Galilee because the time had not arrived for that. They have not wavered in their conviction that Jesus is alive. They have not formulated any plans for the future of Christianity, but are waiting for further developments. The doors are closed again, for the rulers must be kept in ignorance of the present situation. Thomas is there to-night.

Suddenly Jesus stood before them again and speaks to Thomas. He had accepted the challenge of doubt and showed his hands and his side. It was enough and Thomas could only say to him, "My Lord and My God" (John 20:28). If Thomas had doubted longer, his faith now grew faster than that of the rest. He hails Jesus as Lord and God without any reservation. Christ allowed himself to be declared divine, and added that the greatest faith was that which would reach this height without having seen him, the faith of those who "have not seen and yet have believed." This beatitude belongs to all of us who are convinced of the resurrection and deity of Jesus. . . .

7. ALL OF THE APOSTLES

The days went by and the disciples turned to Galilee. The time had not yet come when Jesus would reveal himself to the body of believers (over five hundred, Paul said) on the appointed mountain in Galilee. There was nothing to do but to wait in the midst of the scenes of so much of the work of Christ. At every turn along the beloved lake they would be reminded of Jesus. They had left their all and cast their fortunes with the new teacher on these shores. Had it been worth while? What has the future in store for them now? Truly it had been wonderful. Most of them had been fishermen and so one night Peter took the initiative and said that he was going fishing. That was enough to call back the old days. Six of them at once offered to go with him. They fished all night and had fisherman's luck and caught nothing. They were used to that and were pulling for the shore in the early dawn when they saw a figure in the dim light walking on the shore. A voice came to them that was strangely familiar, though the word "children" as applied to them in address was apparently unusual, but John's fine spiritual sense perceived the truth, he said: "It is the Lord" (John 21:7). The impulsiveness of Peter responded to John's insight and he was soon on the shore beside Jesus.

The scene between Jesus and Peter on the shore in the early morning is wonderful indeed. It was after the breakfast of fish and bread that Christ turned to Simon. One other morning he had sat by a fire and this of itself was significant to Simon, but Jesus was pointed enough to bring the whole scene of the denial back to his all too vivid memory. He seized the right moment to probe Simon's heart by three searching questions. It was Simon who had spoken for the disciples at Caesarea Philippi. It was Simon who had said on the night of the betrayal that, though all men forsook Jesus, yet he would be faithful even unto death. Time makes short work of the boaster and now Simon was in poor shape to say a word. Jesus was gentle, but persistent with Peter, challenging his superior love and even his very love itself with the word chosen by Simon. A question came for each denial and each cut to the heart. The result was gratifying indeed and revealed a humility in Simon not manifest before, but which reappears in I Peter 5:1–11. He is now converted after the sifting by Satan and the prayers of Jesus for him have availed. Jesus exhorts him to feed the sheep and he will later urge the elders to "tend the flock of God" (I Peter 5:2). Once Peter had promised Jesus that he would die a martyr's death, if need be, and then turned and ran in disgrace. But now that he is humble he will have a martyr's death by and by. But Simon is Simon still in his personal characteristics, and his curiosity leads him to ask about John, "And what shall this man do?" (John 21:22). Peter's question bordered upon impertinence and was sharply rebuked by Jesus, though he did not mean that John actually would live till the second coming, a mistake that John takes pains to correct. James and John had once rashly said that they were able to be baptized with Christ's baptism of blood, and James in fact was soon to drink that cup.

8. TO 500 ON A MOUNTAIN IN GALILEE

The location of this mountain we do not know nor the precise date. Doubtless the bulk of the believers are here assembled. There had been time enough for word to reach them. It was a signal occasion, for here were assembled the people who represented the visible fruitage of the ministry of Jesus, something over five hundred disciples (I Cor. 15:6). The grain of mustard-seed had begun to grow and would ultimately cover the earth. This Jesus knew. Some few still doubted, having a hard battle, but most had come already to a militant faith in the Risen Redeemer. Jesus met this goodly company as the Leader of a world-conquering host. No statesman ever outlined such a magnificent programme as Jesus here laid down, the Christian's Charter for the conquest of the world. No general was ever more certain of victory. The sublime optimism of Christ is transcendent when one recalls that his disciples had no money, no weapons, no influence. They had, however, the supreme message and the presence and power of Christ by the Holy Spirit. . . . The disciples are the salt of the earth, the hope of the world, and the future of Christianity rested on their shoulders.

9. JAMES THE BROTHER OF CHRIST

The Apostles now returned to Jerusalem, the scene of their sore discomfiture, yes, but the scene of Christ's triumphant resurrection also. Henceforth Jerusalem, not Galilee, will be the place of their activity. They will seek to win a foothold right in Jerusalem itself, for now they know that God is with them to the end. James, the brother of Jesus, had received a special manifestation and is now a devout believer along with John and the rest. . . .

10. ALL OF THE APOSTLES PLUS A CROWD OF 120

Jesus led the disciples out of the eastern gate, past Gethsemane with its tragic memories, up the familiar slope towards Bethany, beloved Bethany. The view was sublime in every direction, the Jordan, the Dead Sea, Mt. Nebo, Jerusalem, the Mediterranean. "They were looking up" (Acts 1:9) and Jesus was giving them a parting blessing. . . .

11. THE APOSTLE PAUL (I COR. 15:8)

His life and teachings, his death and resurrection, his power over men to uplift and to make god-like, the greatest of all themes, still fill the horizon of the modern world. Science has done wonders, but science is barren beside the life of Jesus. He has stood the searchlight of minute historical investigation. Most of all he endures the test of life. His pitying eye still looks upon us, his powerful hand still reaches out to save. When he came before they crucified him; when he comes again he will be crowned King of Kings and Lord of Lords. Meanwhile let him rule in all our hearts. "Amen: come, Lord Jesus."

∽

LOVE CRUCIFIED AROSE

MICHAEL CARD

Among popular contemporary singers and composers, at least one talent seems to have taken the theological implications of his verses seriously.

Michael Card, contemporary composer, offers us these lyrical arguments
for the importance of the Resurrection in the church.

Long ago He blessed the earth,
Born older than the years.
And in the stall a cross He saw
Through the first of many tears.
A life of homeless wandering,
Cast out in sorrow's way,
The Shepherd seeking for the lost,
His life the price He'd pay.

Throughout Your life You felt the weight
Of what You'd come to give.
To drink for us that crimson cup,
So we might really live.
At last the time to love and die,
The dark appointed day,
That one forsaken moment when
Your Father turned His face away.

Love crucified arose.
The One who lived and died for me
Was Satan's nail-pierced casualty,
Now He's breathing once again.
Love crucified arose.
And the grave became a place of hope,
For the heart that sin and sorrow broke
Is beating once again.

Love crucified arose.
The risen One in splendor;
Jehovah's soul defender;
Has won the victory.
Love crucified arose.
And the grave became a place of hope,
For the heart that sin and sorrow broke
Is beating once again.

RESURRECTION LIFE

WILLIAM L. CRAIG

*It was Paul the apostle who first set forth the logical challenge that
Easter and Christianity are inseparable. Simply put: no Resurrection,
no Easter, no Easter, no Christianity. Christians are not free to debate
the veracity of the Resurrection, for they in truth would be debating
the existence of Christianity. William Craig argues the idea from a
more positive standpoint.*

"THERE AIN'T GONNA be no Easter this year," a student friend remarked
to me.

"Why not?" I asked incredulously.

"They found the body."

Despite his irreverent humor, my friend displayed a measure of
insight often not shared by modern theologians. Many of them are perfectly willing to assert that Jesus died and rotted in the grave, but that the
resurrection still has value as a symbol of "newness of life" or "new
beginning," so that Christianity can go on quite nicely as though nothing
were changed. My friend's joke implied that without the resurrection
Christianity is worthless.

The earliest Christians would certainly have agreed with my friend.
The apostle Paul put it simply: "If Christ has not been raised, then our
preaching is in vain and your faith is in vain. . . . If Christ has not been
raised, your faith is futile and you are still in your sins" (1 Cor 15:14,17).
For the earliest Christians, Jesus' resurrection was an historical fact,
every bit as real as his death on the cross. Without the resurrection,
Christianity would have been simply false. Jesus would have been just
another prophet who had met his unfortunate fate at the hands of the
Jews, and faith in him as Lord, Messiah, or Son of God would have been
stupid.

∾

EASTER

JOHN UPDIKE

*John Updike's poem "Seven Stanzas at Easter" argues that the reality
of Christianity and the reality of the Resurrection are inseparable.*

Make no mistake: if He rose at all
it was as His body;
if the cells' dissolution did not reverse, the molecules reknit, the amino
    acids rekindle,
the Church will fall.

Let us not mock God with metaphor,
Analogy, sidestepping transcendence;
making of the event a parable, a sign painted in the faded credulity of
    earlier ages:
let us walk through the door.
Let us not seek to make it less monstrous,
for our own convenience, our own sense of beauty,
lest, awakened in one unthinkable hour, we are embarrassed by the
    miracle,
and crushed by remonstrance.

∾

NATURE

DR. WERNHER VON BRAUN

Dr. von Braun argues for the continued existence of the soul. Yet somehow the idea seems to lead to some kind of logical reinforcement to the reality of Resurrection.

MANY PEOPLE SEEM to feel that science has somehow made "religious ideas" untimely or old-fashioned. But I think science has a real surprise for the skeptics. Science, for instance, tells us that nothing in nature, not even in the tiniest particle, can disappear without a trace. Nature does not know extinction. All it knows is transformation. Now if God applies this fundamental principle of indestructibility to the most minute and insignificant parts of his universe, does it not make sense to assume that He applies it also to the human soul? I think it does. And everything science has taught me and continues to teach me strengthens my belief in the continuity of our spiritual existence after death. Nothing disappears without a trace.

EASTER WINGS

GEORGE HERBERT

Lord, Who createdst man in wealth and store,
Though foolishly he lost the same
Decaying more and more,
Till he became
Most poor:
With Thee
O let me rise
As larks, harmoniously,
And sing this day Thy victories:
Then shall the fall further the flight in me.

My tender age in sorrow did begin;
And still with sicknesses and shame
Thou didst so punish sin,
That I became
Most thin.
With Thee
Let me combine
And feel this day Thy victory;
For, if I imp my wing on Thine,
Affliction shall advance the flight in me.

THE EVENT NAMED *RESURRECTION*

THOMAS C. ODEN

WHATEVER IT WAS that occurred after Jesus' crucifixion, one thing is absolutely clear: It was *called* "resurrection." Of that there can be no doubt. All who were met by it called it the same thing. However unclear many things may be about alleged meetings with Jesus after his death, there was a consensus in the community that whatever it was that people were experiencing, the correct term for it was *resurrection*. This meant that they had experienced and tasted the first fruits of the expected event at the end time of judgment and redemption.

• • •

This empowered the early Christian community with incredible courage in the face of seemingly impossible obstacles and terrifying threats. Why? Because their trust was not in this broken world but in the risen Christ present to them as they sat together "at the Lord's Table" or faced the wild animals of the Roman Colosseum.

• • •

The earliest church reasoned in this way: In Jesus' resurrection the end is already present, in an anticipated sense. Thus the will of God is finally revealed. So to participate in Christ is already to share in the events of the last days. It all made reasonable sense, seen from within the assumptions of Jewish historical reasoning, transformed by a living encounter with the resurrected Jesus.

We today must learn to think historically in the Hebraic sense if we are to make sense of this central proclamation of Christianity. Seen in this frame of reference, the resurrection is so decisive that the importance of all other theological issues pales beside it. It focuses on nothing less than the final revelation of the will of God in history.

We are searching for the center of the wide circumference of Christian experience. What is the center? *Resurrection* as interpersonal meeting with the living Christ. Not resurrection as idea or past event but resurrection as a currently experienced interpersonal encounter. This is why interpersonal meeting has been the central feature of Christian theology from its inception.

Something so decisive happened anticipatively for human history in the resurrection of Jesus that it does not and cannot fit into our ordinary categories of understanding. We cannot rule out the resurrection of Jesus simply on the grounds (as Troeltsch's law of analogy would require) that nothing like this ever happened to us before. How could it! The event of which Christianity speaks is, like all truly significant interpersonal meeting, an event without analogy.

The least plausible of all explanations of the resurrection was that it was generated out of the despairing imagination of the disciples. For that does not explain why they were willing to risk their lives for it. Nor does it account for one of the most characteristic literary features of the Easter narratives: the report that the beholders were utterly surprised by the appearance of the risen Lord. The "surprise" element of the Easter narratives is too recurrent to be considered an anomaly. It is not likely that one would report being surprised by something that one had previously projected. No. *Something* occurred in Jesus' resurrection. It is quite unconvincing to assume that it could have been nothing. Whatever it was, it was experienced as the resurrected or spiritual or glorified body of Jesus and understood as the final self-disclosure of God.

TURIN

STEPHEN BROWN

Stephen Brown argues for the shroud in a mode quite different from other writers. But most outstanding in his argument is his marshalling of William Buckley to join in his concurrence. Buckley suggests that in matters of faith it is not faith that dies hard, but agnosticism. Whether or not the shroud is authentic may be up for grabs, but the outraged cries of atheists makes one wonder if the volume of the negative outcry is not evidence in itself. They do protest too much, perhaps?

ONE OF THE most fascinating occurrences of our time is the scientific interest generated by the Shroud of Turin. Many believe it is the shroud in which the corpse of Jesus was wrapped before His resurrection. The shroud's history is complex, and many details are obscure. Its existence was not generally known until 1357, when it was exhibited in the French provincial town of Lirey.

In 1898, Secondo Pia was allowed to photograph the shroud for the first time. To his astonishment, when he looked at the negatives of his pictures, he found they presented a highly detailed picture of a man who had been crucified.

The next showing of the shroud took place in 1931, when detailed photographs were taken by Giuseppe Enrie. The photographs he took that year became the basis of study by physicians and scientists in France, England, Italy, Germany, and the United States. Their conclusions were not unanimous in every detail, but they all agreed on one matter: the imprints in the shroud are those of a human corpse in a pronounced state of rigor mortis.

In 1978, there was a major development in the study of the shroud. A team of scientists, known as the Shroud of Turin Research Project, converged on Turin, Italy. The Catholic church had allowed an object of faith to be inspected with the neutral analytical tools of modern science, and it was an opportunity not to be missed. Dozens of scientists of every religious belief and unbelief were invited to examine the shroud to settle once and for all its authenticity. It was the most thorough examination of a religious relic by the scientific community in history. Millions of dollars in sophisticated testing equipment was taken to the Renaissance reception room in the royal palace of the House of Savoy. For five days, the most rigorous and detailed testing of the shroud took place. Then the results were tested and retested in the laboratories of scientists in Europe and the United States. The preliminary results are nothing less than astounding.

First, the shroud and the image on it are not counterfeit. The shroud contained a corpse of a crucified man about five feet ten inches tall. The facial expression is peaceful, especially compared to the tortured and punctured body.

Second, the anatomy pictured on the shroud shows details that weren't even known until the eighteenth century. In other words, an artist would have had to travel six hundred years into the future to learn the information necessary to produce a counterfeit.

Third, there are actual blood stains on the fourteen-foot shroud. There is also an amazing accuracy in terms of blood flow and consistency. The corpse in the shroud died with nails through the upper part of his hands, and a nail was driven through his feet. The blood stains show there was a crown of thorns or a similar object on his forehead. There was a lance wound in his side.

Fourth, pollen discovered in the threads of the shroud has been shown to be from first-century Palestine.

Fifth, there has been a computer enhancement of the image on the shroud that makes the image three-dimensional. That image is especially interesting, because it shows that coins were placed over the eyes of the corpse. The coins bear an amazing resemblance to those issued by Pontius Pilate in the years A.D. 31–34.

Sixth, the back of the shroud shows small lash marks. The details of these wounds are amazing in that they show exactly the marks that would have been left by a Roman flagrum, an instrument of torture used much like a whip.

I could go on and on.

By far, the most interesting mystery about the Shroud of Turin is how the corpse got out of the shroud. The facts militate against the body's being removed from the shroud by any human means, because the blood stains have not been smudged. Further, the body in the shroud did not decompose while wrapped in it. Pathologists are sure the man was dead, but the scientific tests found no evidence of decomposition beyond the initial signs of death. That of course indicates the body was in the shroud for a very short period.

• • •

Did the Shroud of Turin contain the body of Jesus? Maybe. However, the reaction of many to the scientific data surrounding the shroud is more fascinating than the data itself. Rarely has opposition to a scientific investigation been so shrill. When the facts began to indicate Jesus was the body in the shroud, and when there was indication of a miraculous removal of the body, the forces began to line up on the other side. That was nothing new.

In 1902, Yves Delage, an agnostic professor of comparative anatomy at the Sorbonne, became convinced that the corpse in the shroud was none other than the historic Jesus. When Delage made his findings known to the French Academy of Sciences, many of his colleagues were outraged that he would even discuss the subject, and the Academy refused to publish his work. Delage was understandably surprised and hurt. More recently, numerous articles and editorials, including one in the *New York Times,* have been critical of the authenticity of the shroud and the validity of the Shroud of Turin Research Project.

One magazine, *National Review,* did a generally favorable article on the shroud, and the response they received from their readers was immediate and harsh. In his "Notes and Asides" column, William F. Buckley answered:

> As for us, we fail to understand the manifest hostility toward the Shroud on the part of some Christians. Would they be equally interested or ostensibly uninterested in a possible or problem portrait of Xerxes? of Alexander the Great? Is it possible that the details of the Shroud are just too "literal" for an enlightened liberal sensibility? Is it somehow bad manners to suggest that Christian claims about what happened to Jesus are, in fact, true?

❧

GOD'S SON

LOIS A. CHENEY

Once upon a time
There was a God
Who so loved the world
That he gave his son
His only son.

And they took that son
And they hung him on a cross
And that son died
And they buried the son—
Sealed him up tight.

But God said,
"Oh no you don't"
And he rolled back the rock
He unsealed his son
And his son came out
Came out walking and breathing
And he was Alive.

And he's alive today
And he walks around
And he stalks around
Breathing life and life
Every morning, just before dawn
For thousands of years
Little grim people—
Preachers and bankers and
Storekeepers and students—
Sneak up to the grave and
Roll back the stone
To seal it up tight.

And every morning
God roars
"Oh no you don't!"
And he flings back
the stone.

❧

EASTER

GEORGE HERBERT

Rise heart; thy Lord is risen. Sing His praise
    Without delays,
Who takes thee by the hand, that thou likewise
    With Him mayst rise:
That as His death calcined thee to dust,
His life may make thee gold, and much more, just.

Awake, my lute, and struggle for thy part
 With all thy art.
The cross taught all wood to resound His Name,
 Who bore the same.
His stretchèd sinews taught all strings what key
Is best to celebrate this most high day.

Consort both heart and lute, and twist a song
 Pleasant and long:
Or, since all music is but three parts vied
 And multiplied,
O let Thy blessed Spirit bear a part,
And make up our defects with His sweet art.

THE CROSS

CALVIN MILLER

BECAUSE OF THE CROSS, we are unafraid. For after Christ's cruel death he
went to be with his Father. Indeed, he died saying to a thief, "Today, you
will be with me in paradise" (Luke 23:43). It is the glorious triumph of
his cross that announces that to be absent from the body is to be present
with the Lord (2 Cor. 5:8). Death is but the gateway to the automatic
entrance into heaven. Now we know the truth of the matter. We but trade
heartbeat for glory, and it will be most exciting. We shall go from the
instant pain of our passing to the full presence of knowing the Lord face
to face. "Hallelujah!" cries the spirit of that old Negro hymn:

> "Sit down, brother."
> "Can't sit down."
> "Sit down, brother."
> "Can't sit down."
> "Sit down, brother."
> "Can't sit down. I just got to Heaven
> And I can't sit down!"

JESUS AND SOCRATES

JEAN-JACQUES ROUSSEAU

Jesus lived in a definite historical time, but he cannot be discussed as one might discuss any other great personage of history. History is the story of man, but the gospels are the story of the God-man, Jesus. So it was Rousseau who pointed this out. The German theologians had a word for that special kind of history that we have wherever God gets involved in the historical scene. The word is Heilsgeschichte, *which means* holy, *or* saving, history. *Jesus is as real as Pilate; both were in history. But, while Pilate is only history, Jesus stands both inside and outside of history. Jesus' life is verifiable like history, but its significance is not limited to any era or group of people. Christ is cosmic, Pilate only mortal.*

WHAT A TOUCHING grace in His instruction! What sweetness, yet what purity, in His manners! What loftiness in His maxims! What profound wisdom in His discourses! What presence of mind, what delicacy of art, yet what justice, in His replies! What an empire over His passions! Where is the man, where the sage, who knows thus to act, to suffer, and to die, without weakness, and without ostentation? What prejudice, what blindness, must be in him who dares to compare the son of Sophroniscus with the Son of Mary? What a distance lies between them! . . . Greece abounded in virtuous men before he (Socrates) had define virtue. But whence had Jesus drawn for His disciples that exalted and pure morality of which He alone has presented at once the lessons and the example? Out of the midst of the fiercest fanaticism the highest wisdom made itself heard, and the artlessness of the most heroical virtues glorified the vilest of all the nations. The death of Socrates, philosophizing quietly with his friends, is the pleasantest that one could desire: that of Jesus, expiring amid torments, insulted, railed at, cursed by a whole nation, is the most horrible that anyone could fear. Socrates, taking the poisoned cup, blesses him who presents it, and who weeps beside him. Jesus, in the midst of a frightful anguish, prays for his maddened executioners. Yes! if the life and the death of Socrates are those of a philosopher, the life and the death of Jesus are those of a God.

IX

JESUS:

~

HIS CONTINUING REIGN

$\mathcal{T}$HE central teaching of the church has always been this: God is in charge of the world. The church refers to this idea as the sovereignty of God. People of faith believe they are not in life alone. Christ is the unforsaking presence (Hebrews 13:5) who walks with them. Christ rules over life to help them make sense of every baffling circumstance. He has gone through every facet of the human pilgrimage through which we must also travel (1 Corinthians 10:13). Further, he promises those who believe that he is in charge (Colossians 1:18) of all things and that even those events of our lives that appear random and unconnected are never haphazard. All things are working together for good to those who love God (Romans 8:28). Further, said the apostle Paul, even persecution and death take on a special significance as the faithful begin to realize that the nightmares of the human pilgrimage are sent "on schedule" to serve God's inscrutable purposes in the continuing reign of Christ.

Russell Conwell's "Acres of Diamond" was a sermon preached and printed thousands of times to remind us that God has a plan for every life, which is never haphazard. We always live under his watchful eye. "His eye is on the sparrow," says the hymn, "and I know he watches me."

In the gospel of John (1.48) Jesus shocks Nathanael by reminding him that he knew him even while Nathanael was unaware of him. Jesus' most profound teaching was that we never can live beyond God's watchful care. The hairs of our heads are numbered (Matthew 10:30). "Are not sparrows two a penny," he said, "yet not a one of them falls to the earth without his knowledge" (Matthew 10:29).

Regarding the last judgment, Jesus taught that the sins we commit against the needy are remembered and we are all held accountable (Matthew 25:44). An old African-American song held the words "My god's a-writing all the time." In the book of Revelation, Jesus says, "I know your works" (3:15). This saying of Jesus indicates that his surveying of his world never stops.

What Job said of God is also true of Christ: "He knows the way that I take and where he has tried me I shall come forth as gold" (Job 23:10). Jesus rules over his church and his rule is never ending. He provides all in his church with the power to meet their needs (Philippians 4:19). He is the confident ruler of all lives in all times. Jesus cares, and his continued care is the confidence of his church that whatever harm or evil may come upon us, Christ will be with us.

Finally, he is sovereign over death. His Resurrection made of him the great enabler. He has conquered the grave. This conquest is the hope of all who follow him.

> "All this time and money wasted on fashion—do you think it makes that much difference? Instead of looking at the fashions, walk out into the fields and look at the wildflowers. They never primp or shop, but have you ever seen color and design quite like it? The ten best-dressed men and women in the country look shabby alongside them.
>
> "If God gives such attention to the appearance of wild-flowers—most of which are never even seen—don't you think he'll attend to you, take pride in you, do his best for you?"
>
> Matthew 6:28–32

"What's the price of a pet canary? Some loose change, right? And God cares what happens to it even more than you do. He pays even greater attention to you, down to the last detail— even numbering the hairs on your head! So don't be intimidated by all this bully talk. You're worth more than a million canaries."

Matthew 10:29–31, *The Message*

∾

"I Am the Way"

ALICE MEYNELL

Christians are not mere champions of tomorrow, glutted on sky pie. Most Christians feel gratitude that they know they will live in the "sweet by-and-by," but they were drawn to faith in Jesus because he seems to them to make life livable in the nitty-gritty now. Alice Meynell confesses what most Christians feel: they would be Christians if Christianity held no promises of tomorrow. What Jesus does for them in the living of life day to day makes it all worthwhile. The momentary Christ with his immense daily counsel is reason enough to believe.

Thou art the Way.
Hadst thou been nothing but the goal,
   I cannot say
If thou hadst ever met my soul.

   I cannot see—
I, child or process—if there lies
   An end for me,
Full of repose, full of replies.

   I'll not reproach
The road that winds, my feet that err.
   Access, approach
Art thou, Time, Way, and Wayfarer.

THE MARTYRDOM OF JIM ELLIOT

ELISABETH ELLIOT

When I was a young student in college, Jim Elliot and a group of his companions were martyred by Indians in Ecuador. The deaths of these missionaries attracted worldwide attention. I was much moved by their heroic and noble altruism, and much of my next few years were motivated by the example of these martyrs. But what I have most appreciated about Jim Elliot was that for him Christ was the source of all strength for daily living and the only sensible confidence for dying.

Elisabeth Elliot immortalized the heroic exploits of her martyred husband, Jim. In the years since, her own spiritual pilgrimage has grown world-wide in its influence. Her enormously popular books have become the counsel to millions in their pilgrimage of faith.

WHEN JIM WAS a college student in 1949 he wrote these words:

"He is no fool who gives what he cannot keep to gain what he cannot lose."

Seven years later, on a hot Sunday afternoon, far from the dormitory room where those lines were written, he and four other young men were finishing a dinner of baked beans and carrotsticks. They sat together on a strip of white sand on the Curaray River, deep in Ecuador's rain forest, waiting for the arrival of a group of men whom they loved, but had never met—savage Stone Age killers, known to all the world now as Aucas.

Two days before, the hope of years had been partially fulfilled. Three of these Indians had met them on the beach where they now sat. The first friendly contact, long anticipated and carefully prepared for, had been completely successful. The young man and his two women companions stepped off the jungle green on the other side of the river, and after slight hesitation, accepted the hand of Jim Elliot, who led them across the river to the other white men. At first the naked tribespeople were distrustful, and with reason. They had known of white men who flew in great birds similar to that which now stood beside them on the sand, who had proved that they could not be trusted. But somehow they had sensed, throughout the long weeks when these five men had attempted to show them their friendship, that there was no "catch" here.

• • •

Back at the beach on the Curaray, the five men waited eagerly the next day for the return of their friends. Pacing the beach as before, they shouted the few phrases they had learned of the Auca language, phrases elicited from an escaped member of the tribe who lived on a hacienda near one of the mission stations. But their calls were answered only by the stillness of the virgin jungle on both sides of the winding river. Once a tree fell, alerting them all to tense expectancy. Nothing happened. Finally Jim Elliot looked at his watch.

"Okay, boys—I give them five minutes. If they don't show up, I'm going over!"

Wisdom prevented his carrying out this threat, but the long afternoon brought no reward for their vigil.

The "neighbors" were apparently in conference—should they return and invite the white men to their village? Who should go? They could not know with what eagerness and longing they were awaited.

Sunday morning dawned clear. Again God had answered prayer. The river had not risen to obliterate the little landing strip, and the skies were good for flying. Nate, the pilot, took off. After circling the Indian village, he spotted about ten Aucas making their way along the beach in the direction of the four foreigners.

"This is it, guys!" he shouted as the Piper bounced onto the beach. "They're on their way!"

Nate's wife was informed by radio of the expected contact and was asked to stand by again at 4:30 P.M.

Lunch over, the men busied themselves fixing up a miniature "jungle" and model house in the sand, with the intention of demonstrating to the savages how to build an airstrip, should they be interested enough to want the white men to come and live among them. Then the five missionaries sang together, as they had so often done, spontaneously and joyously:

"We rest on Thee, our Shield and our Defender,
We go not forth alone against the foe.
Strong in Thy Strength, safe in Thy keeping tender,
We rest on Thee, and in Thy name we go.

"Yea, in Thy name, O Captain of Salvation,
In Thy blest name, all other names above,
Jesus our Righteousness, our sure Foundation,
Our Prince of Glory, and our King of Love.

"We go in faith, our own great weakness feeling,
And needing more each day Thy grace to know,
Yet from our hearts a song of triumph pealing,
We rest on Thee, and in Thy name we go.

"We rest on Thee, our Shield and our Defender,
Thine is the battle, Thine shall be the praise
When passing through the gates of pearly splendor,
Victors, we rest with Thee through endless days."

Committing themselves and all their carefully laid plans to Him who had so unmistakably brought them thus far, they waited for the Aucas.

Before four-thirty that afternoon the quiet waters of the Curaray flowed over the bodies of the five comrades, slain by the men they had come to win for Christ, whose banner they had borne. The world called it a nightmare of tragedy. The world did not recognize the truth of the second clause in Jim Elliot's credo: "He is no fool who gives what he cannot keep to gain what he cannot lose."

∾

THE CONVERSION OF BORIS KORNFELD

CHARLES COLSON

It is not possible for American Evangelicals to talk about the dramatic conversions of this century without mentioning Charles Colson. In the wake of the Nixon Watergate scandal, Colson was sentenced to prison, where he was influenced by many evangelical writers and thinkers. The writings of the late C. S. Lewis were especially influential in turning Colson toward Jesus. In this selection Colson celebrates the conversion of a Russian physician. Typical in Protestant and Evangelical tradition has been the public sharing of the testimony. The testimony in less traditional worship is a personal and confessional account of how the narrator became a Christian. These accounts are inevitably the most moving parts of Evangelical worship. The relating of the testimony is rather like the events that transpire during a meeting of Alcoholics Anonymous. The center of A. A. is the testimonies of how the various members are struggling and winning the war one day at a time. Colson's autobiographical account of his conversion was contained in his book Born Again. *The quickness of that account is found in his relating of the testimony of Boris Kornfeld.*

No REPORTERS HAVE visited the prison camps of Soviet Russia, unless they have gone as prisoners. So to this day we have little information about the millions who have lived, suffered, and died there, especially during Stalin's reign of terror. Most will remain nameless for all time, remembered only in the hearts of those who knew and loved them. But from time to time, scraps of information have filtered out about a few. One of those few was Boris Nicholayevich Kornfeld.

Kornfeld was a medical doctor. From this we can guess a little about his background, for in post-revolutionary Russia such education never went to families tied in any way to czarist Russia. Probably his parents were socialists who had fastened their hopes on the Revolution. They were also Jews, but almost certainly not Jews still hoping for the Messiah, for the name Boris and the patronymic Nicholayevich indicate they had taken Russian names in some past generation. Probably Kornfeld's fore-bears were *Haskalah,* so-called "enlightened Jews," who accepted the philosophy of rationalism, cultivated a knowledge of the natural sciences, and devoted themselves to the arts. In language, dress, and social habits they tried to make themselves as much like their Russian neighbors as possible.

It was natural for such Jews to support Lenin's revolution, for the czars' vicious anti-Semitism had made life almost unendurable for the prior two hundred years. Socialism promised something much better for them than "Christian" Russia. "Christian" Russia had slaughtered Jews; perhaps atheistic Russia would save them.

Obviously Kornfeld had followed in his parents' footsteps, believing in Communism as the path of historical necessity, for political prisoners at that time were not citizens opposed to Communism or wanting the Czar's return. Such people were simply shot. Political prisoners were believers in the Revolution, socialists or communists who had, nevertheless, not kept their allegiance to Stalin's leadership pure.

We do not know what crime Dr. Kornfeld committed, only that it was a political crime. Perhaps he dared one day to suggest to a friend that their leader, Stalin, was fallible; or maybe he was simply accused of harboring such thoughts. It took no more than that to become a prisoner in the Russia of the early 1950s; many died for less. At any rate, Kornfeld was imprisoned in a concentration camp for political subversives at Eki-bastuz.

Ironically, a few years behind barbed wire was a good cure for Communism. The senseless brutality, the waste of lives, the trivialities called criminal charges made men like Kornfeld doubt the glories of the system. Stripped of all past associations, of all that had kept them busy and secure, behind the wire prisoners had time to think. In such a place, thoughtful men like Boris Kornfeld found themselves reevaluating beliefs they had held since childhood.

So it was that this Russian doctor abandoned all his socialistic ideals. In fact, he went further than that. He did something that would have horrified his forebears.

Boris Kornfeld became a Christian.

• • •

While few Jews anywhere in the world find it easy to accept Jesus Christ as the true Messiah, a Russian Jew would find it even more difficult. For two centuries these Jews had known implacable hatred from the people who, they were told, were the most Christian of all. Each move the Jews made to reconcile themselves or accommodate themselves to the Russians was met by new inventions of hatred and persecution, as when the head of the governing body of the Russian Orthodox Church said he hoped that as a result of the Russian pogroms, "one-third of the Jews will convert, one-third will die, and one-third will flee the country."

Yet following the Revolution a strange alignment occurred. Joseph Stalin demanded undivided, unquestioning loyalty to his government; but both Jews and Christians knew their ultimate loyalty was to God. Consequently people of both faiths suffered for their beliefs and frequently in the same camps.

Thus it was that Boris Kornfeld came in contact with a devout Christian, a well-educated and kind fellow prisoner who spoke of a Jewish Messiah who had come to keep the promises the Lord had made to Israel. This Christian—whose name we do not know—pointed out that Jesus had spoken almost solely to Jewish people and proclaimed that He came to the Jews first. That was consistent with God's special concern for the Jew, the chosen ones; and, he explained, the Bible promised that a new kingdom of peace would come. This man often recited aloud the Lord's Prayer, and Kornfeld heard in those simple words a strange ring of truth.

The camp had stripped Kornfeld of everything, including his belief in salvation through socialism. Now this man offered him hope—but in what a form!

To accept Jesus Christ—to become one of those who had always persecuted his people—seemed a betrayal of his family, of all who had been before him. Kornfeld knew the Jews had suffered innocently. Jews were innocent in the days of the Cossacks! Innocent in the days of the czars! And he himself was innocent of betraying Stalin; he had been imprisoned unjustly.

But Kornfeld pondered what the Christian prisoner had told him. In one commodity, time, the doctor was rich.

Unexpectedly, he began to see the powerful parallels between the Jews and this Jesus. It had always been a scandal that God should entrust Himself in a unique way to one people, the Jews. Despite centuries of persecution, their very existence in the midst of those who sought to destroy them was a sign of a Power greater than that of their oppressors. It was the same with Jesus—that God would present Himself in the form of a man had always confounded the wisdom of the world. To the proud and powerful, Jesus stood as a Sign, exposing their own limitations and sin. So they had to kill Him, just as those in power had to kill the Jews, in order to maintain their delusions of omnipotence. Thus, Stalin, the new god-head of the brave new world of the Revolution, had to persecute both Jew and Christian. Each stood as living proof of his blasphemous pretensions to power.

Only in the gulag could Boris Kornfeld begin to see such a truth. And the more he reflected upon it, the more it began to change him within.

Though a prisoner, Kornfeld lived in better conditions than most behind the wire. Other prisoners were expendable, but doctors were scarce in the remote, isolated camps. The authorities could not afford to lose a physician, for guards as well as prisoners needed medical attention. And no prison officer wanted to end up in the hands of a doctor he had cruelly abused.

Kornfeld's resistance to the Christian message might have begun to weaken while he was in surgery, perhaps while working on one of those guards he had learned to loathe. The man had been knifed and an artery cut. While suturing the blood vessel, the doctor thought of tying the thread in such a way that it would reopen shortly after surgery. The guard would die quickly and no one would be the wiser.

The process of taking this particular form of vengeance gave rein to the burning hatred Kornfeld had for the guard and all like him. How he despised his persecutors! He could gladly slaughter them all!

And at that point, Boris Kornfeld became appalled by the hatred and violence he saw in his own heart. Yes, he was a victim of hatred as his ancestors had been. But that hatred had spawned an insatiable hatred of his own. What a deadly predicament! He was trapped by the very evil he despised. What freedom could he ever know with his soul imprisoned by this murderous hate? It made the whole world a concentration camp.

As Kornfeld began to retie the sutures properly, he found himself, almost unconsciously, repeating the words he had heard from his fellow prisoner. "Forgive us our trespasses, as we forgive those who trespass against us." Strange words in the mouth of a Jew. Yet he could not help praying them. Having seen his own evil heart, he had to pray for cleansing. And he had to pray to a God who had suffered, as he had: Jesus.

• • •

Now Boris Kornfeld wanted to tell someone about his discovery, about this new life of obedience and freedom. The Christian who had talked to him about Jesus had been transferred to another camp, so the doctor waited for the right person and the right moment.

One gray afternoon he examined a patient who had just been operated on for cancer of the intestines. This young man with a melon-shaped head and a hurt, little-boy expression touched the soul of the doctor. The man's eyes were sorrowful and suspicious and his face deeply etched by the years he had already spent in the camps, reflecting a depth of spiritual misery and emptiness Kornfeld had rarely seen.

So the doctor began to talk to the patient, describing what had happened to him. Once the tale began to spill out, Kornfeld could not stop.

The patient missed the first part of the story, for he was drifting in and out of the anesthesia's influence, but the doctor's ardor caught his concentration and held it, though he was shaking with fever. All through the afternoon and late into the night, the doctor talked, describing his conversion to Christ and his new-found freedom.

Very late, with the perimeter lights in the camp glazing the window-panes, Kornfeld confessed to the patient: "On the whole, you know, I have become convinced that there is no punishment that comes to us in this life on earth which is undeserved. Superficially, it can have nothing to do with what we are guilty of in actual fact, but if you go over your life with a fine-tooth comb and ponder it deeply, you will always be able to hunt down that transgression of yours for which you have now received this blow."

Imagine! The persecuted Jew who once believed himself totally innocent now saying that every man deserved his suffering, whatever it was.

The patient knew he was listening to an incredible confession. Though the pain from his operation was severe, his stomach a heavy, expansive agony of molten lead, he hung on the doctor's words until he fell asleep.

The young patient awoke early the next morning to the sound of running feet and a commotion in the area of the operating room. His first thought was of the doctor, but his new friend did not come. Then the whispers of a fellow patient told him of Kornfeld's fate.

During the night, while the doctor slept, someone had crept up beside him and dealt him eight blows on the head with a plasterer's mallet. And though his fellow doctors worked valiantly to save him, in the morning the orderlies carried him out, a still, broken form.

But Kornfeld's testimony did not die.

The patient pondered the doctor's last, impassioned words. As a result, he, too, became a Christian. He survived that prison camp and went on to tell the world what he had learned there.

The patient's name was Alexander Solzhenitsyn.

❧

THE CROSS AND THE HUMAN NEED FOR LOVE

ALISTER MCGRATH

Alister McGrath has addressed the age-old existential issue of trying to find meaning when we are but a speck on the cosmic flywheel. In a universe where human beings are about halfway between the atom and the universe in size, how shall we find any significance in our being? McGrath seems convinced that Christ is the place to look for human significance in the cosmic machine. In becoming a human being, Jesus conferred upon humanity a sense of significance that cannot be diminished merely by the gigantic dimensions of our starry environment.

MANY PEOPLE FEEL lost in the immensity of the universe. We all need to feel loved, to feel that we are important to someone else. Yet at the root of the lives of many, there is a virtual absence of any meaning. President John F. Kennedy once remarked that "modern American youth has everything—except a reason to live." And the words of Jean-Paul Sartre express this point with force: "Here we are, all of us, eating and drinking to preserve our precious existences—and yet there is nothing, nothing, absolutely no reason for existing." We could even give a name to this feeling of meaninglessness—we could call it an "existential vacuum." But that doesn't solve the problem. We still feel lonely and lost, in a vast universe which threatens to overwhelm us.

It is this feeling of meaninglessness which is transformed through the electrifying declaration that God—the same God who created the universe—loves us. Love gives meaning to life, in that the person loved becomes special to someone, assumes a significance which he otherwise might not have. Christianity makes the astonishing assertion—which it bases upon the life, death and resurrection of Jesus Christ—that God is profoundly interested in us and concerned for us. We mean something to God; Christ died for us; we are special in the sight of God. Christ came to bring us back from the "far country" to our loving and waiting father. In the midst of an immense and frightening universe, we are given meaning and significance by the realisation that the God who called the world into being, who created us, also loves us and cares for us, coming down from heaven and going to the cross to prove the full extent of that love to a disbelieving and wondering world. Once more, a human experience (a sense of loneliness and meaninglessness) is addressed, and transformed into a sense of being dearly loved and given a sense of purpose.

∾

ONE SOLITARY LIFE

AUTHOR UNKNOWN

This selection discusses the mysterious yet certain impact of Jesus. We cannot grant to Jesus a widely traveled, cosmopolitan existence, nor can we deny the global impact of his provincial life.

HE WAS BORN in an obscure village, the child of a peasant woman. He worked in a carpentry shop until he was thirty, and then for three years he was an itinerant preacher.

When the tide of popular opinion turned against him, his friends ran away. He was turned over to his enemies. He was tried and convicted. He was nailed upon a cross between two thieves. When he was dead, he was laid in a borrowed grave.

He never wrote a book. He never held an office. He never owned a home. He never went to college. He never traveled more than two hundred miles from the place where he was born. He never did one of the things that usually accompanies greatness.

Yet all the armies that ever marched, and all the governments that ever sat, and all the kings that ever reigned, have not affected life upon this earth as powerfully as has that One Solitary Life.

THE MEMOIRS OF A MADMAN

LEO TOLSTOY

I have abridged this splendid autobiographical short story. Tolstoy's coming to faith was accomplished during the foment of Bolshevism. Nothing he ever wrote has stirred the human spirit like his account of coming to faith.

I REMEMBER THAT once when going to bed, at the age of five or six, my nurse Eupraxia, a tall thin woman who wore a brown dress and a cap and had flabby skin under her chin, was undressing me and lifting me up to put me into my cot. "I will get into bed by myself—myself!" I said, and stepped over the side of the cot.

"Well, lie down then. Lie down, Fedya! Look at Mitya. He's a good boy and is lying down already," she said, indicating my brother with a jerk of her head.

I jumped into my bed still holding her hand and then let it go, kicked about under my bedclothes, and wrapped myself up. And I had such a pleasant feeling. I grew quiet and thought: "I love Nurse; Nurse loves me and Mitya; and I love Mitya, and Mitya loves me and Nurse. Nurse loves Taras, and I love Taras, and Mitya loves him. And Taras loves me and Nurse. And Mamma loves me and Nurse, and Nurse loves Mamma and me and Papa—and everybody loves everybody and everybody is happy!"

Then suddenly I heard the housekeeper run in and angrily shout something about a sugar-basin and Nurse answering indignantly that she had not taken it. And I felt pained, frightened, and bewildered, and horror, cold horror, seized me, and I hid my head under the bedclothes but felt no better in the dark.

I also remembered how a serf-boy was once beaten in my presence, how he screamed, and how dreadful Foka's face looked when he was beating the boy. "Then you won't do it any more, you won't!" and went on beating him.

And then it came upon me! I began to sob, and went on so that they could not quiet me for a long time. That sobbing and despair were the first attacks of my present madness.

I remember another attack when my aunt told us about Christ. She told the story and was about to go away, but we said: "Tell us some more about Jesus Christ!"

"No, I have no time now," she said.

"Yes, do tell us!"

Mitya also asked her to, and my aunt began to repeat what she had told us. She told us how they crucified, beat, and tortured him, and how he went on praying and did not reproach them.

"Why did they torment him, Auntie?"

"They were cruel people."

"But why, when he was good?"

"There, that's enough. It's past eight! Do you hear?"

"Why did they beat him? He forgave them, then why did they hit him? Did it hurt him, Auntie? Did it hurt?"

"That will do! I'm going to have tea now."

"But perhaps it isn't true and they didn't beat him?"

"Now, now, that will do!"

"No, no! Don't go away!"

And again I was overcome by it. I sobbed and sobbed and began knocking my head against the wall.

That was how it befell me in my childhood.

• • •

In the tenth year of my married life I again had an attack—the first since my childhood.

My wife and I had saved money—some inherited by her and some from the bonds I, like other landowners, received from the Government at the time of the emancipation of the serfs—and we decided to buy an estate. I was much interested, as was proper, in the growth of our property and in increasing it in the shrewdest way—better than other people. At that time I inquired everywhere where there were estates for sale, and read all the advertisements in the papers. I wanted to buy an estate so that the income from it, or the timber on it, should cover the whole purchase price and I should get it for nothing. I looked out for some fool who did not understand business and thought I had found such a man.

An estate with large forests was being sold in Penza province. From all I could learn about it, it seemed that its owner was just such a fool as I wanted and the timber would cover the whole cost of the estate. So I got ready and set out.

• • •

Night came and we still went on. We grew drowsy. I fell asleep but suddenly awoke feeling that there was something terrifying. As often happens, I woke up thoroughly alert and feeling as if sleep had gone for ever. "Why am I going? Where am I going to?" I suddenly asked myself. It was not that I did not like the idea of buying an estate cheaply, but it suddenly occurred to me that there was no need for me to travel all that distance, that I should die here in this strange place, and I was filled with dread.

• • •

We were nearing the town of Arzamas.

"Shall we put up here and rest a bit?"

"Why not? Splendid!"

"Are we still far from the town?"

"About five miles from the last mile-post."

The driver was a respectable man, careful and taciturn, and he drove rather slowly and wearily.

We drove on. I remained silent and felt better because I was looking forward to a rest and hoped that the discomfort would pass.

• • •

At last we came up to a small house with a post beside it. The house was white but appeared terribly melancholy to me, so much so that it seemed uncanny and I got out of the carriage slowly.

Sergey briskly took out all that would be wanted, running clattering up the porch, and the sound of his steps depressed me. I entered a little corridor. A sleepy man with a spot on his cheek (which seemed to me terrifying) showed us into a room. It was gloomy. I entered, and the uncanny feeling grew worse.

"Haven't you got a bed-room? I should like to rest."

It was a small square room, with whitewashed walls. I remember that it tormented me that it should be square. It had one window with a red curtain, a birchwood table, and a sofa with bent-wood arms. We went in. Sergey prepared the samovar and made tea, while I took a pillow and lay down on the sofa. I was not asleep and heard how Sergey was busy with the tea and called me to have some. But I was afraid of getting up and arousing myself completely, and I thought how frightful it would be to sit up in that room. I did not get up but began to doze. I must have fallen asleep, for when I awoke I found myself alone in the room and it was dark. I was again as wide awake as I had been in the chaise. I felt that to sleep would be quite impossible. "Why have I come here? Where am I betaking myself? Why and whither am I escaping?"

• • •

I had gone into the corridor thinking to escape from what tormented me. But *it* had come out with me and cast a gloom over everything. I felt just as filled with horror or even more so.

"But what folly this is!" I said to myself. "Why am I depressed? What am I afraid of?"

"Me!" answered the voice of Death, inaudibly. "I am here!"

A cold shudder ran down my back. Yes! Death! It will come—here it is—and it ought not to be. Had I been actually facing death I could not have suffered as much as I did then. Then I should have been frightened. But now I was not frightened. I saw and felt the approach of death, and at the same time I felt that such a thing ought not to exist.

• • •

Something was tearing within that yet could not be torn apart. A painful, painfully dry and spiteful feeling, no atom of kindliness, but just a dull and steady spitefulness towards myself and towards that which had made me.

What created me? God, they say. God . . . what about prayer? I remembered. For some twenty years I had not prayed, and I did not believe in anything, though as a matter of propriety I fasted and went to communion every year.

• • •

I lay down. But I had only to lie down and close my eyes for the same feeling of terror to knock and rouse me. I could bear it no longer. I woke the hotel servant and Sergey, gave orders to harness, and we drove off again. The fresh air and the drive made me feel better.

• • •

I returned home safely. I did not buy the estate—I had not enough money—and I continued to live as before, only with this difference, that I began to pray and went to church. As before—it seemed to me, but I now remember that it was not as before—I lived on what had been previously begun. I continued to go along the rails already laid by my former strength, but I did not undertake anything new. And I took less part in those things I had previously begun. Everything seemed dull to me and I became pious. My wife noticed this and scolded and nagged me on account of it. But my spleen did not recur at home.

But once I had unexpectedly to go to Moscow. I got ready in the afternoon and left in the evening. It was in connection with a lawsuit. I arrived in Moscow cheerful. On the way I had talked with a landowner from Kharkov about estate-management and banks, and about where to put up, and about the theatre. We both decided to stop at the Moscow Hotel on the Myasnitsky Street and to go to see *Faust* that same evening.

When we arrived I was shown into a small room. The oppressive air of the corridor filled my nostrils . . . And suddenly I was seized with an attack of the same horror as in Arzamas. "My God! How can I say here all night" I thought.

"Yes, uncord, my good fellow," I told the porter to keep him longer in the room. "I'll dress quickly and go to the theater."

• • •

All was well, and I quite forgot my oblong room with its partition. In the theatre, too, it was pleasant. After the opera the Kharkov landowner suggested that we should have supper. That was contrary to my habit, but just then I again remembered the partition in my room and accepted his suggestion.

We got back after one. I had had two glasses of wine, to which I was unaccustomed, but in spite of that I felt cheerful.

• • •

I had suffered all night unbearably. Again my soul and body were being painfully torn asunder. "I am living, have lived, and ought to live, and suddenly—here is death to destroy everything. Then what is life for? To die? To kill myself at once? No, I am afraid. To wait for death till it comes? I fear that even more. Then I must live. But what for? In order to die?" And I could not escape from that circle. I took up a book, read, and forgot myself for a moment, but then again the same question and the same horror. I lay down in bed and closed my eyes. It was worse still!

God has so arranged it. Why? They say: "Don't ask, but pray!" Very well. I prayed, and prayed as I had done at Arzamas. Then and afterwards I prayed simply, like a child. But now my prayers had a meaning. "If Thou dost exist, reveal to me why and what I am!" I bowed down, repeated all the prayers I knew, composed my own, and added: "Then reveal it!" and became silent, awaiting an answer. But no answer came. It was just as if there were no one who could give an answer. And I remained alone with myself. And in place of Him who would not reply I answered my own questions. "Why? In order to live in a future life," I said to myself. "Then why this obscurity, this torment? I cannot believe in a future life. I believed when I did not ask with my whole soul, but now I cannot, I cannot. If Thou didst exist Thou wouldst speak to me and to all men. And if Thou dost not exist there is nothing but despair. And I do not want that. I do not want that!"

I became indignant. I asked Him to reveal the truth to me, to reveal Himself to me. I did all that everybody does, but He did not reveal Himself. "Ask and it shall be given you," I remembered, and I had asked and in that asking had found not consolation but relaxation. Perhaps I did not pray to Him but repudiated Him. "You recede a span and He recedes a mile," as the proverb has it. I did not believe in Him but I asked, and He did not reveal anything to me. I was balancing accounts with Him and blaming Him. I simply did not believe.

The next day I did all in my power to get through my ordinary affairs so as to avoid another night in the hotel. Although I did not finish every-thing, I left for home that evening. I did not feel any spleen. That night in

Moscow still further changed my life which had begun to change from the time I was at Arzamas. I now attended still less to my affairs and became apathetic. I also grew weaker in health. My wife insisted that I should undergo a treatment. She said that my talks about faith and God arose from ill health. But I knew that my weakness and ill health were the effect of the unsolved question within me.

• • •

One winter day a neighboring huntsman came with his wolf-hounds. I rode out with him. When we reached the place we put on snow-shoes and went to the spot where the wolf might be found. The hunt was unsuccessful, the wolves broke through the ring of beaters. I became aware of this from a distance and went through the forest following the fresh tracks of a hare. These led me far into a glade, where I spied the hare, but it jumped out so that I lost it. I went back through the thick forest. The snow was deep, my snowshoes sank in, and branches of the trees entangled me. The trees grew ever more and more dense. I began to ask myself: "Where am I?" The snow had altered the look of everything.

Suddenly I realized that I had lost my way. I was far from the house, and from the hunters too, and could hear nothing. I was tired and bathed in perspiration. If I stopped I should freeze. If I went on my strength would fail me. I shouted. All was still. No one answered. I turned back, but it was the same again. I looked around—nothing but trees, impossible to tell which was east or west. Again I turned back. My legs were tired. I grew frightened, stopped, and was seized with the same horror as in Arzamas and Moscow, but a hundred times worse. My heart palpitated; my arms and legs trembled. "Is this death? I won't have it! Why death? What is death?" Once again I wanted to question and reproach God, but here I suddenly felt that I dare not and must not do so, that it is impossible to present one's account to God, that He had said what is needful and I alone was to blame. I began to implore his forgiveness, and felt disgusted with myself.

The horror did not last long. I stood there for awhile, came to myself, went on in one direction and soon emerged from the forest. I had not been far from its edge, and came out on to the road. My arms and legs still trembled and my heart was beating, but I felt happy. I found the hunting party and we returned home. I was cheerful, but I knew there was something joyful which I would make out when alone. And so it was. I remained by myself in my study and began to pray, asking forgiveness and remembering my sins. There seemed to me to be but few, but when I recalled them they became hateful to me.

After that I began to read the scriptures. The Old Testament I found unintelligible though enchanting, but the Gospels moved me profoundly. But most of all I read the Lives of the Saints, and that reading consoled me, presenting examples that it seemed more and more possible to follow. From that time forth farming and family matters occupied me less and less. They even repelled me. They all seemed to me wrong. What it was that was "right" I did not know, but what had formerly constituted my life had now ceased to do so. This became plain to me when I was going to buy another estate.

Not far from us an estate was for sale on very advantageous terms. I went to see it. Everything was excellent and advantageous; specially so was the fact that the peasants there had no land of their own except their kitchen-gardens. I saw that they would have to work on the landlord's land merely for permission to use his pastures. And so it was. I grasped all this and by old habit felt pleased about it. But on my way home I met an old woman who asked her way. I had a talk with her, during which she told me about her poverty. I got home, and when telling my wife of the advantages that estate offered, I suddenly felt ashamed and disgusted. I told her I could not buy it because the advantages we should get would be based on the peasants' destitution and sorrow. As I said this I suddenly realized the truth of what I was saying—the chief truth, that the peasants, like ourselves, want to live, that they are human beings, our brothers, and sons of the Father as the Gospels say. Suddenly something that had long troubled me seemed to have broken away, as though it had come to birth. My wife was vexed and scolded me, but I felt glad.

That was the beginning of my madness. But my utter madness began later—about a month after that.

It began by my going to church. I stood there through the liturgy and prayed well, and listened and was touched. Then suddenly they brought me some consecrated bread: after that we went up to the Cross, and people began pushing one another. Then at the exit there were beggars. And it suddenly became clear to me that this ought not to be, and not only ought not to be but in reality was not. And if this was not, then neither was there either death or fear, and there was no longer the former tearing asunder within me and I no longer feared anything.

Then the light fully illumined me and I became what I now am. If there is nothing of all that—then it certainly does not exist within me. And there at the church door I gave away to the beggars all I had with me —some thirty-five rubles—and went home on foot talking with the peasants.

A REVERSAL OF MEEKNESS

RICHARD FOSTER

THE MOST RADICAL social teaching of Jesus was his total reversal of the contemporary notion of greatness. Leadership is found in becoming the servant of all. Power is discovered in submission. The foremost symbol of this radical servanthood is the cross. "He [Jesus] humbled himself and became obedient unto death, even death on a cross" (Phil. 2:8). But note this: Christ not only died a "cross-death," he lived a "cross-life." The way of the cross, the way of a suffering servant was essential to his ministry. Jesus lived the cross-life in submission to all human beings. He was the servant of all. He flatly rejected the cultural givens of position and power when he said, "You are not to be called rabbi. . . . Neither be called masters . . ." (Matt. 23:8–10). Jesus shattered the customs of his day when he lived out the cross-life by taking women seriously and by being willing to meet with children. He lived the cross-life when he took a towel and washed the feet of his disciples. This Jesus who easily could have called down a legion of angels to his aid chose instead the cross-death of Calvary. Jesus' life was the cross-life of submission and service. Jesus' death was the cross-death of conquest by suffering.

❧

FRIENDSHIP WITH US

CHARLES COLSON

GOD OFTEN USES what we least expect for His divine purposes. That has certainly proved to be true for me. Out of the depths of my prison experience came the vision for Prison Fellowship's ministry, which now involves thousands of volunteers and brings the hope of Christ to prisoners throughout the U.S. and abroad.

As I sorted through some forty cartons of papers, I came across writings from my first days at Maxwell Federal Prison after my ten-week stint at Fort Holabird prison in Baltimore. Because these formerly unpublished letters and journal entries give such candid glimpse of what life in prison is really like, I thought it would be appropriate to share them with my readers. In the context of all that has happened in the past ten years, I believe these writings from prison bear witness to God's sovereignty, even times of emptiness and pain.

JOURNAL ENTRIES, UNDATED; first impressions of Maxwell Federal Prison.

. . . I HAD A good collection of Christian books that I had stuffed into my bag. They [prison officials] examined each paper, each book, and each personal item, one by one . . .

My wallet would be packed in the suitcase and returned home. I protested momentarily on the grounds that I might be called back to Washington anytime to testify and I would certainly need my identification with me. Officer B—— explained that if I were taken back to Washington I would be in the custody of marshals with a set of government orders, a government-provided ticket and that I would need no identification.

The wallet, curiously enough, was one of the most difficult things to part with. It sounds like a small point, but psychologically it's a major one. One has no way of proving to anyone who he is, and if he should suddenly be granted his freedom, he would be totally dependent on someone else, some impersonal set of orders, or some marshal. I was faced with the disquieting feeling that I was to become no more than an anonymous number. Simply another face among a whole mass of faces.

. . . As the final act I was handed a set of dark brown, very well-worn surplus Air Force work clothes. The shirt was too tight and the pants too baggy. But at this point it made little difference. I was now a full-fledged federal prisoner. A member of what is euphemistically called "the population."

. . . Within a few moments I was ushered into the control room, the nerve center of the prison camp. It is a large square room with thick plate glass windows on three sides, overlooking the central courtyard. I was at once struck by the eerie feeling that everyone in the camp was being watched at all times.

. . . Looking out from the control room at the drab brown bodies moving about slowly, most of them hunched over, was the first real depressing awareness I had of the emptiness—the empty souls, the barrenness of the inside of a prison.

EXCERPTS FROM LETTER of September 18, 1974, to my fellowship prayer group in Washington, written my first day at Maxwell after nearly three months at Fort Holabird in Baltimore.

DEAR BROTHERS,

. . . I am badly qualified after twenty-four hours to speak with much authority on life in the Maxwell Prison Camp. But I didn't want a day to pass without writing to let you know I am glad I came here. It is an experience I think will be important to us, however long it must last.

This is *no* country club, nor is it like boot camp, as some have suggested. It is a prison and the conditions are really worse than I expected (I will not tell Patty that; her burdens are enough already). The "barracks" aren't the way you guys remember from your military days—there is everything here from lifelong, hardened criminals to young drug offenders.

The reason I am glad to be here, however, is the sudden realization of how many needs there are here—spiritual needs and the need for people to establish their own identity and dignity as human beings. My heart has ached for so many while I am here; more important, when I leave I hope I can do something about the concept of rehabilitation and punishment. All its high sounding names—deterrence, rehabilitation— are untrue. If it is punishment, so be it; but maybe it is more humane to whip a man's body than destroy his soul slowly.

. . . It helps me to write you now before I get calloused to it. I want you brothers to read this letter back to me when I am out of here and have forgotten what the initial shock was like—and in the event I ever forget I have an obligation to try to improve the fate and circumstances of man in this plight.

. . . 8:45 P.M.: I have been asked by six inmates and one guard if I'd share my witness with them. It is encouraging; I am convinced the Lord has planned this for me and will use me for His purpose. I first had to learn who I was in relation to God; now I'm learning who I am in relation to others, and how the Lord works through us to reach others in need.

. . . I'll write as often as I can. Patty will be here this weekend and can tell you all the visiting arrangements. Give my love to all the brothers —I miss you all, but I want you to know I am fine.

In His love, Chuck

EXCERPTS FROM LETTER of October 23, 1974, also to the prayer group.

DEAR BROTHERS,

Forgive me for being so slow in responding to your wonderful birthday messages. You helped mightily in supporting me last week. Special days like birthdays do add to the anxieties of being confined.

. . . I decided when I came here that I would offer no help to people as a lawyer. The demand is great and I was asked by many for assistance. In the last few weeks I've been helping some if I believed there was an opportunity to talk to them about Christ.

I have really had some magnificent experiences, particularly with some who cannot read or write and desperately need help—legally and spiritually. You can't imagine how much it opens a man's heart just to help in something as simple as writing a letter to his judge. I found that the man in the next bunk had tried for two weeks to compose a letter to his probation officer. He worked on it every night; I finally asked him what he was doing. When he told me, I helped him, and in a half hour it was done. Now he is borrowing my Bible.

Three other Christians and I have been meeting each night at 9:30 for a half-hour of fellowship and prayer.

We have a larger fellowship group on Monday evenings, fifteen or twenty men, and we're using that for a Bible study as well. It really is exciting when I think back; five weeks ago people were ridiculed for carrying a Bible. There was nothing like a fellowship. The Christians didn't even know one another. But none of this is a result of planning or conscious organizing. The Lord has worked through me and others, and this is happening because of Him, not us.

Apart from the separation from Patty, who is waiting faithfully for the gates to open each visiting day, my only real sorrow is being away from all of you. I miss you, but I am comforted in the assurance that all of this is by His plan; Christ's bonds are so great that our love cannot be affected by the distance which separates us. You are all in my prayers.

In His love, Chuck

∽

THE LIGHT OF CHRIST

GEORGE FOX

George Fox summed up what the end of all the mysteries of God should be. It does little good to have wonderful worship experiences within the church and not see the hurting in the world beyond the church's walls. Fox, the inspired founding luminary of Quakers, defined for them the truth that mystical experience is no good unless it results in helping others who are in need. Quakers have excelled among nontraditional churches in caring about the need of the dispossessed and needy.

Now was I come up in spirit through the flaming sword, into the paradise of God. All things were new, and all the creation gave another smell unto me than before, beyond what words can utter. I knew nothing but pureness, and innocency, and righteousness, being renewed up into the image of God by Christ Jesus, to the state of Adam, which he was in before he fell . . . Great things did the Lord lead me into, and wonderful depths were opened unto me beyond what can by words be declared . . . He shewed me that the physicians were out of the wisdom of God, by which the creatures were made; and so knew not their virtues . . . He shewed me that the priests were out of the true faith, which Christ is the author of; the faith which purifies and gives victory, and brings people to have access to God, and by which they please God . . . He shewed me also, that the lawyers were out of the equity, and out of the true justice, and out of the law of God . . . And as the Lord opened these things unto me, I felt his power went forth over all, by which all might be reformed, if they would receive and bow to it. The priests might be reformed and brought into the true faith, which was the gift of God. The lawyers might be reformed and brought into the law of God, which answers that of God which is transgressed in everyone, and brings to love one's neighbour as himself . . . The physicians might be reformed and brought into the wisdom of God by which all things were made and created, that they might receive a right understanding of the creatures and understand their virtues . . .

These things I did not see by the help of man, nor by the letter, though they are written in the letter, but I saw them in the light of the Lord Jesus Christ, and by his immediate spirit and power, as did the holy men of God by whom the Holy Scriptures were written. Yet I had no slight esteem of the Holy Scriptures, but they were very precious to me, for I was in that Spirit by which they were given forth; and what the Lord opened to me I afterwards found was agreeable to them . . . With and by this divine power and Spirit of God, and the light of Jesus, I was to bring people off from all their own ways, to Christ, the new and living way; and from their own churches, which men had made and gathered, to the church in God, the general assembly written in heaven which Christ is the head of . . . And I was to bring people off from all the world's religions, which are vain; that they might know the pure religion, might visit the fatherless, the widows, and the strangers, and keep themselves from the spots of the world; that there would be not so many beggars, the sight of whom often grieved my heart, to see so much hard-heartedness amongst them that professed the name of Christ.

HIS ENDURING WORDS

ELTON TRUEBLOOD

In this selection and the next, Trueblood points out that the church has survived beyond Greco-Roman forms and intellectual structures by a single focus on changing the world. One can fault the Christian church with periods of gross corruption and heartless struggles and competitions. It is easy to see that often the church in doctrinal purges of one kind or another has killed her own Christians. But the dream of Christ that Trueblood exalts in these two passages reminds us that before Jesus came, the common people were often considered unworthy of education. The first asylums and hospitals were often established in the name of Christ. So were schools. In truth, missionaries in any century never took just Jesus to their new converts; they took also schools and alphabets and ultimately science and self-understanding.

CHRIST'S DISCIPLES WERE in a remote part of the Roman Empire, having no standing, no money, no prestige, no worldly power, no education. Consequently, from a human point of view, the chance of their enduring was very slight, while the idea that they could redeem or save the civilization of the world was obviously fantastic.

In spite of all such considerations, Jesus made His tremendous prediction. His statement was paradoxical (Matt. 5:13), but what is far more paradoxical is the fact. Nearly all of the rest of the things on which men depended did actually decay. The Roman Empire did come to an end; Plato's Academy finally closed; the great library at Alexandria was finally burned; the legions were scattered; the schools of the Stoics and the Epicureans faded out. But the little redemptive society which Christ instituted as the divine preservative went on. It entrenched itself in the Greco-Roman world; it penetrated Caesar's household; it carried men through the Dark Ages; it survived the Renaissance, the Reformation, the Enlightenment, and the Industrial Revolution, as it is now surviving the Atomic Revolution. Your presence here thousands of miles from the place where the original pronouncement was made, is one modest evidence that it is still going on. The incredible has occurred.

GOD'S UNDERGROUND

ELTON TRUEBLOOD

WHAT A GREAT event the selecting of the Twelve was! Much of the future history of the world hinged on the decision about these men. If all should prove to be unfaithful, as Judas did, what then would happen to the plan for saving mankind from ultimate decay? According to Luke's account, Christ took the decision about the appointment of the Twelve so seriously that he spent all of the previous night alone in the hills, in prayer. This is not really surprising, when we realize how momentous the occasion was. He was already withdrawing from the crowds, and now it was these or nobody. From then on the great majority of his reported effort was expended upon the careful preparation of these men for their subsequent testing. What was needed was a society hard enough to penetrate thick barriers, something which an amorphous mass can never do.

There is a strange irony in the fashion in which the modern Communist movement has taken over some of the features of Christianity, directing some of the same strategy to other and different ends. One of the really critical moments came in London more than fifty years ago, when, at an international Communist meeting, Lenin barely won out in his struggle to limit the membership of their group to a small, disciplined and deeply committed body of men. If Lenin had not won at that point, the subsequent history of mankind would undoubtedly have been very different. To this day the victories of militant communism are won, in every case, not by a majority, but by a highly disciplined, unyielding, and dedicated minority. Always it is the prepared task force which takes over.

The more we meditate upon Christ's method, the more we realize that the Twelve and those closely associated with them had many of the characteristics of an underground movement. Only on the basis of this understanding can we explain the frequent injunctions concerning secrecy. Even the account of the preparations for the final meal with the Twelve sounds like a contemporary story of a secret meeting of a rebel group under the very eyes of the police. There was, above all, a prearranged signal concerning the place of meeting. "Behold, when you have entered the city, a man carrying a jar of water will meet you; follow him into the house which he enters, and tell the householder, 'The Teacher says to you, Where is the guest room?'" This is precisely the kind of procedure we expect in the meeting of a secret society. How else, except on the basis of a good deal of secrecy, can we explain the necessity of paying a large bribe to Judas to act as an informer? If all of the operations of the little company were as open as Christ's visits to the temple area were, no canny group of leaders would have paid any money at all, for they could have found the group themselves. We are drawn to the conclusion that, while some of the operations of the Twelve were public, others were not. In any case all of the members of the group were highly aware that they were engaged in an enterprise as risky as it was important.

The lesson of all this for our day and generation is the lesson that there are times when we too must withdraw from the crowds. We can be glad that we live in a period in which church attendance is more common than it has been for a long time, and in which mass evangelism has been renewed, but we ought to be aware that there is no spiritual security in this kind of success. It is easy to get crowds and it is likewise easy to lose them. There are predictable circumstances in which we *shall* lose them.

༄

DAILY PRAYER

MOTHER TERESA OF CALCUTTA

DEAREST LORD, MAY I see you today and every day in the person of your sick, and, whilst nursing them, minister unto you.

Though you hide yourself behind the unattractive disguise of the irritable, the exacting, the unreasonable, may I still recognize you, and say: "Jesus, my patient, how sweet it is to serve you."

Lord, give me this seeing faith, then my work will never be monotonous. I will ever find joy in humouring the fancies and gratifying the wishes of all poor sufferers.

O beloved sick, how doubly dear you are to me, when you personify Christ; and what a privilege is mine to be allowed to tend you.

Sweetest Lord, make me appreciative of the dignity of my high vocation, and its many responsibilities. Never permit me to disgrace it by giving way to coldness, unkindness, or impatience.

And O God, while you are Jesus my patient, deign also to be to me a patient Jesus, bearing with my faults, looking only to my intention, which is to love and serve you in the person of each one of your sick.

Lord, increase my faith, bless my efforts and work, now and for evermore, Amen.

THE ART OF BECOMING LIKE CHRIST

PROFESSOR MOMERIE

IF YOU DO not love Him, it must be because you do not know Him. Either He is seldom in your thoughts, or you think of Him as a dogma rather than a person. Try and picture Him to yourself as of old He lived, and talked, and worked in Palestine. Remember how wonderfully, like no one before or since, He combined all conceivable excellences. He had the tenderness of the most womanly woman, and at the same time the strength of the manliest man. Though invincible by the temptations which assailed Himself, He was always ready to make the most generous allow-ance for those who failed and fell. He lived much with God, but this seemed to bring Him only nearer to man. He delighted in solitary commu-nion with the Father, but He was fond also of mingling with His neighbours at their social meetings and festivities. He was keenly alive to the paramount importance of the Spirit and eternity; and yet no one was ever so thoughtfully considerate for men's temporal and bodily welfare— He ministered to them in their bereavements and in their diseases, He was not unmindful even of their hunger and thirst. He had the most sensitive nature, which yearned inexpressibly for sympathy, and yet He never, for the sake of sympathy, swerved from the path of duty. Though all His followers deserted Him, under the conviction that their confidence had been misplaced, He persevered unto the end. He avoided no effort, He shirked no sacrifice, He shrank from no anguish, by which He might serve the race in revealing God and reconciling man. Think of this and much more in that sad, beautiful, sublime career. Think of Him till you love Him and your love has made you like Him. Nothing short of this will make you what Christ would call a Christian. "Except ye eat the flesh and drink the blood of the Son of man, ye have no life in you."

WAR AND PEACE

CHARLES H. SPURGEON

"I did not come to bring peace but a sword."
Matthew 10:34

CHRISTIANS WILL MAKE enemies. If doing right and believing the truth causes us to lose every earthly friend, it will be only a small loss, for our great heavenly Friend will be friendlier and more gracious than ever.

You who have taken up His cross know what your Master said: "I have come to set a man against his father, a daughter against her mother, . . . and a man's enemies will be those of his own household" (Matthew 10:35–36).

Christ is the great peacemaker, but before peace He brings war. When the light comes the darkness must depart. Where truth is, the lie must flee. If the lie remains, there will be a severe conflict, because truth cannot and will not lower its standard.

If you follow Christ, all the hounds of the world will yelp at your heels. Count on this, if you live for Jesus Christ, the world will not speak well of you. "Do you not know that friendship with the world is enmity with God?" (James 4:4). If you are true and faithful to the Most High, people will resent your unflinching devotion because it is a testimony against their iniquity.

Regardless of the consequences, you must do what is right. You will need the courage of a lion to pursue a course that could turn your best friend into your fiercest foe. For the sake of Jesus Christ, you must be courageous.

Risking your reputation and emotions for the truth requires a degree of moral principle that only the Spirit of God can work into you. Do not turn back, do not be a coward; be a hero of the faith. Follow in your Master's steps. He walked this rough way before you.

Better a brief warfare and eternal rest than false peace and everlasting torment.

MORNING PRAYERS

DIETRICH BONHOEFFER

In me there is darkness,
But with you there is light;
I am lonely, but you do not leave me;
I am feeble in heart, but with you there is help;
I am restless, but with you there is peace.
In me there is bitterness, but with you there is patience;
I do not understand your ways,
But you know the way for me.

Lord Jesus Christ,
You were poor
and in distress, a captive and forsaken as I am.
You know all man's troubles;
You abide with me
when all men fail me;
You remember and seek me;
It is your will that I should know you and turn to you.
Lord, I hear your call and follow;
Help me.

THE BISHOP OF SOULS

HERBERT C. GABHART

*"Ye were as sheep going astray; but are now returned unto the
Shepherd and Bishop of your souls"*
1 Peter 2:25

A LITTLE GIRL, when asked how she was able to ward off the devil, said,
"When the devil knocks at the door of my heart, I take Jesus by the hand.
I ask him to go with me to answer the door. When I open the door, the
devil sees me and Jesus standing hand in hand and he says, 'Excuse me, I
must be at the wrong place.' He leaves."

Jesus plays a similar role with all believers. As Bishop of souls he is the spiritual Overseer of His flock. He is the Good Shepherd looking after the flock including the one that goes astray. His Holy Spirit is the "Paraclete" to guide us into all truth.

Since Christians have been cleansed by His blood, loosed from their sins, and made to become kings and priests, Christ is, to them, their Bishop. He wears no particular garb as bishops of the Greek, Roman, or Anglican churches. He wears only the robes of righteousness. Like the bishops of those churches, He does have special duties and powers over the priests. It is His purpose and mission to see that His followers grow and mature into the fullness of Himself.

His diocese is the kingdom of God where the rules of love, grace, mercy, and forgiveness place supreme responsibilities upon the priesthood of believers.

C. Austin Miles, a hymn writer of the early part of the twentieth century, expresses in the chorus of his hymn "In the Garden" what I consider to be a warm and pertinent relationship that exists between the Bishop of souls and His followers:

> And He walks with me, and He talks with me,
> And He tells me I am His own;
> And the joy we share, as we tarry there,
> None other has ever known.

What a glorious relationship. It makes the heart sing!

❧

A PRAYER

HENRY WADSWORTH LONGFELLOW

> My Redeemer and my Lord,
> I beseech Thee, I entreat Thee,
> Guide me in each act and word,
> That hereafter I may meet Thee,
> Watching, waiting, hoping, yearning,
> With my lamp well trimmed and burning!

Interceding
With these bleeding
Wounds upon Thy hands and side,
For all who have lived and erred
Thou hast suffered, Thou hast died,
Scourged, and mocked, and crucified,
And in the grave hast Thou been buried!

If my feeble prayer can reach Thee,
O my Saviour, I beseech Thee,
Even as Thou hast died for me,
More sincerely
Let me follow where Thou leadest,
Let me, bleeding as Thou bleedest,
Die, if dying I may give
Life to one who asks to live,
And more nearly,
Dying thus, resemble Thee!

ON LEAVING HOME

CHARLES DICKENS

Charles Dickens drafted a note to his youngest child when the boy was leaving England to join his older brother in Australia.

TRY TO DO to others as you would have them do to you, and do not be discouraged if they fail sometimes. It is much better for you that they should fail in obeying the greatest rule laid down by our Saviour than that you should. I put a New Testament among your books for the very same reasons, and with the very same hopes, that made me write an easy account of it for you, when you were a little child. Because it is the best book that ever was, or will be, known in the world; and because it teaches you the best lessons by which any human creature, who tries to be truthful and faithful to duty, can possibly be guided. As your brothers have gone away, one by one, I have written to each such words as I am now writing to you, and have entreated them all to guide themselves by this Book, putting aside the interpretations and inventions of Man. You will remember that you have never at home been harassed about religious observances, or mere formalities, I have always been anxious not to weary my children with such things, before they are old enough to form opinions respecting them. You will therefore understand the better that I now most solemnly impress upon you the truth and beauty of the Christian Religion, as it came from Christ Himself, and the impossibility of your going far wrong if you humbly but heartily respect it.

THIS TRANSITORY LIFE

AUTHOR UNKNOWN

FIX THOU OUR steps, O Lord, that we stagger not at the uneven motions of the world, but steadily go on to our glorious home; neither censuring our journey by the weather we meet with, nor turning out of the way for anything that befalls us.

The winds are often rough, and our own weight presses us downwards. Reach forth, O Lord, thy hand, thy saving hand, and speedily deliver us.

Teach us, O Lord, to use this transitory life as pilgrims returning to their beloved home; that we may take what our journey requires, and not think of settling in a foreign country.

WITH HOW GREAT REVERENCE

CHRIST IS TO BE RECEIVED

THOMAS À KEMPIS

COME TO ME all you who labor and are heavily burdened, and I will refresh you, says our Lord. And the bread that I will give you will be My

Flesh, for the life of the world. Take you and eat: for it is My Body that will be given for you to sacrifice. Do this in remembrance of Me, for whoever eats My Flesh and drinks My Blood, he will dwell in Me, and I in him. These words I have said to you are spirit and life.

O my Lord Jesus Christ, Eternal Truth, these words are Your words, although they were not spoken in one same time or written in one same place. And because they are Your words, I will thankfully and faithfully accept them. They are Your words and you have spoken them, and they are mine also, for You have said them for my salvation. I shall gladly receive them from Your mouth to the end that they may be better sown and planted in my heart. Your words of such great pity, full of sweetness and love, greatly stir me. But, Lord, my sins put me in great fear and my conscience, not pure to receive so great a mystery, holds me sadly aback. The sweetness of Your words stirs me, but the multitude of my offenses weighs most heavily upon me. You command me to come unto You faithfully, if I will have part with You, and to receive the nourishment of immortality, if I yearn to obtain the glory of everlasting life. Lord, You say: Come to me you who labor and are heavily burdened, and I will refresh you. Oh, how sweet and how friendly a word is this in the ear of a sinner, that You, Lord God, will bid me, so poor and needy, to the communion of Your most holy Body. But what am I, Lord, that I dare presume to come to You. Lo, heaven and earth may not comprehend You, and yet You say: Come all of you to Me.

What is the meaning of this humble familiarity and this lovely and friendly invitation? How shall I, who do not know that I have done anything well, dare come to You? How shall I, who have so often offended before Your face, bring You into my house? Angels and archangels honor you and just men fear You, yet You say: Come all of you to Me. Except that You, Lord, said it, who would believe it to be true? Except that You commanded it, who would dare approach?

∾

RESULTS OF THE ATONEMENT

BILLY GRAHAM

FIRST: IT REDEEMS—1 Peter 1:18–19: "Forasmuch as ye know that ye were not redeemed with corruptible things, as silver and gold, from your vain conversation received by tradition from your fathers; but with the precious blood of Christ, as of a lamb without blemish and without spot."

Second: It brings us nigh—Ephesians 2:13: "But now in Christ Jesus ye who sometimes were far off are made nigh by the blood of Christ."

Third: It makes peace—Colossians 1:20: "And having made peace through the blood of his cross, by him to reconcile all things unto himself; by him, I say, whether they be things in earth, or things in Heaven."

Fourth: It justifies—Romans 5:9: "Much more then, being now justified by his blood, we shall be saved from wrath through him."

Fifth: It cleanses—1 John 1:7: "But if we walk in the light, as he is in the light, we have fellowship one with another, and the blood of Jesus Christ his Son cleanseth us from all sin."

∾

HIS PILGRIMAGE TO DEATH

SIR WALTER RALEIGH

Give me my scallop-shell of quiet,
My staff of faith to walk upon,
My scrip of joy, immortal diet,
My bottle of salvation,
My gown of glory, hope's true gage;
And thus I'll take my pilgrimage.

Blood must be my body's balmer,
    No other balm will there be given;
Whilst my soul, like quiet palmer,
    Travelleth towards the land of heaven;
Over the silver mountains,
Where spring the nectar fountains;
    There will I kiss
    The bowl of bliss,
And drink mine everlasting fill
Upon every milken hill.
My soul will be a-dry before,
But after, it will thirst no more.

• • •

From thence to heaven's bribeless hall,
Where no corrupted voices brawl,
No conscience molten into gold,
No forged accuser bought or sold,
No cause deferred, no rain-spent journey;
For there Christ is the King's Attorney,
Who pleads for all without degrees,
And He hath angels, but no fees;
And when the grand twelve-million jury
Of our sins, with direful fury,
Against our souls black verdicts give,
Christ pleads His death, and then we live.

THE CONVERSION OF CHARLES COLSON

CHARLES COLSON

Here is Colson's own testimony. Here is the dramatic account of a person who won the prestigious Templeton Award because he was able to learn from Christ that those who serve are really greatest in the Kingdom of God.

I WORRIED WHETHER there had been something smug and self-righteous in saying "I *have* been converted." Can anyone really be sure that in fact he has been? Certainly I had accepted and fervently believed certain truths. Yet I was hardly a transformed person. All I could honestly say was that I was seeking, searching, trying, learning, failing and falling short, recovering and continuing to try—all the time reaching for a relationship with Jesus Christ. The change was in my spirit, in my attitudes, in the set of my will. Why should anyone believe me when I described it, and why should anyone accept my word that indeed the conversion was permanent? The skeptics had every right to say, "Let him show us by his deeds not by words."

I've discovered that the term *conversion* is misunderstood by many people. St. Paul's experience on the Damascus Road is the best known in all of history and books written about other conversions are similarly dramatic. Yet I am sure that most are simple, undramatic, and not newsworthy.

I was troubled, too, by the popular assumption that to be converted to Christ one must be driven to it by the most heinous and sinful past, one's conscience must be so guilt-ridden, his mischief so great that in an act of desperation he thrusts himself upon God's mercy. For days after the initial rash of stories, many, including the prosecutors, believed that I was on the verge of stepping forward to confess to all of the most dastardly sins of Watergate.

In a meeting that took place in Mr. Jaworski's office in late December, attended by Mr. Merrill and several young assistants, the subject of my much-publicized conversion was brought up.

"We've read about your experience," Merrill said. "We believe that you are sincere and that *now* you do want to come forward and tell us everything."

Merrill was sitting across from me at the big conference table in Jaworski's office. He lowered his eyes as he spoke, as if he wanted to spare me the embarrassment of staring at me while I told all. I looked to my left at Leon Jaworski; there was a faint enigmatic smile on his round face.

I knew, of course, what they expected. If my conversion was real I should tell them how guilty I had really been all this time. The only difficulty was that I had been trying to tell them the truth from the outset. They didn't believe it and hoped perhaps that God had now joined the Special Prosecutor's force to open me up. They were also saying, or so it seemed to me, that I could only prove the sincerity of my religious conviction by confessing to something I had previously withheld.

Anger welled up in me. "I didn't seek this publicity about my religion," I responded to Merrill. "And I don't intend to use it, but it shouldn't be used against me." Merrill quickly changed the subject; but I knew then and there that the publicity about my conversion had further eroded what little was left of my credibility with the prosecutors.

The other reactions ran the whole gamut. My mother was irate. "His father and I raised our boy as a good Christian. He was baptized and confirmed in the Episcopal Church. We taught him every Christian principle. Imagine saying he's just now become a Christian!" she lamented to a neighbor.

I tried to explain to my parents that while their efforts had been sincere, nothing had happened to me. It was my fault, not theirs.

One relative believed that the strain of Watergate had been too much. "I'm afraid poor Chuck has snapped, gone over the edge. This kind of religious fervor is often the sign of mental instability," she wrote a mutual friend.

The sharpest blow of all was inflicted on Wendell, then in his sophomore year at Princeton. He was, as he later recounted, studying quietly in his room when one of the girls down the hall (yes, coed dorms at Princeton), an active Campus Crusader, pounded excitedly on his door. "I just saw your father on television!" she exclaimed. "He is one of us; he has accepted Jesus Christ as his personal Saviour!"

It was for Wendell the last straw. It had been hard enough for a nineteen-year-old college student struggling for acceptability on campus to have a father accused day after day of one crime after another. But he was not prepared for this. Slapping his hand against his forehead he sighed, "Oh, no! Dad's a Jesus freak."

Dave Shapiro was predictably irate, storming into my office the morning after the first stories broke. "You've done it this time, Colson, you've really done it. I hope He [I assumed he meant Christ] can save your butt now because I can't."

"Calm yourself, Dave," I said. "I couldn't do a thing about it this time. We should have expected it one of these days."

"Calm myself?" he screamed, pounding his beefy fist on my desk. "Just when I thought we had the Ellsberg thing licked, just when you've been out of the press for a month, now this. It looks like the biggest 'dirty trick' you've ever pulled, the final big play for sympathy. It probably is. As far as I'm concerned they ought to indict you for this one." With that he stomped out of my office past Holly, whose fingers were plugged in her ears.

Old friends had the toughest time understanding it. Brad Morse, under-secretary-general of the United Nations, who thought he knew me as well as anyone, was visited one day by Jonathan Moore, my assistant in Saltonstall days and best man when Patty and I were married. Brad glared at Jonathan. "What's all this Jesus stuff about Colson: I have only been double-crossed twice in my life, both times by Christians. Do you think Chuck is okay?"

An intensely serious Harvard law student who had worked for me as an intern in the White House put it very bluntly: "Some of us knew, admired, and respected the Colson that 'was.' All this conversion talk, in addition to being pontifical, I frankly resent." The young man took it as a renunciation of my past, of which he considered himself a part.

Teamster President Frank Fitzsimmons, himself a deeply religious Catholic, was furious. "Those _____ in the press, nothing is sacred, nothing. Writing about a man's religion; that is the dirtiest, lowest thing of all."

And yet some of the press coverage was surprisingly sympathetic. Bill Greider, a reporter for the *Washington Post* authored a page-one feature article, detailing the history of my conversion, the relationship with

Hughes and the Monday prayer group. The Lord's ways are mysterious indeed: it had to be my sworn enemies on the *Post* who would write the first serious treatment of the subject. "Colson's spiritual awakening may not remedy any of his problems with the Watergate Grand Jury," Greider wrote, "but it does satisfy one group, the men who meet with him regularly for prayer at Harold Hughes' home." The understanding *Post* article, along with a sympathetic UPI story written by a young Christian, Wes Pippert, were carried in hundreds of papers across the country.

On Monday, December 17, Eric Sevareid devoted his entire commentary on the CBS evening news to the blizzard which had struck Washington that day—and the Colson conversion. An act of God, the snowstorm, he opined, had done more to save energy and to cleanse Washington's air than all the conservation legislation Congress was then scrambling to enact. As for the conversion, the other act of God, he said, "Mr. Charles Colson, once the toughest of the White House tough guys, and a man believed by many to be standin' in the need of prayer as well as a good defense lawyer, Mr. Colson has made page one with the news of his conversion to religion. He is not repenting of any alleged sin of a juridical nature, but he does confess that he was just too big for his britches. The new Colson does not claim the capacity to walk on water, but he has given up walking on grandmothers. A good many people here, anxious to believe in something, are quite willing to take Colson's change of heart as real. After all, that kind of change is what innumerable critics have been demanding all along. . . . Mr. Colson is clearly on the right track in more ways than one. An act of Congress has its place, but it's a simple act of God that gets results."

∾

JOHN WOOLMAN IS DEAD

JOHN WOOLMAN

The following is excerpted from Woolman's account of a vision he had during a time of serious illness.

I THEN HEARD a soft, melodious voice, more pure and harmonious than any I had heard with my ears before; I believed it was the voice of an angel who spoke to the other angels. The words were, "John Woolman is dead." I greatly wondered what that heavenly voice could mean.

I was then carried in spirit to the mines, where poor oppressed people were digging rich treasures for those called Christians, and heard them blaspheme the name of Christ, at which I was grieved, for his name to me was precious. Then I was informed that these heathens were told that those who oppressed them were the followers of Christ, and they said among themselves, "If Christ directed them to use us in this way, then Christ is a cruel tyrant."

All this time the song of the angel remained a mystery, and I was very desirous to get so deep that I might understand this mystery.

[After some physical recovery] . . . at length I felt divine power prepare my mouth that I could speak, and then I said, "I am crucified with Christ, nevertheless I live; yet not I, but Christ liveth in me, and the life I now live in the flesh [is] by faith in the Son of God, who loved me and gave himself for me" (Gal. 2:20, KJV). Then the mystery was opened, and I perceived there was joy in heaven over a sinner who had repented, and that the language "John Woolman is dead" meant no more than the death of my own will.

⌀

A SYMPOSIUM ON CHRIST'S LORDSHIP

JOHN BLANCHARD

As Christ is the root by which a saint grows, so is he the rule by which a saint walks.

Anonymous

He values not Christ at all who does not value Christ above all.

Saint Augustine

The Lord who vacated his tomb has not vacated his throne.

G. R. Beasley-Murray

Christ with anything would have satisfied me; nothing without Christ would do it.

Thomas Boston

Miss Christ and you miss all.

Thomas Brooks

The rattle without the breast will not satisfy the child; the house without the husband will not satisfy the wife; the cabinet without the jewel will not satisfy the virgin; the world without Christ will not satisfy the soul.

Thomas Brooks

They do not love Christ who love anything more than Christ.

Thomas Brooks

Jesus cannot be our Saviour unless he is first our Lord.

Hugh C. Burr

The system of human mediation falls away in the advent to our souls of the living Christ. Who wants stars, or even the moon, after the sun is up?

A. B. Cave

Christ is either both Saviour and Lord, or he is neither Saviour nor Lord.

John R. DeWitt

You cannot have the gifts of Christ apart from the government of Christ.

A. Lindsay Glegg

A Christ supplemented is a Christ supplanted.

William Hendriksen

Tomorrow's history has already been written . . . at the name of Jesus every knee must bow.

Paul E. Kauffman

There's not a thumb's breadth of this universe about which Jesus Christ does not say, "It is mine."

Abraham Kuyper

Seek Christ, and you will find him, and with him everything else thrown in.

C. S. Lewis

When Jesus Christ utters a word, he opens his mouth so wide that it embraces all heaven and earth, even though that word be but in a whisper.

Martin Luther

When we come to Jesus for salvation, we come to the one who is Lord over all. Any message omitting this truth cannot be called the gospel according to Jesus.

John F. MacArthur Jr.

I have a great need for Christ; I have a great Christ for my need.

Charles H. Spurgeon

To present Christ's lordship as an option leaves it squarely in the category of stereo equipment for a new car.

Dallas Willard

∾

PRAISE

CONSTANTINE THE GREAT

Constantine made Christianity the official religion of Rome following his conversion and victorious military campaigns at the beginning of the fourth century.

THUS DO WE render thanks to Thee, according to our feeble power, our God and Saviour, Christ; supreme Providence of the mighty Father, Who both savest us from evil, and impartest to us Thy most blessed doctrine: thus we essay, not indeed to celebrate Thy praise, but to speak the language of thanksgiving. For what mortal is he who shall worthily declare Thy praise, of Whom we learn that Thou didst from nothing call creation into being, and illumine it with Thy light: that Thou didst regulate the confusion of the elements, by the laws of harmony and order! But chiefly we mark Thy loving-kindness in that Thou hast caused those whose hearts inclined to Thee, to desire earnestly a divine and blessed life; and hast provided that, like merchants of true blessings, they might impart to many others the wisdom and happiness which they had received—themselves, meanwhile, reaping the everlasting fruit of virtue.

SAVED BY GRACE

KARL BARTH

In 1917, when allied forces were pounding the little German village of Safenwil, Karl Barth was the pastor of a church. At that time Barth was a very liberal churchman. He had been trained in theological schools that had taught him to doubt much of the biblical view of who Jesus was. Barth of his own confession had such a weak view of the divinity of Christ that he was not able to help the poor suffering people of his war-torn parish to overcome their difficulties and problems. Only as he came back to a view of Jesus that was more biblical was he able to give his people a view of Christ sufficient to help them in their time of need. In this inclusion, Barth shows us this new Christ that he gave not only to the people in his parish but to all throughout the Western world.

SOMEONE ONCE SAID to me, "I need not go to church. I need not read the Bible. I know already what the church teaches and what the Bible says: 'Do what is right and fear no one!'" Let me say this at this point: if this were the message at stake, I would most certainly not have come here. My time is too precious and so is yours. To say that, neither prophets nor apostles, neither Bible, Jesus Christ nor God are needed. Anybody is at liberty to say this to himself. By the same token this saying is void of any new, of any very special and exciting message. It does not help anyone. I have never seen a smile on the face of a person reassuring himself with this kind of talk . . . Let us hear therefore what the Bible says and what we as Christians are called to hear together: By grace you have been saved! No man can say this to himself. Neither can he say it to someone else. This can only be said by God to each one of us. It takes Jesus Christ to make this saying true . . .

You probably all know the legend of the rider who crossed the frozen Lake of Constance by night without knowing it. When he reached the opposite shore and was told whence he came, he broke down, horrified. This is the human situation when the sky opens and the earth is bright, when we may hear: By grace you have been saved! In such a moment we are like that terrified rider. When we hear this word we involuntarily look back, do we not, asking ourselves: Where have I been? Over an abyss, in mortal danger! What did I do? The most foolish thing I ever attempted! What happened? I was doomed and miraculously escaped and now I am safe! . . .

Look once again to Jesus Christ in his death upon the cross. Look and try to understand that what he did and suffered, he did and suffered for you, for me, for us all. He carried our sin, our captivity and our suffering, and did not carry it in vain. *He carried it away.* He acted as the captain of us all. He broke through the ranks of our enemies. He has already won the battle, our battle. All we have to do is to follow him, to be victorious with him. Through him, in him we are saved. Our sin no longer has any power over us. Our prison door is open . . . When he, the Son of God, sets us free, we are *truly* free.

❧

A PRESENT AND AN ARGUMENT

WILLIAM GRIFFIN

JESUS AND HIS friends were invited to Lazarus's house. Martha served dinner to the crowd. Everyone was relaxing after the meal when Mary came in from the kitchen with a pretty bottle.

"Aren't you going to clean the table?" asked Martha.

"I hope that's the dessert," said Lazarus.

Without saying a word, Mary went to Jesus and knelt down in front of him.

"Oooooh, that's cold," said Jesus.

She was pouring a bottle of perfume over his feet, and the smell filled the whole room.

"It cost a lot of money," said Judas. "I can tell by the smell."

Mary was wiping Jesus's feet dry with her hair.

"I just knew she'd pull a stunt like this," said Martha.

Mary whispered something to Jesus and then ran from the room.

"What was that all about?" asked Judas.

"Mary gave me a gift," said Jesus.

"Some gift that was," sniffed Judas. "She poured it all out, and now it's gone."

"What would you have done with the perfume?" asked Jesus.

"I would have sold it and given the money to the poor," said Judas.

"You can always give to the poor. . . ."

"But the money she paid for that bottle of perfume could have fed a family of four for eight weeks," said Judas.

"You won't be able to give me a present much longer," said Jesus.

"I don't know what you're talking about," said Judas.

"What Mary gave me was a goodbye present."

"She's crazy," said Judas.

"What are you going to give me before I say goodbye?" asked Jesus.

"You're crazy," said Judas.

"I just thought I'd ask."

"They're all crazy," said Judas as he stormed out into the night.

IF ANY REASON BE IN CHRIST

W. M. MACGREGOR

IT IS THOUGHTS of God's thinking which we need to set us right and, remember, they are not as our thoughts. A man cannot come to the great God and remain himself, little and mean and suspicious; he has to give up something, to clear his mind of something, to get another heart and other eyes. When a man does come to God, it is as if he looked from the other side of the sky, seeing the same things but from another standpoint. His fault which seemed excusable in a trivial earth is now serious and great; repentance, I suppose, is nothing else than the sight, for a moment, of sin as God sees it. And Jesus, the dim far-off figure, with a kind of idyllic charm and pathos about it, is seen with other eyes, seen now as God sees Him, in whom it pleased the Father that all fullness should dwell.

When my thoughts about life are put away that I may get God's thoughts, Christ becomes the gift of God's heart to me, a Deliverer in whom the power of my new life consists, an Enlightener from whom I learn how to think of God and man. "If any man be in Christ," says Paul, "he is a new creature: old things have passed away, behold they have become new." His former judgements, his estimate of great and small, are changed; he finds himself in a new washen earth. It is no power of earth that can work a change like that, but the redeeming will of God, who is able also to subdue all things unto Himself.

LOOKING BACK

JOHN CLIFFORD

LOOKING BACK UPON my past, upon these sixty years spent in Jesus Christ's school, I see many lessons badly learned, many blunders, innumerable faults, yet, scientifically interpreting the whole of the past, I say, with the full assurance of understanding, that all that there is in me, and has been in me, throughout these years, of any good, is due to Jesus Christ . . . whatsoever of value there has been in my life is due entirely to Him, whatsoever of service I have been able to perform for my generation owes all its inspiration, all its strength, to His indwelling. All the conceptions I have formed of God, the answers I am able to give for myself as to what is religion, human duty, human destiny, all that man may hope for, I get from Him who is the Way, the Truth, and the Life.

❧

THE MARTYRDOM OF POLYCARP

JOHN R. W. STOTT

The martyrs of the church are numerous. All Saints' Day, November 1, is the day given to the celebration of all who have been canonized as the great heroes of the faith and above all those who have paid for their faith with their blood. John R. W. Stott relates the tale of one of those who stood for Christ in the second century.

IT WAS 22 February, probably in the year A.D. 156. The venerable bishop, who had fled from the city at the entreaty of his congregation, was tracked down to his hiding-place. He made no attempt to flee. Instead, he offered food and drink to his captors and asked permission to retire for prayer, which he did for two hours. Then, as they drove into the city, the officer in charge urged him to recant. "What harm can it do," he asked, "to sacrifice to the emperor?" Polycarp refused. On arrival, he was roughly pushed out of the carriage, and brought before the proconsul in the amphitheatre, who addressed him: "Have respect to your old age . . . Swear by the genius of Caesar . . ." And again, "Swear, and I will release you; revile the Christ." To which Polycarp replied: "Eighty and six years have I served Him, and He has done me no wrong; how then can I blaspheme my King who saved me?" The proconsul persisted: "Swear by the genius of Caesar. . . . I have wild beasts; if you will not change your mind, I will throw you to them. . . ." "Bid them be brought. . . ." "As you despise the beasts, unless you change your mind, I make you to be destroyed by fire." Infuriated Jews and Gentiles gathered wood for the pile. Polycarp stood by the stake, asking not to be fastened to it, and prayed, "O Lord, Almighty God, the Father of Thy beloved Son Jesus Christ, through whom we have received a knowledge of Thee. . . . I thank Thee that Thou hast thought me worthy, this day and this hour, to share the cup of Thy Christ among the number of Thy witnesses!" The fire was kindled, but as the wind drove the flames away from him and prolonged his agony, a soldier's sword put an end to his misery.

HOW TO REIGN WITH CHRIST

AUTHOR UNKNOWN

FOCUS YOUR EYES as if you were looking at [your heart], right through the wall of your chest cavity. Try to visualize it as vividly as possible in your mind, and with your ears listen to the steady rhythm of its beating. When you have succeeded with this, then begin to repeat the words of the prayer, in accompaniment to each beat of your heart, keeping your eyes focused on it all the while. Thus with the first beat you will say, verbally or mentally, the word *Lord;* with the second, *Jesus;* with the third, *Christ;* with the fourth, *have mercy;* with the fifth, *on me.* Repeat this over and over again. It should be easy for you, since you have already learned the basics of the prayer of the heart. Eventually, when you get used to it, then you can begin to repeat the full Jesus Prayer in your heart, in time with a steady rhythm of inhaling and exhaling, as the Fathers taught. As you inhale, you visualize your heart and say, "Lord Jesus Christ." As you exhale, you say, "have mercy on me!" Do this as much and as often as you can, and soon you will experience a delicate but pleasant soreness in your heart, which will be followed by warmth and a warming tenderness in your heart. If you do this, with God's help you will attain to the delightful self-acting interior prayer of the heart. However, as you do all this, guard against mental imagings and any sort of visions. Reject everything your imagination produces, for the holy Fathers strictly teach that interior prayer must be a visionless exercise, lest one fall into delusion.

I MISSED HIM...FOUND HIM

GEORGE MACDONALD

I missed Him when the sun began to bend;
I found Him not when I had lost his rim;
With many tears I went in search of Him,
Climbing high mountains which did still ascend,
And gave me echoes when I called my friend;
Through cities vast and charnel-houses grim,
And high cathedrals where the light was dim,
Through books and arts and works without an end,
But found Him not—the friend whom I had lost.
And yet I found Him—as I found the lark,
A sound in fields I heard but could not mark;
I found Him nearest when I missed Him most;
I found Him in my heart, a life in frost,
A light I knew not till my soul was dark.

OPERATIONS OF DIVINE GRACE

JOHN WOOLMAN

THUS TIME PASSED ON: my heart was replenished with mirth and wantonness, and pleasing scenes of vanity were presented to my imagination, till I attained the age of eighteen years; near which time I felt the judgements of God in my soul like a consuming fire; and looking over my past life, the prospect was moving. I was often sad and longed to be delivered from these vanities; then again my heart was strongly inclined to them and there was in me a sore conflict; at times I turned to folly, and then again sorrow and confusion took hold of me. In a while, I resolved totally to leave off some of my vanities; but there was a secret reserve in my heart of the more refined part of them, and I was not low enough to find true peace. Thus for some months I had great troubles; there remaining in me an unsubjected will, which rendered my labours fruitless, till at length through the merciful continuance of heavenly visitations, I was made to bow down in spirit before the Lord. I remember one evening I had spent some time in reading a pious author; and, walking out alone, I humbly prayed to the Lord for His help, that I might be delivered from all those vanities which so ensnared me. Thus, being brought low, He helped me; and as I learned to bear the Cross, I felt refreshment to come from His presence; but, not keeping in that strength which gave victory I lost ground again; the sense of which greatly affected me; and I sought deserts and lonely places, and there with tears did confess my sins to God and humbly craved help of Him. And I may say with reverence, He was near to me in my troubles, and in those times of humiliation opened my ear to discipline. I was now led to look seriously at the means by which I was drawn from pure truth, and learned this—that if I would live in the life which the faithful servants of God lived in, I must not go into company as heretofore in my own will; but all the cravings of sense must be governed by a divine principle.

∽

CHRIST IN ME

MAJOR W. IAN THOMAS

IT IS OUR solemn responsibility, not only to present the Lord Jesus Christ as the One Who died historically to redeem sinners through His atoning sacrifice, but as a contemporary experience NOW—as the living Rock, the source of that "pure river of water of life, clear as crystal, proceeding out of the throne of God and of the Lamb" (Revelation 22: 1).

I am deeply grateful to those who introduced me to the Lord Jesus Christ as my Redeemer, but the one thing that they did not make adequately clear to me (because in all probability it was inadequately clear to them) was that the Christ who died *for* me, rose again to live *in* me. So, knowing Christ experientially only as the Way, it took seven weary years to come to know Him as my Life.

At the age of nineteen, training at London University to become a doctor in order to serve as a missionary in Africa, I knew that my life as a Christian was ineffective. I did not know of one single soul whom it had been my privilege to lead to Christ. I engaged in more than my share of Christian activity, and with genuine enthusiasm, but I knew that if I ever went as a missionary to Africa, I would be just as useless there.

It was out of a deep sense of need, as I despaired of my Christian life, that I made the startling discovery that for seven years I had missed the whole point of my salvation, that Christ had not died just to save me from hell and one day get me to heaven but that I might become available to Him—for Him to live His life through me.

For all those years I had known only the shadow of the smitten in Horeb, but now at last in the bright light of day, I stepped out by faith to speak to the living Rock, and life for me as a Christian was transformed; the rivers of living water began to flow.

∾

SAY, WHAT SAW YOU?

LIONEL JOHNSON

Say, what saw you, Man?
   And say, what heard?
I saw while Angels sang,
   Jesus the Word.

Saw you aught else, Man?
   Aught else heard you?
I saw the Son of Man,
   And the wind blew.

Saw you beside, Man?
   Or heard beside?
I saw, while murderers mocked
   The Crucified.

Nay! what is this, Man?
   And who is He?
The Holy Child must die
   For you and me.

Oh! say, Brother! Oh! say, Brother!
   What then shall be?
Home in his Sacred Heart
   For you and me.

Oh! what can we give, Brother!
   For such a thing?
Body and soul, Brother!
   To Christ the King.

FOR MY PART

DAVID LIVINGSTONE

David Livingstone is truly one of the remarkable missionaries of all time. Not only did he seek to bring Christ to the continent of Africa; he also succeeded at great personal cost in making maps and blazing the trail into the little known heart of what was then called the dark continent. But for all of his remarkable work in education and explora-tion, his heart remained captive to Jesus. So much so that when he died, at his own wish, his heart was buried in Africa.

FOR MY OWN part, I have never ceased to rejoice that God has appointed me to such an office. People talk of the sacrifice I have made in spending so much of my life in Africa. Can that be called a sacrifice which is simply paid back as a small part of a great debt owing to our God, which we can never repay? Is that a sacrifice which brings its own blest reward in healthful activity, the consciousness of doing good, peace of mind, and a bright hope of a glorious destiny hereafter? Away with the word in such a view, and with such a thought! It is emphatically no sacrifice. Say rather it is a privilege. Anxiety, sickness, suffering, or danger, now and then, with a foregoing of the common conveniences and charities of this life, may make us pause, and cause the spirit to waver, and the soul to sink; but let this be only for a moment. All these are nothing when compared with the glory which shall hereafter be revealed in, and for, us. I never made a sacrifice. Of this we ought not to talk, when we remember the great sacrifice which He made who left His Father's throne on high to give Himself for us; "who being the brightness of that Father's glory, and the express image of his person, and upholding all things by the word of his power, when he had by himself purged our sins, sat down on the right hand of the Majesty on high."

∾

CHRIST'S CONTINUED REIGN

FRANK C. LAUBACH

WE SEE OURSELVES on trial with Jesus. He could walk into the jaws of death to do His blessed work for others. He could dare to speak out against wrong and take the consequences. He could receive floggings, could allow men to spit in His face, could endure the agony of thorns in His head, could be taunted without a word or even a thought of anger, could think of His mother while writhing on the cross, could cry, "Father, forgive them, they know not what they do." I have read books which said that these words were evidently imaginary for nobody could say anything when suffering the excruciating torture of hanging by nails. But Jesus was such an "impossible" person more than once in His life. This scene fits into His whole character. True, nobody else can think of others when suffering like that, but Jesus was better than the rest of us. Tragedy, magnificent horror! The best man who ever lived dying because He was too good to run away.

That would have driven humanity more deeply into despair. They might or might not have remembered Jesus. I think they would have tried to forget Him. For humanity wants to believe that God is good, and the crucifixion portrays God forsaking the finest example of loyalty we can find. God was betraying His staunchest defender. That cross alone is horrible. The God who would allow the drama to stop there would be a monster. "My God, why . . ."

So we cannot believe in a good God unless we have Easter. It is a difficult story to believe, because we have had nothing else quite like it before or since. But it is only the difficulty of believing the unprecedented. On the other hand to doubt it is far more difficult. I must either rule out the whole story of the life of Jesus or else rule out any intelligence or heart from the universe. And if I do that my troubles are far more than intellectual—they become moral. I cannot actually sacrifice myself for others, at least not to death, for, noble as it may sound, it is folly. The act of Jesus becomes not only rash and useless but misleading to the rest of mankind.

"How it is proved? It isn't proved, you fool! It can't be proved. How can you prove a victory before it's won? How can you prove a man who leads to be a leader worth following unless you follow to the death, and out beyond mere death, which is not anything but Satan's lie upon eternal life. . . . And you? You want to argue. Well, I won't. It's a choice, and I choose Christ."

That last sentence is the crux of the whole matter; it is a choice, and while choosing Christ brings mystery, rejecting Him brings despair.

THE LIVING ONE

CHARLES H. SPURGEON

LOOK TO THE living One for life. Look to Jesus for all you need between the gate of hell and the gate of heaven.

∾

QUO VADIS?

HENRYK SIENKIEWICZ

Outside of Rome on the Appian Way, there exists a small chapel called the Chapel of the Quo Vadis. In this small chapel is a pair of footprints cast in hard form, which are believed by many to be the footprints of Christ. The story gathers around a tale of Christian persecution under Nero. It is said that as Nero's persecutions grew intense, the church became intensely concerned about the leadership of Peter, the apostle. They believed that ultimately Peter, who would have been considered a real prize by the Praetorian Guard, would be put to death. Peter's martyrdom would hamstring the church, depriving it of real leadership. The church urged Peter to leave the city and return once the mass killings were over. Peter obeyed. On the way out of the city, however, he was met by the Savior, who was apparently going into the city. "Where are you going, Master?" ("Quo vadis, Domine?") Peter asked him. Jesus replied that he was going back into the city to be killed all over again if Peter left Rome. Peter therefore returned to Rome, where he was soon captured and martyred by inverted crucifixion. Henryk Sienkiewicz, the Polish novelist (1846–1916), took this tale and wove it into his powerful classic, Quo Vadis?

FOR A LONG time Apostle Peter did not venture to appear at the house of Petronius, but when one evening Nazarius announced his arrival, Lygia and Vinicius ran to meet him, fell to his feet, and greeted him with great alarm. Few Christians remained and they feared for his safety. Vinicius insisted on his going with them to Naples, where they would meet Pomponia, and then to Sicily, but the Apostle stoutly resisted the temptation, although he was in danger of being momentarily apprehended. Petronius brought the terrible news that letters were found upon one of Caesar's freedmen from Peter, Paul of Tarsus, Judas, and John. Peter's coming to Rome was known to Tigellinus, but he was supposed to have perished with the other Christians. Now it was determined to uproot and exterminate the remainder of the hated sect by consigning the two leaders to the cross.

Vinicius, when he heard of it, went with Ursus to Miriam's house on the edge of the Trans-Tiber, where he found Peter surrounded by a group of the faithful. Timothy, Paul's assistant, and Linus were also at his side. It appearing unsafe, they all went to the quarry in a waste part of the land. There they tried to persuade the Apostle of the necessity of saving himself by going to Sicily.

With tears in their eyes they surrounded him and entreated in the name of Christ,—

"Hide thyself, teacher, and lead us away from the power of the 'Beast.'"

"Look at our tears!"

Tears came to the eyes of Peter. He rose, stretched his hands over the kneeling Christians, and said:

"May the name of the Lord be blessed, and may His will be done!"

At dawn of the following day, two dark figures were moving along the Appian road toward the ruins of the Campania.

They were Nazarius and Peter, leaving Rome and their coreligionists, who were destined to end their days in torture.

The sun appeared from behind the mountains, and at the same time the Apostle was staggered by a strange vision. It seemed to him that the golden circle, instead of rising, was coming down the mountain and advancing on the road.

Peter stopped and asked:

"Dost thou see the light approaching us?"

"I do not see anything," answered Nazarius.

Peter shaded his eyes with his hand, and after a while said:

"Some one is approaching us in the glare of the sun."

But not the slightest sound was heard. Perfect stillness reigned. He looked at the Apostle, and exclaimed with alarm,—

"Teacher! What ails thee?"

The staff fell from Peter's hand, his eyes looked immovably forward, his lips parted, and wonder, gladness and ecstasy were depicted on his face. Suddenly he fell on his knees, stretched forward his hand, and cried:

"Christ! Christ!"

And he threw himself on the ground, as if to kiss some one's feet.

He was silent for a long time, then were heard the words of the old man, broken by sobs,—

"Quo vadis, Domine?"

A sad and gentle voice reached his ears,—

"If thou hast deserted my people, then I am going to Rome to be crucified anew."

The Apostle lay on the ground without motion or speech. Nazarius thought that he had died or fainted, but Peter finally rose, and, taking his staff, turned toward the seven hills of the city.

The boy, seeing this, repeated,—

"Quo vadis, Domine?"

"To Rome," answered the Apostle, in a low voice.

❧

BETRAYED

CHARLES H. SPURGEON

"Are you betraying the Son of Man with a kiss?"
Luke 22:48

"THE KISSES OF an enemy are deceitful" (Proverbs 27:6). We need to be on guard when the world puts on a loving face. For just as the world betrayed our Master, it will betray us with a kiss.

Whenever people are about to stab Christianity they often profess a great reverence for it. Beware of the sleek-faced hypocrisy that is the armorbearer of heresy and infidelity. Be aware of how deceptive the unrighteous are and be "wise as serpents" (Matthew 10:16), in order to detect and avoid the plans of the enemy.

The young man without understanding was led astray by the kiss of a strange woman (Proverbs 7:13). May we be graciously instructed today so that the "flattering lips" of the world will not affect us (Proverbs 7:21). Holy Spirit, do not let us be betrayed with a kiss!

What if I should be guilty of the same accursed sin as Judas? I have been baptized in the name of the Lord Jesus. I am a member of His visible church. I take communion. All of these are kisses of my lips. Am I sincere? If not, I am a base traitor.

Do I live in the world as carelessly as unbelievers and yet profess to follow Jesus? If so, then I expose my belief to ridicule and cause people to speak evil of the holy name by which I am called. Surely if I act inconsistently I am a Judas, and "it would have been good for that man if he had never been born" (Mark 14:21).

Oh Lord, make me sincere and true. Preserve me from every false way. Never let me betray my Savior. I love you Jesus, and though I often grieve You my desire is to be faithful to death. Amen.

Oh God, forbid that I would be a high soaring professing Christian and then fall into the lake of fire (Revelation 20:10) because I betrayed my Master with a kiss. Amen.

❧

Now It Is Our Turn

CARDINAL JOHN HENRY NEWMAN

In this inclusion Cardinal John Henry Newman reminds the church that we are to follow Christ even unto the giving of our lives.

ONCE IT WAS the Apostles' turn. It was St. Paul's turn once. He had all cares upon him all at once; covered from head to foot with cares, as Job with sores. And, as if all this were not enough, he had a thorn in the flesh added—some personal discomfort ever with him. Yet he did his part well —he was as a strong and bold wrestler in his day, and at the close of it was able to say, "I have fought a good fight, I have finished my course, I have kept the faith." And after him, the excellent of the earth, the white-robed army of martyrs, and the cheerful company of confessors, each in his turn, each in his day, have likewise played the man. And so down to this very time, when faith has well-nigh failed, first one and then another have been called out to exhibit before the Great King. It is as though all of us were allowed to stand round his throne at once, and He called on first this man, and then that, to take up the chant by himself, each in his turn having to repeat the melody which his brethren have before gone through. Or as if we held a solemn dance to His honour in the courts of heaven, and each had by himself to perform some one and the same solemn and graceful movement at a signal given. Or as if it were some trial of strength or of agility, and, while the ring of bystanders beheld and applauded, we in succession, one by one, were actors in the pageant. Such is our state; angels are looking on, Christ has gone before—Christ has given us an example, that we may follow in His steps. He went through far more, infinitely more, than we can be called to suffer. Our brethren have gone through much more; and they seem to encourage us by their success, and to sympathize in our essay. Now it is our turn; and all ministering spirits keep silence and look on. O let not your foot slip, or your eye be false or your ear dull, or your attention flagging!

❧

CHRIST IN THE LIFE

THOMAS EDWARD BROWN

The poet Brown, it is said, was walking along the beach one day when he spied a conch lying in the sand. He picked the shell up and passed it to his ear to "hear the sea roar." But as he passed the supposedly empty shell past his face the spidery little legs of a sand crab came out of the shell and nearly nipped his cheek as it passed his face. He removed the shell to arm's length and studied the shell carefully. He realized that the old monopod who had originally lived in and built the strong shell had died. A much more fragile creature, realizing how secure he might be in such a strong house, had moved in and taken a step in favor of his own security and endurance. The poet considered this incident to be a metaphor of the Christian life and wrote the following poem.

If thou couldst empty all thyself of self,
Like to a shell dishabited,
Then might He find thee on the Ocean shelf,
And say—"This is not dead,"—
And fill thee with Himself instead.

But thou art all replete with very *thou,*
And hast such shrewd activity,
Then, when He comes, He says:—"This is now
Unto itself—T'were better let it be:
It is so small and full, there is no room for me."

HOW WE BLOCK CHRIST'S ADVANCE

WILLIAM TEMPLE

HOW, IN FACT, do we block His advance? Partly, of course, by sheer resistance. We definitely desire that He should not yet take charge of some parts of our lives; we are like St. Augustine when he caught himself praying, "Give me chastity, but not yet." We want to indulge a little longer. There is no need to dwell on this. We know that it is wrong, and at least in our better moments set ourselves to undermine the barriers which in our worse moments we erect. But there is another way of blocking the divine grace. We block it by failure of expectation. Of course this is just one form of lack of faith. But it is so purely negative that it escapes detection. Moreover, there is a common belief among devout people that if we are personally devoted to Christ, His Presence will entirely purify us and put us right in every relation of life. Experience shows that this is simply not true. Devotion to Christ will win from Him purification from those faults of which we are already aware; it will also quicken our consciences and make us aware of others besides. But it does not at all invariably do this with completeness, especially where sins of omission are concerned. It was possible during the war to hear utterances from unquestionably devout and even holy persons, which showed that they had no inkling of the fact that Christ commanded them to feel charity for the Germans. We look back now with amazement to the attitude adopted by such saints as Wilberforce and Hannah More towards the sufferings of the poor in the early days of the Industrial Revolution. For saints they were; but they none the less had their blind spots; and blind they remained despite their saintliness.

❧

JOSEPH THE MASAI

MICHAEL CARD

JOSEPH IS A tall, slender man, like most Masai. He is a warrior. His face bears the ritual scars every young man receives after killing his first lion with only a spear and shield. But the scars on his face and his ordeal with the lion are not what make Joseph special.

• • •

The story began when Joseph, who was walking along one of those hot, dusty African roads, met someone who shared the good news of Jesus Christ with him. Then and there he accepted Jesus as his Lord and Savior. The power of the Spirit began transforming his life. He was filled with such excitement and joy that the first thing he wanted to do was return to his own village and share the good news with the members of his local tribe.

Joseph began going door-to-door, telling everyone he met about the cross of Jesus and the salvation it offered, expecting to see their faces light up the way his had. To his amazement the villagers not only didn't care, they became hostile. The men of the village seized him, holding him to the ground, while the women began to beat him with strands of barbed wire. He was dragged from the village and left to die alone in the bush.

Joseph somehow managed to crawl to a water hole, and there, after two days of passing in and out of consciousness, found he had the strength to get up. He still wondered about the hostile reception he had received from the people he had known all his life. He decided he must have left something out or told the story of Jesus wrong. After rehearsing the message he had first heard he decided to go back to the village and share his faith once more.

Joseph limped back into the circle of huts and began again to proclaim the good news about Jesus. "He died for you, so that you might find forgiveness and come to know the living God," he pleaded. Once again he was grabbed by the men of the village and held while the women beat him a second time, opening up wounds that had only just begun to heal. Once more they dragged him, unconscious, from the village and left him to die.

To have survived the first beating was truly remarkable. To live through the second was a miracle. Again, days later, Joseph awoke in the wilderness, bruised and scarred and yet determined to go back.

For the third time he returned to the small village. This time he found everyone waiting for him. They attacked him before he even had a chance to open his mouth. As they began to flog him for the third and probably last time, he began again to speak to them of Jesus Christ, the Lord, who had the power to forgive sin and give them new life. The last thing he remembered before he passed out was seeing the women who were beating him begin to weep.

This time he awoke in his own bed, not in the wilderness. The very ones who had so severely beaten him were now trying to save his life and nurse him back to health. The entire village had come to Christ.

DEATH OF DR. JOHNSON

JAMES BOSWELL

FOR SOME TIME before his death all his fears were calmed and absorbed by the prevalence of his faith, and his trust in the merits and *propitiation* of Jesus Christ.

He talked to me often about the necessity of faith in the *sacrifice* of Jesus, as necessary beyond all good works whatever, for the salvation of mankind.

He pressed me to study Dr. Clarke and to read his Sermons. I asked him why he pressed Dr. Clarke, an Arian. "Because," said he, "he is fullest on the propitiatory sacrifice."

Johnson having thus in his mind the true Christian scheme, at once rational and consolatory, uniting justice and mercy in the DIVINITY, with the improvement of human nature, previous to his receiving the Holy Sacrament in his apartment, composed and fervently uttered this prayer:

"Almighty and most merciful Father, I am now, as to human eyes, it seems, about to commemorate, for the last time, the death of thy Son Jesus Christ, our Saviour and Redeemer. Grant, O Lord, that my whole hope and confidence may be in His merits, and Thy mercy; enforce and accept my unperfect repentance; make this commemoration available to the confirmation of my faith, the establishment of my hope, and the enlargement of my charity; and make the death of Thy Son Jesus Christ effectual to my redemption. Have mercy upon me, and pardon the multitude of my offences. Bless my friends; have mercy upon all men. Support me, by Thy Holy Spirit, in the days of weakness, and at the hour of death; and receive me, at my death, to everlasting happiness, for the sake of Jesus Christ. Amen."

Having, as has been already mentioned, made his will on the 8th and 9th December, and settled all his worldly affairs, he languished till Monday, the 13th of that month, when he expired, about seven o'clock in the evening, with so little apparent pain that his attendants hardly perceived when his dissolution took place.

AMAZING GRACE!

JOHN NEWTON

John Newton among all the hymnists has a most colorful background. He was of his own testimony a lecherous and foul-mouthed sailor who later became a slaver, buying and transporting and selling slaves in other parts of the world. But during a storm at sea, when his life seemed all but gone, he cried out to Jesus, who saved him from his sin and wasted life. He gave up his slaving and other debaucheries and became not just a Christian but ultimately an Anglican cleric. Yet he seemed never able to stop being overwhelmed by the grace, the unde-served love, of God, which was a lifelong theme of his. Out of that deep gratitude to Jesus for changing all of his degradation for salvation and a calling in the church, he wrote the poem "Amazing Grace." Once a hymn, it became perhaps the best-known hymn in the world, sung by all Christians of all denominations. It has been bagpiped in Scotland and harped in symphony halls. It has been popularly recorded and sung at state funerals. It is apparent that most Christians agree with John Newton on the subject of the joyous, if undeserved, love of God.

Amazing grace! how sweet the sound
That saved a wretch like me!
I once was lost, but now am found,
Was blind, but now I see.

'Twas grace that taught my heart to fear,
And grace my fears relieved;
How precious did that grace appear
The hour I first believed!

Through many dangers, toils, and snares
I have already come;
'Tis grace hath brought me safe thus far,
And grace will lead me home.

When we've been there ten thousand years,
Bright shining as the sun,
We've no less days to sing God's praise
Than when we first begun.

POTENTATE

HERBERT C. GABHART

*"Which in his times he shall shew, who is the blessed
and only* Potentate.*"*
1 Timothy 6:15

A POTENTATE is one who possesses great power, who can rule with independent right and absolute authority. Has there ever been one of earth? No! Only Jesus. I shall mention, however, for comparison, three who tried.

King Tutankhamen of Egypt tried to leave his mark by the elegance of his throne and the richness which attended his funeral. Howard Carter, in 1922, unearthed part of his tomb. King Tut was buried in three coffins, one of solid gold surrounded by precious jewels. Jesus was buried in a borrowed tomb.

Louis XIV, called the Grand Monarch, the "Sun King," reigned seventy-two years—the longest in French history and possibly the world to date. He built the renowned Palace of Versailles. Jesus lived to the age of thirty-three with only three years of public service. He had not where to lay His head.

Ivan IV, called "Ivan the Terrible," was the first ruler of Russia to take the title of Czar. He did much for his country, cruel as he was. In his later years, he became violent and fierce. He accidentally killed his son and in repentance became a monk shortly before he died. God gave His son who did not withdraw from the world but walked among the poor, the downtrodden and the sinful.

The only kingdom Jesus sought to expand was the kingdom of God within the hearts of His followers. He built no palace to be remembered by. He extended no physical boundary lines. He is building heavenly mansions for us and extending the horizons of our souls.

What a loving and gracious Potentate!

A SELF-DEDICATION

JONATHAN EDWARDS

SATURDAY, 12 JANUARY 1723, in the morning. I have this day solemnly renewed my baptismal covenant and self-dedication, which I renewed when I was received into the communion of the church. I have been before God; and have given myself, all that I am and have to God, so that I am not in any respect my own. I can claim no right in myself, no right in this understanding, this will, these affections that are in me; neither have I any right to this body or any of its members; no right to this tongue, these hands nor feet; no right to these senses, these eyes, these ears, this smell or taste. I have given myself clear away. . . . This I have done. And I pray God, for the sake of Christ, to look upon it as a self-dedication; and to receive me now as entirely His own, and deal with me in all respects as such; whether He afflicts me or prospers me, or whatever He pleases to do with me, who am His. Now henceforth I am not to act in any respect as my own. I shall act as my own, if I ever make use of any of my powers to anything that is not to the glory of God, or do not make the glorifying of Him my whole and entire business; if I murmur in the least at afflictions; if I grieve at the prosperity of others; if I am any way uncharitable; if I am angry because of injuries; if I revenge my own cause; if I do anything purely to please myself, or avoid anything for the sake of my ease, or omit anything because it is great self-denial; if I trust to myself; if I take any of the praise of any good that I do, or rather God does by me; or if I am in any way proud.

❧

LOVE (III)

GEORGE HERBERT

Love bade me welcome: yet my soul drew back,
　　Guilty of dust and sin.
But quick-eyed Love, observing me grow slack
　　From my first entrance in,
Drew nearer to me, sweetly questioning
　　If I lacked anything.

"A guest," I answered, "worthy to he here":
　　Love said, "You shall be he."
"I, the unkind, ungrateful? Ah, my dear,
　　I cannot look on thee."
Love took my hand, and smiling did reply,
　　"Who made the eyes but I?"

"Truth, Lord; but I have marred them; let my shame
　　Go where it doth deserve."
"And know you not," says Love, "who bore the blame?"
　　"My dear, then I will serve."
"You must sit down," says Love, "and taste my meat."
　　So I did sit and eat.

❧

ON HIS BAPTISMAL BIRTHDAY

SAMUEL TAYLOR COLERIDGE

In this selection Coleridge celebrates, not his physical birthday, but his spiritual birthday. Christians who come to faith often distinguish the day they were born from the day they were born again (John 3:3). The teaching of the church has always been that those who are born again become brothers and sisters with Christ by adoption (Romans 8:15–16). At that moment of becoming a Christian, one becomes a part of the family of God. It is that moment, Coleridge's baptismal moment, that he celebrates as a birthday of joy.

God's child in Christ adopted—Christ my all—
What that earth boasts were not lost cheaply, rather
Than forfeit that blessed name, by which I call
The Holy One, the Almighty God, my Father?
Father! in Christ we live, and Christ in thee,
Eternal Thou, and everlasting we.
The heir of heaven, henceforth I fear not death;
In Christ I live! in Christ I draw the breath
Of the true life! Let then, earth, sea, and sky
Make war against me; on my front I show

Their mighty Master's seal. In vain they try
To end my life, that can but end its woe.
Is that a deathbed where a Christian lies?
Yes, but not his—'Tis death itself there dies.

ﾠ

THE WIDENESS OF GOD'S MERCY

JOHN DONNE

As THOSE BLESSED Fathers of tender bowels enlarged themselves in this distribution and apportioning [of] the mercy of God that it consisted best with the nature of His mercy, that as His saints had suffered temporal calamities in this world, in this world they should be recompensed with temporal abundances, so did they enlarge this mercy farther, and carry it even to the Gentiles, to the pagans that had no knowledge of Christ in any established Church. You shall not find a Trismegistus, a Numa Pompilius, a Plato, a Socrates, for whose salvation you shall not find some Father, or some ancient and reverend author, an advocate. . . . St. Dionyse the Areopagite says that from the beginning of the world God hath called some men of all nations, and of all sorts, by the ministry of angels, though not by the ministry of the Church. To me, to whom God hath revealed His Son, in a Gospel, by a Church, there can be no way of salvation but by applying that Son of God, by that Gospel, in that Church. Nor is there any other foundation for any, nor other name by which any man can be saved, but the name of Jesus. But how this foundation is presented, and how this name of Jesus is notified, to them amongst whom there is no Gospel preached, no Church established, I am not curious in inquiring. I know God can be as merciful as those tender Fathers present Him to be; and I would be as charitable as they are. And therefore, humbly embracing that manifestation of His Son which He hath afforded me, I leave God to His unsearchable ways of working upon others, without further inquisition.

JESUS' CONTINUING REIGN

BLAISE PASCAL

In 1654 Pascal seems to have experienced an immersion in the joy of Christ. While he never spoke of this during his lifetime, the following testimony was found as a written item sewed into the lining of his coat. It was discovered only after his death.

The year of grace 1654.

   Monday, 23 November, feast of Saint Clement, Pope and Martyr, and
      of others in the Martyrology.
   Eve of Saint Chrysogonus, Martyr, and others.
   From about half past ten in the evening until half past midnight.
                                    Fire
         "God of Abraham, God of Isaac, God of Jacob," not of
      philosophers and scholars.
   Certainty, certainty, heartfelt, joy, peace.
   God of Jesus Christ.
   God of Jesus Christ.
   My God and your God.
   "Thy God shall be my God."
   The world forgotten, and everything except God.
   He can only be found by the ways taught in the Gospels.
   Greatness of the human soul.
   "O righteous Father, the world has not known thee, but I have known
      thee."
   Joy, joy, joy, tears of joy.
   I have cut off myself from him.
   They have forsaken me, the fountain of living waters.
   "My God wilt thou forsake me?"
   Let me not be cut off from him for ever!
   "And this is life eternal, that they might know thee, the only true
      God, and Jesus Christ whom thou has sent."
   Jesus Christ.
   Jesus Christ.
   I have cut myself off from him, shunned him, denied him, crucified him.
   Let me never be cut off from him!
   He can only be kept by the ways taught in the Gospel.
   Sweet and total renunciation.
   Total submission to Jesus Christ and my director.
   Everlasting joy in return for one day's effort on earth.
   I will not forget thy word. Amen.

GOD'S RIGHT

SAINT BERNARD OF CLAIRVAUX

GOD CERTAINLY IS well within His rights in claiming to Himself the works of His own hands, the gifts Himself has given! How should the thing made fail to love the Maker, provided that it have from Him the power to love at all? How should it not love Him with all its powers, since only by His gift has it got anything? Man, called into being out of nothing by God's free act and raised to such high honour, how patent is his debt of love to God's most just demand! How vastly God has multiplied His mercy too, in saving man and beast in such a way! Why, we had turned our glory into the likeness of a calf that eateth hay; our sin had brought us to the level of the beasts that know not God at all! If then I owe myself entire to my Creator, what shall I give my Re-creator more? The means of our remaking too, think what they cost! It was far easier to make than to redeem; for God had but to speak the word and all things were created, I included; but He who made me by a word, and made me once for all, spent on the task of my re-making many words and many marvellous deeds, and suffered grievous and humiliating wrongs.

What reward therefore shall I give the Lord for all the benefits that He has done to me? By His first work He gave me to myself; and by the next He gave Himself to me.

∽

O FOR A THOUSAND TONGUES

CHARLES WESLEY

Charles Wesley, brother to John Wesley who founded Methodism, seems to have been the most poetic in the family, writing thousands of poems, many of which ultimately became hymns for all Christian churches.

> O for a thousand tongues to sing
> My great Redeemer's praise,
> The glories of my God and King,
> The triumphs of His grace.

My gracious Master and my God,
O help me to proclaim,
To spread through all the earth abroad
The honors of Thy name.

Jesus! the Name that charms our fears,
That bids our sorrows cease;
Tis music in the sinner's ears,
Tis life and health and peace.

He breaks the power of canceled sin,
He sets the prisoner free;
His blood can make the foulest clean;
His blood availed for me.

Hear Him, ye deaf; His praise, ye dumb,
Your loosened tongues employ;
Ye blind, behold your Savior come,
And leap, ye lame, for joy!

SOMETIMES TO BE RECKLESS

W. M. MACGREGOR

JESUS DID LOVE a man who was able, sometimes, to be reckless. He did not care for the rulers as a class, but when one of them forgot his dignity, and ran after a peasant teacher and fell on the road at His feet, we read that "Jesus, seeing him, loved him." He did not choose for His disciples discreet and futile persons, but a man whose temper was not always under control, and whose tongue was rough when he was roused, and another who might have been a saint, but his life got twisted and he betrayed his Lord. He saw a widow flinging into the treasury all that she had, which no doubt was a very foolish action, but it stirred His heart with gladness to see somebody venturing herself simply upon God. He wanted life in men, energy, impulse; and in His Church He has often found nothing but a certain tame decorum, of which even He can make little.

• • •

He sought out in the world all people of affluent nature, not chilled by learning or manners, but with some voice of the heart in them, and where He found such He had hope. I wish His Church could learn the lesson from Him, and could make access easier for the multitude of enjoying natures in whose companionship He found such pleasure. For about them He held the conviction that, even though they may have fallen to be last, it is in them by His grace to be first, true saints, the splendour and light of His kingdom.

∾

I MET THE MASTER

AUTHOR UNKNOWN

This poem expresses the missionary impact of conversion. Almost all who discover any great truth or person are anxious to make others aware of their good fortune. This popular Christian poem celebrates the missionary fervor that follows conversion.

I had walked life's way with an easy tread,
Had followed where comfort and pleasures led.
Until one day in a quiet place
I met the Master face to face.

With station and rank and wealth for my goal,
Much thought for my body but none for my soul,
I had entered to win in life's mad race,
When I met the Master face to face.

I met Him, and knew Him and blushed to see
That His eyes full of sorrow were fixed on me;
And I faltered and fell at His feet that day,
While my castles melted and vanished away.

Melted and vanished and in their place
Naught else did I see but the Master's face.
And I cried aloud, "Oh, make me meet
To follow the steps of Thy wounded feet."

My thought is now for the souls of men,
I have lost my life to find it again,
E'er since one day in a quiet place
I met the Master face to face.

❧

PALM SUNDAY

MARTIN LUTHER

LOOK AT CHRIST. He rides not upon a horse which is a steed of war. He comes not with appalling pomp and power but sits upon an ass, which is a gentle beast to bear burdens and to work for men. From this we see that Christ comes not to terrify, to drive, and oppress, but to help and to take for himself our load. We read further that he came from the Mountain of Olives. Now the oil of the olive was the symbol of that which soothes. His entry was marked not by the clash of weapons and the cries of war, but by singing, praise, rejoicing, and the blessing of God.

"THY KING COMETH UNTO THEE."

Observe that he comes. You do not seek him; he seeks you. You do not find him; he finds you. The preachers come from him, not from you, and their preaching comes from him and not from you. Your faith comes, not from you, but from him.

He is lowly. This brings us from faith to the example of love. Christ gives you faith with all its benefits, and you are to give your neighbor love with all its benefits. You may then ask what are the good works which you should do for your neighbor? They have no name. Just as the good works which Christ has done for you have no name, so the good works which you do for your neighbor have no name. How, then, are they to be recognized? Answer: they have no name for this reason, lest they be divided and this done and that left undone. Rather you must give yourself to your neighbor utterly, just as Christ did not confine himself to prayer and fasting for you. These are not the works which he did for you, but he gave himself completely not only with prayer and fasting, with all works and suffering, so that there was nothing in him that was not made yours and done for you. So this is not your good work, that you should give alms or pray, but rather that you should give yourself entirely to your neighbor, as he needs and as you can, with alms, prayer, fasting, counsel, comfort, teaching, appeal, reproof, pardon, clothes, food, and also suffering and death on his behalf. But tell me, where in all Christendom are such works?

∾

JOHN WESLEY'S HEART STRANGELY WARMED

JOHN WESLEY

Wesley was a wandering Oxford scholar always eager to learn more and more about God and at the same time eager to experience the bliss of inner relationship with Christ. His hungers led him to form the Holy Club while at Oxford. This group of devout young scholars prayed and studied God's word so that they might "draw ever closer" to Jesus. This hunger to know Jesus in greater levels of spiritual intimacy and love at last called Wesley to Georgia, where he purposed to convert the Indians to Christ. But he was not effective as a missionary, because the hunger for Jesus he felt had never led him to a real conversion. On his way back to England, he fell in with Moravians, who during a storm at sea gave evidence of having great inner peace when the rest of the passengers were in a fearful state of panic. Wesley determined that he wanted the peace that these Moravian missionaries knew, and he felt very guilty about his failure to be an effective missionary. His hungers of heart were all resolved when he passed a Moravian chapel in Aldersgate. There he finally came to know the experience of genuine conversion. His new life in Christ inflamed Wesley with evangelism and zeal, and millions were ultimately received into what became known as the Methodist church. Wesley's experience is taken from his journal. He kept this journal all his life. In it he faithfully wrote down his adventurous life as a seeker, a Christian, and finally a preacher.

I THINK IT was about five this morning that I opened my Testament on those words, "There are given unto us exceeding great and precious promises, even that ye should be partaken of the divine nature." Just as I went out, I opened it again on those words, "Thou art not far from the kingdom of God." In the afternoon I was asked to go to St. Paul's. The anthem was, "Out of the deep have I called unto thee, O Lord. O let thine ears consider well the voice of my complaint. If thou, Lord, wilt be extreme to mark what is done amiss, O Lord, who may abide it? For there is mercy with thee; therefore shalt thou be feared. O Israel, trust in the Lord: for with the Lord there is mercy, and with him is plenteous redemption. And he shall redeem Israel from all his sins."

In the evening I went very unwillingly to a society in Aldersgate Street, where one was reading Luther's preface to the Epistle to the Romans. About a quarter before nine, while he was describing the change which God works in the heart through faith in Christ, I felt my heart strangely warmed. I felt I did trust in Christ, Christ alone, for my salvation; and an assurance was given me that He had taken away my sins, even mine, and saved me from the law of sin and death.

❧

JESUS SHALL REIGN WHERE'ER THE SUN

ISAAC WATTS

Jesus shall reign where'er the sun
Does his successive journeys run;
His Kingdom stretch from shore to shore,
Till moons shall wax and wane no more.

People and realms of every tongue
Dwell on His love with sweetest song,
And infant voices shall proclaim
Their early blessings on His Name.

Blessings abound where'er He reigns;
The prisoner leaps to lose his chains,
The weary find eternal rest,
And all the sons of want are blest.

Let every creature rise and bring
Peculiar honors to our King,
Angels descend with songs again
And earth repeat the loud Amen!

THY RIGHTEOUSNESS IS IN HEAVEN

JOHN BUNYAN

BUT ONE DAY, as I was passing in the field, and that too with some dashes on my conscience, fearing lest yet all was not right, suddenly this sentence fell upon my soul, *Thy righteousness is in heaven;* and methought withal, I saw, with the eyes of my soul, Jesus Christ at God's right hand. There, I say, was my righteousness; so that wherever I was, or whatever I was adoing, God could not say of me, *He wants my righteousness,* for that was just before Him. I also saw, moreover, that it was not my good fame of heart that made my righteousness better, nor yet my bad fame that made my righteousness worse; for my righteousness was Jesus Christ Himself, *the same yesterday, and today, and for ever.*

Now did my chains fall off my legs indeed; I was loosed from my affliction and irons; my temptations also fled away; Now went I also home rejoicing, for the grace and love of God. So when I came home, I looked to see if I could find that sentence, *Thy righteousness is in heaven,* but could not find such a saying; wherefore my heart began to sink again; only that was brought to my remembrance, *He is made unto us of God wisdom, and righteousness, and sanctification and redemption;* by this word I saw the other sentence true.

For by this Scripture I saw that the Man Christ Jesus, as He is distinct from us, as touching His bodily presence, so He is our righteousness and sanctification before God. Here, therefore, I lived for some time, very sweetly at peace with God through Christ. Oh methought, Christ! Christ! there was nothing but Christ that was before my eyes: I was not now only for looking upon this and the other benefits of Christ apart, as of His blood, burial, or resurrection, but considered Him as a whole Christ; as He in whom all these, and all other His virtues, relations, offices, and operations met together, and that as He sat on the right hand of God in heaven.

THE LOSS OF THE *SANTA MARIA*
Christmas Day 1492

CHRISTOPHER COLUMBUS

I RECOGNIZED THAT our Lord had caused me to run aground at this place so that I might establish a settlement here. And so many things came to hand here that the disaster was a blessing in disguise.

• • •

I also feel great anxiety because of the two sons I have in Cordoba at school, if I leave them orphaned of father and mother in a foreign land. And I am concerned because the Sovereigns do not know the service I have rendered on this voyage and the very important news I am carrying to them, which would move them to help my sons.

TOLSTOY'S CONVERSION

LEO TOLSTOY

FIVE YEARS AGO I came to believe in Christ's teaching, and my life suddenly changed; I ceased to desire what I had previously desired, and began to desire what I formerly did not want. What had previously seemed to me good seemed evil, and what had seemed evil seemed good. It happened to me as it happens to a man who goes out on some business and on the way suddenly decides that the business is unnecessary and returns home. All that was on his right is now on his left, and all that was on his left is now on his right; his former wish to get as far as possible from home has changed into a wish to be as near as possible to it. The direction of my life and my desires became different, and good and evil changed places. . . .

I, like that thief on the cross, have believed Christ's teaching and been saved. And this is no far-fetched comparison, but the closest expression of the condition of spiritual despair and horror at the problem of life and death in which I lived formerly, and of the condition of peace and happiness in which I am now. I, like the thief, knew that I had lived and was living badly. . . . I, like the thief, knew that I was unhappy and suffering. . . . I, like the thief to the cross, was nailed by some force to that life of suffering and evil. And as, after the meaningless sufferings and evils of life, the thief awaited the terrible darkness of death, so did I await the same thing.

In all this I was exactly like the thief, but the difference was that the thief was already dying, while I was still living. The thief might believe that his salvation lay there beyond the grave, but I could not be satisfied with that, because besides a life beyond the grave life still awaited me here. But I did not understand that life. It seemed to me terrible. And suddenly I heard the words of Christ and understood them, and life and death ceased to seem to me evil, and instead of despair I experienced happiness and the joy of life undisturbed by death.

∾

HE WHO WOULD BE GREAT AMONG YOU

LUCI SHAW

You whose birth broke all the
social and biological rules—
son of the poor who accepted
the worship due a king—
child prodigy debating with
the Temple Th.D.'s—you
were the kind who used
a new math
to multiply bread, fish, faith.
You practiced a
radical sociology:
rehabilitated con men and
call girls. You valued women
and other minority groups.
A G.P., you specialized in
heart transplants.
Creator, healer,
shepherd, innovator,
storyteller, weather-maker,
botanist, alchemist,
exorcist, iconoclast,
seeker, seer, motive-sifter,

you were always beyond,
above us. Ahead
of your time, and ours.

And we would like
to be *like* you. Bold
as Boanerges, we hear ourselves
demand: "Admit us
to your avant-garde.
Grant us degree
in all the liberal arts of heaven."
Why our belligerence?
Why does this whiff of fame
and greatness smell so sweet?
Why must we compete
to be first? Have we forgotten
how you took simply, cool water
and a towel for our feet?

∾

THE GOD OF CHRISTIANS

BLAISE PASCAL

THE GOD OF Christians is not a God who is simply the author of mathematical truths, or of the order of the elements, as is the god of the pagans and of Epicureans. Nor is He merely a God who providentially disposes the life and fortunes of men, to crown His worshippers with length of happy years. Such was the portion of the Jews. But the God of Abraham, the God of Isaac, the God of Jacob, the God of Christians, is a God of love and consolation, a God who fills the souls and hearts of His own, a God who makes them feel their inward wretchedness and His infinite mercy, who unites Himself to their inmost spirit, filling it with humility and joy, with confidence and love, rendering them incapable of any end other than Himself.

All who seek God apart from Jesus Christ, and who rest in nature, either find no light to satisfy them, or form for themselves a means of knowing God and serving Him without a Mediator. Thus they fall either into atheism or into deism, two things which the Christian religion almost equally abhors.

The God of Christians is a God who makes the soul perceive that He is her only good, that her only rest is in Him, her only joy in loving Him; who makes her at the same time abhor the obstacles which withhold her from loving Him with all her strength. Her two hindrances, self-love and lust, are insupportable to her. This God makes her perceive that the root of self-love destroys her, and that He alone can heal.

The knowledge of God without that of our wretchedness creates pride. The knowledge of our wretchedness without that of God creates despair. The knowledge of Jesus Christ is the middle way, because in Him we find both God and our wretchedness.

∾

SAVING LIFE OF CHRIST

MAJOR W. IAN THOMAS

IN II PETER 1:3,4 we read, "According as his divine power hath given unto us all things that pertain unto life and godliness, through the knowledge of him that hath called us to glory and virtue: Whereby are given unto us exceeding great and precious promises, that by these ye might be partakers of the divine nature."

I may say to a glove, "Glove, pick up this Bible," and yet, somehow, the glove cannot do it. It has got a thumb and fingers, the shape and form of a hand, and yet it is unable to do the thing I command it to do. You may say, "Well, of course not. You have never told the glove how!" But I may preach to and instruct that glove until my patience is exhausted, but the glove, try as it will, still cannot pick up that Bible. Yet I have a glove at home that has picked up my Bible dozens of times!—but never once before I put my hand into it! As soon, however, as my hand comes into that glove, the glove becomes as strong as my hand. Everything possible to my hand becomes possible to that glove—but only in the measure in which the glove is prepared simply to clothe the activity of my hand.

That is what it is to have Christ, by His Spirit, dwelling within your redeemed humanity. You are the glove, Christ is the Hand! Everything that is possible to Him becomes possible to you, and with Paul you may say, "I have strength for all things that pertain to life and godliness, all that you need to live a life of righteousness and nobility of character."

PILGRIM'S PROGRESS

JOHN BUNYAN

I AM GOING now to see the Head that was crowned with thorns, and that face that was spit upon, for me. I have formerly lived by hear-say, and faith, but now I go where I shall live by sight, and shall be with Him, in whose company I delight myself.

∾

DEATH

GEORGE HERBERT

Death, thou wast once an uncouth hideous thing,
    Nothing but bones,
   The sad effect of sadder groans:
Thy mouth was open, but thou couldst not sing.

For we considered thee as at some six
    Or ten years hence,
   After the loss of life and sense,
Flesh being turned to dust, and bones to sticks.

We looked on this side of thee, shooting short;
    Where we did find
   The shells of fledge souls left behind,
Dry dust, which sheds no tears, but may extort.

But since our Savior's death did put some blood
    Into thy face,
   Thou art grown fair and full of grace,
Much in request, much sought for as a good.

For we do now behold thee gay and glad,
    As at doomsday;
   When souls shall wear their new array,
And all thy bones with beauty shall be clad.

> Therefore we can go die as sleep, and trust
> > Half that we have
> > Unto an honest faithful grave,
> Making our pillows either down or dust.

❧

WITH JESUS FOREVER

J. C. POLLOCK

JESUS HAS WON the race! He has lit the torch. It's all over! You may have hope! He is the first-born from the dead that in all things he might have the preeminence!

Hudson Taylor rejoiced in this truth as his wife lay dying.

"My hair is so hot!" she said.

"Oh, I will thin it out for you, shall I?" Hudson knew she did not like to have her hair cut short because it could not be done nicely in the Chinese way.

Her hair was matted and tangled with sweat. He began to cut it all off except for an inch of fuzz.

"Would you like a lock of it sent to each of the three children? What message shall I send with it?"

"Yes, and tell them to be sure and be kind to dear Miss Blatchly . . . and . . . and . . . to love Jesus."

When he stopped cutting she put a hand to her head.

"That's what you call thinning out?" she smiled. "Well, I shall have the comfort and you have all the responsibility as to looks."

• • •

"My darling, are you conscious that you are dying?" She replied with evident surprise, "Dying? Do you think so? What makes you think so?"

"I can see it, Darling."

"What is making me die?"

"Your strength is giving way."

"Can it be so? I feel no pain, only weakness."

"Yes, you are going Home. You will soon be with Jesus."

"I am sorry . . ."

"You are not sorry to go to be with Jesus?"

• • •

"It's not that. You know, my Darling, that for ten years there has not been a cloud between me and my Saviour."

• • •

"I cannot be sorry to go to Him," she whispered. "But it does grieve me to leave you alone at such a time. Yet . . . He will be with you and meet all your needs."

Soon after nine, the breathing sank lower. Hudson knelt down. With full heart, one of the watches wrote, he committed her to the Lord; thanking Him for having given her and for the twelve and a half years of happiness they had had together; thanking Him, too, for taking her to His own blessed Presence, and solemnly declaring himself anew to His service . . .

JESUS, KING

CALVIN MILLER

I'm all desire by stinginess annoyed.
Can I afford to call this Jesus, King?
I'd like to follow Him and yet avoid
Cross lugging and a naked death. I sing
Therefore in church. I sing of all
I'll eat at lunch when singing's done. Born twice,
By hundreds then we gather at the mall
And bless and praise, applaud and criticize.

Grace by installment—total faith—and we
Can spot a bargain when there's one in town,
Picking up the maximum of love,
With nothing but the minimum paid down.
It makes his love so interest-free! Not hard!
Like taking up your cross by MasterCard.

BARNFLOOR AND WINEPRESS

GERARD MANLEY HOPKINS

"And he said, 'If the Lord do not help thee, whence shall I help thee?
Out of the barnfloor, or out of the winepress?'"
II Kings 6:27

Thou that on sin's wages starvest,
Behold we have the joy in harvest;
For us was gathered the firstfruits,
For us was lifted from the roots,
Sheaved in cruel bands, bruised sore,
Scourged upon the threshing floor;
Where the upper millstone roofed His head,
At morn we found the heavenly Bread,
And, on a thousand altars laid,
Christ our Sacrifice is made!

Those whose dry plot for moisture gapes,
We shout with them that tread the grapes;
For us the Vine was fenced with thorn,
Five ways the precious branches torn;
Terrible fruit was on the tree
In the acre of Gethsemane;
For us by Calvary's distress
The wine was rackèd from the press;
Now in our altar-vessels stored
Is the sweet Vintage of our Lord.

In Joseph's garden they threw by
The riven Vine, leafless, lifeless, dry;
On Easter morn the Tree was forth,
In forty days reached Heaven from earth;
Soon the whole world is overspread;
Ye weary, come into the shade.

The field where He has planted us
Shall shake her fruit as Libanus,
When He has sheaved us in His sheaf,
When He has made us bear His leaf.

We scarcely call that banquet food,
But even our Savior's and our blood,
We are so grafted on His wood.

∾

JESUS

LOIS A. CHENEY

There was a place
Where the unbelief was so great
That Jesus
Jesus, the Son of God,
Could not heal and help
And so he left them.

Has anyone seen Jesus lately?

∾

HOW SWEET THE NAME

JOHN NEWTON

How sweet the Name of Jesus sounds
In a believer's ear!
It soothes his sorrows, heals his wounds,
And drives away his fear.

It makes the wounded spirit whole
And calms the troubled breast;
'Tis manna to the hungry soul,
And to the weary rest.

Dear Name! the Rock on which I build,
My Shield and Hiding-place,
My never-failing Treasury filled
With boundless stores of grace.

By Thee my prayers acceptance gain,
Although with sin defiled;
Satan accuses me in vain,
And I am owned a child.

Jesus! my Shepherd, Husband, Friend,
My Prophet, Priest, and King;
My Lord, my Life, my Way, my End,
Accept the praise I bring.

Weak is the effort of my heart
And cold my warmest thought;
But when I see Thee as Thou art,
I'll praise Thee as I ought.

Till then I would Thy love proclaim
With every fleeting breath;
And may the music of Thy Name
Refresh my soul in death.

❧

GOING HOME

WILLIAM GRIFFIN

"THIS IS GOODBYE," said Jesus.

Peter and the other men had walked from Jerusalem. Jesus had met them on a mountainside in Galilee. Together they strolled the grassy slopes.

"I'm going home," said Jesus. "My Father in heaven is waiting for me."

"Don't go just yet," said James. "Stay awhile."

"We can get something to eat, build a fire, have good talks," said Nathaniel Bartholomew.

"Like old times," said Peter.

"No more old times," said Jesus. "There are only new times from now on."

"Don't leave us alone," said John.

"I may be leaving," said Jesus, "but I'll never be far away."

"How can you go away and stay behind at the same time?" asked Thomas.

"I'll be with you when you bless bread and wine the way I did," said Jesus.

"I forgot about that," said Thomas.

"I'll be with you when you talk about me and the things I've done."

"But what'll we do when you're gone?" asked Philip.

"Work," said Jesus. "You have to spread the word."

"I didn't know we had to do that," said Simon.

"We could be very good at doing that," said Andrew.

"You have to teach the world what I've taught you," said Jesus.

"I could write it all down," said Matthew.

"So could I," said John.

"The people who listen to you," said Jesus, "you should baptize in the name of the Father and the Son and the Holy Spirit."

"What if they don't listen?" asked James the Younger.

"Bop them on the head," said Thaddeus.

"Don't bop them on the head," said Jesus. "You must tell them again and again and again until they do listen."

"But what if? . . ."

"No more questions," said Jesus.

"But . . ."

"My last words to you are *go* and *do*."

He went around, hugged each, whispered a special word.

Then he blessed them. They fell to the ground. He smiled. They wept.

• • •

Sometime later the men pulled themselves together and got to their feet. They headed for Jerusalem, talking at first, then singing songs.

They knew from that moment on they would be walking in Jesus's footsteps, saying the things he said, doing the things he did. They knew also that, when it was their time to go home, Jesus, their brother, their friend, their Lord and Master, would be waiting for them with arms outstretched.

CHRIST IS MY SAVIOUR

SADHU SUNDAR SINGH

CHRIST IS MY Saviour. He is my life. He is everything to me in heaven and earth. Once while travelling in a sandy region I was tired and thirsty. Standing on the top of a mound I looked for water. The sight of a lake at a distance brought joy to me, for now I hoped to quench my thirst. I walked toward it for a long time, but I could never reach it. Afterwards I found out that it was a mirage, only a mere appearance of water caused by the refracted rays of the sun. In reality there was none. In a like manner I was moving about the world in search of the water of life. The things of this world—wealth, position, honour and luxury—looked like a lake by drinking of whose waters I hoped to quench my spiritual thirst. But I could never find a drop of water to quench the thirst of my heart. I was dying of thirst. When my spiritual eyes were opened I saw the rivers of living water flowing from His pierced side. I drank of it and was satisfied. Thirst was no more. Ever since I have always drunk of that water of life, and have never been athirst in the sandy desert of this world. My heart is full of praise.

X

JESUS:

HIS SECOND COMING

"*T*HE world is coming to an end!" someone once said to Mark Twain. Twain replied, "Good, we can get along without it!"

Once a network anchorperson promised if the world came to an end on Tuesday, NBC would have a full report on Wednesday. Still, this doomsday rhetoric is coupled with the Second Coming and meshed deeply in the fabric of Christianity.

On the day of the Ascension two men dressed in white stood by Jesus as he began to float upward. Naturally the squinting crowd watched as Jesus went ever higher into the burning blue of the sky. When at last Jesus could be seen no longer, these two men turned and spoke to the observers still staring at the place he disappeared. "Men of Galilee," they asked, "why do you stand here looking into the sky? This same Jesus, who has been taken from you into heaven, will come back in the same way you have seen him go into heaven" (Acts 1:11). This Ascension prophecy has described the future of the church since it began.

In every age Jesus' Second Coming again occupied the attention of the church. Even now in the contemporary church it is the only mystery of Christian history yet to unfold. The other mysteries of Christianity are rooted in events that now lie faraway in the past. The Second Coming is still there reminding us that all Christians yet believe the future holds a final major Christian event. The creeds all proclaim that Jesus, who is now at the right hand of the Father, will come at some future, unsuspected moment.

Throughout the centuries, various groups of believers, including some Adventist groups and the Branch Davidians, have built elaborate schemes of prophecies deciding when the event would occur. Often these millennial groups have ended on some mountaintop, a bit embarrassed that Jesus didn't show at the widely publicized moment they expected. Sometimes, as in the case in Jonestown or Waco, the mass martyrdom of these sky watchers has left the world aghast.

Jesus taught that nobody knows when he is coming (Mark 13:32). Only his Father knows the date for sure. The New Testament seems to teach that his Second Coming will be in fiery display, but also like a thief in the night (2 Peter 3:10). In that section of scripture known as the Little Apocalypse (Matthew 24–25), Jesus says his coming will be preceded by natural disasters, cosmic destruction, and wars and rumors of wars.

Around the issue of the thousand-year reign of Christ, Evangelicals have divided into premillennials, postmillennials, and amillennials. These viewpoints as to when Christ will come again have left congregations and denominations sometimes querulously divided over their views. The various schools of thought usually come from differing interpretations of the prophecies of Revelations, Daniel, or Ezekiel.

Doomsday has always been a part of the general recipe of final things. But "The world is coming to an end" seems to hold a special intrigue for the church. It has, from time to time, been a negative proposition. But for the most part it has remained the all-consuming hope of the church.

Christians have not so much believed that the world is coming to an end as to a beginning. This beginning will be the hopeful and joyous reign of Christ. The utopian pictures of Jesus' coming are overwhelmingly seen as a time of joy for his followers. The apostle Paul saw it a part of the ultimate triumph of the church over the personal crisis of death.

But let me tell you something wonderful, a mystery I'll probably never fully understand. We're not all going to die—*but* we are all going to be changed. You hear a blast to end all blasts from a trumpet, and in the time that you look up and blink your eyes—it's over. On signal from the trumpet from heaven, the dead will be up and out of their graves, beyond the reach of death, never to die again. At the same moment and in the same way, we'll all be changed. In the resurrection scheme of things, this has to happen: everything perishable taken off the shelves and replaced by the imperishable, this mortal replaced by the immortal. Then the saying will come true:

"Death swallowed by triumphant Life!
Who got the last word, oh, Death?
Oh, Death, who's afraid of you now?"

1 Corinthians 15:51–55, *The Message*

∾

WATCH, THEREFORE

BOB BENSON AND MICHAEL W. BENSON

Watching is seen to be the business of the church till Jesus comes again. Jesus said that his disciples were never to lose interest in the subject of his Second Coming. "Watch, for you do not know the hour" (Matthew 24:42), said Jesus. On another occasion he said, "Watch and pray so that you do not fall" (Luke 22:46). The Bensons in this occasion celebrate the church's enduring expectancy for this historically climactic event.

"WATCH, THEREFORE." FOR life in time is not a stumbling from one ecstatic epiphany to another. The enormous task is to keep your eyes open, your wick trimmed, your lamp filled, your powder dry. Even when the bridegroom tarries. Even when the sky falls into the pond and the pond itself is sucked down some sewer of time that comes to nothing. Even when it all flattens out to triviality. Or the midnight cry, "Behold, the bridegroom cometh!" will catch you sleeping, your lamp overturned, the oil spilled out.

And then it is better if you had never been born. The moment you've been waiting for, the end for which you were made—your time —flies without you. Instead of going out to meet the bridegroom, glorious and infinitely desirable, you're in town haggling with the oil dealers. Life himself passes you by. The light dies out. The pond turns its back, closes the door. Depart. It doesn't know you anymore.

There are no two ways about it. You've got your eyes open or you don't. You're watching at midnight or you're not. You must be ready when it comes flying at you, skimming swiftly over the surface of time.

The cares of this world are no excuse. Not father, mother, wife, nor children. Not burials or births or weddings. Not fixing formula, scrubbing the toilet, peddling pills or prose. Whatever the great human enterprise currently in hand, the point is to watch. All the rest is addenda.

∾

THE HARLEQUIN CHRIST

HARVEY COX

THE DEVIL, NIETZSCHE claims, is "the spirit of gravity." And a Christian mystic in the tradition of St. Bernard once wrote these lines:

> Jesus the dancers' master is,
> A great skill at the dance is his,
> He turns to right, he turns to left;
> All must follow his teaching deft.

The appearance in our time of Christ the harlequin and the Lord of the Dance should provide a double cause for rejoicing. Not only does he draw us in to the dance of life, he also restores an essential aspect of our faith that in the awful seriousness of our age we had nearly forgotten.

• • •

But why a clown Christ in a century of tension and terror? The clown represents different things to different people. For some he is the handy butt of our own fears and insecurities. We can jeer at his clumsy failures because they did not happen to us. For some he shows what an absurd clod man really is, and he allows us on occasion to admit it. For others he reveals to us our stubborn human unwillingness to be encaged forever within the boundaries of physical laws and social proprieties. The clown is constantly defeated, tricked, humiliated, and tromped upon. He is infinitely vulnerable, but never finally defeated.

In representing Christ as a clown our generation probably senses, at least intuitively, that the painted grin and motley suit carry all these multiple meanings, and more. The very ambiguity of the cap and bells somehow suits our wistful ironic attitude toward Christ. To Christ's pointed question of Peter, "Who do you say that I am?" we can no longer conscientiously spout the conventional replies. So we clothe Christ in a clownsuit, and that way we express many things at once: our doubts, our disillusionment, our fascination, our ironic hope.

But we say something else too, something more distinctively contemporary. We say that our whole relation to Christ, to any faith at all, and to the whole of existence for that matter, is one of conscious play and comic equivocation. Only by assuming a playful attitude toward our religious tradition can we possibly make any sense of it. Only by learning to laugh at the hopelessness around us can we touch the hem of hope. Christ the clown signifies our playful appreciation of the past and our comic refusal to accept the spectre of inevitability in the future. He is the incarnation of festivity and fantasy.

$$\backsim$$

WHAT JESUS HAD TO SAY ABOUT THE
END OF THE WORLD

EUGENE PETERSON

Jesus' most dramatic teachings on the end of the world are recorded in Matthew's gospel. In this passage the term monster of desecration *is used to denote the powerful Antichrist who will appear as a world power at the end of time. In other versions of the Bible the term is translated* abomination of desolation. *This monster of desecration refers to that time in Jewish history——recorded in the book of Daniel ——when one of Alexander's successors, Antiochus Epiphanes, sacrificed a pig on the altar of the Jewish temple. This was a loathsome violation of the Jewish taboos of unclean offerings. But its offense wasn't just because swine were not kosher to the Jews; the whole Greek way of life was threatening to supplant Jewish faith and culture. The sacrifice occurred in June of 168 B.C. but was so odious that it marked*

Jewish doomsday literature from then on. The Antichrist of the book of Revelation is seen to be a new Antiochus Epiphanes, who would again desecrate the temple with unclean sacrifices. Some interpreters believe that this Antichrist is whom the apostle Paul is referring to when he uses the term man of lawlessness *(2 Thessalonians 2:3–4). The image suggests that there would have to be a new temple built in Jerusalem for this abomination to occur. Hence, the rebuilding of the temple in Jerusalem is a prophecy—yet to be fulfilled—that is cherished by some branches of the Evangelical church.*

Eugene Peterson has translated and paraphrased his way to the most important version of the Bible in a decade. These excerpts are all taken from his version of the New Testament, which is called The Message.

THEN JESUS LEFT the temple. As he walked away, his disciples pointed out how very impressive the temple architecture was. Jesus said, "You're not impressed by all this sheer size, are you? The truth of the matter is that there is not a stone in that building that is not going to end up in a pile of rubble."

Later as he was sitting on Mount Olives, his disciples approached and asked him, "Tell us, when are these things going to happen? What will be the sign of your coming, that the time's up?"

Jesus said, "Watch out for doomsday deceivers. Many leaders are going to show up with forged identities, claiming 'I am Christ, the Messiah.' They will deceive a lot of people. When reports come in of wars and rumored wars, keep your head and don't panic. This is routine history; this is no sign of the end. Nation will fight against nation and ruler against ruler, over and over. Famines and earthquakes will occur in various places. This is nothing compared to what's coming.

"They are going to throw you to the wolves and kill you, everyone hating you because you carry my name. And then, going from bad to worse, it will be dog-eat-dog, everyone at each other's throat, everyone hating each other.

"In the confusion, lying preachers will come forward and deceive a lot of people. For many others, the overwhelming spread of evil will do them in—nothing left of their love but a mound of ashes.

"Staying with it—that's what God requires. Stay with it to the end. You won't be sorry, and you'll be saved. All during this time, the good news—the Message of the kingdom—will be preached all over the world, a witness staked out in every country. And then the end will come.

"But be ready to run for it when you see the monster of desecration set up in the Temple sanctuary. The prophet Daniel described this. If you've read Daniel, you'll know what I'm talking about. If you're living in Judea at that time, run for the hills; if you're working in the yard, don't return to the house to get anything; if you're out in the field, don't go back and get your coat. Pregnant and nursing mothers will have it especially hard. Hope and pray this won't happen during the winter or on a Sabbath.

"This is going to be trouble on a scale beyond what the world has ever seen, or will see again. If these days of trouble were left to run their course, nobody would make it. But on account of God's chosen people, the trouble will be cut short.

"If anyone tries to flag you down, calling out, 'Here's the Messiah!' or points, 'There he is!' don't fall for it. Fake Messiahs and lying preachers are going to pop up everywhere. Their impressive credentials and dazzling performances will pull the wool over the eyes of even those who ought to know better. But I've given you fair warning.

"So if they say, 'Run to the country and see him arrive!' or 'Quick, get downtown, and see him come!' don't give them the time of day. The arrival of the Son of Man isn't something you go to see. He comes like swift lightning to you! Whenever you see crowds gathering, think of carrion vultures circling, moving in, hovering over a rotten carcass. You can be sure that it's not the living Son of Man pulling in those crowds.

"Following those hard times,

'Sun will fade out,
     moon will cloud over,
Stars fall out of the sky,
     cosmic powers tremble.'

"Then the arrival of the Son of Man! It will fill the skies—no one will miss it. Unready people all over the world, outsiders to the splendor and power, will raise a huge lament as they watch the Son of Man blazing out of heaven. At that same moment, he'll dispatch his angels with a trumpet-blast summons, pulling in God's chosen from the four winds, from pole to pole.

"Take a lesson from the fig tree. From the moment you notice its buds form, the merest hint of green, you know summer's just around the corner. So it is with you: When you see all these things, you'll know he's at the door. Don't take this lightly. I am not just saying this for some future generation, but for all of you. This age continues till all these things take place. Sky and earth will wear out, my words won't wear out.

"But the exact day and hour? No one knows that, not even heaven's angels, not even the Son. Only the Father knows.

"The Son of Man's arrival will be like that: Two men will be working in the field—one will be taken, one left behind; two women will be grinding at the mill—one will be taken, one left behind. So stay awake, alert. You have no idea what day your Master will show up. But you do know this: You know that if the homeowner had known what time of night the burglar would arrive, he would have been there with his dogs to prevent the break-in. Be vigilant just like that. You have no idea what time the Son of Man is going to show up."

Matthew 24:1–44

෬

SECOND COMING

JOHN BUNYAN

THE TALK THAT they had with the Shining Ones was about the Glory of the place, who told them, that the Beauty and Glory of it was inexpressible. There, said they, is *Mount Sion, the Heavenly Jerusalem, the innumerable Company of Angels, and the Spirits of just men made Perfect.* You are going now, said they, to the Paradise of GOD, wherein you shall see the *Tree of Life,* and eat of the never-fading Fruits thereof; and when you come there you shall have white Robes given you, and your walk and talk shall be every day with the KING, even all the days of Eternity. There you shall not see again such things as you saw when you were in the lower region upon the earth, to wit, Sorrow, Sickness, Affliction, and Death, *for the former things are passed away.* You are going now to *Abraham, Isaac,* and *Jacob,* and to the Prophets, men that God hath taken away from the Evil to come, and that are now resting upon their beds, each one walking in his Righteousness. The men then asked, What must we do in the Holy Place? To whom it was answered, You must there receive the Comfort of all your Toil, and have Joy for all your Sorrow; you must reap what you have sown, even the fruit of all your Prayers and Tears, and Sufferings for the King by the Way. In that place you must wear Crowns of Gold, and enjoy the perpetual sight and vision of the *Holy One, for there you shall see him as he is.* There also you shall serve him continually with Praise, with Shouting, and Thanksgiving, whom you desired to serve in the World, though with much difficulty because of the Infirmity of your Flesh. There your eyes shall be delighted with seeing, and your ears with hearing the pleasant Voice of the *Mighty One*. There you shall enjoy your Friends again, that are gone thither before you; and there you shall with joy receive even every one that follows into the Holy Place after you. There also you shall be clothed with Glory and Majesty, and put into an equipage fit to ride out with the *King of Glory*. When he shall come with Sound of Trumpet in the Clouds, as upon the wings of the Wind, you shall come with him; and when he shall sit upon the Throne of Judgment, you shall sit by him; yea, and when he shall pass Sentence upon all the workers of Iniquity, let them be Angels or men; you also shall have a voice in that Judgment, because they were his and your Enemies. Also when he shall again return to the City, you shall go too with sound of Trumpet, and be ever with him.

HEAVEN

AUTHOR UNKNOWN

Think of—
Stepping on shore, and finding it Heaven!
Of taking hold of a hand, and finding it God's hand.
Of breathing a new air, and finding it celestial air.
Of feeling invigorated, and finding it immortality.
Of passing from storm to tempest to an unbroken calm.
Of waking up, and finding it Home.

THE PARABLE OF THE TENANTS

CLARENCE JORDAN

It's LIKE A businessman who was leaving town for a long time and called in his assistants and turned over his investments to them. He made one responsible for about five hundred thousand dollars, another two hundred thousand, and another a hundred thousand—according to each one's ability—and then he left town. Right away the man with the five hundred grand got to work and made five hundred more. The man with the two hundred grand did the same and made another two hundred. But the guy with the hundred G's went and rented a safe-deposit box and put his boss' money in it. After a long time the boss returned and called his assistants together for an accounting. The one with the five hundred thousand brought his other five hundred thousand and said, 'Sir, you let me have five hundred grand; look, I've made another five hundred.' The boss said, 'Splendid, you good and responsible worker! You were diligent with the smaller sum; I'll entrust you with a larger one. You'll be a partner in my business.' Then the one with the two hundred G's came and said, 'Sir, you let me have two hundred thousand; look, I've made another two hundred.' The boss said, 'Splendid, you good and responsible worker! You were diligent with the smaller sum, I'll entrust you with a larger one. You'll be a partner in my business.' Well, the hundred-grand man came up and said, 'Sir, I know you are a hard-nosed man, squeezing pennies you haven't yet made and expecting a profit before the ink has dried. I was plain scared to take any chances, so I rented a safe-deposit box and put your money in it. Look, you've got every cent.' But his boss replied, 'You sorry, ornery bum! You knew that I squeeze pennies I haven't yet made, and expect profits before the ink dries. Then you should have turned my money over to the bank so that upon my return I would get back at least my principal with interest. So then, y'all take the money away from him and give it to the one with the million. For it will be given to everyone who has the stuff, and he'll have plenty, but the man who doesn't have the stuff will have even what he has taken away from him. Now as for this useless critter, throw him in the back alley. That'll give him something to moan and groan about.'

∽

THE HOPE OF HIS COMING

BILLY GRAHAM

THE GREAT CREEDS of the church teach that Christ is coming back. The Nicene Creed states, "He shall come again with glory to judge both the living and the dead." Charles Wesley wrote seven thousand hymns, and in five thousand he mentioned the Second Coming of Christ. When Queen

Elizabeth II was crowned by the Archbishop of Canterbury, he laid the crown on her head with the sure pronouncement, "I give thee, O sovereign Lady, this crown to wear until He who reserves the right to wear it shall return."

But till that time, one of America's best-known columnists summed it up when he said, "For us all, the world is disorderly and dangerous; ungoverned, and apparently ungovernable." The question arises: Who will restore order? Who can counter the danger of the nuclear holocaust? Who can bring an end to AIDS and the other epidemics of our time? Who alone can govern the world? The answer is Jesus Christ!

The Psalmist asked centuries earlier: "Why do the nations conspire and the peoples plot in vain? The kings of the earth take their stand and the rulers gather together against the LORD and against his Anointed One. 'Let us break their chains,' they say, 'and throw off their fetters.' The One enthroned in Heaven laughs; the Lord scoffs at them. Then he rebukes them in his anger and terrifies them in his wrath, saying, 'I have installed my King'" (Psalm 2:1–6). He promises the Anointed One, "I will make the nations your inheritance, the ends of the earth your possession. You will rule them with an iron scepter. . . . Therefore, you kings, be wise; be warned, you rulers of the earth. Serve the LORD with fear and rejoice with trembling" (Psalm 2:11). Then He advises the whole earth, "Blessed are all who take refuge in him" (verse 12).

Yes, God has promised this planet to His Son, Jesus Christ, and someday it will be His. He will bring an end to all the injustice, the oppression, the wars, the crime, the terrorism that dominates our newspapers and television screens today. But before that time comes, the four horsemen are going to vent their storm of fury across the pages of history.

For the Christian believer, the return of Christ is comforting, for at last men and women of faith will be exonerated. They will be avenged. The nonbeliever will see and understand why true Christians marched to the sound of another drum. But for the sinful unbeliever, the triumphant return of Christ will prove disastrous, because Christ's return ensures final judgment.

LAST THINGS

C. S. LEWIS

Once again the Second Coming may be best seen through the literary eye. On the Second Coming, as on nearly every other significant doctrine, C. S. Lewis immortalized both himself and Christ's teaching. Here, for children, for all, is truth made beautiful and simple.

THEN THE GREAT giant raised a horn to his mouth. They could see this by the change of the black shape he made against the stars. After that—quite a bit later, because sound travels so slowly—they heard the sound of the horn: high and terrible, yet of a strange, deadly beauty.

Immediately the sky became full of shooting stars. Even one shooting star is a fine thing to see; but these were dozens, and then scores, and then hundreds, till it was like silver rain: and it went on and on. And when it had gone on for some while, one or two of them began to think that there was another dark shape against the sky as well as the giant's. It was in a different place, right overhead, up in the very roof of the sky as you might call it. "Perhaps it is a cloud," thought Edmund. At any rate, there were no stars there: just blackness. But all around, the downpour of stars went on. And then the starless patch began to grow, spreading further and further out from the centre of the sky. And presently a quarter of the whole sky was black, and then a half, and at last the rain of shooting stars was going on only low down near the horizon.

With a thrill of wonder (and there was some terror in it too) they all suddenly realized what was happening. The spreading blackness was not a cloud at all: it was simply emptiness. The black part of the sky was the part in which there were no stars left. All the stars were falling: Aslan had called them home.

❧

BATTLE HYMN OF THE REPUBLIC

JULIA WARD HOWE

In 1861, Julia Ward Howe composed, to the tune of "John Brown's Body," the hymn text that would immortalize her name. One cannot miss the strong sense of the righteous cause that the hymn extols. But equally clear is the powerful and Biblical imagery of Jesus' second coming.

Mine eyes have seen the glory of the coming of the Lord:
He is trampling out the vintage where the grapes of wrath are stored;
He hath loosed the fateful lightning of His terrible swift sword:
   His truth is marching on.

I have seen Him in the watch-fires of a hundred circling camps;
They have builded Him an altar in the evening dews and damps;
I can read His righteous sentence by the dim and flaring lamps:
   His day is marching on.

I have read a fiery gospel writ in burnished rows of steel:
"As ye deal with my contemners, so with you my grace shall deal;
Let the Hero, born of woman, crush the serpent with his heel,
   Since God is marching on."

He has sounded forth the trumpet that shall never call retreat;
He is sifting out the hearts of men before His judgment-seat;
Oh, be swift, my soul, to answer Him! be jubilant, my feet!
   Our God is marching on.

In the beauty of the lilies Christ was born across the sea,
With a glory in his bosom that transfigures you and me:
As he died to make men holy, let us die to make men free,
   While God is marching on.

THE WORLD'S LAST NIGHT

C. S. LEWIS

IN *KING LEAR* (III:vii) there is a man who is such a minor character that Shakespeare has not given him even a name: he is merely "First Servant." All the characters around him—Regan, Cornwall, and Edmund—have fine long-term plans. They think they know how the story is going to end, and they are quite wrong. The servant has no such delusions. He has no notion how the play is going to go. But he understands the present scene. He sees an abomination (the blinding of old Gloucester) taking place. He will not stand it. His sword is out and pointed at his master's breast in a moment: then Regan stabs him dead from behind. That is his whole part: eight lines all told. But if it were real life and not a play, that is the part it would be best to have acted.

The doctrine of the Second Coming teaches us that we do not and cannot know when the world drama will end. The curtain may be rung down at any moment: say, before you have finished reading this paragraph. This seems to some people intolerably frustrating. So many things would be interrupted. Perhaps you were going to get married next month, perhaps you were going to get a raise next week; you may be on the verge of a great scientific discovery; you may be maturing great social and political reforms. Surely no good and wise God would be so very unreasonable as to cut all this short? Not *now,* of all moments!

But we think thus because we keep on assuming that we know the play. We do not know the play. We do not even know whether we are in Act I or Act V. We do not know who are the major and who the minor characters. The Author knows. The audience, if there is an audience, (if angels and archangels and all the company of heaven fill the pit and the stalls) may have an inkling. But we, never seeing the play from outside, never meeting any characters except the tiny minority who are "on" in the same scenes as ourselves, wholly ignorant of the future and very imperfectly informed about the past, cannot tell at what moment the end ought to come. That it will come when it ought, we may be sure; but we waste our time in guessing when that will be. That it has a meaning we may be sure, but we cannot see it. When it is over, we may be told. We are led to expect that the Author will have something to say to each of us on the part that each of us has played. The playing it well is what matters infinitely.

The doctrine of the Second Coming, then, is not to be rejected because it conflicts with our favorite modern mythology. It is, for that very reason, to be the more valued and made more frequently the subject of meditation. It is the medicine our condition, especially, needs.

And with that, I turn to the practical. There is a real difficulty in giving this doctrine the place which it ought to have in our Christian life without, at the same time, running a certain risk. The fear of that risk probably deters many teachers who accept the doctrine from saying very much about it.

We must admit at once that this doctrine has, in the past, led Christians into very great follies. Apparently many people find it difficult to believe in this great event without trying to guess its date, or even without accepting as a certainty the date that any quack or hysteric offers them. To write a history of all these exploded predictions would need a book, and a sad, sordid, tragi-comical book it would be. One such prediction was circulating when St. Paul wrote his second letter to the Thessalonians. Someone had told them that "the Day" was "at hand." This was apparently having the result which such predictions usually have: people were idling and playing the busybody. One of the most famous predictions was that of poor William Miller in 1843. Miller (whom I take to have been an honest fanatic) dated the Second Coming to the year, the day, and the very minute. A timely comet fostered the delusion. Thousands waited for the Lord at midnight on March 21st, and went home to a late breakfast on the 22nd followed by the jeers of a drunkard.

Clearly, no one wishes to say anything that will reawaken such mass hysteria. We must never speak to simple, excitable people about "the Day" without emphasizing again and again the utter impossibility of prediction. We must try to show them that that impossibility is an essential part of the doctrine. If you do not believe our Lord's words, why do you believe in his return at all? And if you do believe them must you not put away from you, utterly and forever, any hope of dating that return? His teaching on the subject quite clearly consisted of three propositions: (1) That he will certainly return. (2) That we cannot possibly find out when. (3) And that therefore we must always be ready for him.

Note the *therefore*. Precisely because we cannot predict the moment, we must be ready at all moments. Our Lord repeated this practical conclusion again and again; as if the promise of the Return had been made for the sake of this conclusion alone. Watch, watch, is the burden of his advice. I shall come like a thief. You will not, I most solemnly assure you you will not, see me approaching. If the householder had known at what time the burglar would arrive, he would have been ready for him. If the servant had known when his absent employer would come home, he would not have been found drunk in the kitchen. But they didn't. Nor will you. Therefore you must be ready at all times. The point is surely simple enough.

WE SHALL HEAR

JUDITH DEEM DUPREE

We shall hear a Voice of splendor echo through our halls,
Shake the portals of our being—
Separate the walls.
We shall hear a breathless Whisper creep across the air,
Mitigate our rasping edges,
Strip our fictions bare.
We shall hear a Song come sifting,
Shifting down from scale to scale,
Tuning earth to strings that shiver, timbres that impale.
We shall hear the Sound of heaven rumble over space,
Making room beyond the heavens
For His day of Grace.

❧

OUR COOPERATION WITH GOD

DESMOND M. TUTU

MY FRIENDS, THAT is what God has accomplished in Jesus Christ, and it is this in which we are given a share—this ministry of reconciliation. The church must be the forgiving fellowship of the forgiven; it must be the reconciling *koinonia* of the reconciled. In this way it is the first fruits of the kingdom and becomes a *verbum visibile,* a kind of audiovisual aid for the sake of the world. It shows what human society should be as God intended it to be.

Some might think that reconciliation is a soft or easy option. But look at what it cost God. True reconciliation does not mean crying, "'Peace, peace' where there is no peace." No, true reconciliation occurs when we confront people with the demands of the gospel of Jesus Christ for justice and peace and compassion and caring. It means taking sides on behalf of the weak and the downtrodden, the voiceless ones. We cannot be neutral in situations of injustice and oppression and exploitation.

Be careful if you say that you want reconciliation and that you are a minister of reconciliation. Be sure you know what you are about because reconciliation involves suffering and even death. Reconciliation cannot happen apart from the cross. A Christian who does not suffer for the sake of Christ and the sake of the kingdom cannot be a Christian. These are the words of Jesus, "Unless you take up your cross and follow me you cannot be my disciple." He says this quite categorically. A church that does not suffer for Christ's sake and the gospel's cannot be the church of Jesus Christ.

As Christians, we cannot sit about wringing our hands in help-lessness. We are not impotent. We can work mightily for justice, peace, and reconciliation. After all, we are the instruments of God's peace. Let us go out in the power of the Holy Spirit to work for God's justice, God's peace, God's love and reconciliation. If we are true to our vocation to be Christ's ambassadors, then we shall help to bring to pass that wonderful vision contained in Revelation:

> After this I looked and saw a vast throng, which no one could count, from every nation, of all tribes, peoples, and languages, standing in front of the throne and before the Lamb. They were robed in white and had palms in their hands, and they shouted together: "Victory to our God who sits on the throne, and to the Lamb!" And all the angels stood round the throne and the elders and the four living creatures, and they fell on their faces before the throne and worshipped God, crying: "Amen! Praise and glory and wisdom, thanksgiving and honour, power and might, be to our God for ever and ever! Amen."
>
> Revelation 7:9–12 (NEB)

THE PARABLE OF THE TEN VIRGINS

CLARENCE JORDAN

"THE GOD MOVEMENT, then, may be compared to ten young ladies who got their lanterns and went out to join a wedding party. Five of them were giddy-witted and five were cool. The giddy-wits took their lanterns but no oil, while the cool ones took extra oil for their lanterns. The wedding procession was late in coming, so they all started nodding and napping. Along about midnight someone yelled, 'Hey, the procession is coming! Jump up and join it!' So all the girls woke up and got their lanterns in order. The giddy-wits said to the cool gals, 'Our lanterns are going out; please let us have some of your oil.' But the smart ones said, 'We can't; there isn't enough for both of us. You'd better go to the store and buy some for yourselves.' While they were gone to the store, the procession came and those who were all set went along into the ballroom, and the doors were closed. Later on, the other girls came running and said, 'Mister, Mister, let us in!' But he replied, 'I don't recognize you.' So keep your eyes open, because you never know the day or hour.

NOTES

❧

PAGE

35 Barclay, William, *Jesus As They Saw Him* (London: SCM Press, Ltd., 1962), 12.

35 Lucado, Max, *When God Whispers Your Name* (Dallas: Word Publishing, 1994), 23–25.

38 Tabb, John Bannister, "Christ and the Pagan," from *Later Poems,* in *Anthology of Jesus,* arr. and sel. Sir James Marchant, ed. Warren W. Wiersbe (1926; Grand Rapids: Kregel Publications, 1981), 244.

38 Gabhart, Herbert C., *The Name Above Every Name* (Nashville: Broadman Press, 1986), 109.

40 Jordan, Clarence, *The Cotton Patch Version of Matthew and John* (New York: Association Press, 1970), 108–9.

41 Barclay, William, *Jesus As They Saw Him* (London: SCM Press Ltd., 1962) 79–83.

45 Josephus, Flavius, *Antiquities of the Jews,* book XVIII, in *Anthology of Jesus,* arr. and sel. Sir James Marchant, ed. Warren W. Wiersbe (1926; Grand Rapids: Kregel Publications, 1981), 190.

45 Trueblood, D. Elton, *Confronting Christ* (New York: Harper & Brothers Publishers, 1960), 5–6.

46 Lacordaire, Jean-Baptiste-Henri, "Jesus Christ, God, God and Man," in *Anthology of Jesus,* arr. and sel. Sir James Marchant, ed. Warren W. Wiersbe (1926; Grand Rapids: Kregel Publications, 1981), 98–99.

47 Baillie, John, "Excerpt from a Diary of Private Prayer," in *Devotional Classics: Selected Readings for Individuals and Groups,* comp. Richard J. Foster and James Bryan Smith (San Francisco: HarperSanFrancisco, 1993), 128–29.

48 Spurgeon, Charles H., *Morning and Evening,* ed. Roy H. Clarke (Nashville: Thomas Nelson Publishers, 1994), May 8, morning.

49 Dostoyevsky, Fyodor Mikhaylovich, *The Brothers Karamazov,* in *Anthology of Jesus,* arr. and sel. Sir James Marchant, ed. Warren W. Wiersbe (1926; Grand Rapids: Kregel Publications, 1981), 82.

50 Graham, Billy, *The Faithful Christian, An Anthology of Billy Graham,* comp. William Griffin and Ruth Graham Dienert (New York: McCracken Press, 1994), 30–31.

51 Didon, Père, *Jesus Christ,* Introduction, in *Anthology of Jesus,* arr. and sel. Sir James

Marchant, ed. Warren W. Wiersbe (1926; Grand Rapids: Kregel Publications, 1981), 5.

52   Blanchard, John, *Gathered Gold* (Durham, Eng.: Evangelical Press, 1984), 168–169.

54   Garvie, A. E., *The Christian Doctrine of the Godhead,* chap. I, in *Anthology of Jesus,* arr. and sel. Sir James Marchant, ed. Warren W. Wiersbe (1926; Grand Rapids: Kregel Publications, 1981), 309–10.

55   Miller, Calvin, "A Gathering of Angels."

58   Author Unknown, *Apples of Gold,* quoted in John R. Rice, *Sword of the Lord,* 1960.

59   Pascal, Blaise, *Thoughts on Religion,* chap. XIV, in *Anthology of Jesus,* arr. and sel. Sir James Marchant, ed. Warren W. Wiersbe (Grand Rapids: Kregel Publications, 1981), 273–74.

60   Fairbairn, Andrew Martin, "Christ in Galilee," in *Treasury of the World's Great Sermons,* comp. Warren W. Wiersbe (Grand Rapids: Kregel Publications, 1977), 211–12.

61   Goodspeed, Edgar J., *Modern Apocrypha* (Boston: Beacon Press, 1956), 88–89.

62   Stott, John R. W., *Basic Christianity* (Downers Grove, Ill.: InterVarsity Press, 1958), 81.

63   Bonaparte, Napoleon, "Conversations with General Bertrand at St. Helena," in *Anthology of Jesus,* arr. and sel. Sir James Marchant, ed. Warren W. Wiersbe (1926; Grand Rapids: Kregel Publications, 1981), 260.

64   Fletcher, Giles, *Christ's Victory and Triumph* (London: Griffith, Farran, Okeden & Welsh, 1640) 58.

64   Lewis, C. S., *The Screwtape Letters* (New York: Macmillan Publishing Co., 1961), 106–80.

66   Buttrick, George A., *Jesus Came Preaching* (New York: Charles Scribner's Sons, 1931), 16–17.

67   Lewis, C. S., *God in the Dock,* ed. Walter Hooper (Grand Rapids: William B. Eerdmans Publishing Company), 160.

67   Buechner, Frederick, *A Room Called Remember* (San Francisco: Harper & Row, 1984), 84–85.

68   Buttrick, George A., *Jesus Came Preaching* (New York: Charles Scribner's Sons, 1946), 50–51.

69   Graham, Billy, *The Faithful Christian, An Anthology of Billy Graham,* ed. William Griffin and Ruth Graham Dienert (New York: McCracken Press, 1994), 15–16.

70   Wangerin, Walter, *Ragman and Other Cries of Faith* (San Francisco: Harper & Row Publishers, 1984), 3–6.

73   I. F., "The Son of Man Came Eating and Drinking," in *The Poet's Life of Christ,* comp., arr., and dec. Norman Ault (London: Humphrey Milford, Oxford University Press, 1922), 101.

74   Teresa, Mother, *Mother Teresa: Contemplative in the Heart of the World,* comp. Angelo Devananda (Ann Arbor: Servant Books, 1985), 114.

74   Palmer, Earl, *The 24-Hour Christian* (Downers Grove, Ill.: InterVarsity Press, 1987), 25.

75   Cheney, Lois A., *God is No Fool* (Nashville: Abingdon, 1969), 21–22.

75   Bryan, William Jennings, *The Prince of Peace* (Chicago: Reilly and Briton Company, 1909), 20–27.

78 Dostoyevsky, Fyodor, *The Brothers Karamazov,* trans. Constance Garnett, ed. Manuel Komroff (New York: New American Library, 1957), 227–42.

88 Rahner, Karl, *Encounters with Silence,* trans. James M. Demske (Westminister, Md.: Christian Classics, 1984), 5.

88 Asch, Sholem, *Mary* (New York: Carroll & Graf Publishers, Inc., 1985), 302–303.

90 Oxenham, John, "Child Jesus," in *Portrait of Jesus,* ed. Peter Seymour (Kansas City, Mo.: Hallmark Cards, 1972), 16.

91 Campbell, Dr. R. J., *The Life of Christ,* note A, in *Anthology of Jesus,* arr. and sel. Sir James Marchant, ed. Warren W. Wiersbe (1926; Grand Rapids: Kregel Publications, 1981), 87–89.

97 Lucado, Max, *He Still Moves Stones* (Dallas: Word Publishing, 1993), 175–77.

99 Brown, Elijah P., *The Real Billy Sunday* (Dayton: Otterbein Press, 1914), 272–82.

106 Lacordaire, Jean-Baptiste-Henri, "Jesus Christ, God, God and Man," in *Anthology of Jesus,* arr. and sel. Sir James Marchant, ed. Warren W. Wiersbe (1926; Grand Rapids: Kregel Publications, 1981), 20–21.

107 Lucado, Max, *God Came Near* (Portland, Ore.: Multnomah Press, 1987), 43–44.

108 Edersheim, Alfred, *The Life and Times of Jesus the Messiah* (Oxford: Longmans, Green and Co., 1883), 180–81.

108 Luther, Martin, *Sermons of Martin Luther,* vol. I, ed. and trans. John Nicholas Leuker (Grand Rapids: Baker Book House) 135–44.

112 Hale, Sir Matthew, "I Have a Room," in *A Diary of Readings,* ed. John Baillie (New York: Collier Books, 1955), 326.

112 Lucado, Max, *God Came Near* (Portland, Ore.: Multnomah Press, 1987), 23.

113 Jordan, Clarence, *The Cotton Patch Version of Matthew and John* (New York: Association Press, 1970), 16–17.

114 Whitley, Pam, *This Precious Christ of Christmas* (Oklahoma City: Send the Light)

117 Edwards, Gene, *The Birth* (Auburn, Maine: Seed Sowers, 1990), 111–26.

119 L'Engle, Madeleine, *A Stone for a Pillow* (Wheaton, Ill.: Harold Shaw Publishers, 1986), 107–8.

120 Wangerin, Walter, *Ragman and Other Cries of Faith* (San Francisco: Harper & Row Publishers, 1984), 9–11.

122 Augustine, Saint, "Christmas," in "To Illustrate . . . Christmas," *Leadership* magazine, Fall 1987, p. 45.

123 Miller, Calvin, *The Singer* (Downers Grover, Ill.: InterVarsity Press, 1975), 32–35.

124 Merton, Thomas, "The Flight into Egypt," in *Portrait of Jesus,* ed. Peter Seymour (Kansas City, Mo.: Hallmark Cards, 1972), 14.

125 Edersheim, Alfred, *The Life and Times of Jesus the Messiah* (Oxford: Longmans, Green and Co., 1883), 183–84.

126 Blake, William, "The Lamb," quoted in Malcolm Muggeridge, *A Third Testament* (New York: Ballantine Books, 1988), 84.

127 Crashaw, Richard, "Herod's Suspicions," in *Portrait of Jesus,* ed. Peter Seymour (Kansas City, Mo.: Hallmark Cards, 1972), 13.

128 Edersheim, Alfred, *The Life and Times of Jesus the Messiah* (Oxford: Longmans, Green and Co., 1983), 187–88.

128 Wallace, Lew, *Ben-Hur* (New York: Dodd, Mead & Company, 1953), 63–65.

130 Card, Michael, "Joseph's Song," from the tape *The Promise, A Celebration of Christ's Birth* (Brentwood, Tenn.: Sparrow Corporation, 1991).

132 Matthew, Saint, "Genealogy of Jesus," in Robert E. Webber, *The Book of Family Prayer* (Nashville: Thomas Nelson Publishers, 1986), 55–56.

133 Gariepy, Henry, *100 Portraits of Christ* (Wheaton, Ill. Victor Books, 1987), 56.

133 Eliot, T. S., *The Complete Poems and Plays, 1909–1950* (New York: Harcourt Brace & Co., 1980), 68–69.

134 Rossetti, Christina, "In the Bleak Mid-Winter," in *Portrait of Jesus,* ed. Peter Seymour (Kansas City, Mo.: Hallmark Cards, 1972), 11.

135 Edersheim, Alfred, *The Life and Times of Jesus the Messiah* (Oxford: Longmans, Green and Co., 1883), 217–18.

136 Bishop, Jim, "The Holy Birth," in *Portrait of Jesus,* ed. Peter Seymour (Kansas City, Mo.: Hallmark Cards, 1972), 6.

137 Milton, John, "The Hymn," in *The Country of the Risen King, An Anthology of Christian Poetry,* comp. Merle Meeter (Grand Rapids: Baker Book House, 1978), 356–60.

143 Murray, James R., "Away in a Manger," in *The Reader's Digest Merry Christmas Songbook* (Pleasantville, N.Y.: The Reader's Digest Association, 1981), 29.

144 Van Dyke, Henry, "A Christmas Prayer for the Home," in *A Treasury of Christmas Stories,* ed. James S. Bell Jr. (Wheaton, Ill.: Harold Shaw Publishers, 1993), 115–116.

145 Shakespeare, William, *Hamlet,* 1.1.139–45, in *An Oxford Anthology of Shakespeare,* sel. Stanley Wells (Oxford: Clarendon Press, 1987), 221.

146 Author Unknown, "The Coventry Carol," in *The Reader's Digest Merry Christmas Songbook* (Pleasantville, N.Y.: The Reader's Digest Association, 1981), 190.

147 Gire, Ken, *Intimate Moments with the Savior* (Grand Rapids: Zondervan Publishing House, 1989), 3–6.

149 Edersheim, Alfred, *The Life and Times of Jesus the Messiah* (Oxford: Longmans, Green and Co., 1883), 221.

149 Van Dyke, Henry, "The Birth of Jesus," in *A Treasury of Christmas Stories,* ed. James S. Bell Jr. (Wheaton, Ill.: Harold Shaw Publishers, 1993), 81.

150 Author Unknown, "Bring a Torch, Jeannette, Isabella," in *The Reader's Digest Merry Christmas Songbook* (Pleasantville, N.Y.: The Reader's Digest Association, 1981), 186.

150 Wesley, Charles, "Hark! The Herald Angels Sing," in *The Country of the Risen King, An Anthology of Christian Poetry,* comp. Merle Meeter (Grand Rapids: Baker Book House, 1978), 410.

151 Virgil, "Virgil's Star," quoted in Calvin Miller, *A Thirst for Meaning* (Grand Rapids: Zondervan Publishing House, 1973), 57–58.

152 Wilde, Oscar, "Ave Maria Gratia Plena," in *Portrait of Jesus,* ed. Peter Seymour (Kansas City, Mo.: Hallmark Cards, 1972), 5.

152 Jonson, Ben, "A Hymn on the Nativity of My Savior," in *The Country of the Risen King, An Anthology of Christian Poetry,* comp. Merle Meeter (Grand Rapids: Baker Book House, 1978), 353.

153 Miller, Calvin, *A Thirst for Meaning* (Grand Rapids: Zondervan Publishing House, 1973), 58–59.

154 Stauffer, Ethelbert, *Jesus and His Story* (New York: Alfred A. Knopf, 1959), 32–33.

155 Milton, John, "Ode on the Morning of Christ's Nativity," in *The Jesus of the Poets, An Anthology,* sel. and ed. Leonard R. Gribble (New York: Richard R. Smith, 1930), 95.

161 Lucado, Max, *He Still Moves Stones* (Dallas: Word Publishing, 1993), 194–95.

162 Trueblood, D. Elton, *The Yoke of Christ and Other Sermons* (New York: Harper & Brothers, 1958), 11–12, 84–85.

163 Augustine, Saint, "On Meeting Christ," in *The Joy of the Saints,* ed. Robert Llewelyn (Springfield, Ill.: Templegate Publishers, 1988), 240.

164 Jordan, Clarence, *The Cotton Patch Version of Matthew and John* (New York: Association Press, 1970), 107–8.

165 Crashaw, Richard, "The Centurion," in *The Poet's Life of Christ,* comp., arr., and dec. Norman Ault (London: Humphrey Milford, Oxford University Press, 1922), 101.

165 South, Robert, Sermon XIV, in *A Diary of Readings,* ed. John Baillie (New York: Collier Books, 1955), 299.

166 Bangley, Bernard, *Growing in His Image* (Wheaton, Ill.: Harold Shaw Publishers, 1983), 67.

167 Lewis, C. S., *The Weight of Glory* (Grand Rapids: William B. Eerdmans Publishing Company, 1949), 1–2.

168 Carlile, J. C., *Portraits of Jesus Drawn by Himself* (London: Religious Tract Society, n.d.), 90–95.

169 Buttrick, George A., *Jesus Came Preaching* (New York: Charles Scribner's Sons, 1946), 46.

170 Graham, Billy, *Unto the Hills* (Dallas: Word Publishing, 1986), 123–24.

170 Kierkegaard, Søren, *Journals,* trans. Alexander Dru (1938), §§974, 248, in *A Diary of Readings,* ed. John Baillie (New York: Collier Books, 1955), 21.

171 Author Unknown, "Letter from Jesus," *Good News* magazine, October 1977.

172 Fosdick, Harry Emerson, "Jesus' Love of Children," in *Portrait of Jesus,* ed. Peter Seymour (Kansas City, Mo.: Hallmark Cards, 1972), 48.

173 Cheney, Lois A., *God Is No Fool* (Nashville: Abingdon, 1969), 51–52.

174 Baxter, Richard, *The Saints' Everlasting Rest,* chap. XIII, in *A Diary of Readings,* ed. John Baillie (New York: Collier Books, 1955), 20.

175 Cowper, William, "Longing to Be with Christ," in *The Country of the Risen King, An Anthology of Christian Poetry,* comp. Merle Meeter (Grand Rapids: Baker Book House, 1978), 306.

176 Bonhoeffer, Dietrich, *Life Together,* in *Devotional Classics: Selected Readings for Individuals and Groups,* comp. Richard J. Foster and James Bryan Smith (San Francisco: HarperSanFrancisco, 1993), 294–95.

177 Miller, Calvin, "No Hurry," in *Couples' Devotional Bible NIV,* ed. staff of *Marriage Partnership* magazine (Grand Rapids: Zondervan Publishing House, 1994), 935.

177 Markham, Edwin, "How the Great Guest Came," in *The Best Loved Poems of the American People,* sel. Hazel Felleman (Garden City, N.Y.: Garden City Books, 1936), 296–97.

179 Dickens, Charles, "His Mercy and Love," in *Portrait of Jesus,* ed. Peter Seymour (Kansas City, Mo.: Hallmark Cards, 1972), 43.

180 Cheney, Lois A., *God Is No Fool* (Nashville: Abingdon, 1969), 53–54.

181 Nee, Watchman, *What Shall This Man Do?* in *Devotional Classics: Selected Readings for Individuals and Groups,* comp. Richard Foster and James Bryan Smith (San Francisco: HarperSanFrancisco, 1993), 341–42.

182 Thurman, Howard, "Lord, Lord, Open unto Me," in Richard Foster, *Prayers from the Heart* (New York: HarperCollins Publishers, 1994), 31.

183 Spurgeon, Charles H., *Spiritual Revival, The Want of the Church,* in *Devotional Classics: Selected Readings for Individuals and Groups,* comp. Richard Foster and James Bryan Smith (San Francisco: HarperSanFrancisco, 1993), 333–34.

183 Miller, Calvin, "Adore the Savior," in *Couples' Devotional Bible NIV,* ed. staff of *Marriage Partnership* magazine (Grand Rapids: Zondervan Publishing House, 1994), 414.

184 Powers, Margaret Fishback, "Footprints." (HarperCollins Publishers Ltd., 1964) Canada.

185 Griffin, William, *Jesus for Children* (Minneapolis: Winston Press, 1985), 75–76.

185 Lawrence, Brother, *The Practice of the Presence of God* (Mount Vernon, N.Y.: Peter Pauper Press, 1963), 30–35.

188 Cheney, Lois A., *God Is No Fool* (Nashville: Abingdon, 1969), 55–56.

189 Patrick, Saint, "Christ with Me, Christ Before Me," in Richard J. Foster, *Prayers from the Heart* (New York: HarperCollins Publishers, 1994), 84.

190 Rolle, Richard, "Develop in Me a Longing That Is Unrestrained," in Richard J. Foster, *Prayers from the Heart* (New York: HarperCollins Publishers, 1994), 52.

190 Cheney, Lois A., *God Is No Fool* (Nashville: Abingdon, 1969), 57–58.

191 Coleridge, Hartley, "Jesus Praying," in *Portrait of Jesus,* ed. Peter Seymour (Kansas City, Mo.: Hallmark Cards, 1972), 35.

192 Irenaeus of Lyons, Saint, "The Sanctification of Each Stage of Life," in *Documents of the Christian Church,* sel. and ed. Henry Bettenson (London: Oxford University Press, 1963), 30.

192 Long, James, "Jesus, the Righteous Husband," in *Couples' Devotional Bible NIV,* ed. staff of *Marriage Partnership* magazine (Grand Rapids: Zondervan Publishers, 1994), 1044.

193 Thompson, Francis, *Selected Poems of Francis Thompson* (London: Methuen and Co., 1909), 51–56.

198 Augustine of Hippo, Saint, "Late Have I Loved You," in Richard J. Foster, *Prayers from the Heart* (New York: HarperCollins Publishers, 1994), 50.

199 Fosdick, Harry Emerson, "Women Disciples," in *Portrait of Jesus,* ed. Peter Seymour (Kansas City, Mo.: Hallmark Cards, 1972), 34.

205 Dawson, William J., *The Life of Christ* (Philadelphia: George W. Jacobs & Co., 1901), 24–25.

206 Trueblood, D. Elton, *Confronting Christ* (New York: Harper & Brothers Publishers, 1960), 14.

206 Milman, Henry Hart, "God with Us," *The Jesus of the Poets, An Anthology,* sel. and ed. Leonard R. Gribble (New York: Richard R. Smith, 1930), 94.

207 Evely, Louis, *That Man Is You,* trans. Edmond Bonin (New York: Paulist, 1963), 3.

207 Billheimer, Paul E., *Don't Waste Your Sorrows* (Fort Washington, Pa.: Christian Literature Crusade, 1977), 82–83.

208 Thomas, Major W. Ian, *The Saving Life of Christ* (Grand Rapids: Zondervan Publishing House, 1961), 141–43.

211 Eckhart, Meister, *Meditations with Meister Eckhart* (Santa Fe, N.M.: Bear & Company, 1983), 100.

211 Lewis, C. S., *Letters to Malcolm: Chiefly on Prayer* (New York: Harcourt Brace Jovanovich, 1963), 70–71.

211 Card, Michael, *Immanuel* (Nashville: Thomas Nelson, 1990), 27.

212 Lucado, Max, *God Came Near* (Portland, Ore.: Multnomah Press, 1987), 54.

212 Swanson, Donna, *Mind Song* (Nashville: Upper Room, 1978), 90.

213 Muggeridge, Malcolm, *The Green Stick* (New York: William Morrow & Co., Inc., 1972) 82.

214 Bunyan, John, *The Riches of Bunyan,* selected from his works by Rev. Jeremiah Chaplin (New York: American Tract Society, 1850), 102.

214 Card, Michael, *Immanuel* (Nashville: Thomas Nelson, 1990), 120; *Things We Leave Behind* (Brentwood, TN: EMI Christian Music Publishers, 1982).

216 Hester, H. I., *The Heart of the New Testament* (Nashville: Broadman Press, 1963), 111–12.

217 Bayley, Joseph, *Psalms of My Life* (Elgin, Ill.: David C. Cook Publishing Co., 1987), 37–38.

218 Donne, John, "Jesus in the Temple," in *Portrait of Jesus,* ed. Peter Seymour (Kansas City, Mo.: Hallmark Cards, 1972), 20.

218 Alphonsus Maria de Liguori, Saint, *Book of Novenas* (New York: John J. Crawley & Co., 1956), 11–12.

219 Packer, J. I., *Knowing God* (Downers Grove, Ill.: InterVarsity Press, 1973), 18.

220 Alphonsus Maria de Liguori, Saint, *Book of Novenas,* (New York: John J. Crawley & Co., 1956), 2–4.

221 Hession, Roy, *The Calvary Road* (Fort Washington, Pa.: Christian Literature Crusade, 1964), 15.

221 Shakespeare, William, *Richard II,* 3.3.142–82, in *An Oxford Anthology of Shakespeare,* sel. Stanley Wells (Oxford: Clarendon Press, 1987), 264–65.

222 Thielicke, Helmut, *Christ and the Meaning of Life,* quoted in Calvin Miller, *Once upon a Tree* (Grand Rapids: Baker Book House, 1967), 169.

223 Adams, Nate, "Only Begotten Son," in *Couples' Devotional Bible NIV,* ed. staff of *Marriage Parnership* magazine (Grand Rapids: Zondervan Publishing House, 1994), 1151.

224 Bayley, Joseph, *Psalms of My Life* (Elgin, Ill.: David C. Cook Publishing Co., 1987), 73.

225 Muggeridge, Malcolm, *Jesus: The Man Who Lives* (New York: Harper & Row, 1975), 29.

226 Alphonsus Maria de Liguori, Saint, *Book of Novenas* (New York: John J. Crawley & Co., 1956), 5–6.

226 Milton, John, "The Angels' Song," in *The Jesus of the Poets, An Anthology,* sel. and ed. Leonard R. Gribble (New York: Richard R. Smith, 1930), 97–98.

233 Crashaw, Richard, "Steps," in *Anthology of Jesus,* arr. and sel. Sir James Marchant, ed. Warren W. Wiersbe (1926; Grand Rapids: Kregel Publications, 1981), 43.

233 Griffin, William, *Jesus for Children* (Minneapolis: Winston Press, 1985), 39–40.

234 Borg, Marcus J., *Jesus, A New Vision* (San Francisco: HarperCollins Publishers, 1987), 60–70.

238   Luther, Martin, *Luther's Meditations on the Gospels,* trans. and arr. Roland H. Bainton (Philadelphia: Westminster Press, 1962), 64–65.

239   Oursler, Fulton, "Loaves and Fishes," in *Portrait of Jesus,* ed. Peter Seymour (Kansas City, Mo.: Hallmark Cards, 1972), 45.

240   Tennyson, Alfred, Lord, *In Memoriam* (1850), xxxi, xxxii, in *A Diary of Readings,* ed. John Baillie (New York: Collier Books, 1955), 54.

241   Bryan, William Jennings, *The Prince of Peace* (Chicago: Reilly & Britton Company, 1909), 13–14.

242   MacDonald, George, "The Woman Who Came Behind Him in the Crowd," in *Portrait of Jesus,* ed. Peter Seymour (Kansas City, Mo.: Hallmark Cards, 1972), 42.

243   Griffin, William, *Jesus for Children* (Minneapolis: Winston Press, 1985), 42–43.

244   Oursler, Fulton, "The Storm" in *Portrait of Jesus,* ed. Peter Seymour (Kansas City, Mo.: Hallmark Cards, 1972), 41.

245   Ludwig, Emil, "The Cure in the Synagogue," in *Portrait of Jesus,* ed. Peter Seymour (Kansas City, Mo.: Hallmark Cards, 1972), 39.

245   Edwards, Gene, *The Birth* (Auburn, Maine: Seed Sowers, 1990), 45–47.

247   Merton, Thomas, "Cana," in *Portrait of Jesus,* ed. Peter Seymour (Kansas City, Mo.: Hallmark Cards, 1972), 39.

248   Dickens, Charles, *The Life of Our Lord* (New York: Simon & Schuster, 1934), 27–33.

250   Griffin, William, *Jesus for Children* (Minneapolis: Winston Press, 1985), 53–54.

251   Graham, Billy, *The Faithful Christian, An Anthology of Billy Graham,* comp. William Griffin and Ruth Graham Dienert (New York: McCracken Press, 1994), 32.

251   Oursler, Fulton, "Healing," in *Portrait of Jesus,* ed. Peter Seymour (Kansas City, Mo.: Hallmark Cards, 1972), 30.

252   Marshall, Peter, *Mr. Jones Meet the Master* (New York: Fleming H. Revell, a division of Baker Book House Company, 1949), 177–88.

259   Longfellow, Henry Wadsworth, "Blind Bartimeus," in *Anthology of Jesus,* arr. and sel. Sir James Marchant, ed. Warren W. Wiersbe (1926, Grand Rapids: Kregel Publications, 1981), 47–48.

260   Griffin, William, *Jesus for Children* (Minneapolis: Winston Press, 1985), 60–62.

267   Bonhoeffer, Dietrich, *The Cost of Discipleship* (New York: Collier Books, 1959), 47–49.

268   Capon, Robert Farrar, *The Parables of Judgment* (Gran Rapids: William B. Eerdmans Publishing Company, 1989), 51–54.

271   Brown, Elijah P., *The Real Billy Sunday* (Dayton: Otterbein Press, 1914), 244–47.

274   Phillips, J. B., *Your God Is Too Small* (New York: Macmillan Publishing Company, 1961), 92–93.

275   Cho, Dr. David Yonggi, *The Fourth Dimension* (Plainfield, N.J.: Logos International, 1979), 103–4.

276   Snow, Laura A. Barter, "This Thing Is From You," in Paul E. Billheimer, *Don't Waste Your Sorrows* (Ft. Washington, Pa.: Christian Literature Crusade, 1977), 65–66.

277   Garvie, A. E., "The Christian Doctrine of the Godhead," in *Anthology of Jesus,* arr. and sel. Sir James Marchart, ed. Warren W. Wiersbe (1926; Grand Rapids: Kregel Publications, 1981), 64–65.

278   Spurgeon, Charles H., *Morning and Evening*, ed. Roy H. Clarke (Nashville: Thomas Nelson Publishing, 1994), December 5, morning.

279   Luther, Martin, *Luther's Meditations on the Gospels*, trans. and arr. Roland H. Bainton (Philadelphia: Westminster Press, 1962), 71–73.

280   Strauss, Lehman, *The Day God Died* (Grand Rapids: Zondervan Publishing House, 1965), 27–28, 37–38, 49–50, 59–61, 71–72, 81–82, 93–94.

280   Dickens, Charles, *The Life of Our Lord* (New York: Simon & Schuster, 1934), 59–62.

281   Griffin, William, *Jesus for Children* (Minneapolis: Winston Press, 1985), 67.

282   Jordan, Clarence, *The Cotton Patch Version of Matthew and John* (New York: Association Press, 1970), 62–63.

283   Spurgeon, Charles H., *Morning and Evening*, ed. Roy H. Clarke (Nashville: Thomas Nelson Publishers, 1994), March 17, evening.

284   Luther, Martin, *Table-Talk*, Hazlitt's trans., §§ 198, 212, 231, in *A Diary of Readings*, ed. John Baillie (New York: Collier Books, 1955), 353.

284   Brown, Elijah P., *The Real Billy Sunday* (Dayton: Otterbein Press, 1914), 77–78.

286   Phillips, J. B., *Your God Is Too Small* (New York: Macmillan Publishing Company, 1961), 112–14.

287   á Kempis, Thomas, *The Imitation of Christ* (New York: Doubleday, Image Books, 1955), 103–4, 217–18, 191–93.

290   Blanchard, John, *Gathered Gold* (Durham, Eng.: Evangelical Press, 1984), 174–75.

291   Jordan, Clarence, *The Cotton Patch Version of Matthew and John* (New York: Association Press, 1970), 72–73.

291   Luther, Martin, *Table Talk*, in *Devotional Classics: Selected Readings for Individuals and Groups*, comp. Richard Foster and James Bryan Smith (San Francisco: HarperSanFrancisco, 1993), 133–34.

292   Laubach, Frank C., *Letters by a Modern Mystic* (Westwood, N.J.: Fleming H. Revell Co., 1958), 47–48.

293   Kingsley, Charles, *Two Years Ago* (1857), chap. xi, in *A Diary of Readings*, ed. John Baillie (New York: Collier Books, 1955), 337.

294   Spurgeon, Charles H., *Morning and Evening*, ed. Roy H. Clarke (Nashville: Thomas Nelson Publishers, 1994), March 12, morning.

295   Jordan, Clarence, *The Cotton Patch Version of Matthew and John* (New York: Association Press, 1970), 74.

295   Luther, Martin, *Luther's Meditations on the Gospels*, trans. and arr. Roland H. Bainton (Philadelphia: Westminster Press, 1962), 116–18.

297   Willard, Dallas, *The Spirit of the Disciplines*, in *Devotional Classics: Selected Readings for Individuals and Groups*, comp. Richard Foster and James Bryan Smith (San Francisco: HarperSanFrancisco, 1993), 15.

297   Bushnell, Horace, *Christian Nurture* (1847), part ii, chap. i, in *A Diary of Readings*, ed. John Baille (New York: Collier Books, 1955), 320.

298   Cheney, Lois A., *God Is No Fool*, (Nashville: Abingdon, 1969), 23.

299   Griffin, William, *Jesus for Children* (Minneapolis: Winston Press, 1985), 69–71.

300   Fénelon, François, *Christian Perfection*, in *Devotional Classics: Selected Readings for Individuals and Groups*, comp. Richard Foster and James Bryan Smith (San Francisco: HarperSanFrancisco, 1993), 48.

301   Graham, Billy, *The Faithful Christian, An Anthology of Billy Graham*, comp. William Griffin and Ruth Graham Dienert (New York: McCracken Press, 1994), 33–34.

301 Brooks, Phillips, *Sermons,* vol. i, in *A Diary of Readings,* ed. John Baillie (New York: Collier Books, 1955), 305.

302 Wenham, David, *The Parables of Jesus* (Downers Grove, Ill.: InterVarsity Press, 1989), 94–95.

303 Stott, John R. W., *Christ the Controversialist* (Downers Grove, Ill.: InterVarsity Press, 1970), 93–94.

304 Bonhoeffer, Dietrich, *Letters and Papers from Prison* (1953), in *A Diary of Readings,* ed. John Baillie (New York: Collier Books, 1955), 239.

305 Bushnell, Horace, *Christian Nurture* (1847), part i, chap. iii, in *A Diary of Readings,* ed. John Baillie (New York: Collier Books, 1955), 209.

306 Rolle, Richard, *The Mending of Life,* Misyn's translation (1434), amended by Francis Comper (1914), in *A Diary of Readings,* ed. John Baillie (New York: Collier Books, 1955), 177.

307 Stott, John R. W., *Basic Christianity* (Downers Grove, Ill.: InterVarsity Press, 1958), 23–25.

309 Teresa, Mother, *Mother Teresa: Contemplative in the Heart of the World,* comp. Angelo Devananda (Ann Arbor: Servant Books, 1985), 75.

310 Francis of Assisi, Saint, *The Little Flowers of St. Francis,* in *Devotional Classics: Selected Readings for Individuals and Groups,* comp. Richard Foster and James Bryan Smith (San Francisco: HarperSanFrancisco, 1993), 314–17.

313 Bonhoeffer, Dietrich, *The Cost of Discipleship,* in *A Diary of Readings,* ed. John Baillie (New York: Collier Books, 1955), 167.

314 Graham, Billy, *The Faithful Christian, An Anthology of Billy Graham,* comp. William Griffin and Ruth Graham Dienert (New York: McCracken Press, 1994), 35.

315 Cheney, Lois A., *God Is No Fool* (Nashville: Abingdon, 1969), 24–25.

316 Schweitzer, Albert, *Memories of Childhood and Youth,* in *A Diary of Readings,* ed. John Baillie (New York: Collier Books, 1955), 45.

317 Miller, Calvin, "The Seven Great I Am's of Jesus," from *The Holy Bible: Contemporary English Version* (New York: American Bible Society, 1995).

319 Tillich, Paul, *The Shaking of the Foundations* (1949), (New York: Charles Scribner's Sons, 1955), 53.

319 *The Holy Bible* (The New Scofield Reference Bible), ed. C. I. Scofield, D. D. (New York: Oxford University Press, 1967), 997–1003.

325 Hare, J. C. and Augustus, *Guesses at Truth* (1827), in *A Diary of Readings,* ed. John Baillie (New York: Collier Books, 1955), 59.

325 Wenham, David, *The Parables of Jesus* (Downers Grove, Ill.: InterVarsity Press, 1989), 151.

326 Miller, Calvin, "The Stories of Jesus" from *The Living Bible* (Wheaton, Ill.: Tyndale House Publishers, 1971).

341 Cheney, Lois A., *God Is No Fool* (Nashville: Abingdon, 1969), 23–27.

342 Bonhoeffer, Dietrich, *The Cost of Discipleship,* in *A Diary of Readings,* ed. John Baillie (New York: Collier Books, 1955), 103.

347 Lewis, C. S., *The Lion, the Witch and the Wardrobe* (New York: Macmillan Publishing Co., 1950), 145–52.

351 Coleman, Robert E., *Songs of Heaven* (Old Tappan, N.J.: Fleming H. Revell Co., 1980), 50–60.

352 Llewelyn, Robert, ed., *The Joy of the Saints* (Springfield, Ill.: Templegate Publishers, 1988), 77.

352 Spurgeon, Charles H., *Morning and Evening,* ed. Roy H. Clarke (Nashville: Thomas Nelson Publishers, 1994), February 23, evening.

354 Author Unknown, "Meditation on the Cross," in *Eerdmans' Book of Famous Prayers,* comp. Veronica Zundel (Grand Rapids: William B. Eerdmans Publishing Company, 1983), 64.

354 Milton, John, "The Passion," in *The Jesus of the Poets, An Anthology,* sel. and ed. Leonard R. Gribble (New York: Richard R. Smith, 1930), 96.

355 Athanasius, Saint, *De Incarnatione Verbi Dei,* Robertson's translation (1884), xliii, in *A Diary of Readings,* ed. John Baillie (New York: Collier Books, 1955), 17.

356 Farmer, H. H., *The Healing Cross* (1938), in *A Diary of Readings,* ed. John Baillie (New York: Collier Books, 1955), 338.

357 Anselm, Saint, *Meditations,* trans. E. B. Pusey (1856), Meditation ix, in *A Diary of Readings,* ed. John Baillie (New York: Collier Books, 1955), 222.

358 Blanchard, John, *Gathered Gold* (Durham, Eng.: Evangelical Press, 1984), 166–67.

360 Griffin, William, *Jesus for Children* (Minneapolis: Winston Press, 1985), 83–84.

361 Lewis, C. S., *Letters to Malcolm: Chiefly on Prayer* (New York: Harcourt Brace Jovanovich, 1963), 42–43.

362 Ker, John, *Thoughts for Heart and Life,* in *A Diary of Readings,* ed. John Baillie (New York: Collier Books, 1955), 296.

362 Goodspeed, Edgar J., *Modern Apocrypha* (Boston: Beacon Press, 1956), 92–93.

364 Dickens, Charles, *The Life of Our Lord* (New York: Simon & Schuster, 1934), 109–11.

365 Catherine of Siena, Saint, *The Dialogue,* in *Devotional Classics: Selected Readings for Individuals and Groups,* comp. Richard Foster and James Bryan Smith (San Francisco: HarperSanFrancisco, 1993), 287–90.

368 à Kempis, Thomas, *The Imitation of Christ* (Chicago: Moody Press Edition, 1980), 166.

368 Spurgeon, Charles H., *Evening by Evening* (Whitaker House, 1984), 157.

369 Cairns, D. S., *The Faith That Rebels* (1928), in *A Diary of Readings,* ed. John Baillie (New York: Collier Books, 1955), 10.

370 Cheney, Lois A., *God Is No Fool* (Nashville: Abingdon, 1969), 105.

371 Luther, Martin, *Table-Talk,* Hazlitt's translation, §§1619, 1806, 1564, 1537, in *A Diary of Readings,* ed. John Baillie (New York: Collier Books, 1955), 185.

371 Penn-Lewis, Jessie, *The Cross of Calvary* (England: Overcomer Literature Trust, n.d.), 5–11.

375 Andrews, C. F., *The Prospects of Humanism* (1931), in *A Diary of Readings,* ed. John Baillie (New York: Collier Books, 1955) 23.

376 Luther, Martin, *Luther's Meditations on the Gospels,* trans. and arr. Roland H. Bainton (Philadelphia: Westminster Press, 1962), 135–37.

378 Elliot, Elisabeth, *Shadow of the Almighty* (San Francisco: Harper & Row Publishers, 1970), 61–62, citing L. E. Maxwell, *Born Crucified* (Chicago: Moody Press).

378 Graham, Ruth Bell, *Sitting by My Laughing Fire* (Minneapolis: World Wide Publications, 1977), 118.

380 Marvell, Andrew, in *A Diary of Readings,* ed. John Baillie (New York: Collier Books, 1955), 72.

381 Browning, Elizabeth Barrett, "The Look" and "The Meaning of the Look," in *The Country of the Risen King, An Anthology of Christian Poetry,* comp. Merle Meeter (Grand Rapids: Baker Book House, 1978), 300.

382 Miller, Calvin, *Once upon a Tree* (Grand Rapids: Baker Book House, 1967), 54–55.

383 Thomas Aquinas, Saint, trans. Gerard Manley Hopkins, in *A Diary of Readings,* ed. John Baillie (New York: Collier Books, 1955), 33.

384 Author Unknown, "The Entry into Jerusalem," in *Portrait of Jesus,* ed. Peter Seymour (Kansas City, Mo.: Hallmark Cards, 1972), 49.

385 Bunyan, John, *The Pilgrim's Progress.* (Westwood, N.J.: Christian Library, 1984).

386 Dupree, Judith Deem, *Going Home* (Palm Springs, Calif.: Ronald N. Haynes Publishers, 1984), 72.

387 Watts, Isaac, "Alas! And Did My Savior Bleed," in *The Country of the Risen King, An Anthology of Christian Poetry,* comp. Merle Meeter (Grand Rapids: Baker Book House, 1978), 405.

387 Edwards, William D., "On the Physical Death of Jesus Christ" (Rochester, Minn.: *JAMA,* March 21, 1986), 1457–63.

391 Lanier, Sidney, "A Ballad of Trees and the Master," in *The Best Loved Poems of the American People,* sel. Hazel Felleman (New York: Doubleday, 1965), 345.

391 Watts, Isaac, "When I Survey the Wondrous Cross," in *The Country of the Risen King, An Anthology of Christian Poetry,* comp. Merle Meeter (Grand Rapids: Baker Book House, 1978), 406.

392 Goudge, Elizabeth, "In Gethsemane," in *Portrait of Jesus,* ed. Peter Seymour (Kansas City, Mo.: Hallmark Cards, 1972), 53.

393 Campbell, Joseph, with Bill Moyers, *The Power of Myth* (New York: Doubleday Books, 1988), 109.

394 Miller, Calvin, "The Form of a Servant," August 3, 1986.

394 Bates, Katharine Lee, "Alone into the Mountain," in *Portrait of Jesus,* ed. Peter Seymour (Kansas City, Mo.: Hallmark Cards, 1972), 54.

395 Jonson, Ben, "A Hymn to God the Father," in *The Country of the Risen King, An Anthology of Christian Poetry,* comp. Merle Meeter (Grand Rapids: Baker Book House, 1978), 353.

396 Davidman, Joy, *Smoke on the Mountain* (Philadelphia: Westminster Press, 1954), 20.

397 Miller, Calvin, *Once upon a Tree* (Grand Rapids: Baker Book House, 1967), 62–63.

398 Isaac Watts, "Am I a Soldier of the Cross?" in *The Country of the Risen King, An Anthology of Christian Poetry,* comp. Merle Meeter (Grand Rapids: Baker Book House, 1978), 406.

399 Robinson, Edwin Arlington, "Calvary," in *Portrait of Jesus,* ed. Peter Seymour (Kansas City, Mo.: Hallmark Cards, 1972), 56.

399 Miller, Calvin, *Once upon a Tree* (Grand Rapids: Baker Book House, 1967), 82–83.

400 Bayley, Joseph, *Psalms of My Life* (Elgin, Ill.: David C. Cook Publishing Co., 1987), 39.

401 Miller, Calvin, *Once upon a Tree* (Grand Rapids: Baker Book House, 1967), 90.

402 Buechner, Frederick, *Wishful Thinking* (New York: Harper & Row Publishers, 1973), 44–46.

403 Graham, Ruth Bell, *Sitting by My Laughing Fire* (Minneapolis: World Wide Publications, 1977), 47.

403 Miller, Calvin, *Once upon a Tree* (Grand Rapids: Baker Book House, 1967), 138.

404   Cowper, William, "The Blood of Christ," in *The Jesus of the Poets, An Anthology,* sel. and ed. Leonard R. Gribble (New York: Richard R. Smith, 1930), 51.

411   Gaither, William J. and Gloria, "Because He Lives," (Gaither Copyright Management, 1971).

412   Nouwen, Henri J. M., *Letters to Marc About Jesus* (San Francisco: Harper & Row Publishers, 1988), 23–25.

413   Lewis, C. S., *The Lion, the Witch and the Wardrobe* (New York: Macmillan Publishing Company, 1950), 158–61.

415   Capon, Robert Farrar, *The Parables of Grace* (Grand Rapids: William B. Eerdmans Publishing Company, 1988), 106.

416   Kelsey, Morton, *Resurrection, Release from Oppression* (New York: Paulist Press, 1985), 18–19.

417   Goethe, Johann Wolfgang von, Easter hymn from *Faust,* in *Anthology of Jesus,* arr. and sel. Sir James Marchant, ed. Warren W. Wiersbe (1926; Grand Rapids: Kregel Publications, 1981), 194.

418   Robinson, C. H., *Studies in the Resurrection of Christ* (1909), in *A Diary of Readings,* ed. John Baillie (New York: Collier Books, 1955), 76.

419   Robertson, A. T., *Epochs in the Life of Jesus* (New York: Charles Scribner's Sons, 1907), 174–90.

424   Card, Michael, *Immanuel* (Nashville: Thomas Nelson, 1990), 187.

426   Craig, William L., *Knowing The Truth About the Resurrection, Our Response to the Empty Tomb* (Ann Arbor: Servant Books, 1981), 125.

426   Updike, John, "Seven Stanzas at Easter," quoted in D. Bruce Lockerbie, *The Liberating Word: Art and the Mystery of the Gospel* (Grand Rapids: William B. Eerdmans, 1974), 104–5.

427   von Braun, Dr. Wernher, *Reader's Digest,* June 1960, cited in Ravenhill, *Tried and Transfigured,* 86.

428   Herbert, George, "Easter Wings" found in *The Country of the Risen King,* compiled by Merle Meeter (Grand Rapids: Baker Book House, 1978), p. 327.

428   Oden, Thomas C., *Agenda for Theology After Modernity . . . What?* (Grand Rapids: Zondervan Publishing House, 1990), 134–36.

430   Brown, Stephen, *If Jesus Has Come* (Grand Rapids: Baker Book House, 1992), pp. 99–102.

432   Cheney, Lois A., *God Is No Fool* (Nashville: Abingdon, 1969), 114–15.

433   Herbert, George, "Easter," in *The Country of the Risen King, An Anthology of Christian Poetry,* comp. Merle Meeter (Grand Rapids: Baker Book House, 1978), 326.

434   Miller, Calvin, *Once upon a Tree* (Grand Rapids: Baker Book House, 1967), 127.

435   Rousseau, Jean-Jacques, *Emile,* in *Anthology of Jesus,* arr. and sel. Sir James Marchant, ed. Warren W. Wiersbe (1926; Grand Rapids: Kregel Publications, 1981), 54–55.

441   Meynell, Alice, "I Am the Way," in *Eerdman's Book of Christian Poetry,* comp. Pat Alexander (Grand Rapids: William B. Eerdmans Publishing Company, 1981), 73.

442   Elliot, Elisabeth, *Shadow of the Almighty* (San Francisco: Harper & Row Publishers, 1958), 15, 18–19.

444   Colson, Charles, *Loving God* (Grand Rapids: Zondervan, 1983), 27–30, 33–34.

449   McGrath, Alister, *Understanding Doctrine* (Grand Rapids: Zondervan Publishing House, 1990), 165.

449   Author Unknown, "One Solitary Life," taken from a bookmark.

451   Tolstoy, Leo, "The Memoirs of a Madman," translated by Louise and Aylmer Maude, taken from the Worlds Classics Series (New York: Oxford University Press, 1965), pp. 248–260.

458   Foster, Richard J., *Celebration of Discipline* (San Francisco: Harper & Row, 1988), 115–16.

458   Colson, Charles, *Who Speaks for God?* (Westchester, Ill.: Crossway Books, 1985), 15–19.

461   Fox, George, "The Light of Christ," in *Eerdmans' Book of Christian Classics,* comp. Veronica Zundel (Grand Rapids: William B. Eerdmans Publishing Company, 1985), 63–64.

463   Trueblood, Elton, *The Yoke of Christ and Other Sermons* (New York: Harper & Brothers, 1958), 24–25.

464   Trueblood, Elton, *The Yoke of Christ and Other Sermons* (New York: Harper & Brothers, 1958), 114–15.

465   Teresa, Mother, "Daily Prayer," in *Eerdmans' Book of Famous Prayers,* comp. Veronica Zundel (Grand Rapids: William B. Eerdmans Publishing Company, 1983), 99.

466   Momerie, Professor, *Defects of Modern Christianity,* chap. VI, in *Anthology of Jesus,* arr. and sel. Sir James Marchant, ed. Warren W. Wiersbe (1926; Grand Rapids: Kregel Publications, 1981), 93–94.

467   Spurgeon, Charles H., *Morning and Evening,* ed. Roy H. Clarke (Nashville: Thomas Nelson Publishers, 1994), December 28, evening.

468   Bonhoeffer, Dietrich, *Letters and Papers from Prison* (New York: Collier, 1972).

468   Gabhart, Herbert C., *The Name Above Every Name* (Nashville: Broadman Press, 1986), 37.

469   Longfellow, Henry Wadsworth, "A Prayer," in *The Jesus of the Poets, An Anthology,* ed. Leonard R. Gribble (New York: Richard R. Smith, 1930), 87.

470   Dickens, Charles, "On Leaving Home," in *Anthology of Jesus,* arr. and sel. Sir James Marchant, ed. Warren W. Wiersbe (1926; Grand Rapids: Kregel Publications, 1981), 255–56.

471   Author Unknown, "This Transitory Life," in *Eerdmans' Book of Famous Prayers,* comp. Veronica Zundel (Grand Rapids: William B. Eerdmans Publishing Company, 1983), 64.

471   à Kempis, Thomas, *The Imitation of Christ* (New York: Doubleday, Image Books, 1955), 203–04.

471   Graham, Billy, *The Faithful Christian, An Anthology of Billy Graham,* comp. William Griffin and Ruth Graham Dienert (New York: McCracken Press, 1994), 103.

473   Raleigh, Sir Walter, "His Pilgrimage to Death," in *A Diary of Readings,* ed. John Baillie (New York: Collier Books, 1955), 344.

474   Colson, Charles W., *Born Again* (Old Tappan, N.J.: Fleming H. Revell, 1976), 167–71.

477   Woolman, John, *The Journal of John Woolman,* in *Devotional Classics: Selected Readings for Individuals and Groups,* comp. Richard Foster and James Bryan Smith (San Francisco: HarperSanFrancisco, 1993), 259–60.

478   Blanchard, John, *Gathered Gold* (Durham, Eng.: Evangelical Press, 1984), 171–73.

480   Constantine the Great, from Eusebius's *Life of Constantine,* in *Anthology of Jesus,* arr.

and sel. Sir James Marchant, ed. Warren W. Wiersbe (1926; Grand Rapids: Kregel Publications, 1981), 331–32.

481   Barth, Karl, "Deliverance to the Captives," in *Eerdmans' Book of Christian Classics*, comp. Veronica Zundel (Grand Rapids: William B. Eerdmans Publishing Company, 1985), 98–99.

482   Griffin, William, *Jesus for Children* (Minneapolis: Winston Press, 1985), 77–78.

483   MacGregor, William Malcolm, *Jesus Christ the Son of God* (1907), in *A Diary of Readings*, ed. John Baillie (New York: Collier Books, 1955), 316.

484   Clifford, John, "Looking Back," from his diary, in *Anthology of Jesus*, arr. and sel. Sir James Marchant, ed. Warren W. Wiersbe (1926; Grand Rapids: Kregel Publications, 1981), 334.

484   Stott, John R. W., *What Christ Thinks of the Church* (Downers Grove, Ill.: InterVarsity Press, 1958), 40–41.

485   Author Unknown, *The Way of a Pilgrim*, trans. Olga Savin (Boston: Shambhala Publications, 1991), 135–37.

486   MacDonald, George, "Lost and Found," in *Anthology of Jesus*, arr. and sel. Sir James Marchant, ed. Warren W. Wiersbe (1926; Grand Rapids: Kregel Publications, 1981), 129.

486   Woolman, John, *Journal* (1744), chap. i, in *A Diary of Readings*, ed. John Baillie (New York: Collier Books, 1955), 253.

487   Thomas, Major W. Ian, *The Saving Life of Christ* (Grand Rapids: Zondervan Publishing House, 1961), 121–22.

488   Johnson, Lionel, "Say, What Saw You?" in *A Diary of Readings*, ed. John Baillie (New York: Collier Books, 1955), 240.

489   Livingstone, David, "The Story of His Life," in *Anthology of Jesus*, arr. and sel. Sir James Marchant, ed. Warren W. Wiersbe (1926; Grand Rapids: Kregel Publications, 1981), 223–24.

489   Laubach, Frank C., *Letters by a Modern Mystic* (Westwood, N.J.: Fleming H. Revell Co., 1958), 53–55.

491   Spurgeon, Charles H., quoted in Calvin Miller, *The Table of Inwardness* (Downers Grove, Ill.: InterVarsity Press, 1984), 52.

491   Sienkiewicz, Henryk, *Quo Vadis?* trans. William E. Smith (New York: T. S. Ogilvie Publishing Co., 1898), 391–93.

493   Spurgeon, Charles H., *Morning and Evening*, ed. Roy H. Clarke (Nashville: Thomas Nelson Publishers, 1994), March 25, morning.

494   Newman, Cardinal John Henry, "Warfare the Condition of Life," in *A Diary of Readings*, ed. John Baillie (New York: Collier Books, 1955), 224.

495   Brown, Thomas Edward, "Indwelling," in *Old John and Other Poems* (New York: Macmillan & Co., 1893).

496   Temple, William, *Personal Religion and the Life of Fellowship* (1926), in *A Diary of Readings*, ed. John Baillie (New York: Collier Books, 1955), 198.

496   Card, Michael, *Immanuel* (Nashville: Thomas Nelson, 1990), 172–73.

498   Boswell, James, *Life of Johnson*, December 1784, quoting Dr. Brocklesby's account, in *A Diary of Readings*, ed. John Baillie (New York: Collier Books, 1955), 146.

499   Newton, John, "Amazing Grace," in *Worship His Majesty* (Alexandria, Ind.: Gaither Music Company, 1987), 429.

500   Gabhart, Herbert, *The Name Above Every Name* (Nashville: Broadman Press, 1986), 266.

501   Edwards, Jonathan, *Works* (1844), vol. i, 11, in *A Diary of Readings,* ed. John Baillie (New York: Collier Books, 1955), 132.

501   Herbert, George, "Love (III)," in *The Country of the Risen King, An Anthology of Christian Poetry,* comp. Merle Meeter (Grand Rapids: Baker Book House, 1978), 332.

502   Coleridge, Samuel Taylor, "On His Baptismal Birthday," in *The Jesus of the Poets, An Anthology,* sel. and ed. Leonard R. Gribble (New York: Richard R. Smith, 1930), 60.

503   Donne, John, *Fifty Sermons* (1649), Sermon 50, in *A Diary of Readings,* ed. John Baillie (New York: Collier Books, 1955), 131.

504   Pascal, Blaise, quoted in James W. Sire, *Why Should Anyone Believe Anything at All?* (Downers Grove, Ill.: InterVarsity Press, 1994), 69–70.

505   Bernard of Clairvaux, Saint, *De Diligendo Deo,* in *A Diary of Readings,* ed. John Baillie (New York: Collier Books, 1955), 89.

505   Wesley, Charles, "O for a Thousand Tongues," in *The Baptist Hymnal* (Nashville: Convention Press, 1975), 69.

506   MacGregor, W. M., *Jesus Christ the Son of God* (1917), in *A Diary of Readings,* ed. John Baillie (New York: Collier Books, 1955), 80.

507   Author Unknown, "I Met the Master," in *Best Loved Poems of the American People,* sel. Hazel Fellman (New York: Doubleday, 1965), 337.

508   Luther, Martin, *Luther's Meditations on the Gospels,* trans. and arr. Roland H. Bainton (Philadelphia: Westminster Press, 1962), 91–92.

509   Wesley, John, *Journal,* 24 May 1738, in *A Diary of Readings,* ed. John Baillie (New York: Collier Books, 1955), 73.

510   Watts, Isaac, "Jesus Shall Reign Where'er the Sun," in *The Baptist Hymnal* (Nashville: Convention Press, 1975), 282.

511   Bunyan, John, *Grace Abounding to the Chief of Sinners* (1666), in *A Diary of Readings,* ed. John Baillie (New York: Collier Books, 1955), 63.

512   Fuson, Robert H., *The Log of Christopher Columbus* (Camden, N.J.: International Marine Publishing, 1987), 1–3.

512   Tolstoy, Leo, *What I Believe,* Introduction, trans. Aylmer Maude, in *A Diary of Readings,* ed. John Baillie (New York: Collier Books, 1955), 38.

513   Shaw, Luci, "He Who Would Be Great Among You," in *Polishing the Petoskey Stone* (Wheaton, Ill.: Harold Shaw, 1990) 69–70.

514   Pascal, Blaise, *Pensées,* trans. Kegan Paul, in *A Diary of Readings,* ed. John Baillie (New York: Collier Books, 1955), 37.

515   Thomas, Major W. Ian, *The Saving Life of Christ* (Grand Rapids: Zondervan Publishing House, 1961), 41.

516   Bunyan, John, *The Pilgrim's Progress.* (Chicago: Moody Press) pp. 40–41.

516   Herbert, George, "Death," in *The Country of the Risen King, An Anthology of Christian Poetry,* comp. Merle Meeter (Grand Rapids: Baker Book House, 1978), 334.

517   Pollock, J. C., *Hudson Taylor and Maria: Pioneers in China* (Grand Rapids: Zondervan, 1970), 205–7, quoted in Calvin Miller, *The Table of Inwardness* (Downers Grove, Ill.: InterVarsity Press, 1984), 115–16.

518   Miller, Calvin, *The Discipline of a Servant,* August 5, 1986.

519 Hopkins, Gerard Manley, "Barnfloor and Winepress," in *The Country of the Risen King, An Anthology of Christian Poetry,* comp. Merle Meeter (Grand Rapids: Baker Book House, 1978), 336.

520 Cheney, Lois A., *God Is No Fool* (Nashville: Abingdon, 1969), 98.

520 Newton, John, "How Sweet the Name," in *The Country of the Risen King, An Anthology of Christian Poetry,* comp. Merle Meeter (Grand Rapids: Baker Book House, 1978), 365.

521 Griffin, William, *Jesus for Children* (Minneapolis: Winston Press, 1985), 115–17.

523 Singh, Sadhu Sundar, "Christ Is My Saviour," from B. H. Streeter and A. J. Appasamy, *The Sadhu,* in *Anthology of Jesus,* arr. and sel. Sir James Marchant, ed. Warren W. Wiersbe (1926; Grand Rapids: Kregel Publications, 1981), 233–34.

529 Benson, Bob, and Michael W. Benson, *Disciplines for the Inner Life* (Waco, Tex.: Word Books, 1985), 23.

530 Cox, Harvey, *The Feast of Fools* (New York: Harper & Row, 1969), 66, 170–71.

531 Peterson, Eugene, "What Jesus Had to Say About the End of the World," in *The Message* (Colorado Springs: NavPress, 1993).

534 Bunyan, John, *The Pilgrim's Progress* (Westwood, N.J.: Christian Library, 1984), 184–85.

535 Author Unknown, "Heaven," in *Best Loved Poems of the American People,* sel. Hazel Fellman (New York: Doubleday, 1965), 331.

535 Jordan, Clarence, *The Cotton Patch Version of Matthew and John* (New York: Association Press, 1970), 83–84.

536 Graham, Billy, *The Faithful Christian, An Anthology of Billy Graham,* comp. William Griffin and Ruth Graham Dienert (New York: McCracken Press, 1994), 247–48.

538 Lewis, C. S., *The Visionary Christian, 131 Readings,* sel. Chad Walsh (New York: Collier Books, 1981), 163–64.

538 Howe, Julia Ward, "Battle Hymn of the Republic," in *The Book of Virtues, A Treasury of Great Moral Stories,* ed. William J. Bennett (New York: Simon & Schuster, 1993), 797–98.

539 Lewis, C. S. *The World's Last Night and Other Essays* (New York: Harcourt Brace Jovanovich, 1952), 104–8.

542 Dupree, Judith Deem, *Going Home* (Palm Springs, Calif.: Ronald N. Haynes Publishers, 1984), 74.

542 Tutu, Desmond M., "Allies of God" (adapted from an address given to the Synod in Port Elizabeth, 1981), in *Weavings, A Journal of the Christian Spiritual Life* V, no. 1 (January-February 1990): 41–42.

543 Jordan, Clarence, *The Cotton Patch Version of Matthew and John* (New York: Association Press, 1970), 83.

INDEX